Melissa Paniz

(714) 717-6391

THE OLD TESTAMENT

Its Background, Growth, & Content

The Old Testament

Its Background, Growth, & Content

Steven L. McKenzie
and John Kaltner

WIPF & STOCK · Eugene, Oregon

Wipf and Stock Publishers
199 W 8th Ave, Suite 3
Eugene, OR 97401

The Old Testament
Its Background, Growth, and Content
By Kaltner, John and McKenzie, Steven Linn

ISBN 13: 978-1-62564-264-6
Publication date 8/1/2014
Previously published by Abingdon, 2007

For our students at Rhodes College

CONTENTS

PART ONE: TORAH

PART TWO: FORMER PROPHETS

PART THREE: LATTER PROPHETS

PART FOUR: WRITINGS

Table of Illustrations

Table of Maps

INTRODUCTION

CONTENT

If you were to go into any bookstore with a well-stocked religion section, remove copies of various editions of the Bible from the shelves, and begin to compare the tables of contents for the part labeled "Old Testament" or "Hebrew Bible," chances are you would soon discover an interesting fact—they wouldn't all agree on what the book contains. Some copies would list entire books not found in others. Books would be grouped one way in one Bible and a different way in another. The order of the list of books would not match up in every case. Your proverbial "stack of Bibles" would be just that—a stack of different books that have much in common but are not identical.

Those discrepancies are due to the Bible's role as an officially approved collection of writings for a number of different faith groups. The Bible found in Jewish communities is not the same as that used among Christians, and the various Christian denominations do not all read the same text. Each group has its own canon, or set of accepted writings that are deemed to be authoritative for the community.

The term *canon* comes from the Greek word for a reed, which was often used in the ancient world as an instrument to measure something or to compare the sizes of two objects. When applied to religious writings, a canon refers to those texts that have been set apart and granted special status by a group because of the authority they have over its members. Canonization—the process that determines which writings are in and which are out—is how canons are formed.

This book is an introduction to that part of the Bible called the Old Testament or Hebrew Bible. The two designations are often used interchangeably but, as just noted, they do not always refer to the same set of writings. "Old Testament" is a label that implies the existence of a "New Testament," and so it is a common way many Christians refer to the first part of their Bible. Jews do not consider the New Testament to be part of the canon, and for this reason (as well as the somewhat pejorative connotation of the word "old") they speak of the Old Testament, or Hebrew Bible, as simply "the Bible." Throughout this book all three designations will be used.

The traditional story of how the canon came about describes a meeting of rabbis that took place around the year 90 C.E. in the seacoast town of Jamnia, west of Jerusalem. At this gathering the rabbis, after discussing the pros and cons of the various works that were candidates for inclusion, took a vote that determined the books of the Hebrew Bible. According to this account, the canon was set by the leaders of the Jewish community and it was done in the aftermath of, perhaps in response to, a major tragedy—the destruction of the temple in Jerusalem by the Romans in 70 C.E.

This story is still widely told, and many consider it to be the official version of how the canon of the Hebrew Bible came to be. But most scholars believe that the Jamnia assembly of rabbis is based more on legend than on fact and that it is too simplistic a way of explaining a very complex, drawn-out process like canonization. In all likelihood, some parts of the Hebrew Bible—like the Pentateuch, or first five books—had already achieved authoritative status within the community long before the supposed vote by the rabbis in Jamnia. The details of what occurred over the extended period of time during which the Hebrew Bible canon took shape are impossible to reconstruct, but it is safe to say that its evolution involved many individuals and groups from across the spectrum of Israelite and Jewish society.

The common Jewish term for the Hebrew Bible is Tanak, an acronym whose consonants *T*, *N*, and *K* identify the three parts of the canon. The first is the *Torah* (literally, "instruction"), which is comprised of the first five books: Genesis, Exodus, Leviticus, Numbers, and Deuteronomy. As already noted, these writings are also referred to as the Pentateuch. The second part is the *Nevi'im*, or Prophets. This section is made up of eight books, some of which are divided differently in Christian Bibles. Joshua, Judges, Samuel, and Kings—the latter two are each divided into two books in Christian Bibles—are the Former Prophets. The Latter Prophets are Isaiah, Jeremiah, Ezekiel, and the Book of the Twelve, which is a group of twelve smaller prophetic books that are listed separately in Christian Bibles. The third part is the *Ketuvim*, or Writings. This is a collection of eleven works of different genres: Psalms, Proverbs, Job, Song of Solomon, Ruth, Lamentations, Qoheleth (Ecclesiastes), Esther, Daniel, Ezra–Nehemiah, and Chronicles.

The Tanak (*Torah-Nevi'im-Ketuvim*), then, is a three-part collection of twenty-four books that comprise the sacred scripture of Judaism. Scholars believe that the order of the sections in the Tanak reflects the order in which they were canonized, with the Torah being the first to be officially recognized, and the Writings—which generally are among the latest biblical books to be written—the last to be accepted.

When we turn to the Christian canon, things are a bit more complicated because there are two main ways of understanding it, one for the Protestant churches and the other for the Roman Catholic and Orthodox churches. The Protestant canon has four parts, with the first—called the Pentateuch—identical to that found in the Tanak. The second part is called the Historical Books, and it contains twelve books that are listed in both the Prophets and Writings sections of the Tanak: Joshua, Judges, Ruth, 1–2 Samuel, 1–2 Kings, 1–2 Chronicles, Ezra, Nehemiah, and Esther. The Poetic Books comprise the third section, and they include Job, Psalms, Proverbs, Qoheleth, and Song of Solomon. Finally, the Prophets section of the Protestant canon contains all of the same material found in the third part of the Tanak, in addition to the books of Lamentations and Daniel. It also treats the Book of the Twelve as separate works: Hosea, Joel, Amos, Obadiah, Jonah, Micah, Nahum, Habakkuk, Zephaniah, Haggai, Zechariah, and Malachi. The overall result in the Protestant tradition is a canon of thirty-nine books.

The Roman Catholic/Orthodox canon resembles the Protestant one closely, but differs in a number of ways. Among the Historical Books it includes Tobit, Judith, and 1–2 Maccabees. Wisdom of Solomon and Sirach—the latter work is also known as Ecclesiasticus—are found among the Poetic Books. The only difference in the Prophetic Books is the inclusion of Baruch after the book of Lamentations. Completing the picture, the canon of several Orthodox churches also contains the following works: 1–2 Esdras, The Prayer of Manasseh, Psalm 151, and 3–4 Maccabees.

The content of the Old Testament canon of the Protestant churches is identical to that of the Hebrew Bible for Judaism. The only differences between them concern how the books are divided and the order in which they are found. With the Roman Catholic/Orthodox canon the differences are more profound because it introduces certain writings not found in the other two. The primary reason for this is that the Roman Catholic and Orthodox canons include Greek works, not just those written in Hebrew. The Greek translation of the Hebrew Bible known as the Septuagint, which was done in the third century B.C.E., contains a number of writings not found in the Hebrew Bible that are included in some Christian Bibles. This is so because the Septuagint was a primary source for the Latin translation known as the Vulgate, which has been very influential in the Catholic Church. Of course, the Greek translation has been very important throughout the history of the Orthodox churches because Greek is the official liturgical language of many of them.

Dependence on the Greek text also left its mark on certain books whose content differs from canon to canon. In other words, the Septuagint is not just a translation but also an expansion in places. This can be seen, for example, in the book of Esther. The Septuagint adds a significant portion of material not found in the Hebrew text; most notably it introduces references to God and divine involvement that add a more explicitly theological tone to the work. These sections are found in the Roman Catholic/Orthodox canon but absent from the Jewish and Protestant ones. A similar thing can be seen in the book of Daniel, whose Greek translation includes a number of stories about the main character that are found only in Catholic and Orthodox Bibles. It should be noted that many scholars think these so-called "Greek additions" might be translations of Hebrew or Aramaic originals that are no longer extant.

The Christian order of the canon reflects what is found in the Septuagint, but the Protestant churches did not see fit to include in the Old Testament works or passages that are only found in the Greek translation. This was because they privileged the Hebrew text as the original form of the works and viewed other versions cautiously. Nonetheless, these writings are often included in Protestant Bibles, where they are gathered together between the Old and New Testaments in a section called the Apocrypha (literally, "hidden"). Included in this group are the following works: 1–2 Esdras; Tobit; Judith; the additions to Esther; Wisdom of Solomon; Sirach; Baruch; The Letter of Jeremiah (chapter 6 of Baruch); The Prayer of Azariah and the Song of the Three; Daniel and Susanna; Daniel, Bel and the Snake; The Prayer of Manasseh; and 1–2 Maccabees.

In sum, all three canons agree only on the placement and order of the first five books. The following chart lists the canonical order of the Hebrew Bible/Old Testament for those places where they do not agree.

Jewish Canon	Protestant Canon	Catholic/Orthodox Canon
Nevi'im	*Historical Books*	*Historical Books*
Former Prophets	Joshua	Joshua
Joshua	Judges	Judges
Judges	Ruth	Ruth
1–2 Samuel	1 Samuel	1 Samuel
1–2 Kings	2 Samuel	2 Samuel
	1 Kings	1 Kings
Latter Prophets	2 Kings	2 Kings
Isaiah	1 Chronicles	1 Chronicles
Jeremiah	2 Chronicles	2 Chronicles
Ezekiel	Ezra	Ezra
Book of the Twelve	Nehemiah	Nehemiah
Hosea	Esther	Tobit

Joel
Amos
Obadiah
Jonah
Micah
Nahum
Habakkuk
Zephaniah
Haggai
Zechariah
Malachi

Ketuvim
Psalms
Proverbs
Job
Song of Solomon
Ruth
Lamentations
Qoheleth
Esther
Daniel
Ezra–Nehemiah
1–2 Chronicles

Judith

Poetic Books
Job
Psalms
Proverbs
Qoheleth
Song of Solomon

Prophets
Isaiah
Jeremiah
Lamentations
Ezekiel
Daniel
Hosea
Joel
Amos
Obadiah
Jonah
Micah
Nahum
Habakkuk
Zephaniah
Haggai
Zechariah
Malachi

Esther
1 Maccabees
2 Maccabees

Poetic Books
Job
Psalms
Proverbs
Qoheleth
Song of Solomon
Wisdom of Solomon
Sirach

Prophets
Isaiah
Jeremiah
Lamentations
Baruch
Ezekiel
Daniel
Hosea
Joel
Amos
Obadiah
Jonah
Micah
Nahum
Habakkuk
Zephaniah
Haggai
Zechariah
Malachi

This book adopts the four-part division of the Jewish canon with sections on the Torah, Former Prophets, Latter Prophets, and Writings. The first three sections of the book each have three subsections, and the final one has two subsections. The first part of the Torah section discusses Genesis 1–11, which is commonly referred to as the "Primeval History" and contains myths and legends that treat the period from the creation of the world to the time of Abraham. This is followed by a study of the patriarchal narratives in Genesis 12–50 that describe events in the lives of key figures like Abraham, Jacob, and Joseph. The final part of the Torah section considers biblical traditions from the period between the Israelites' escape from Egypt, known as the exodus, and their entry into the land promised to them by God. During this time the law is given to Moses on Mt. Sinai and the people experience a forty-year period of wandering in the wilderness.

The section on the Former Prophets begins with a consideration of the book of Deuteronomy. Although it has been traditionally identified as part of the Pentateuch, there is good reason to group Deuteronomy with the books that come after it rather than with those that precede it. This section presents a history of the Israelite people from the time they enter the promised land to their loss of it with the Babylonian invasion of 586 B.C.E., which begins a period known as the exile. The first part of this section examines traditions about how Joshua led the Israelites into the land and how they interacted with the local population under the leadership of figures known as judges. The time of the united monarchy under kings Saul, David, and Solomon is the focus of the next subsection. With Solomon's death the kingdom split into two to usher in the period known as the divided monarchy, which is the subject of the third part of the Former Prophets. Prior to the invasion of the southern kingdom of Judah by the Babylonians in 586, the northern kingdom, known as Israel, was overrun by the Assyrians in 721 B.C.E.

The section on the Latter Prophets is divided chronologically based on when the individual prophets were active in relation to the Babylonian exile. The preexilic prophets directed their messages to both the northern and southern kingdoms and attempted to warn the people of the impending threat posed by their enemies if they did not reorient their lives and have faith in God. The exilic prophets were responding to the period just prior to the Babylonian exile and its aftermath. Jeremiah reports on the final years leading up to that tragic event before he himself was forced to leave Jerusalem, while Ezekiel writes from his perspective as one of the exiled Israelites in Babylon. His book, like the writings of Second Isaiah (chs. 40–66), communicates a message of hope that the people will one day be allowed to return to the land. The postexilic prophetic books are a set of six short works from the Book of the Twelve that all date from the later part of the exile or, in some cases, after the return to the land under the Persians in 539 B.C.E.

The final section of the book discusses the Writings. The first part of this section treats the Wisdom literature, a set of three books (Job, Proverbs, and Qoheleth) that address issues related to common human experience and the meaning of life. These works offer advice and rules to live by, in the case of Proverbs, and explore such themes as innocent suffering (Job) and the seeming absurdity of human existence (Qoheleth). This is followed by the remaining books of the Writings, a potpourri of styles and genres that includes prayer and hymns (Psalms), historiography (Chronicles, Ezra–Nehemiah), short story (Ruth, Esther), erotica (Song of Solomon), dirge (Lamentations), and apocalyptic (Daniel).

GROWTH

The diverse nature of the contents of the Hebrew Bible/Old Testament shows that it did not originate as a single book but as a collection, or anthology, of writings. In that sense, it is exactly like a stack of books on a bookstore table. In fact, that's what the word *bible* means. It is Greek (*biblia*) for "small scrolls." The process by which this collection—this particular table of books—grew into the single book that we know as the Bible was a long and complicated one spanning thousands of years. It may be helpful to conceive of the process as taking place in three general stages: composition, transmission, and translation.

Composition

Many of the stories and traditions in the Bible were probably passed down orally before they were written down. These are difficult to identify with any precision, because all we have today are the written materials. However, biblical scholars have employed interpretive methods borrowed from folklore studies in order to attempt to isolate originally oral sources. Certain texts, such as the "Song of Moses" (Exod 15) and the "Song of Deborah" (Judg 5), are explicitly called songs. These two poems in particular have been identified by some scholars as the earliest written documents in the Bible, dating from the twelfth and eleventh centuries, respectively. Even after poems and songs—and stories as well—began to be recorded in writing, they might well have continued in oral form too, particularly if the majority of people could not read or write.

The writers of the Bible compiled the various sources at their disposal—oral and written, prose and poetry—into extended written works. Here again, though, the process was complicated. Scholars often identify the composers of the biblical books more as "redactors," or editors, than as authors. For example, the standard model for the composition of the Pentateuch, or Torah (the first five books of the Bible), has been the "Documentary Hypothesis," which holds that originally independent and somewhat parallel narrative documents were edited together in several stages by redactors. This model has recently come under fire, and the consensus about it has begun to dissipate. However, scholars who adopt other models agree that the process of composition was complex, at the least involving numerous interpolations and later additions. The Pentateuch contains numerous instances of multiple variants of the same texts and stories that are frequently in tension with one another, and such models represent attempts to explain this phenomenon.

In other portions of the Bible, there is also ample evidence of an extended process of composition. The book of Kings, for example, refers the reader to source documents—"the book of the annals of the kings of Israel/Judah," which is usually assumed to be some sort of official, royal record, though it has not been found. Scholars have sometimes argued for the existence of additional narrative sources not explicitly mentioned in the present book of Kings. The book of Chronicles furnishes good reason to posit such narrative sources, because its author used the book of Kings as one of its main sources without clear acknowledgement. Scholars have also been prone to suggest that the book of Kings went through two or more stages of editing in different centuries.

The book of Psalms contains five separate collections or "books" (Pss 1–41, 42–72, 73–89, 90–106, 107–150), and the headings of the psalms ascribe them to many different authors—some prominent (Moses, David, Solomon), others less so (Asaph, the Korahites, Ethan). Many of the psalms are anonymous.

Similarly, the book of Proverbs has separate sections assigned to Solomon (1–9 and 10:1–22:16), "the wise" (22:17–24:22 and 24:23-34), other proverbs of Solomon copied by the officials of Hezekiah (25–29), Agur son of Jakeh, and King Lemuel. The latter two are probably not even Israelites.

Perhaps the best example of this complicated process of development is the prophetic book of Isaiah, which most scholars see as three books or three successive stages of writing combined. Chapters 1–39 house the prophecies of the eighth-century prophet Isaiah, though there are later materials as well. Chapters 40–55 were added by a writer at the end of the exile two centuries later. Chapters 56–66 are an even later collection of materials, which are difficult both to characterize and to date with precision. Each stage of composition, in Isaiah as in other books, represents not just supplementation but reinterpretation as well.

The end of this process of composition is equally difficult to determine. One aspect of this difficulty has been suggested already by the discussion of canonization. Since Jews and Christians, and indeed, Catholics and Protestants, do not share the same canon, the end of the process of composition of the Bible/Old Testament differs for each group. For the books we are treating in this introduction, the end of the process of composition might be considered about 165 B.C.E., the approximate time scholars date the setting in which the latest books (for example, Daniel) were written or edited. But there are still problems separating the process of composition from that of transmission, as the Dead Sea Scrolls have made clear.

Transmission

The Dead Sea Scrolls are copies of biblical books and other ancient writings. They were found in 1947 at the site of Khirbet Qumran near the northern end of the Dead Sea. Qumran was occupied from ca. 150 B.C.E. to

68 C.E., and the people who lived there spent much of their time copying these writings. Thus, multiple copies of several Old Testament books were discovered there. The problem is that these copies are not exact duplicates. Rather, they are variant versions, and sometimes they differ significantly. In the case of the book of Jeremiah, for instance, one version contains about a third more textual content than the others. Yet there is every indication that the different versions were all equally revered by those who copied them. This situation shows that the line between the composition and writing of biblical books and their transmission through copying was not clean. They continued to be augmented (or shortened), some would say "edited," even in the latter stage.

It was not until the canonization of the Hebrew Bible in the first century C.E.—and perhaps considerably beyond that—that a particular version of each book was adopted and standardized. The criteria for choosing one particular version of a given book over another are not clear. It is clear, though, that they were not the criteria employed by modern scholars doing textual criticism (see below under "Interpretation"), since the version regarded by textual critics as the best text of a given book is not always the one that was adopted in the Masoretic Text (see below). This situation may seem unsettling at first, but it is comparable to other phases of the Bible's history. For instance, the Old Testament of early Christians was not the Hebrew Bible but the Septuagint. Along similar lines, the New Testament translation of the initial King James Version of the English Bible was based on what are universally recognized today as inferior manuscripts. Yet for many people the KJV was and is *the* Bible.

The canonization of the Old Testament was also a process. Even if there was a meeting of rabbis at Jamnia in 90 C.E., it was, at most, just the capstone of a gradual process spanning hundreds of years. The canon, the writings considered sacred and authoritative by a given faith community, is determined by the community itself through its practice and life. It is the collection of writings that the members of such a community consult and cite for divine guidance and direction. The eventual formation of the canon of the Old Testament, in other words, was not a list of texts decided upon by religious authorities at the beginning of Judaism and issued as a decree for all Jewish believers. Rather, it was a confirmation of what adherents to Judaism had already determined—the writings they were already using in their synagogues and daily lives.

Development of the Hebrew Bible also continued in a sense long after the set of canonical books had been determined. During the second half of the first millennium, families of scribes known as Masoretes (from the Hebrew word for "tradition") continued editing the text of the Hebrew Bible. Their work consisted mainly of adding a system of vowels to the consonantal text along with marginal notes about such matters as pronunciation and spelling of words. Their edited version of the Hebrew Bible is known as the Masoretic Text. The earliest exemplars of the Masoretic Text of the full Hebrew Bible that we possess today date from ca. 900–1000 C.E. They serve as the basis for modern, printed editions of the Hebrew Bible and for most modern translations of it into English and other languages. The existence of variant versions that had been present a thousand years earlier was unknown until the discovery of the Dead Sea Scrolls in 1947, though it was sometimes surmised from the differences in ancient translations, such as the Septuagint. It is worth noting that there is disagreement among the earliest lists and exemplars of the Masoretic Text about the order of the books in the Hebrew Bible, indicating that by as late as the end of the first millennium C.E., and even beyond, it was flexible.

Translation

A final issue to consider regarding growth is that of translation. Returning to our hypothetical bookstore, imagine that you were to open up several different Bibles and read the same passage in each of them. While their overall sense and meaning would be quite close, you would most likely be struck by how different they were in style and wording. Differences among translations are another reason why the contents can vary from one Bible to the next.

As early as 250 B.C.E., the Hebrew Bible, or at least significant parts of it, was translated into Greek. That translation, the Septuagint, as already mentioned, was the Bible of early Christians. The Bible has continued to be translated into other languages over the centuries for the simple reason that very few people are able to read it in its original languages—Hebrew and a little bit of Aramaic in the Old Testament and Greek in the New Testament. In fact, no other book has been translated into more languages than the Bible. According to the United Bible Societies, translation projects are currently underway in 495 different languages. Many of those languages have more than one translation of the Bible, and some, like English, have a large number of versions from which a person may choose.

The differences among those versions are due to different philosophies and methods of translation. One of the most important distinctions is that between formal equivalence and dynamic equivalence. A translation that is based on formal equivalence pays particular attention to the original, or source, language and tries to preserve as many of its features and characteristics as possible in the target language. Dynamic equivalence looks in the opposite direction and is more interested in rendering the text in language that reflects the norms and characteristics of everyday usage. Of course, every translation must be intelligible to its audience, so dynamic equivalence is always a concern. It is ultimately a question of how much influence the original language exerts on the way the target language is used to convey the text's meaning.

Throughout history Bibles reflecting different translation methods have appeared in the English language. The first translation into English was the one done by John Wycliffe and his associates at the end of the fourteenth century, which was based on the Vulgate, or Latin version of the text. The first English Bible translated from the original Hebrew and Greek was that of William Tyndale in the first half of the sixteenth century. The most celebrated of all English Bibles is the famous King James Version (KJV), which was published in 1611 as the result of the effort of six teams totaling fifty-four people who had been commissioned by the king of England to produce a translation that would be as close to the Hebrew and Greek as possible. The success of that project is seen in the fact that the KJV became the standard version of the Bible in the English-speaking world for about 250 years.

The late nineteenth and twentieth centuries saw a flurry of translation activity that continues into the present day. The results are too numerous to mention, but some deserve brief comment. The Revised Version (RV) appeared in the late nineteenth century as a replacement for the KJV with modernized language. This was followed in the early twentieth century by the American Standard Version (ASV), which was meant to serve the interests and purposes of American communities. The Revised Standard Version (RSV) was published between 1946 and 1957 and was updated by the New Revised Standard Version (NRSV) in 1990. The NRSV translation was able to take into account the archaeological discoveries and the advancements in the study of ancient languages that had taken place in the decades since the RSV had been published. It also attempted to make the language of the text more gender neutral where appropriate. It is the version most frequently used by scholars when quoting the Bible in English, and it is the one used throughout this book unless otherwise specified.

Other translations of note in recent times have been the products of teams of scholars working from common faith perspectives. The versions listed above were done by Christians, but Jewish scholars under the auspices of the Jewish Publication Society (JPS) produced their own English translation throughout the course of the twentieth century. It was published in its entirety in 1985 with the title *Tanakh: A New Translation of the Holy Scriptures According to the Traditional Hebrew Text*. Protestant scholars produced the New English Bible (NEB) in 1970, revised about twenty years later as the Revised English Bible (REB). In the Roman Catholic world, the Jerusalem Bible (JB), which is based on a translation published by French-speaking scholars in Jerusalem, came out in 1966. The Catholic Biblical Association of America published The New American Bible in

1970, a translation that is in the process of being revised. Finally, a team of evangelical scholars produced the New International Version (NIV), which was completed in 1978.

Each of these English translations, and the many others that have not been mentioned, has its strengths and weaknesses. When trying to decide among the many options, it is helpful to keep a few guidelines in mind. First, translations that are the result of a team effort are generally superior to those that are the work of one person. Such group projects usually have a system in place to evaluate alternative translations and to correct errors. Second, translations with footnotes and explanatory comments are to be preferred. A translator's work always entails assessing evidence and making decisions; a Bible with notes at the bottom of the page can give the reader a sense of how those decisions were reached. Third, go with a Bible that gives an idea of the broader context of the text. This can come in the form of introductory essays, historical background, commentary, maps, or charts. Such aids allow the reader to better appreciate the wider world of which the text is just a part.

CONTEXT

Like all literature, the Hebrew Bible can only be appreciated and understood when properly contextualized. Different aspects of its ancient context must be considered, especially the geographical setting of ancient Israel, the historical context of the events it describes and in which it was written, and its cultural environment.

Geographical Context

To understand the geographical and topographical setting of ancient Israel is to comprehend much of the history and culture that shaped it and the Hebrew Bible. The region of Israel was a part of what is known today as the Middle East. Scholars typically refer to the Middle East as the ancient Near East. It encompasses the modern countries of Egypt, Israel, Jordan, Lebanon, Syria, Turkey, Iraq, Iran, and Saudi Arabia, among others. However, these modern countries do not usually match the ancient ones in either their names or their boundaries.

The Fertile Crescent

Another name sometimes used for the ancient Near East is the "Fertile Crescent." A glance at a climate map reveals why. Perhaps the most prominent feature of the region is the great Arabian Desert, which is bordered on the north by a crescent-shaped band of fertile land extending from northern Africa and the eastern shore of the Mediterranean Sea to the head of

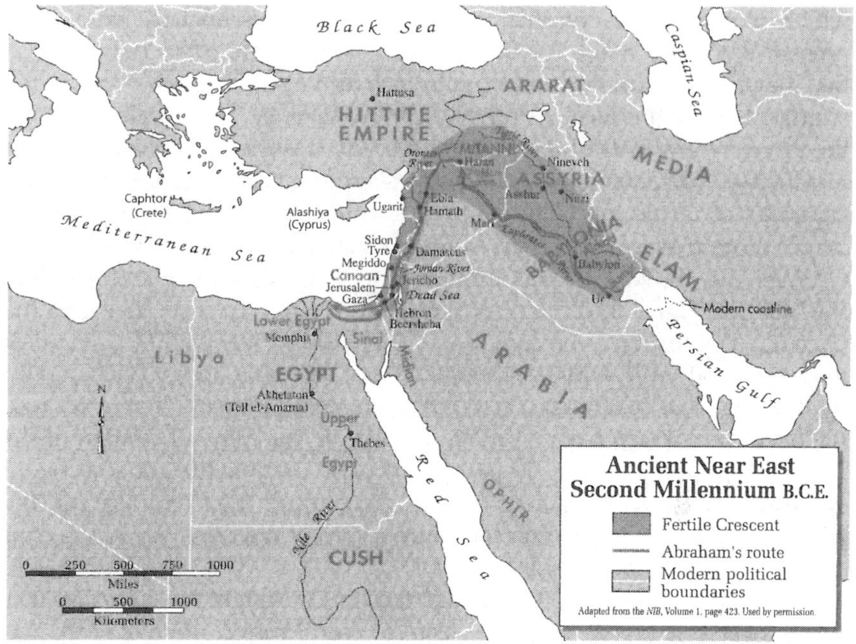

the Persian Gulf. Ancient Israel was part of this Fertile Crescent, a rather small part, actually. The traditional boundaries of ancient Israel—from Dan in the north to Beersheba in the south, and from the Mediterranean to the Jordan—mark off an area roughly the size of the state of Vermont.

The crescent is really comprised of three geological features involving rivers. The first is the lush valley watered by the Nile River, which runs south to north in northern Africa. Its fertile delta beginning at Memphis and emptying into the Mediterranean accounts for the wealth and antiquity of Egyptian civilization. The second is the Great Rift Valley, a deep geological fault dividing the African and Arabian tectonic plates. It extends some 3,000 miles from the Orontes River valley in northwest Syria through the Gulf of Aqaba and the Red Sea and on into Africa as far as Mozambique. The Jordan River valley, including the Sea of Galilee and the Dead Sea, is part of this rift. In fact, the Dead Sea is the lowest place in altitude on the face of the globe. Paleontologists have discovered the earliest human remains in this great valley system. The third part of the Fertile Crescent is the Mesopotamian plain between and including the Tigris and Euphrates river valleys in southern Iraq. (*Mesopotamia* is Greek for "between rivers.")

There are various names for the central section of the Fertile Crescent, which is our major concern, since it incorporates ancient Israel. The present-day Arab name for it is "Sham." Westerners often refer to it as the "Levant," a term derived from French and alluding to the land of the sunrise, that is, the East. Another common term is "Syria-Palestine." Of the three components of the Fertile Crescent, it is the narrowest and least productive. The Nile delta and broad Mesopotamian plain both provided expanses of fertile land. By contrast, the fertility in the central section comes more from rainfall than from its river. The fertility brought by the Orontes and the Jordan was limited. They are both much smaller than the Nile, the Tigris, and the Euphrates, and the Jordan is smaller than the Orontes. The Jordan is bounded on either side by steep cliffs, a result of the geological fault, which prevents it from watering a very wide swath. And rather than concluding in a delta or watered plateau, it empties into the Dead Sea, which has no outlet. As a result, the mineral content of the Dead Sea is so high (over 30 percent) that no organic life can survive in it—hence its name. Furthermore, the area around the Dead Sea and the portion of the Great Rift from the southern tip of the Dead Sea to the Gulf of Aqaba are dry and desolate.

The Levant, in fact, is quite varied in terrain. One might conceptualize it as a kind of checkerboard. There are distinct vertical bands, running north and south, which are in turn dissected to a certain extent by horizontal, i.e., east and west, zones. In general, the further south one goes, the dryer and less conducive to agriculture the climate becomes, and the same is true as one moves east of the Jordan. From west to east, the five vertical bands are the plain along the coast of the Mediterranean, the central highlands or hill country, the Great Rift Valley itself, the eastern mountains or plateau, and the desert.

Moving north to south, the Orontes valley is a wide, lush plain. As the river flows south, the highlands rise on its east, so that in the modern country of Lebanon, the beautiful Beqaa Valley sits between two ranges, the Lebanon and Ante-Lebanon mountains. The water from these mountains provides the sources for the Jordan beginning around Dan, the traditional northernmost city of ancient Israel. From there, the water flows into the Huleh basin, once a swamp, which in turn drains into the Jordan and the Sea of Galilee. The rolling hills and farmland of the Galilee region come to an end with the wide, rich Jezreel Valley (also called the Esdraelon Plain). This was the most prosperous agricultural area in ancient Canaan/Israel, as its name (Jezreel = "God plants") indicates. The southern line of the Jezreel is formed by the mountain chain of the central highlands, which made up the territory of ancient Israel and Judah proper, with their capitals in Samaria and Jerusalem. Most of the stories in the Hebrew Bible are set in these highlands. West and south of Jerusalem, the coastal plain, which was the territory of the Philistines, widens and then gives way to the lowlands or

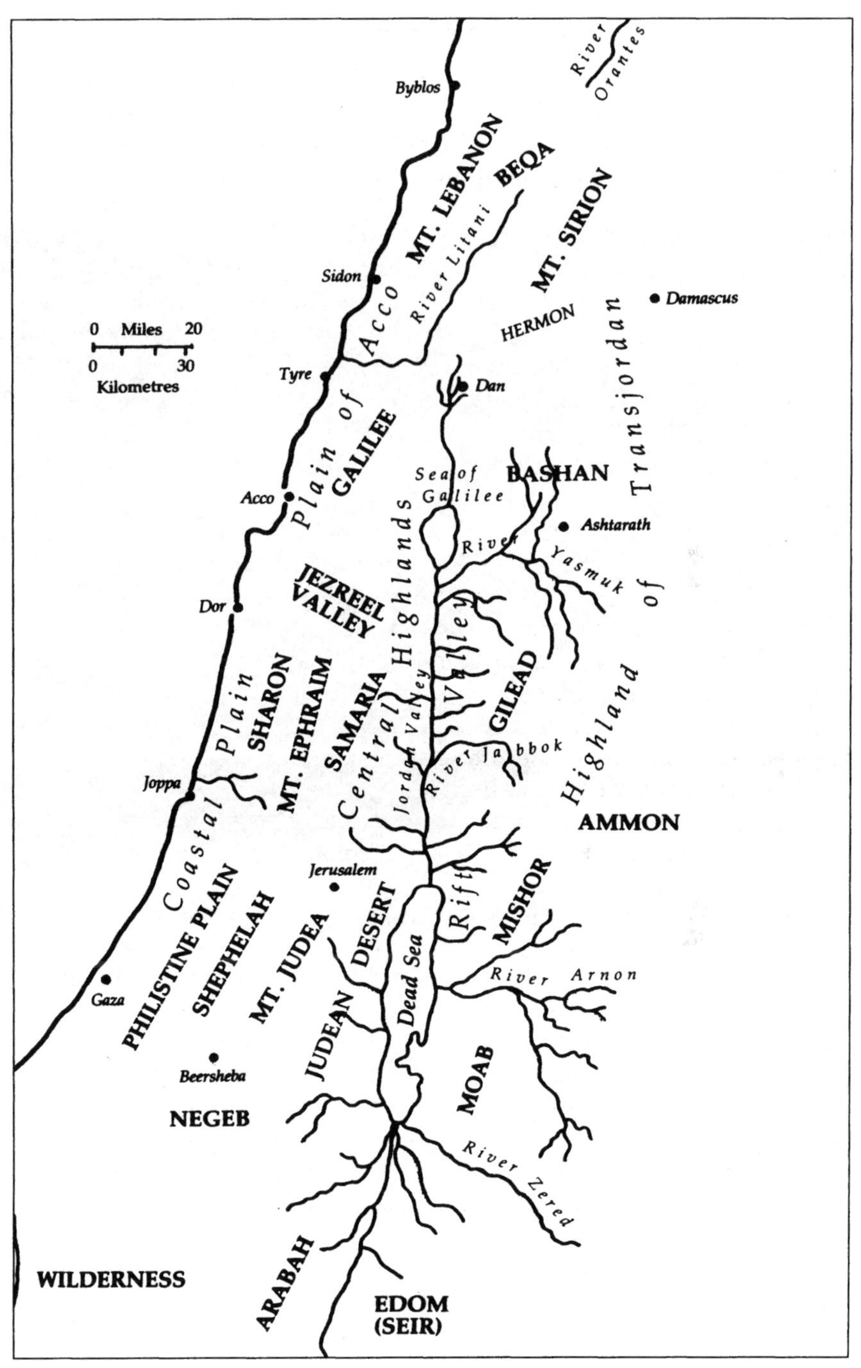

Map of the Levant, also called Syria-Palestine.

Shephelah. Due east of Jerusalem is the northern tip of the Dead Sea. Roughly at its southern tip the highlands play out and the Negeb begins. This was the badlands of ancient Israel, a dry steppe—though not a full desert—unsuitable for agriculture and thus sparsely populated.

View of the Jabbok River. Photograph by Steven L. McKenzie.

The plain east of the Jordan is broken by four *wadis* emptying into the Jordan River. (*Wadi* is the term for a ravine cut by a stream or river.) These are, from north to south, the Yarmuk, Jabbok (modern Zerqa), Arnon (modern Mujib), and Zered (modern Hesa). The latter three all play some role in biblical stories (the Yarmuk is not mentioned in the Bible). The Jabbok is the setting for the story of Jacob wrestling with God or an angel. The Arnon is the "Grand Canyon" of the modern country of Jordan and sometimes served in antiquity as a natural border between countries, that is, Ammon and Moab.

The geographical features of the ancient Near East help explain why Egypt and Mesopotamia produced the two earliest and greatest civilizations of that region, and of all human history. These countries had the natural resources that would attract the earliest humans and afford the kind of prosperity to build civilizations and empires.

Wadi Mujib, known as the Arnon River in the Bible.
Photograph by Steven L. McKenzie.

Geography also helps account for much of Israel's history. While Syria-Palestine could not produce civilizations of the same power and grandeur as the Nile delta and Mesopotamian plain, it was of great interest to the residents of these other parts of the Fertile Crescent. Egyptian and Mesopotamian (and subsequently Persian and Roman) interest in Israel and its near neighbors was occasioned by two factors. First, since travel through the Arabian Desert was difficult if not impossible, commerce between the great powers had to travel through Syria-Palestine. There were three major routes through the area: via the coast, through the Jordan Valley, and along the plateau east of the Jordan. The coastal route turned eastward through the Jezreel Valley. All three ascended northeast through Damascus and on to Mesopotamia. Since the Palestinian coast had no natural harbor, Egyptian ships typically landed further north at Tyre, Sidon, or Ugarit before heading east. The lack of a natural harbor is one of the main reasons Israel's history interacts so little with that of Greece and so much more with the landed peoples to its east.

The great powers of Egypt and Mesopotamia were not just interested, however, in Syria and Palestine as a throughway. They also

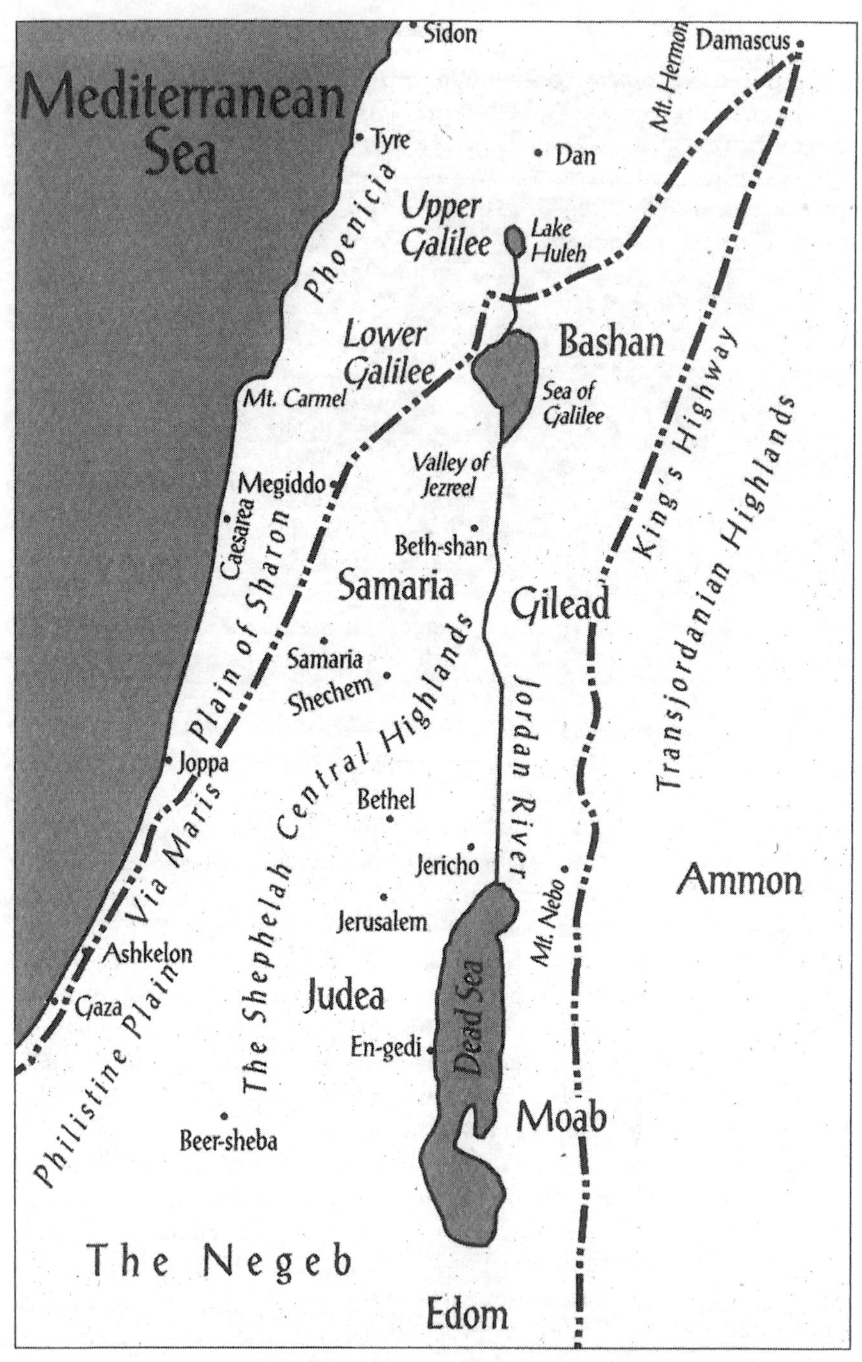

Map of ancient trade roads through Palestine.

exploited their intermediate neighbor for the products that they themselves could not produce. Chief among such products were wine and olive oil. The latter was especially valued for its medicinal, hygienic, luminary, and culinary uses, and neither Egypt nor Mesopotamia was conducive to the cultivation of grapes or olive trees. The climate and terrain of Egypt and Mesopotamia did not actually favor the growing of trees of any kind. So wood from Syria-Palestine, especially the "cedars of Lebanon," was another product of particular interest to them. This difference is reflected in certain stories in the Hebrew Bible. For instance, the tower of Babel episode (Gen 11:1-9), which is set in southern Mesopotamia, remarks that the people make a tower of bricks (not lumber). Similarly, the Hebrew slaves are forced to make bricks and even to gather their own straw for them in order to carry out building projects for their Egyptian overlords (Exod 5).

The trade routes through Syria and Palestine also became the roads traveled by armies from Egypt and Mesopotamia, eager to protect and expand commercial and imperial interests. Their forces and those of other great powers, such as the Hittites, met on more than one occasion in the Jezreel Plain. In fact, the reputation of this plain as a battleground was so pronounced that its western end, which was overseen by the elevated fortress at the town of Megiddo, lent its name (Hebrew *har megiddo*) to the legendary site of the world's final battle—Armageddon.

Aerial view of Tel Megiddo with the Jezreel Valley in the background. Photograph by Z. Radovan/www.BibleLandPictures.com.

The name well symbolizes how so much of Israel's history and culture were shaped by its geographical setting, caught between the world powers of its day. The commercial interest in Syria-Palestine meant that it was dominated throughout its history by foreign powers. For most of the second millennium (2000–1000 B.C.E.) it was under the aegis of Egypt. Egyptian control was loose, represented by military outposts and occasional Pharaonic visits, but exercised only when Egyptian interests were threatened. Then for much of the first millennium B.C.E., Syria-Palestine was dominated by Mesopotamian powers—first the Assyrians, then the Babylonians (followed by the Persians, Greeks, and Romans).

The stories in the Hebrew Bible generally reflect this history, early Israel being intimately involved with Egypt—the period of captivity and the exodus. Then after a period of "independence" for Syria-Palestine, during which David and Solomon were able to establish their own small "empires," the kingdoms of Israel and Judah became subject first to the Assyrian empire (eighth–seventh centuries) and then to the Babylonian (sixth century). Yet the Egyptian proximity loomed as an intimidating presence, even in the heyday of the Mesopotamian powers. At certain times in their histories, Israel and Judah tried to play the Egyptians and Mesopotamians off against one another. The Hebrew prophets warned against such practices and called for trust in Yahweh rather than in foreign powers. The prophets both explained and threatened invasion and destruction by a foreign army as the ultimate punishment for disobedience to God. It may be that, in the end, part of the reason Judah lasted longer as an independent kingdom than did Israel was simply because Judah was closer to Egypt.

Historical Context

It will be helpful to list a handful of dates as a framework for the historical context of the Hebrew Bible. All of these dates are approximate and B.C.E. A number of other dates will be introduced in the discussion to follow, but the dates listed below are basic to Israel's setting in ancient Near Eastern history.

925 Invasion of Syria-Palestine by Sheshonq I (Shishak) of Egypt
721 Assyrian destruction of Samaria and end of the kingdom of Israel
586 Babylonian destruction of Jerusalem, end of the kingdom of Judah, and beginning of the Babylonian exile
539 End of Babylonian exile; beginning of the Persian Empire
333 Alexander the Great's conquest of Syria-Palestine
64 Beginning of the Roman Empire

As was mentioned earlier, Syria-Palestine was under Egyptian aegis for most of the second millennium. In fact, by the end of the second millennium, when Israel was just getting started, Egypt's real glory days had passed, and Egypt was already approaching its decline on the world stage. Egypt was one of the world's earliest and greatest civilizations, dating back to well before 3000 B.C.E. By 2000 B.C.E., the first ten dynasties of Egyptian royal history—divided into the "Old Kingdom" and the "First Intermediate Period"—were completed. The great pyramids built by the earliest pharaohs were already centuries old. This period from ca. 3000–2000 B.C.E. is also known as the Early Bronze Age.

Much the same situation pertained for Mesopotamia in the Early Bronze Age. The first great, literate civilization of Mesopotamia, the Sumerians, thrived at the beginning of the third millennium. In the middle of that millennium, Sargon the Great established a new kingdom at Akkad in central Mesopotamia. Sargon was not a Sumerian but a member of a different race of people who spoke a Semitic language. The Akkadian people and their language were the forebears of the Assyrians and Babylonians and their respective languages. The last third of the millennium witnessed a resurgence of Sumerian hegemony in southern Mesopotamia, which then gave way for good to the Semites.

Throughout the entirety of the third and second millennia, Syria-Palestine was within the sphere of Egyptian influence and domination. Egyptian control was loose, as previously noted. Canaan was not a single socio-political entity but was ruled from ca. 2000 B.C.E. on by city-states, which were often at odds with each other and appealed to Egypt to resolve their disputes. This is the situation reflected in the "Amarna" letters from fourteenth-century Canaanite kings to the Egyptian court at el-Amarna. There was a constant flow of traffic and commerce between Canaan and Egypt—so much so that following the Egyptian Middle Kingdom (ca. 2000–1650 B.C.E.), Egypt fell under several dynasties of rulers from Syria-Palestine known collectively as the "Hyksos." These "rulers of foreign lands" were thoroughly Egyptianized culturally but were of non-Egyptian stock. The Hyksos Period, or Second Intermediate Period, lasted only about a century before the succeeding rulers drove them out and attempted to efface their memory from Egyptian records. There have been attempts to associate this episode with the biblical story of Joseph and the exodus.

Table of Egyptian Dynasties

Dynasties I–II (3200–2780 B.C.E.)
Old Kingdom, Dynasties III–VI (2780–2258 B.C.E.)
  Pyramid Age
First Intermediate Period, Dynasties VII–X (2258–2052 B.C.E.)
Middle Kingdom, Dynasties XI–XII (2134–1786 B.C.E.)
Second Intermediate Period, Dynasties XIII–XVII (1786–1570 B.C.E.)
  Egypt ruled by foreigners called Hyksos
New Kingdom, Dynasties XVIII–XX (1570–1085 B.C.E.)
  Dynasty XXIII (1570–1314) includes Amarna period under Akhenaten
  Dynasty XIX (1314–1197) includes Ramesses II and Merneptah
Third Intermediate Period, Dynasties XXI–XXIV (1085–715)
Late Period, Dynasties XXV–XXXI (730–332 B.C.E.)
Conquest by Alexander the Great and rule of Macedonian kings (331–304 B.C.E.)
Hellenistic Period, Ptolemaic Dynasty (304–30 B.C.E.)
Roman Period (30 B.C.E.–640 C.E.)

Mesopotamia also experienced a period of rule under ethnically foreign leaders in the first half of the second millennium, or Middle Bronze Age. These were people known as "Amorites," a term that means "Westerners." Prominent among them was Hammurapi, who is well known today for the stele (an inscribed monolith) in which he describes the law given to him by the sun god and his task as king to ensure justice for all people in his land.

The second half of the second millennium, or Late Bronze Age, was a period of tremendous upheaval in the ancient Near Eastern and Mediterranean worlds. This was the period of Egypt's New Kingdom and the time of its greatest dominance, first under Thutmose III in the fifteenth century (ca. 1479–1425) and then under Ramesses II "the Great" in the thirteenth century (ca. 1279–1213). Between them, in the fourteenth century, ruled Akhenaten, who tried to radically transform Egyptian religion to worship the one god, Aten, the sun disk. Again, there have been attempts to associate all three pharaohs with stories in the Bible. Thutmose and Ramesses especially have been identified as the pharaoh of the exodus, while Akhenaten's religious reforms have been perceived as influencing Moses' monotheism. For reasons to be discussed later, biblical scholars have grown increasingly skeptical of these connections. The Bible is extremely vague about historical details surrounding the exodus story—including the identity of the ruling Egyptian pharaoh—making it impossible to pinpoint a historical setting for the purported event.

Egypt faced several rivals during its New Kingdom. Around 1500 B.C.E., the Hurrian kingdom of Mitanni began to expand in upper Mesopotamia and Syria. Thutmose III recorded accounts of several battles against the Hurrians. They were conquered in the fourteenth century by the Hittites, who were headquartered in central Anatolia. They also grew to challenge Egypt. A famous battle for control of Syria-Palestine took place ca. 1274 B.C.E. between Ramesses II and the Hittite king Muwatallis II at the site of Kadesh on the Orontes River. The two armies fought to a standstill and drew up a treaty, copies of which remain extant today in both Egyptian and Hittite.

One of the factors leading to the collapse of the Hittite empire at the end of the Bronze Age was the invasion of the "Sea Peoples" from the Western Mediterranean. The movement of the Sea Peoples was one of the symptoms of the turmoil taking place in the Greek sphere at this period. This was also the time of the Trojan War of which Homer sang in the *Iliad* and *Odyssey*. The Sea Peoples tried to enter Egypt in the twelfth century but were repulsed and moved up into Canaan. A leading tribe of the Sea Peoples was the Philistines, who brought with them a sophisticated culture, despite the boorishness that the modern adjective *philistine* has come to imply. The Bible depicts them as entering Canaan from the west as Israel came in from the east. The clash between the two was inevitable, and the Bible describes them as Israel's principal enemy at this time.

It was at the threshold between the Late Bronze and early Iron Ages that Israel emerged as a people and then a nation in Canaan. Israel's first real king, David, came to the throne ca. 1000 B.C.E., during a kind of power vacuum in the ancient Near East, when the great empires of Egypt and Mesopotamia, following centuries of dealing with rivals, were focused inward, rebuilding. David was thus able to forge a small empire in Syria-Palestine that continued under his son, Solomon, though the actual extent of this empire remains open to question.

A large measure of David's and Solomon's success may have been their uniting of two distinct political entities, Israel and Judah, into one. At any rate, after Solomon's death, the united nation (re)divided into two separate kingdoms. The Bible (1 Kgs 14:25) dates this division five years before the invasion of Pharaoh Shishak (= Sheshonq I). This invasion, celebrated by Sheshonq himself in a relief on the temple of the god Amun in Thebes, occurred ca. 925 B.C.E. It provides one of the chronological pegs for biblical and ancient Near Eastern history. Sheshonq founded Egypt's twenty-second dynasty and led a brief resurgence of Egyptian prestige. But for most of the rest of the Third Intermediate Period (Dynasties 21–25, 1085–715 B.C.E.), Egypt was focused on internal rivalries and posed little threat to Syria-Palestine.

A more serious menace was looming on the horizon—the Assyrian or Neo-Assyrian Empire. Gathering force in the ninth century, it reached its zenith in the eighth and seventh centuries. Correspondingly, the northern kingdom of Israel was at its strongest point in terms of international reputation in the first half of the ninth century, during the dynasty of Omri, though it quickly declined thereafter. Thus, in 853 B.C.E., King

Shalmaneser III of Assyria met a formidable coalition of Syro-Palestinian kings in battle at Qarqar in northwestern Syria. Although there is no account of this battle in the Bible, Shalmaneser's annals describe King Ahab of Israel, the son of Omri, as one of the major contributors to the coalition. A dozen years later, Assyrian records portray the founder of the next Israelite dynasty, Jehu, submitting to and paying tribute to Shalmaneser. Israel would effectively remain a vassal of Assyria until it was destroyed by the Assyrian army in 721 B.C.E.

In actuality, for much of the dynasty of Jehu and beyond, Israel seems to have been little more than a puppet of its nearer neighbor, Aram or Syria. The same is true for Judah and is illustrated by the events surrounding the "Syro-Ephraimitic Crisis" in 734 B.C.E., the occasion of the famous "Immanuel oracle" of the prophet Isaiah (Isa 7; cf. 2 Kgs 16:1-9). Israel under King Pekah was compelled to join the Aramean king, Rezin, in resistance to one of Assyria's greatest kings, Tiglath-pileser III. The two kings tried to force Ahaz of Judah to join the resistance, but he refused, choosing instead to seek aid from Tiglath-pileser. The ultimate result was that first Aram (732) and then Israel (721) met their destruction at the hands of the Assyrians, and Judah became an Assyrian vassal. In 701, Hezekiah tried to break free of this vassalage but quickly repented upon the arrival of Sennacherib, who decimated Judah's countryside and also razed the ancient and revered city of Babylon. Sennacherib boasted of his conquest of one of Hezekiah's fortified cities, Lachish, in his annals and on a relief in his palace in Nineveh.

Assyria's hold on the Near East remained firm for another century, through the reigns of Esarhaddon (681–669) and Ashurbanipal (669–627), two of its most powerful kings. The former even invaded and conquered Egypt in 671, a unique feat for an Assyrian king. After the latter's reign, however, Assyria quickly declined. Its ancient capital, Ashur, fell to the Babylonians in 614, and the later capital, Nineveh, fell in 612. As Assyria declined, Egypt and Babylonia jockeyed for position to replace it, and Judah was once more caught in the middle. This predicament was well illustrated in the death of King Josiah, who in 609 B.C.E. met his death at the hands of Pharaoh Neco II, whom he was trying to prevent from marching to meet the Babylonians in battle. Josiah's death occurred at, yes, Megiddo (2 Kgs 23:29-30).

Following Josiah's death, there was disagreement and vacillation in the royal court of Judah about whether to give allegiance to Egypt or Babylonia. The decision made by the last kings of Judah to opt for Egypt proved fatal for the kingdom. After several forays into Judah to deal with rebel kings, Nebuchadrezzar II finally destroyed Jerusalem in 586 B.C.E. The last chapters of the books of 1–2 Kings and 1–2 Chronicles recount this destruction and exile (2 Kgs 25:1-21; 2 Chr 36:17-21). Nebuchadrezzar's siege and conquest of Jerusalem, in which he took its most prominent citizens captive to Babylon, is recounted both in the Bible (2 Kgs 24:10-17) and in the summary of Nebuchadrezzar's reign in the "Babylonian Chronicles." The latter dates this event precisely to March 15 or 16, 597 B.C.E., making it another of the pegs for the chronology of Israel's history.

The Babylonian empire declined following Nebuchadrezzar and was conquered in 539 B.C.E. when the city of Babylon fell without battle to Cyrus II of Persia. The former kingdom of Judah became the Persian province of Yehud. The stories in the biblical books of Ezra-Nehemiah, Esther, and Daniel are set during the Persian period, the latter two in the Persian court. However, much more of the Hebrew Bible was likely written or attained its final form during this period.

Persian domination over the Near East lasted until the coming of Alexander the Great in 333. Originally from Macedon, Alexander united the Greek city-states against Persia. He crossed the Hellespont in 334, defeating a Persian force at the Granicus River and the next year met and defeated the Persians under Darius III at Issus on the northeastern shore of the Mediterranean. Alexander died a scant decade later in 323, leaving his empire to be divided among his generals (the Diadochi). One of them, Seleucus I Nicator, became king of the eastern regions, more or less modern Syria, Lebanon, Iraq, Iran, and Afghanistan, and established the Seleucid dynasty. Another, Ptolemy I Soter, took control of Egypt and Palestine as satrap and eventually king, ruling from Alexandria. The Ptolemies were a particularly enlightened family of rulers. Ptolemy I adopted and fostered Egyptian culture, and his dynasty produced a number of women monarchs, the most famous of whom was Cleopatra VII. More important for our present concerns, Ptolemy's son, Ptolemy II Philadelphus (ca. 285–247 B.C.E.), commissioned the translation of the Hebrew Bible into Greek (the "Septuagint" or LXX) to add to the library that he established in Alexandria.

In the first half of the second century, the Seleucid ruler Antiochus IV Epiphanes came to power (175–164 B.C.E.). He invaded and overran Egypt in 168 and would have taken Alexandria if it had not been for Roman intervention. His importance for the Hebrew Bible lies in the fact that he subsequently tried to Hellenize Judea by force, abolishing Jewish rituals, holidays, and scriptures, and compelling the worship of Zeus, whose idol he erected on the altar in the temple in Jerusalem. His actions occasioned the Jewish revolt of 167–166 B.C.E., led by the high priest Mattathias and his sons, especially Judas, who were known collectively as the Maccabees. The events surrounding this revolt are recounted in the Apocryphal, or Deuterocanonical, book of 1 Maccabees. It is probably best known as the origin of the Jewish holiday of Hanukkah. The Maccabean revolt was also the setting for the writing of the book of Daniel (especially chs. 7–12), the last clearly dateable work of the Hebrew Bible.

Cultural Context

The prosperity of the early civilizations in Egypt and Mesopotamia led to a need for systems of record keeping, which in turn produced writing. Long before 2000 B.C.E., both of these civilizations had invented sophisticated writing systems and myriads of texts, many of which have been preserved across the millennia due to the durability of the writing materials and the nature of the climates involved. Official documents were often inscribed in stone. Egypt's aridity preserved its venerable papyri. In Mesopotamia, writing was done by styluses pressing into damp clay tablets, which were then hardened by baking, making them as durable as stone.

Both systems were originally pictographic. Their fundamental element was drawings or pictures of items. The pictures then became symbolic for categories, and additional signs were contrived to indicate grammatical function. The Sumerian pictures were stylized into configurations of wedges made by a triangular-headed stylus, and this system is known today as "cuneiform" or "wedge writing." Similarly, Egyptian hieroglyphs were stylized into a cursive form known as hieratic. But pen and ink did not require the replacement of pictographs as in Mesopotamia, so that hieroglyphic and hieratic writing were used simultaneously.

Both systems were complex. The Akkadians—Assyrians and Babylonians—borrowed the Sumerian signs and used them to represent syllables, with some signs having tens of possible meanings. The multiplicity of potential values was true also of Egyptian hieroglyphs. The complicated nature of these systems meant that most people—including kings—could not read or write. (Ashurbanipal was a notable exception who proved the rule.) Writing was the property of an elite, trained group of individuals—a scribal class—that could read and write. Later, in Syria-Palestine of the Late Bronze Age, the alphabet was invented based on the acrophonic principle of a single symbol for each sound. It would eventually prove to be revolutionary for Western culture. The revolution, however, was not immediate in the ancient Near East. Akkadian was the language of international communication, and only scribes were trained to use it. Even though reading and writing were easier with the alphabet, literacy among the population as a whole was minimal. There may also have been less to read. Far fewer written texts have been found in Syria-Palestine than in Egypt and Mesopotamia. This may be due partly to a difference in writing materials. The climate in most parts of Syria-Palestine is too humid for papyrus or parchment (animal skin) to endure. But there have also been fewer royal and hence stone inscriptions found. In fact, no inscription from any king of Israel or Judah bearing his name has yet been found.

Ugaritic tablet displaying writing of the ancient Near East.
Photograph by Wayne T. Pitard.

The ancient Near Eastern documents that have been found yield valuable insight into the cultural setting of ancient Israel and the Hebrew Bible. These documents are of different genres. Royal annals and monumental inscriptions, especially the annals of Assyrian and Babylonian kings, furnish much of the data about the historical setting of ancient Israel described above. They also afford useful parallels to the biblical account of the reigns of the kings of Israel and Judah in the books of Kings and Chronicles. Correspondence, such as the Amarna letters mentioned previously, illuminate the social and political situation. Treaties between monarchs not only clarify the historical setting but also aid our understanding of the Bible's depiction of the covenant between God and Israel. Other legal documents, especially contracts, do the same. Marriage contracts provide background to the relationships between the patriarchs and their wives in the Genesis stories and shed light on social customs, such as adoption, and family relationships. Law codes, like that of Hammurapi, provide parallels to the Bible's Torah. Mythological texts preserved in Ashurbanipal's library but often originating much earlier help to account for the origin of portions of Genesis 1–11. The Mesopotamian classic, the Gilgamesh Epic, bears similarities to the Genesis story of Adam and Eve, and its growth over time may be analogous to the composition of the Pentateuch. One of the most important discoveries for the study of the Bible, the tablets from Ugarit, a cosmopolitan city on the northeastern Mediterranean coast, affords our only clear glimpse of Canaanite religion for comparison with Israel's beliefs and practices. The Ugaritic texts also clarify some of the grammar and vocabulary of biblical Hebrew. Wisdom and erotic literature attest some of the same themes and images encountered in the biblical books of Job, Proverbs, Ecclesiastes, and Song of Solomon and augment our understanding of education in the ancient Near East.

The Israelite walled city of Arad, partially reconstructed.
Photograph by Steven L. McKenzie.

In addition to the attention long given to the ancient Near East, scholars in recent years have begun to devote more attention to materials from Greece and Persia as resources for cultural parallels to the Bible. They have focused especially on the question of the Bible's composition, finding similarities in the development of the Homeric classics, the *Iliad* and *Odyssey*, and noting the likelihood that much of the Bible, however it originated, achieved its final form during the Persian Empire.

The prominence of literary parallels strongly suggests that the Hebrew Bible is predominately the product of the upper classes. This is, in itself, an extremely important point, and it raises a host of questions about the intended audience of this literature and how it was used. These questions remain unanswered for the time being, as scholars continue to grapple with them.

Nevertheless, the authors of biblical books make frequent allusions to the daily life of common citizens—farmers, shepherds, merchants, and so on. An important resource—perhaps even more important than written documents—for understanding daily life in ancient Israel is archaeology. Archaeologists have uncovered the ruins of ancient cities, for example, so that when Amos (Amos 5:15) talks about establishing justice in the gate, we have the remains of benches inside city gateways and know that is

Set of oil lamps from different periods, the oldest being a simple bowl. Photograph by Gamla Excavations/Danny Syon.

where legal proceedings took place. We know also that city gates were thick and often housed chambers and residences, such as that ascribed to Rahab (Josh 2:15). We have samples of weapons and can piece together the tactics used to attack and defend city walls. Because of archaeology, we know what ancient temples looked like, even though Solomon's has not been found and probably never will be because it was leveled for new construction. We know that the "horns of the altar" (1 Kgs 2:28) refers to the raised corners used to tie down sacrifices. We have installations for the production of wine and oil and numerous examples of oil lamps. Indeed, archaeologists can trace the evolution of lamps from simple bowls with wicks on the side to elaborately decorated "Aladdin-shaped" vessels. And they can assign dates to their discoveries based on the typological development of lamps and other pottery.

Archaeology is more than just material remains. It involves interpretation in light of other evidence, including parallels from other cultures. We have a good idea what Israelite houses were like, so that when the woman at Endor fetches a calf in the house to feed Saul (1 Sam 28:24), we understand that livestock were kept on the ground floor for protection,

Typical Israelite period rural house.
Photograph by Z. Radovan/www.BibleLandPictures.com.

convenience and warmth. But we need more than the remains of a house to comprehend fully the conventions of hospitality in ancient Israel. Indeed, we may never comprehend such matters. Still, it helps to read biblical texts with cultural sensitivity. Thus, the breaches of hospitality envisioned in Genesis 19 and Judges 19 become especially horrific when one realizes that travel was basically by foot and there were no hotels or inns.

The culture that produced the Bible is distant and foreign to modern readers. Still, the Bible's cultural context can and must be discerned, at least to some extent, by the reader as well as discovered by scholars and archaeologists. Pausing to consider cultural setting, therefore, will be a profitable exercise even for the beginning reader.

INTERPRETATION

In the final part of each chapter of this book, we address some interpretive issue or problem related to the biblical material being considered. A number of different approaches are employed in those interpretation sections. In some places, a particular passage is chosen because of an unusual or interesting element it contains. In other places, more general comments are made about an entire biblical book or certain themes within it. Elsewhere, the way a book or a passage has been understood by readers, or specific groups of readers, is the topic. The perspectives adopted in these discussions range from the historical to the literary to the theological, among others.

This range of methods and points of view is a reminder of how complex and varied the process of interpretation is. Every written work—and every section of every written work—must be interpreted in order for it to make sense to its reader(s). The Hebrew Bible is no different, but there is no single "right" way to read and interpret it or any text. Throughout history, many different interpretive methods have been developed, and most of them continue to be used by readers into the present day. The important thing to keep in mind is that each method has a particular objective that can be realized only if the reader brings a specific set of questions to the text.

Evidence of interpretive activity can be seen within the Hebrew Bible itself. It contains two accounts of the history of Israelite kingship, one in the books of 1–2 Samuel and 1–2 Kings—which are part of a larger work scholars refer to as the Deuteronomistic History—and the other in 1–2 Chronicles. A comparison of these two accounts shows that they do not agree with one another, and careful study of the texts indicates that each presents a modified version of the events that suits its own interests. In other words, in both cases history is being interpreted in order to support and further a particular agenda. Another example of interpretation within the Hebrew Bible can be seen in the reuse of the wilderness motif. According to the biblical narrative, after escaping from Egypt the Israelites wandered in the wilderness for forty years before they were allowed to enter the promised land. Several of the prophetic books draw upon these wilderness traditions and cite them as a way of addressing the concerns of their own day and age. Here, too, the texts have been reinterpreted to meet the needs of later authors and audiences.

Similarly, whenever the Hebrew Bible is translated into another language, it is an act of interpretation. Anyone who has studied a language other than their own knows that all the nuances and subtleties that are found in the original language can never be completely conveyed in the target language. The translator must often choose from among many options to render a Hebrew word in another language, and it is never possible to find a perfect semantic equivalent to the original. This is as true today as it was when the earliest translations of the Hebrew Bible were done, like the Targums in Aramaic, the Septuagint in Greek, and the Vulgate in Latin. Therefore, we should always keep in mind that when we are reading the Bible in English we are reading an interpretation.

Another place in which we see interpretation of the Hebrew Bible going on is in certain extra-canonical Jewish writings that refer to or rework the biblical tradition. Some of these works are part of a collection of writings known as the Pseudepigrapha, a Greek term that means "false writings" and refers to noncanonical books that claim to have been written by prominent figures of the past. A good example is the book of Jubilees, a second-century B.C.E. work that was originally written in Hebrew but now survives only in Greek, Latin, and Ethiopic translations. Jubilees is a retelling of the book of Genesis and a portion of Exodus that purports to come from Moses. It places a great deal of emphasis on the law in its interpretation of the biblical story.

Early Forms of Interpretation

In Judaism, many of the writings of the rabbis contain interpretations of biblical books and passages. The Mishnah, a work that reached its final form around the year 200 C.E., preserves what is referred to as the "oral law," the spoken counterpart of the written law given to Moses on Mt. Sinai that is preserved in the Hebrew Bible. The traditions found in the Mishnah often provide the framework and basis upon which interpretations of the written biblical law are made. Over several centuries the rabbis studied and analyzed the Mishnah carefully, resulting in a body of commentary upon it that is known as the Gemara, or "completion."

Eventually, the Mishnah was joined with the Gemara to form the Talmud, which preserves the record of rabbinic discussion of the law, ethics, and traditions from the Bible. It is a major source of early biblical interpretation and continues to play a very influential role in Jewish life into the present day. There are two versions of the Talmud, one from Jerusalem compiled in the fourth century C.E. and the other from Babylon in the seventh century C.E.

Another important body of work containing rabbinic interpretation of the Hebrew Bible is the midrash, an umbrella term that includes a number of different interpretive methods and approaches. Midrash usually takes the form of an analytical or homiletical discussion of a passage that attempts to elucidate its message. Often the meaning the rabbis discover in the text is not immediately obvious to the reader, and the treatment of a single word or phrase can lead to a lengthy esoteric or theoretical exposition on its hidden sense. The two main forms of midrash are *halakha*, which addresses legal matters, and *aggada*, which treats non-legal content like narratives. Midrashic writings—in the form of commentaries on the Hebrew Bible and its parts—can be traced back to the second century C.E.

On the Christian side, we see interpretation of the Hebrew Bible throughout the New Testament. This is often done to substantiate and support the christological claims made in the texts. The New Testament authors consulted the scriptures (i.e., the Hebrew Bible) and searched for passages that could be cited as proof of their assertions about Jesus. Sometimes this was done overtly through direct quotations, and other times it was done more subtly through allusion. By connecting the events of Jesus' life to the sacred writings of the past, the authors were able to validate their beliefs about who he was and, in the process, develop a way of using the Hebrew Bible that would prove extremely popular for future generations of Christians.

To cite one example, Matthew's Gospel is different from the other three in its frequent use of prophetic fulfillment citations. At key moments in Jesus' life the author states that a certain event took place in order to fulfill what had been spoken by an earlier prophet, and then quotes the prophet's words (see, for example, Matt 1:22; 2:15; 2:17; 12:17-21; 21:4-5). This technique is employed to persuade the reader to see Jesus as the one about whom the prior prophets spoke, and is thereby meant to legitimate the author's Christology. This has an impact not only on how Matthew's Gospel is read, it also influences the reader's attitude toward the prophetic writings—and the Hebrew Bible as a whole—as a source that can be combed for predictions about the coming of Jesus. As noted above, this is an understanding of the Hebrew Bible that many Christians through the centuries have warmly embraced.

Related to this is a form of interpretation known as typology, which has a long history in Christianity, beginning with the New Testament. It is a way of reading the Hebrew Bible that sees its characters and events as somehow predicting or prefiguring Jesus and key aspects of Christianity. One of the most well-known examples of this is the Hebrew Bible story of Jonah being swallowed by the great fish. A typological interpretation of that story sees the fish as the equivalent of the tomb, and Jonah's three-day stay in the fish's belly as prefiguring the three days Jesus spent in the tomb before his resurrection. In this reading Jonah is a type for Jesus, an identification that is often made in medieval artwork, where Jonah and the fish become symbols for Jesus' resurrection from the dead.

Within the New Testament such typological interpretation is present. In Matthew's Gospel Jesus himself endorses the connection between Jonah's three-day stay in the belly of the fish and his own death (Matt 12:38-41). Paul refers to Adam as a "type of the one who was to come," Jesus, the new Adam (Rom 5:14). Here, too, the use of this kind of interpretation in the New Testament gave it legitimacy, allowing later Christians to adopt it in their own reading of the Hebrew Bible.

Closely associated with typology is allegory, in which texts are interpreted in a symbolic, nonliteral way. In an allegorical reading, the characters and events of a story represent other things. For example, one might read the story of Adam and Eve and their expulsion from the garden of Eden as a story that is really about the individual soul and its alienation from God. In this reading, the serpent would symbolize those people who exert a negative influence and prevent one from following God's will, and the forbidden fruit would represent the temptations that entice one and cause one to fall short despite the desire to act properly. The main point behind allegory is that the biblical text is so rich and full of meaning that it should not be reduced to its literal sense. One need only open one's mind to the possibility of hidden meanings, and then entirely new ways of understanding a text become possible. Among the most well-known practitioners of allegory are Philo of Alexandria (20 B.C.E.–40 C.E.), an influential Jewish philosopher, and Origen (182–251), a prominent early Christian theologian who was also from Alexandria, the center of allegorical exegesis. Allegory was very popular within Christianity for many centuries because, like typology, it allowed Christians to interpret the Hebrew Bible in Christian terms. But it has often been criticized because of its lack of controls that ultimately leaves interpretation up to the creative whim of the individual reader.

The various methods of biblical interpretation that were developed in the early centuries of Christianity eventually led to the idea of the "four senses of scripture." According to this schema, one can take any section of the Bible and, depending on the way it is analyzed, glean four different meanings from it: (1) the *historical sense* is the literal meaning of the text; (2) the *allegorical sense* is the symbolic meaning of the text; (3) the *tropological sense* is the moral meaning of the text; and (4) the *anagogical sense* is the mystical meaning of the text.

The garden of Eden can be taken as an example that illustrates the differences among these four senses. Historically (at least for ancient readers), it refers to the place God created as a habitat for Adam and Eve. It can be understood allegorically as a description of the ideal human-divine relationship in which God meets all our needs and completely provides for us. The tropological meaning of the garden of Eden highlights the importance of responsible human behavior. It represents a state of perfect harmony with God that can be realized only by avoiding temptation and being completely obedient to the divine will. The anagogical sense sees the garden of Eden as the eternal heavenly reward that awaits every person who remains faithful and does not surrender to sin.

This fourfold division is something that emerged within the Christian community, but it reflects in a general way some of the major interpretive approaches within Judaism that were developing at the same time. In other words, Jewish study of the Hebrew Bible also exhibited interest in the literal text, its symbolic meanings, its ethical dimension, and its otherworldly aspects. One area in which Jewish scholars were particularly adept in comparison to their Christian counterparts was study of the languages of the Hebrew Bible. There were some Christians who made significant contributions in this area, like the aforementioned Origen, whose Hexapla was one of the first critical studies of the Greek and Hebrew texts of the Old Testament, and Jerome (342–420), who was responsible for the Latin Vulgate translation of the Bible from the original Hebrew and Greek. But Jewish involvement in language study was generally more advanced and prolific than what was found among Christians.

During the medieval period, in particular, study of Hebrew flourished, and this had a direct bearing on biblical interpretation. One reason for this attention to language was the strong influence of Islam in Babylon, Western Europe, and other places with a strong Jewish presence. Soon after the founding of their religion in the seventh century C.E., Muslim scholars began to study very carefully the Arabic language of their sacred text, the Qur'an. They wrote and compiled grammars, concordances, and lexicons that served as the models for similar works by Jewish scholars seeking to come to a better understanding of their own scriptures. Sa'adiya (882–942), working in Babylon, and the Spaniard Abraham Ibn Ezra (1089–1164) were two important figures indebted to Arab scholarship in their own linguistic work. Another beneficiary of developments in

Arabic was David Kimchi (1160–1235), who, along with his predecessors Rashi (1040–1105) and Rashbom (1080–1174), were major Jewish exegetes of the Middle Ages. While they all made significant contributions of their own, much of their work involved systematizing the midrash and other rabbinic writings from previous centuries.

The monastery was an institution closely associated with biblical scholarship in the Christian world in the medieval period. In addition to their involvement in producing and copying biblical manuscripts, monks like the Venerable Bede (673–725) wrote commentaries and other study aids that were disseminated throughout Europe. With the rise of universities in the thirteenth century a new era of biblical scholarship began. Thomas Aquinas (1225–74) was a scholastic theologian who had been greatly influenced by Aristotle. His biblical commentaries, which tended to be more literal in their orientation, were among the most widely read and consulted during this period.

Two important developments in the medieval period that had an impact on biblical scholarship were the invention of the printing press and the Protestant Reformation. Johannes Gutenberg's invention of the printing press in the mid-fifteenth century made possible the mechanical production and distribution of written works that prior to that time had to be copied manually, a painstaking and slow process that kept books in the hands of relatively few people. For the first time, people were able to own their own copies of the Bible, and commentaries and other works of scholars could reach a wider audience.

The role of the Bible was one of the central issues in the debates between Protestants and Catholics. Martin Luther (1483–1546) and the other reformers believed that the Bible was the supreme authority in matters of faith, and he sought to make it available to as many Christians as possible by translating it into the German vernacular of his time. He and John Calvin (1509–64), another major Reformation figure, wrote many commentaries on the Bible that are still frequently studied and read. In their interpretation, they tend to avoid allegorical interpretation, although their view of the Hebrew Bible is such that they rely a great deal on typological and christological readings. For its part, the Catholic Church attempted to defend its views on the papacy and the role of church authority by appealing explicitly to the Bible, particularly the New Testament.

The Rise of Critical Scholarship

By the late seventeenth century the wheels were in motion that would lead to more critical approaches of study of the Bible. The seeds of this development can be seen already in the Renaissance, when the external authority of institutions like the church was called into question and replaced by that of the individual as a rational, independent subject. The idea of the Bible as divine speech was being challenged in some quarters, and more objective methods of studying the Hebrew Bible—freed from the constraints of religion and entrenched custom—were taking shape.

A distinction is often made in biblical scholarship between "lower criticism" and "higher criticism." Lower criticism tries to determine the precise wording of the original text. This entails studying the available manuscripts and other sources, and then evaluating the evidence they contain in an effort to discover what the oldest, and presumably most authentic, reading is. Sometimes called textual criticism, lower criticism consults translations like the Septuagint and other versions of the Bible and tries to establish the literary and chronological relationships among the various witnesses to the textual tradition. The goal of lower criticism is identification of the text itself, and it does not try to get at the text's meaning or interpretation.

That is a concern of higher criticism, which studies the origin of a text. Issues of authorship, sources, place and date of composition, and content are of paramount importance in the attempt to discern how a text came to be. Also sometimes called historical criticism, higher criticism provides the methods and tools to establish meaning and interpret a text. The rise of modern biblical scholarship can be traced through advances in higher criticism that resulted in an approach that came to be known as the historical-critical method. Some of the most important figures in that development are the Frenchman Jean Astruc of the mid-eighteenth century, the Germans Wilhelm M. L. de Wette and K. H. Graf of the early nineteenth century, and the German Julius Wellhausen of the late nineteenth and early twentieth centuries.

As its name implies, the historical-critical method attempts to understand a text within its historical setting and the various contexts that helped shape it. It asks questions about the author(s) of the text. Who wrote it? When was it written? Where was it written? Is there evidence of more than one author? Are there any signs of editorial activity? It is also interested in the text's audience. To whom is the text written? What can we know about that audience? What might the text tell us about the audience's situation? The text's wider literary context is also considered. Is the text similar to others found in the Bible? Does it have anything in common with writings from other parts of the ancient Near East? What does a comparison of this text with those other texts suggest? These and similar questions try to reconstruct both the context(s) from which the text emerged and the context(s) to which it responded.

Rather than see the historical-critical method as a one-size-fits-all approach that is applied to each text in the exact same way, it is better to think of it as a toolkit from which different instruments can be taken out and used depending on the nature of the work to be done. They all share the same goal of elucidating the origin of the text, but each goes about that task in a different way. The three main "tools" that are used in the historical-critical method are source criticism, redaction criticism, and form criticism.

Source criticism seeks to discern the possible sources behind a biblical text. Virtually every book in the Bible appears to be a single entity at first glance, and that initial impression appears to hold up in many cases under closer scrutiny. But scholars believe that the vast majority of the books in the Hebrew Bible are composite works that bring together material from different authors and sources. Source criticism is the method by which those sources can be identified and analyzed. Certain features like repetition, multiple versions of the same story, and alternate names for the same individual or place are often a strong indication of sources in narratives. In other types of writing, like prophetic oracles, references to historical figures or events that do not fit the context of the author or the audience can be another clue. Elsewhere, a message or theme that is at odds with what is found in other parts of a book might be indicative of multiple authorship. The Pentateuch, specifically the book of Genesis, is the place where some of these features were first recognized and studied, but source criticism has been applied to every book in the Hebrew Bible.

Redaction criticism is related to source criticism, but it looks at the opposite end of the process of composition. While source criticism seeks to break down a text to its constitutive parts and study each on its own, redaction criticism considers how those various elements have been edited and brought together to form the text we now have. It tries to find where the seams are between sources and to reconstruct the manner in which they were joined together to create a whole. The different ways you might view a finished jigsaw puzzle can serve as a helpful analogy to appreciate the difference between source criticism and redaction criticism. As you admire your finished product you might focus on the individual pieces and consider each one in isolation from the others. You pause over each piece as an individual entity, and you study its shape, color, and size. This is similar to what the source critic does as each source is isolated and studied. An alternative would be for you to look at the entire puzzle and to pay attention to how the various pieces have come together as parts of the whole. You are aware of the existence of the individual pieces, but your attention is on how they each contribute to the entire puzzle that is now before you. You note how the absence of even one piece would disrupt the whole work. This is the approach of the redaction critic, who studies how the various sources of a text have been brought together and arranged.

Form criticism is an approach toward biblical texts that was developed by Hermann Gunkel (1862–1932), a German scholar who was one of the most influential Old Testament scholars of the first half of the twentieth century. It attempts to discover the *Sitz im Leben* ("situation in life") of a composition by determining how it functioned in society or daily life. In this way the sociological context of the text is brought to the fore through an identification of the institutions and situations in which it would have been most at home in ancient Israel. For example, a prophetic oracle that has the qualities of a lawsuit in which God accuses the people of violating the terms of the covenant can be associated with the judicial context of a court proceeding. Or a proverb that is presented as words of wisdom passed on from a father to his son reflects a setting in the family home, where the parents are involved in the moral and ethical education of their children. Form criticism is more appropriate for some types of writing than others since certain texts or passages can be more easily tied to a particular context than others. For instance, Gunkel's initial work in form criticism concentrated on the psalms, many of which appear to be related to the cultic (worship) activity centered on the temple in Jerusalem. Form criticism has proved to be a helpful tool that exposes the wider cultural setting of biblical texts, and Gunkel's attention to the sociological context anticipated approaches that would become popular later in the twentieth century.

As noted earlier, these three types of analysis—source criticism, redaction criticism, and form criticism—are the primary tools of the historical-critical method, and they can be used independently of one another. The nature of the text being studied and the scholar's reason for studying it determine which type of criticism is most appropriate, but it is often the case that more than one kind is used. As we will see throughout this book, another important dimension of historical-critical methodology entails comparing the biblical material with texts from other parts of the ancient Near East. If the primary goal is to determine as precisely as possible a text's origin, a vital part of that process is to consider the relationship between the Bible and similar literature that predates it from its neighboring cultures. Therefore, written works from Mesopotamia, Egypt, and other places in Canaan like Ugarit must be examined to consider what influence, if any, they exerted on the formation of the Bible.

The historical-critical method remained the dominant way scholars studied the Hebrew Bible through much of the twentieth century. Most graduate schools taught their students to analyze the text in this fashion, and it was also a major component of the training programs for ministry in all but the most conservative of seminaries. It continues to be an approach used by many, as seen in the fact that a majority of the articles published in the most highly respected journals in the field employ some aspects of the method. The historical-critical method is not in danger of becoming obsolete, but beginning in the second half of the twentieth century it has sometimes come under attack. One of the criticisms frequently leveled against it is that its claims to objectivity and impartiality are hollow. A number of other ways of studying the Hebrew Bible have emerged over the past few decades that offer alternative models of interpretation.

Recent Developments

The historical-critical method is primarily interested in the formation of the text and in the contexts that helped shape the text. More recent approaches have suggested other avenues of inquiry, with some dismissing outright the attempt to discover the text's origin as misguided and futile. Some claim we should study only the text as we have it, expressing little or no interest in its growth and development. Others try to draw upon research and methods in other disciplines and apply this to study of the Bible in the hope that it will provide a new perspective leading to fresh insights on the text. Elsewhere, the social location of the reader is taken as a determinative factor in interpretation because it is ultimately the reader who gives meaning and significance to a text. The result has been a gradual expansion of the field of biblical studies to the point that the historical-critical method, which once dominated the discipline, is now one of an array of interpretive possibilities.

Literary criticism is an umbrella category that refers to a number of different ways of studying the Bible that are informed by literary studies. Narrative analysis, rhetorical analysis, and reader-response criticism are three of the most commonly used approaches in this method. In narrative analysis, Hebrew Bible stories are studied with an eye toward their narrative structure, as attention is paid to such elements as plot, the role of the narrator, characterization, repetition, and gaps in the reader's knowledge. Rhetorical analysis seeks to understand how the text tries to influence or persuade the reader to hold certain views or to feel a particular way about something. It is therefore keenly interested in the text as a vehicle of communication between the author and the reader. Reader-response criticism highlights the subjective dimension of reading. It is based on the idea that each reader gives meaning to a text, and so it studies how the text gradually reveals information to the reader and how he or she goes about the task of constructing a meaningful "world of the text" from the data provided by the author. Literary approaches like these focus on the text as it exists in the Hebrew Bible and typically do not pursue questions related to its development or possible sources.

Another interpretive model that stresses the final form of the text is canonical criticism, a more recent development most closely identified with the American scholar Brevard Childs. It is centered on the idea that the Bible is a set of canonical writings that are authoritative for Jews and Christians. Even though their original authors did not intend this status for the works, this is now part of the identity of these books, a fact that has profound implications for how they should be interpreted. Canonical criticism claims that the biblical writings should not be read in isolation from one another, but must be seen as part of the larger collection. It is therefore imperative that the reader understand the text within its wider canonical context.

Social-scientific criticism is another broad category that encompasses a range of relatively new ways of studying the Hebrew Bible. Methods and ideas from anthropology, sociology, and other social sciences are applied to the biblical material in order to come to a better understanding of the worlds behind and within the texts. Our understanding of a number of key aspects of ancient Israelite society—the rise of the monarchy and the social role of prophets, to name but two—has been greatly enhanced through such interdisciplinary study. Another contentious point about which social-scientific criticism has provided valuable insight concerns the emergence of Israel in Canaan. The issue continues to be debated, but social-scientific analysis indicates that the Hebrew Bible's description of an invasion from the outside is not supported by the evidence.

Archaeology has long been an important sister-discipline to biblical studies, and that relationship is now bearing more fruit than ever. Archaeologists are less interested in finding evidence that will support the biblical account than they were in the past, and they have turned their attention to the study of lesser-known sites that sometimes provide valuable information on daily life in ancient Israel. That shift, combined with the recent trend among Bible scholars to engage in social-scientific study, has resulted in a more complete and accurate understanding of the world of the Hebrew Bible.

Another important development to note is the rise of methods of biblical study that call attention to the role a reader's social location plays in the process of interpretation. Underlying these approaches is the belief that the perspective, experiences, needs, and values of a person have a profound impact on how he or she reads and understands any text, including the Bible. Feminist interpreters were among the first to explore the implications of this idea in their work. As the product of a male-dominated context, the Hebrew Bible rarely acknowledges or gives voice to the concerns and experiences of women. Feminist scholars have addressed this by adopting a "hermeneutic of suspicion" in relation to the text. This is a term that was coined in the 1970s by the French philosopher Paul Ricoeur, who felt one should always be suspicious of texts because they conceal the political interests of those who wrote them. Ricoeur believed that an interpretation must bring to light those interests and reveal the text's true intention. One of the tasks of feminist interpretation of the Hebrew Bible is to expose the patriarchal agenda behind the text so that it can be recognized and challenged. Feminist scholars have also put forward many analyses of biblical texts that uncover the patriarchy within them and offer insightful alternative readings.

Related to this are liberationist interpretations of the Hebrew Bible, which first arose with the emergence of liberation theology in Latin America in the late 1960s. Most people in that part of the world live in abject poverty while relatively few control all the wealth and power. People turned to the Bible to try to understand this unjust situation and reached the conclusion that its main message is one of liberation and that people must do what they can to achieve freedom from what oppresses them. Here, too, we can see how one's social location shapes interpretation. The exodus story is no longer an ancient story describing what happened to another group of people centuries ago. It becomes a paradigm for people everywhere as a model of liberation and hope. Theologies of liberation have developed among many oppressed peoples and groups throughout the world, and in all of them the Bible plays a central role.

There are many examples of similar cultural/ideological criticisms that have arisen in the past few decades based on the experiences of members of marginalized groups, including Latino/a, African American, Native American, postcolonial, and gay/lesbian readings of Hebrew Bible texts. In addition, growing numbers of biblical scholars have adopted a postmodernist approach in their analysis of texts. These newer methods are ultimately concerned with questions of power and authority. A key issue they each address is that of who has control over these texts and how they are interpreted. For a long time biblical interpretation was the domain of predominantly white European male scholars, who dictated the rules of the game and set the agenda. As more partners have entered the interpretive conversation, the playing field has begun to level and the discussion is moving in new and interesting directions.

A NOTE ON THE BOOK'S FORMAT

All of the chapters in this book follow the arrangement found in this introductory chapter. Each begins with a consideration of the contents of a particular section of the Hebrew Bible. This is followed by a discussion of evidence that points toward the growth of that material by such means as editorial activity or the use of sources. The context section of each chapter attempts to place the biblical text, or some part of it, in its wider literary, social, geographic, or cultural context. Finally, some interpretive aspects of the material are identified and explored. The treatment in these sections is in no way meant to be exhaustive or complete. Rather, our aim is to identify and illustrate some of the most important dimensions of the content, growth, context, and interpretation of the Hebrew Bible.

PART ONE

Torah

INTRODUCTION TO THE TORAH

The first section of the Hebrew Bible is known as the *Torah*, a Hebrew word meaning "instruction," though it is most commonly translated as "law." This section is also sometimes called the Pentateuch, a combination of two Greek words meaning "implement of five" and referring to a case holding the five scrolls or books that comprise the Torah, or Pentateuch. Those five books are Genesis, Exodus, Leviticus, Numbers, and Deuteronomy. These are actually English titles, since Hebrew scrolls had no titles per se but were called by the first word or words of the scroll. Thus, the Hebrew title for Genesis is *bĕrēshît*, the word usually translated "In the beginning."

The Torah recounts ancient Israel's traditions about the beginning of the world and its own earliest history. The major episodes in this set of traditions are the creation of the world and human origins (Gen 1–11); stories about Israel's ancestors, including Joseph and the descent into Egypt (Gen 12–50); enslavement in Egypt and rescue under Moses (Exod 1–19); the giving of the "law" (*torah*) to Moses (Exod 20–Num 10); the forty-year wilderness wandering (Num 11–36); and Moses' rehearsal of the law on the banks of the Jordan River (Deuteronomy). As this list implies, the law is both central to the Torah and its longest constituent member. Hence the name Torah for the entire Pentateuch.

Traditionally, the Torah is attributed to Moses. However, this attribution has been questioned in the modern period since at least the eighteenth century by careful readers who noticed evidence of the composite nature of these books. Initially, these readers were typically clergymen, but their observations launched the academic field of biblical studies. In its early years biblical studies was focused especially on the Pentateuch, and biblical scholars produced a theory about the composition of its five books. The theory is known as the Documentary Hypothesis. As the name suggests, this theory holds that the Pentateuch is a compilation of different source documents. The classic version of the hypothesis was formulated by a German scholar named Julius Wellhausen, who postulated four such documents, abbreviated J, E, D, and P. The letters stand for Jahwist (German) or Yahwist, Elohist, Deuteronomist, and Priestly writer, the titles of the postulated authors of the sources. The first two of these titles come from names of God in the Bible: Yahweh (sometimes rendered "Jehovah") and Elohim (the generic term for God). These sources were dated to different periods of Israel's history, traditionally J to the tenth–ninth centuries B.C.E. (before the common era), E to the ninth–eighth, D to the seventh, and P to the sixth–fifth centuries. According to leading versions of the theory, the sources were combined by one or more editors, or "redactors," at different stages—one redactor combining J and E, another adding D, and still another adding P.

A major adjustment to the Documentary Hypothesis was proposed in the mid-twentieth century and has been widely accepted. It holds that the book of Deuteronomy and thus the D source was not originally part of the Pentateuch but rather introduced an extended history of Israel that incorporated the entry into Canaan and the monarchy. Originally, therefore, there was not a Pentateuch but a Tetrateuch, four books rather than five. Deuteronomy was only later incorporated as part of the (present) Pentateuch. It is, therefore, a "swing" book of sorts between the Torah and the Former Prophets.

The separation of Deuteronomy (D) from the rest of the Pentateuch is only one (and perhaps the most widely accepted) of many variations on the Documentary Hypothesis proposed since the theory's inception. Some scholars have argued in the opposite direction, for including not only Deuteronomy but also Joshua (Hexateuch) or even further books, extending sometimes all the way to the books of Kings. Others have proposed additional sources beside the "standard" four.

These variations on the Documentary Hypothesis were just that—variations, rather than distinct models. Now, however, new models are emerging. In some cases, these are actually adaptations or renewals of older models that preceded or competed with the Documentary Hypothesis. For instance, an alternative that has gained some currency among scholars is the "Supplementary Hypothesis"—the theory that the Pentateuchal "sources" were not separate documents that were combined but rather that an earlier source document (J) was incorporated and supplemented by a later author (P). Adherents of the "Supplementary Hypothesis" typically doubt the existence of a distinct E source. Even more radical or revolutionary are theories that reject the idea of sources altogether and seek to explain the Pentateuch as the bringing together of independent traditions or blocks of narrative.

It should be clear from this brief survey that scholarly analysis of the Pentateuch is very much in a state of flux at present. The Documentary Hypothesis has furnished the reigning explanation among biblical scholars for the composition of the Torah for the past century and a half, but this may no longer be the case. Still, it is probably fair to say that some version of it is still held by the majority of biblical scholars, at least in North America. (European scholars tend to be more diversified in opinion.)

In this textbook we adopt the basic thesis of the Documentary Hypothesis that different sources underlie the Pentateuch. We especially emphasize the presence of J and P material, because the evidence for these writers seems particularly clear and well accepted. We leave open more detailed questions such as the identification of sources beyond J and P, whether P was an independent document or an editor, and precisely when and how Deuteronomy came to be included in the Pentateuch. We have also chosen to treat Deuteronomy with the Former Prophets, with which it seems to have a stronger and clearer original affiliation than with the first four books of the Torah.

What may be most useful for the beginning student at this point is that biblical scholars generally agree that the Torah is not the oldest part of the Hebrew Bible—certainly not the first to be written in its present form. It was, however, probably the first section of the Bible to be recognized as authoritative scripture by early Jewish readers.

Chapter 1

THE PRIMEVAL HISTORY: THE BEGINNING (GENESIS 1:1–2:3)

The first book of the Bible, Genesis, falls easily into four main sections, according to its content: Primeval History (chs. 1–11), Abraham and Sarah (12:1–25:18), Jacob and his family (25:19–36:43), and Joseph (37–50). The first section, the Primeval History, contains some of the Bible's best-known stories and sets the stage well for our survey of the Hebrew Bible. Hence, we devote the first section of this introduction—three chapters—to it.

Genesis 1–11	
1–3	Creation, Adam and Eve in the Garden of Eden
4	The First Murder: Cain and Abel
5	Genealogy from Adam to Noah
6–9	The Flood
10	Peoples Descended from Noah's Three Sons
11:1-9	The Origin of Different Languages: The Tower of Babel
11:10-32	Descendants of Shem to Abram

The first eleven chapters of Genesis are about origins. They relate creation and the origins of different groups of humans as background to the story of Abram and his descendants. They are history, but ancient history rather than modern history. Their purpose is not to recount exactly what happened in the past but to provide a broad context for Israel's history by explaining the origins of the world and of other civilizations. Writing within their culture and worldview, biblical writers made use of legends and myths in the absence of other sources in order to account for the origins of the world. Thus, these chapters of Genesis actually contain not one but several different stories of creation. Their account of origins is heavily influenced by Mesopotamian tradition in which the flood is an extension of creation. The Genesis account of the flood is composite and adapted from Mesopotamian versions. In addition to creation and the flood, these chapters give legendary explanations for the origins of different professions (ch. 5), the different peoples of the known world (ch. 10), and the different languages and cultures (ch. 11).

THE FIRST CREATION STORY (GENESIS 1:1–2:3)

CONTENT

The first chapter of Genesis tells of creation in six days. God's resting on and consecration of the seventh day (2:1-3) presumes and continues this day-by-day account, making it clear that the description in chapter 1 spills over into chapter 2. The division between chapters in this instance is poorly placed. The conclusion of the account does not come until God's blessing of the seventh day in 2:3. The full extent of the textual unit, then, is 1:1–2:3.

The first words of the Bible are ungrammatical in Hebrew. They literally read, "In the beginning of the God created the heavens and the earth." A slight change in the Hebrew vowels is required to make sense of the sentence. The most common solution yields, "In the beginning, God created the heavens and the earth." But another solution is to read these words as a temporal clause: "When God began to create the heavens and the earth . . ." This latter solution is preferable in terms of Hebrew syntax. The sentence begun by the temporal clause is interrupted in 1:2 by a parenthetical description of the condition of the world when God began creation. The sentence then concludes in 1:3 by naming the first item of creation. The full sentence reads:

> When God began to create the heavens and earth (the earth being formless and empty with darkness over the surface of the deep and a divine wind sweeping over the surface of the water), then God said, "Let there be light." (AT)

The view of creation reflected here is that of bringing order out of chaos rather than making something out of nothing (creation *ex nihilo*).

The account of creation for each day contains the same basic set of expressions:

> God said, "Let there be *x*."
> And there was *x*/So God made *x*/And it was so.
> God saw that *x* was good.
> God called *x* "*x*."
> There was evening and morning, day *y*.

The set of expressions accommodates variation, as on the fifth and sixth days when God blessed them (animals, including birds and fish, and humans) with the command, "Be fruitful and multiply." But the basic pattern upon which each day's account of creation is built is still evident.

Remarkably, the basic pattern occurs twice for days three and six. Verses 9-10 read:

> And God said, "Let the waters under the sky be gathered together into one place, and let the dry land appear."
> And it was so.
> God called the dry land Earth, and the waters that were gathered together he called Seas.
> And God saw that it was good.

According to the pattern in the other verses, one expects to read, "And there was evening and there was morning, the third day"(1:13). Instead, the pattern begins again:

> Then God said, "Let the earth put forth vegetation . . ."
> And it was so (1:11) . . .
> And God saw that it was good (1:12).

Only then does the time reference, "And there was evening and there was morning, the third day," occur.

Similarly, for the sixth day, the basic formula occurs in verses 24-25:

> And God said, "Let the earth bring forth living creatures of every kind . . ."
> And it was so . . .
> God made the wild animals of the earth of every kind.

One expects to read, "And there was evening and there was morning, the sixth day." Instead, the formula restarts in verse 26 and is expanded through the end of the chapter:

> Then God said, "Let us make humankind in our image . . ." (1:26)
> So God created humankind in his image . . . (1:27)
> And it was so. (1:30)
> God saw everything that he had made, and indeed, it was very good.
> And there was evening and there was morning, the sixth day. (1:31)

The narrative thus describes the creation of two categories of things, or better, two creative acts for days three and six. The first act on day three is the gathering of the waters to form seas and dry land. This is followed by the creation of vegetation on the dry land. On day six, land animals and humans are created in separate acts. Only one creative act is detailed for every other day.

The structure of the entire account may thus be sketched as follows:

Day 1 – light	Day 4 – sun, moon, stars
Day 2 – dome (sky) in the midst of waters	Day 5 – birds, fish
Day 3 – seas and dry land vegetation	Day 6 – land animals humans

Day 7 – Sabbath

The account is literarily sophisticated and extremely well balanced. The balance is obvious when the two halves of the account (days 1-3 and days 4-6) are compared side-by-side. In addition to having one item or category created on the first two days in each half (1-2, 4-5) and then two items on the third day (3 and 6), there is "horizontal" correspondence between each half: light (day 1) and luminaries (day 4), sky and seas (day 2) and the creatures in them (day 5), dry land and vegetation (day 3) and the animals and humans who live on land and consume its vegetation (day 6).

GROWTH

The structure of this text as just diagrammed suggests that a version of creation in eight installments lies behind Gen 1:1–2:3. The author retained the eight installments in the pattern in which each item or category of creation is narrated. This pattern occurs eight times in the chapter. But instead of having creation take place over eight days, the author compacted it into six days by placing two installments on days three and six, that is, having two categories of things created on those days. The obvious reason for doing this was to leave the seventh day, the Sabbath, as a day of rest for God. The significance that this account invests in the Sabbath is an important clue to its author's identity. Scholars typically assign it to a Priestly author (abbreviated "P") because of the interest that it reflects in ritual matters, specifically the keeping of Sabbath.

CONTEXT

The reading of Gen 1:1-3 just proposed is supported by the fact that other creation accounts from the ancient Near East begin with a temporal clause. One of the best known of these is the Babylonian story of creation called *Enuma Elish* after its beginning two words:

When on high the heaven had not been named,
firm ground below had not been called by name,
there was nothing but primordial Apsu, their begetter,
and Mummu-Tiamat, she who bore them all,
their waters commingling as a single body;
no reed hut had been matted, nor marsh land had appeared,

when no gods whatever had been brought into being,
uncalled by name, their destinies undetermined—
then it was that the gods were formed within them. (*ANET*, 60)

After recounting the generation of the gods, *Enuma Elish* goes on to describe a conflict between the primordial goddess, Tiamat, and the younger gods. The champion of the younger gods, Marduk, defeats Tiamat in battle and then divides her corpse in two, using half of it to create the sky and the other half for the earth. After making the rest of the cosmos, Marduk ingeniously orders the mixing of the blood of a god with clay to form humans so that they can do the work of the gods. The story ends with the gods proclaiming Marduk their king and enthroning him in Babylon, which they have built for him.

Other Bible writers are familiar with a myth like the one in *Enuma Elish*, in which the storm god defeats the sea god in battle and then divides her or his corpse in order to create the cosmos. In Isa 51:9-10 it is Yahweh, the God of Israel, who defeated the god Sea, also known as Rahab:

Awake, awake, dress yourself in strength, O arm of Yahweh.
Awake as in former days, generations of the distant past.
Were not you the one who cleaved Rahab, who pierced Dragon?
Who dried up Sea, the waters of the great Deep? (AT)

Genesis 1:1–2:3 contains several similarities to *Enuma Elish*. The word for "deep" (*tehom*) is the Hebrew version of "Tiamat." Also, the view of the cosmos as a dome over the earth that holds back water (1:6-8) is similar to the idea that it consists of two parts of Tiamat's body. The order of creation (light, sky, land, luminaries, human beings) is the same in both texts, and God's resting in Gen 2:1-3 may be compared to the celebration of the gods at the end of *Enuma Elish*.

At the same time, Gen 1:1–2:3 and *Enuma Elish* are obviously very different documents, especially in their respective theologies. While *Enuma Elish* is polytheistic, there is only one God in Gen 1:1–2:3. Phenomena such as the sun and moon, which are deified in other cultures, are part of God's creation in Genesis. Even the "deep," though in existence when God begins to create (Gen 1:2), is not a deity. What is more, in Gen 1:1–2:3 God creates not by building or forming but by merely speaking or thinking (the Hebrew verb means both) things into existence. If the Priestly author of Gen 1:1–2:3 was in Babylon and knew *Enuma Elish*, as some scholars have suggested, he surely wrote at least in part to counter Babylonian theology.

INTERPRETATION

The expression "evening and morning" (rather than "morning and evening") reflects the ancient Israelite calendar, which marked the beginning of a new day at sunset. (The same calendar continues today in the start of the Jewish Sabbath at sundown on Friday.) This expression already indicates that this text embodies a particular cultural outlook that was different from a modern, scientific one. Its balanced structure indicates that it is a work of literary artistry and creativity rather than a journalistic report of events that have taken place.

The description in this chapter is also at odds with the modern, scientific view of the world in several particulars. The sun and moon are not created until the fourth day. Before that time, there is already light, day and night, and thriving vegetation—all of which we know to be impossible without the sun. The notion of the sky as a "dome" indicates that the author understood the earth to be flat. Day five sees the creation of "dragons," which we know to be mythological creatures (cf. Job 7:12; Ps 74:13; 148:7; Isa 27:1; 51:9; Jer 51:34; Ezek 29:3; 32:2).

Genesis 1:1–2:3 is not a scientific document. Its purpose is theological rather than historical. It makes the point that a supreme God created the world. In contrast to the Babylonian story, there is only one God—the God of Israel. The "us" of Gen 1:26 does not refer to a plurality of deities, as in a pantheon, nor does it refer to the Christian Trinity. Rather, it reflects the metaphor of God as a Near Eastern king surrounded by a court or council of advisors. The creation of humans in God's image likely refers to the dominion that human beings exercise over animals, as 1:26 explains.

The claim that God created the world in six days carries social and political implications as well as theological ones. The Sabbath, the seventh day, is so important, the author claims, that it is engrained in the very order and fabric of the universe. Even God at creation observed the Sabbath. By giving the Sabbath such an exalted role, Gen 1:1–2:3 promoted a particular class in ancient Israel, namely, the priests, who had oversight of the Sabbath and ritual observances. This is one of the reasons that biblical scholars typically speak of the creation account in Gen 1:1–2:3 as a document probably written by a priest (P). This social dimension of Gen 1:1–2:3 is perhaps its most striking similarity to *Enuma Elish*. By promoting the cult of Marduk in Babylon, the latter obviously furthered the cause of the priesthood of Marduk against the priesthoods of other deities in Babylon. Similarly, the stress on the Sabbath in Gen 1:1–2:3 furthered the cause of the priesthood over against other social classes, such as prophets, scribes, and adherents of the royal court.

CHAPTER 2

THE PRIMEVAL HISTORY: ADAM AND EVE (GENESIS 2:4b–3:24)

The story of Adam and Eve is one of the best known in the Bible. It has been the source of common expressions, like "forbidden fruit," and titles of books and movies, like *Paradise Lost, East of Eden*, and *Adam's Rib*. It is at once a simple story about the first humans and at the same time, an extremely complex narrative in what it suggests about such matters as the relationship of men and women, humans and nature, and good and evil.

CONTENT

The famous story of Adam and Eve and the garden of Eden begins with a second account of creation. Its opening is syntactically identical to that of the first creation story: a sentence beginning with a temporal clause is interrupted by a parenthetical description of conditions at the time of God's first creative act and then continues with a description of that act.

	Genesis 1:1-3	Genesis 2:4b-7
Temporal clause	When God began to create the heavens and the earth	When ("in the day") Yahweh God made earth and heavens
Parenthetical description	(the earth being formless and empty with darkness on the surface of the deep and the divine wind/spirit sweeping over the surface of the water)	(before there was any shrub or grass on the earth, since Yahweh God had not brought rain on the earth, nor was there any human to work the ground but a mist came up from the earth and watered the ground's surface)
First deed of creation	God said, "Let there be light," and light came into existence. (AT)	Yahweh God formed the human of dust from the ground and breathed into his nostrils the breath of life so that the human became a living being. (AT)

The story that begins in 2:4b obviously continues at least through the end of chapter 2 and the creation of woman. The same characters (God, the man, and the woman) also continue through chapter 3 with the addition of the serpent. The entire story, therefore, encompasses 2:4b–3:24 and falls into two major episodes—the creation in chapter 2 and the disobedience with its consequences in chapter 3. The next episode in chapter 4 mentions the man and the woman but quickly moves on to their sons, who are the focus of the chapter. The present unit then is Gen 2:4b–3:24.

This second version of creation (Gen 2:4b–3:24) does not exhibit the kind of neat structure found in the first one (1:1–2:3). This illustrates one of the major differences between the two texts. While 1:1–2:3 is formulaic and repetitive—almost a list—2:4b–3:24 is a story. There is no time frame. Following is a summary of the two principal episodes of the story.

Yahweh God fashions a man and places him in a garden that he has planted for the man (2:4b-9). There are two brief excursuses: the location of the garden is identified (2:10-14), and Yahweh God commands the man not to eat from the tree of knowledge in the middle of the garden (2:15-17). Yahweh God sees that it is not good for the man to be alone, so he fashions first the animals and then a woman (2:18-25).

The serpent appears as the wiliest of creatures; it entices the woman to eat of the forbidden tree, and the man follows her lead (3:1-7). Yahweh God interrogates the man and discovers his offense (3:8-13). Yahweh God curses the serpent, the woman, and the man in turn for their respective roles in the disobedience (3:14-21). Yahweh God then drives the couple out of the garden and posts guardians to prevent their reentry (3:22-24).

GROWTH

The details of creation according to Gen 2:4b–3:24 differ markedly from those given in 1:1–2:3. One of the most obvious differences is that they use different names for God: "God" in 1:1–2:3 but "Yahweh God" in 2:4b–3:24. There are also other, more substantial differences. In 1:1–2:3, human beings are the last item of creation, following plants and animals. "Humankind" is created as a whole and not limited to just one pair. In 2:4b–3:24, in contrast, one man is created, followed by the garden for him to inhabit, then the animals in search of a suitable companion, and finally a woman made from the man:

Genesis 1:1–2:3	Genesis 2:4b–3:24
Day 1 – light	the man
Day 2 – dome (sky)	the garden
Day 3 – seas and dry land + vegetation	the animals
Day 4 – sun, moon, stars	the woman
Day 5 – birds, fish	
Day 6 – land animals + humans	
Day 7 – Sabbath	

In addition to these differences in order, the two texts vary significantly in tone and nature. Genesis 1:1–2:3 is very formulaic and repetitive, as we have seen, with the same expressions occurring repeatedly. It is such a well-ordered text that it might almost be called a list of the categories of created items by the day on which each is created. As such, it can easily be outlined. Genesis 2:4b–3:24, in contrast, is a story. There is no time frame or other tight organization. It contains a set of characters that interact with each other and a plot. Genesis 1:1–2:3 has no plot, and God is the only character.

The views of God reflected in these two texts are also quite different. In Gen 1:1–2:3, God is fairly described as omniscient. The action, so to speak, is set in heaven. God creates merely by speaking or thinking things into existence. The universe may not be created out of nothing, but the things in it are. The depiction of Yahweh God in Gen 2:4b–3:24, on the other hand, is *anthropomorphic*. That is, Yahweh God is described as having human characteristics. He does not create by thought or spoken word. Rather, he "forms" the man (2:7) and the animals (2:19) the way a potter would shape clay vessels. He breathes life into the man (2:7). He "builds" the woman, using a bone he has removed from the man (2:21-22). He strolls in the garden (3:8) and holds a conversation with the man and the woman (3:9-12). He even makes garments for the pair (3:21). He also appears to be intimidated by the humans' newfound knowledge, which makes them somehow like God, and he drives them out of the garden to prevent the unthinkable—that they also become immortal (3:22-24).

These differences between Gen 1:1–2:3 and Gen 2:4b–3:24 are the reason that biblical scholars find in them two originally independent creation stories. The first one is typically referred to as the Priestly version (P for short) because of its interest in Sabbath. The second is known as the J version after the divine name Yahweh (written Jahwe by German scholars, who first formulated the theory of different authors). The two versions have been placed together, making it possible to read the second story as the sequel to the first, though in order to do so, one must ignore their differences. The juxtaposition of variant stories about the same thing is a common literary technique among ancient Greek historiographers and may be reflected here as well.

There are two further clues in Genesis 2 about the process of literary growth that led to the present position of these two stories and their relationship to one another. The first of these is the half verse between the two stories, 2:4a, which we have not yet discussed. The verse reads, "These are the generations of the heavens and the earth when they were created." This sentence follows the appropriate conclusion of the first story but precedes the proper beginning of the second. A series of such statements beginning, "These are the generations of . . ." or using a similar phrase are sprinkled throughout the book of Genesis (5:1; 6:9; 10:1; 11:10, 27; 25:12, 19; 36:1; 37:2). There is wide agreement in assigning these statements to P. What is more, they always serve as introductions to the materials that follow them. Thus, Gen 2:4a seems to be a P introduction to the following J story. This is taken by some scholars to indicate that the Priestly author edited and augmented the work of his predecessor, J.

The second clue lies in the consistent use of the double name "Yahweh God" in Gen 2:4b–3:24. The Yahwist (J) typically uses the name Yahweh alone in referring to God rather than the combination "Yahweh God." Its consistent occurrence in Gen 2:4b–3:24 is unique. This suggests that the Priestly author combined the two names as a way of making clear the identification of God (Gen 1:1–2:3) and Yahweh as one and the same. Despite the tensions between them, the two creation stories were combined deliberately and intended to be read together or in sequence.

EXCURSUS ON YAHWEH

The God of the Bible, the God of ancient Israel, has a proper name represented by the Hebrew consonants YHWH. (Only the consonants were originally written in Hebrew.) When the divine name was read in synagogue it was not pronounced out of reverence. Instead, the word *ʾădōnāy* ("my lord") or *hash-shem* ("the name") was substituted. A system of vowels was added to the text of the Bible between 600–1000 C.E. by scribes known as Masoretes. When they came to the divine name, either out of continued reverence or because the original vowels had been forgotten, the Masoretes borrowed the vowels from the word *ʾădōnāy*, producing the vocalization YeHoWaH, or Jehovah. The same practices continue today in public reading and among observant Jews who write the word "God" as "G-d." The divine name is probably a form of the verb "to be" in Hebrew. It is part of a longer title retained in fuller form in the expression *Yahweh ṣebāʾōt*, "Lord of hosts," meaning "he who causes the heavenly armies to be." The divine name, Yahweh, in the NRSV and many other English versions is rendered LORD in capital letters, obscuring the fact that it occurs in the Bible as a proper name.

CONTEXT

As with Gen 1:1–2:3, there is no other ancient Near Eastern story or document quite like Gen 2:4b–3:24. There are, however, stories or myths with comparable themes. One such theme is the loss of immortality by humans. An example is a tale from Mesopotamia known as the Adapa myth, which dates to the fourteenth century B.C.E., if not earlier. In it, the main character, on advice from a god, refuses food and drink offered to him by another deity that would have brought humans eternal life. Another example is the famous Gilgamesh Epic, also from Mesopotamia, which originated before 2000 B.C.E. It tells how Gilgamesh, in search of immortality, is directed to a plant with rejuvenating properties at the bottom of the sea. After retrieving the plant, he stops at a pool to wash the salt water off his body. A snake eats the plant and immediately sheds its skin in rejuvenation. Both of these texts share with Gen 2:4b–3:24 the association of immortality with food or a plant that was once available to human beings but was irretrievably lost. In the Gilgamesh Epic, as in Genesis, the culprit, furthermore, is a snake.

The Gilgamesh Epic also draws a connection between human identity or awareness and sexuality that bears some resemblance to Gen 2:4b–3:24. The Epic begins with the gods creating Enkidu, who is half-man, half-beast, to serve as a match for Gilgamesh. Enkidu becomes fully human only after he spends seven nights with a prostitute. It is the sexual experience that solidifies his identity as a human being. In somewhat the same way, the man and woman in Genesis realize that they are naked only after they have eaten of the tree of knowledge of good and evil. Like children passing through puberty, their awareness of their sexual identities is linked with their recognition of right and wrong.

INTERPRETATION

It is unlikely that the story in Genesis 2–3 was ever intended to be understood as an actual set of events. The symbolic nature of the story would have been clear to its original audience from the very "names" of its characters. "Adam" and "Eve" were not proper names in ancient Israel. They do not occur elsewhere in the Bible for any other characters. *ʾAdam* is the Hebrew word for "man" or "human," and "Eve" (Hebrew *ḥawwah*) is related to the word for "life." *ʾAdam* is thus a symbolic character for humans in general or for all men and *ḥawwah* for all women or womankind.

The story in Genesis 2–3 is a story of origins. It is full of what scholars call "etiologies." An etiology is an explanation of the origin or cause of natural or cultural phenomena. The etiologies in Genesis 2–3 include explanations for why snakes crawl, why humans wear clothes, and why the institution of marriage exists. Recognition of the etiological nature of this story raises a question about the traditional interpretation of the creation of woman, since men and women actually have the same number of ribs. However, the main point seems to be that in contrast to the animals, she is of the same substance as the man—his "bone" and "flesh" (2:23). The etiologies again highlight the fact that this account of creation, just like the one in Gen 1:1–2:3, is not a modern, scientific account of human origins.

The curses at the end of the story both account for and presuppose different social roles in ancient Israelite society. The subordination of women in this story is pervasive. The woman is created second, out of the man, as his companion. It is she who is deceived by the snake and who then leads the man astray. Ultimately, her husband "rules over" her (3:16). The curses are also etiologies. As such, they are *descriptive* rather than *prescriptive*. Therefore, they are not divine mandates for ordering human society for all time. They reflect an effort by the ancient Israelite writer to explain the domestic status quo of that particular society.

It is striking how many elements of the traditional interpretation of this story are actually absent from the story itself. The forbidden fruit is not an apple. The tradition that it was an apple arose because of the similarity of the words for "apple" (*malum*) and "evil" (*malus*) in Latin. The snake is simply that and not the devil. In fact, the term "sin" never occurs in the story. Indeed, the idea that the story recounts "the fall" of humanity is a later, Christian interpretation. The story does seem intended to explain human mortality as the result of disobedience and separation from God, since the man is told, "in the day that you eat of it you shall die" (2:17). But there are complications: The man and woman do not die when they eat the forbidden fruit. Rather, they are driven away from the tree of life at the end of the story. There are other punishments. The hardships of daily survival find their ultimate causes in the disobedience of the first couple. But there are also trade-offs. Humans lose immortality but gain knowledge—and apparently, sexual pleasure. The story does reflect the struggle of human beings to understand life theologically. That is what makes it scripture and, as scripture, the object of centuries of interpretation.

CHAPTER 3

THE PRIMEVAL HISTORY: AFTER THE GARDEN (GENESIS 4–11)

The rest of the Primeval History contains names that have become common in our culture—Cain and Abel, Noah, Methuselah, and Babel. The stories about them fill out the remainder of the "prehistory" that leads to the appearance of Abraham and Sarah, the ancestors of the people of Israel.

CONTENT

These chapters of Genesis consist basically of three stories: Cain and Abel (Gen 4), the flood (Gen 6–9), and the tower of Babel (Gen 11:1-9). In the first, Cain, the oldest son of Adam and Eve, kills his younger brother, Abel, out of envy because God accepts Abel's sacrifice but rejects Cain's. The names of the two are significant. "Cain" sounds like and may come from the Hebrew root meaning "to produce," and he is a farmer. "Abel" means "breath, futility," because he is so short-lived. The story contains several gaps or mysteries, such as why God accepts Abel's offering but not Cain's, what is meant by the mark on Cain (4:15), and where Cain's wife comes from (4:17).

The story of the flood has a beginning that is very difficult to interpret (Gen 6:1-4). It explains how the "sons of God" married human women at a time when the Nephilim, who were warriors of old, were on earth. It also reports Yahweh's resolution not to allow humans to live forever but to limit their days to 120 years. The point of this entire episode and the way in which it serves as a prelude to the flood is perplexing. It appears to be a fragment of mythology explaining the origin of the Nephilim, who are referred to elsewhere in the Bible as a race of giants (Num 13:33; Deut 2:10, 21; 9:2), as the product of interbreeding between human females and supernatural males. As mythology, it may have accounted for the flood as punishment for transgressing the boundary between human and divine. In the present setting, it seems to function to impose the limit of 120 years on human life. This may refer to the length of time before the flood comes rather than the upper limit of an individual's life span.

Following this odd prelude, the flood story proper commences. Human beings have become so evil that God decides to destroy them all except for Noah and his family (6:5-13). God instructs Noah to build a boat—an ark—and to bring some of every kind of animal aboard. God then sends the flood so that all people and animals on earth are obliterated except for those on board the ark. When the flood stops, the ark comes to rest on a mountain. As the water abates, Noah sends out birds to determine how far it has gone down. Finally, Noah and the rest of the passengers on the ark disembark. Noah offers sacrifices to God, and God makes a covenant with Noah, promising never again to destroy the world by flood.

The story has a postscript (9:20-29) that is as strange as its prelude. In addition to being the hero of the flood, Noah is less famous as the inventor of wine, which brings relief to humans from work (compare 5:29 and 9:20). After the flood, he plants a vineyard, makes wine, becomes drunk, and lies naked in his tent. His youngest son, Ham, sees him and reports it to his two older brothers, Shem and Japheth. They respond by covering their father without looking at his naked body. Noah awakes, finds out what Ham has done, and utters a curse of slavery upon Ham's son, Canaan.

The third story is that of the tower of Babel (11:1-9). People gather to build a mud brick city and tower that will reach to heaven. Alarmed by their limitless potential, God halts the project by confusing the languages and scattering people throughout the earth.

These three stories are punctuated by genealogies in chapters 5, 10, and the remainder of chapter 11. The genealogies are each remarkable for different reasons. The first and third are atypical in giving the ages of those inscribed in them. The one in Genesis 5 serves the function of bringing the narrative up to Noah. It ascribes very long life spans to those in it—from as few as 777 (Lamech, the father of Noah) years to as many as 969 (Methuselah). Noah himself is said to be over 500 years when he receives instructions about the ark. Only Enoch fails to attain such a long life, but this is apparently because he does not die! Rather, he is taken by God because he "walked with God." The genealogy in chapter 10 is unique in that it consists of names of places, peoples, countries, and the like rather than individuals. The third genealogy (11:10-32) gives not only the total life span of each man it lists but also his age at the birth of the son who succeeds him in the list. The life spans are much lower than those in chapter 5 but still high by modern standards. They range from 464 to 148 years, decreasing as they approach Abraham.

GROWTH

The same two writers, J and P, who were evident in Genesis 1–3 continue in Genesis 4–11 as well. However, the way in which they are combined is more complex and sophisticated. This is best illustrated in the flood story. Throughout the course of its narrative there are several *doublets*—two versions of the same story or episode or detail within a story. (The two creation stories in Genesis 1 and 2 represent a doublet.) In the flood narrative, these are best summarized in the following chart.

Item	Version One	Version Two
Reason for flood	Wickedness of humankind, evil inclination of hearts (6:5)	Corruption, violence (6:11)
God's decision	Blot out humankind and animals (6:7)	Make an end of all flesh (6:13)
Noah	Found favor in God's eyes (6:8)	Righteous and blameless, walked with God (6:9)
Animals taken aboard the ark	2 of every kind, male and female (6:19-20)	7 pairs of clean animals, 1 pair of unclean (7:2-3)
Time till flood comes	Unknown, but enough time to build the ark (6:14-16)	7 days (7:4)
Source of flood	Rain (7:4)	Fountains of the deep and windows of heaven (7:11)
Duration of flood	150 days (8:3)	40 days (8:6)
Bird sent out	Raven (8:7)	Dove (8:8-12)

These doublets indicate that the Bible's flood story is a composite. Two versions of the story that differ in certain details have been interwoven. Careful attention to the language and ideology used in each of these versions, furthermore, suggests that they are to be identified with the two sources or authors behind the two different creation stories in Genesis 1–3. For instance, the explanation given for the flood in 6:5-8 uses the name "Yahweh" for God. It also refers to Yahweh in anthropomorphic terms as being sorry and grieved to his heart that he had made human beings. Like the creation story in 2:24b–3:24, this version of the flood story is assigned to the Yahwist (J). In contrast, the explanation in 6:11-13 uses the name "God" and is less anthropomorphic; it is assigned to the Priestly author (P). The P version goes on to give a description of the ark and its dimensions (6:14-16) in the kind of detail that is reminiscent of the day-by-day creation account in Genesis 1. It also uses language and terminology that occur in Genesis 1, including "according to their/its kind(s)" (6:20).

Observation of the language, the doublets, and the tensions within the narrative make it possible to trace the two complete versions of the story with relative ease. J = 6:1-8; 7:1-5, 7-8, 10, 12, 16b-17, 23; 8:6-7, 20-22; 9:20-27, while P = 6:9-22; 7:6, 9, 11, 13-16a, 18-22, 24; 8:1-5, 8-19; 9:1-19, 28-29. The prelude about the "sons of God" and human women belongs to J. Yahweh then expresses his regret at having made humans and his decision to blot them out because of the evil intent of their hearts (6:5-7). Noah is the exception, and Yahweh tells him to take seven pairs of clean animals and one pair of unclean animals aboard the ark (7:1-5). The distinction between clean and unclean animals is a ritual one: a clean animal may be sacrificed and eaten while an unclean animal may not (Lev 11). Noah and his family board the ark along with the animals (7:7-8), and seven days later the flood begins (7:10). The water comes in the form of rain for forty days (7:12, 16b-17), and all the animals and people are "blotted out" (7:23). Noah uses a raven, which flies back and forth from the ark, to measure the abatement of the water (8:6-7). Once out of the ark, Noah offers sacrifices of every clean animal (8:20-22). This episode could only make sense in J, which has seven pairs of clean animals on the ark. Otherwise, Noah would have destroyed a species. The J version ends with the strange postscript about Noah's curse on Ham's son, Canaan (9:20-29).

The Priestly author apparently had access to another version of the flood story, which he combined with J's to form the present account in the Bible. P introduced the story with the heading, "These are the generations of Noah" (6:9-10, AT). The reason for the flood in P is that the earth is corrupt and violent (6:11-13). P gives God's detailed instructions to Noah about how to build the ark and its dimensions (6:14-16). In P's version, God tells Noah to bring just one pair, male and female, of every kind of animal (6:17-22; 7:9, 13-16a). It may seem strange, given P's interest in ritual, that he does not make the distinction between clean and unclean. The reason for this is that P understands that distinction and the practice of sacrifice in general to have been introduced later by Moses and the law, not before.

P's chronology for the flood differs from J's. How long it would have taken Noah and his sons to build the ark is unknown, but it certainly would have been longer than the seven days envisioned by J. The flood comes, according to P, in Noah's six-hundredth year (7:6, 11). The source of the water is not rain, as in J, but collapse of the waters above and below the earth (7:11), in accord with P's view of the world as a domed surface surrounded by water (1:6). P's list of creatures killed by the floodwaters (7:18-23) contains terms, such as "creeping things," that match those in the first creation story. The duration of the swelling waters in P—150 days (7:24; 8:4)—is much longer than J's forty days. It is five months to the day that the ark comes to rest on the mountains of Ararat (compare 7:11 and 8:4) and another three months until the mountains reappear (8:5). Instead of a raven, Noah sends out a dove three times at seven-day intervals until the dove does not return (8:8-12). The entire duration of the flood in P's version is nearly a year (8:13), a figure P has evidently reached by including J's forty days in his calculations and assuming a seven-day interval between the sending of the raven and the dove.

P's conclusion to the flood is a covenant between God and Noah (9:1-19). This is the first of a series of covenants in P, each with a covenantal law, sign, and promise or blessing. The sign of this covenant is the rainbow, and the promise is that God will never again destroy the world by flood. The law of this covenant is the law of blood—the prohibition against shedding human blood and against eating the blood of animals.

CONTEXT

The context in which the materials in Genesis 4–11 should be read is of two kinds—literary and geographical. The literary context is formed by documents from ancient Mesopotamia that provide striking parallels to the biblical materials. For example, a Sumerian document that lists the kings of various Sumerian city-states before the flood is similar to the genealogy in Genesis 5 in ascribing longevity to those listed. In fact, the figures for the reigns of the kings in the "Sumerian King List" dwarf those in Genesis, reaching as many as thirty-six thousand years!

> When kingship was lowered from heaven, kingship was first in Eridu. In Eridu, A-lulim became king and ruled 28,800 years. Alalgar ruled 36,000 years. Two kings thus ruled it for 64,800 years.

Excerpt of the Sumerian King List.

Perhaps most important is the Mesopotamian version of the flood story, discovered in 1872, which is very similar to the one in the Bible. The Mesopotamian story originated with the Sumerians before 2000 B.C.E., and is, therefore, much older than the biblical version. The Old Babylonian version of the story (ca. 1800 B.C.E.) was part of a creation myth. Humans had been created to do the work of the gods but proved to be so noisy that they disturbed the sleep of the chief god, Enlil, who determined that they had to be destroyed. The hero, Atrahasis, was warned by a friendly god and told to build a boat in which to preserve human and animal life. The story was adapted for later editions of the

Gilgamesh Epic. Atrahasis, now named Utnapishtim, explains how he and his wife were uniquely granted immortality, which Gilgamesh seeks, by the gods after the flood.

FIRST SPEECH OF EA TO UTA-NAPISHTIM WHO IS SLEEPING IN A REED HUT
O House of reeds, O House of reeds! O Wall. O Wall!
O House of reeds, hear! O Wall, understand!
O man of Shurippak, son of Ubar-Tutu,
Throw down the house, build a ship,
Forsake wealth, seek after life,
Hate possessions, save thy life,
Bring all seed of life into the ship.
The ship which thou shalt build,
The dimensions thereof shall be measured,
The breadth and the length thereof shall be the same.
Then launch it upon the ocean.

UTA-NAPISHTIM'S ANSWER TO EA
I understood and I said unto Ea, my lord:
See, my lord, that which thou hast ordered,
I regard with reverence, and will perform it,
But what shall I say to the town, to the multitude, and to the elders?

SECOND SPEECH OF EA
Ea opened his mouth and spake
And said unto his servant, myself,
Thus, man, shalt thou say unto them:
Ill-will hath the god Enlil formed against me,
Therefore I can no longer dwell in your city,
And never more will I turn my countenance upon-the soil of Enlil.
I will descend into the ocean to dwell with my lord Ea.
But upon you he will rain riches
A catch of birds, a catch of fish
. . . an [abundant] harvest,
. . . the sender of . . .
. . . shall make hail [to fall upon you].

THE BUILDING OF THE SHIP
As soon as [something of dawn] broke . . .
[seven lines broken away.]
The child . . . brought bitumen,
The strong [man] . . . brought what was needed.
On the fifth day I laid down its shape.
According to the plan its walls were 10 gar (i.e. 120 cubits) high,
And the width of its deck (?) was equally 10 gar.
I laid down the shape of its forepart and marked it out (?).
I covered (?) it six times.
. . . I divided into seven,

Its interior I divided into nine,
Caulking I drove into the middle of it.
I provided a steering pole, and cast in all that was needful.
Six sar of bitumen I poured over the hull (?),
Three sar of pitch I poured into the inside.
The men who bear loads brought three sar of oil,
Besides a sar of oil which the tackling (?) consumed,
And two sar of oil which the boatman hid.
I slaughtered oxen for the [work]people,
I slew sheep every day.
Beer, sesame wine, oil and wine
I made the people drink as if they were water from the river.
I celebrated a feast as if it had been New Year's Day.
I opened [a box of ointment], I laid my hands in unguent.
Before the sunset (?) the ship was finished.
[Since] . . . was difficult.
The shipbuilders brought the . . . of the ship, above and below,
. . . two-thirds of it.

THE LOADING OF THE SHIP
With everything that I possessed I loaded it (i.e., the ship).
With everything that I possessed of silver I loaded it.
With everything that I possessed of gold I loaded it.
With all that I possessed of all the seed of life I loaded it.
I made to go up into the ship all my family and kinsfolk,
The cattle of the field, the beasts of the field, all handicraftsmen I made them go up into it.
The god Shamash had appointed me a time (saying)
The sender of . . . . . will at eventide make a hail to fall;
Then enter into the ship and shut thy door.
The appointed time drew nigh;
The sender of . . . . . made a hail to fall at eventide.
I watched the aspect of the [approaching] storm,
Terror possessed me to look upon it,
I went into the ship and shut my door.
To the pilot of the ship, Puzur-Enlil the sailor
I committed the great house (*i.e.,* ship), together with the contents thereof.

THE ABUBU (CYCLONE) AND ITS EFFECTS DESCRIBED
As soon as something of dawn shone in the sky
A black cloud from the foundation of heaven came up.
Inside it the god Adad thundered,
The gods Nabû and Sharru (*i.e.,* Marduk) went before,
Marching as messengers over high land and plain,
Irragal (Nergal) tore out the post of the ship,
En-urta went on, he made the storm to descend.
The Anunnaki brandished their torches,
With their glare they lighted up the land.

The whirlwind (or, cyclone) of Adad swept up to heaven.
Every gleam of light was turned into darkness.
. . . the land . . . as if had laid it waste.
A whole day long [the flood descended] . . .
Swiftly it mounted up . . . [the water] reached to the mountains
[The water] attacked the people like a battle.
Brother saw not brother.
Men could not be known (or, recognized) in heaven.
The gods were terrified at the cyclone.
They shrank back and went up into the heaven of Anu.
The gods crouched like a dog and cowered by the wall.
The goddess Ishtar cried out like a woman in travail.
The Lady of the Gods lamented with a sweet voice [saying]:

ISHTAR'S LAMENT
May that former day be turned into mud,
Because I commanded evil among the company of the gods.
How could I command evil among the company of the gods,
Command battle for the destruction of my people?
Did I of myself bring forth my people
That they might fill the sea like little fishes?

UTA-NAPISHTIM'S STORY CONTINUED
The gods, the Anunnaki wailed with her.
The gods bowed themselves, and sat down weeping.
Their lips were shut tight (in distress) . . .
For six days and nights
The wind, the storm raged, and the cyclone overwhelmed the land.

THE ABATING OF THE STORM
When the seventh day came the cyclone ceased, the storm and battle,
Which had fought like an army.
The sea became quiet, the grievous wind went down, the cyclone ceased.
I looked on the day and voices were stilled,
And all mankind were turned into mud,
The land had been laid flat like a terrace.
I opened the air-hole and the light fell upon my cheek,
I bowed myself, I sat down, I cried,
My tears poured down over my cheeks.
I looked over the quarters of the world, (to] the limits of ocean.
At twelve points islands appeared.
The ship grounded on the mountain of Nisir.
The mountain of Nisir held the ship, it let it not move.

The first day, the second day, the mountain of Nisir held the ship and let it not move.
The third day, the fourth day, the mountain of Nisir held the ship and let it not move.
The fifth day, the sixth day, the mountain of Nisir held the ship and let it not move.
When the seventh day had come
I brought out a dove and let her go free.
The dove flew away and [then] came back;
Because she had no place to alight on she came back.
I brought out a swallow and let her go free.
The swallow flew away and [then] came back;
Because she had no place to alight on she came back.
I brought out a raven and let her go free.
The raven flew away, she saw the sinking waters.
She ate, she waded (?), she rose (?), she came not back.

UTA-NAPISHTIM LEAVES THE SHIP
Then I brought out [everything] to the four winds and made a sacrifice;
I set out an offering on the peak of the mountain.
Seven by seven I set out the vessels,
Under them I piled reeds, cedarwood and myrtle (?).
The gods smelt the savour,
The gods smelt the sweet savour.
The gods gathered together like flies over him that sacrificed.

Excerpt of the Gilgamesh Epic from sacred-texts.com.

There is little doubt that the Bible's story of the flood was borrowed from the Mesopotamian one. They are basically the same. One man receives divine warning about the impending flood and instructions about building a boat in which to save his family and to preserve the varieties of animals. Seven days later the flood comes; there is rain, and the waters, which are understood to surround the earth, are loosed. All life not on board the boat is lost. As the waters abate, the boat comes to rest on a mountain. Birds are sent out to determine when it is safe to disembark. The occupants of the boat leave and offer sacrifices. The deity/deities are gratified by the pleasing odor and promise not to destroy the world by flood again. The major difference between the Bible and Atrahasis is theological. In the Bible, the flood is God's response to human wickedness rather than the reaction of a sleep-deprived deity to noisy people, as in the Mesopotamian version.

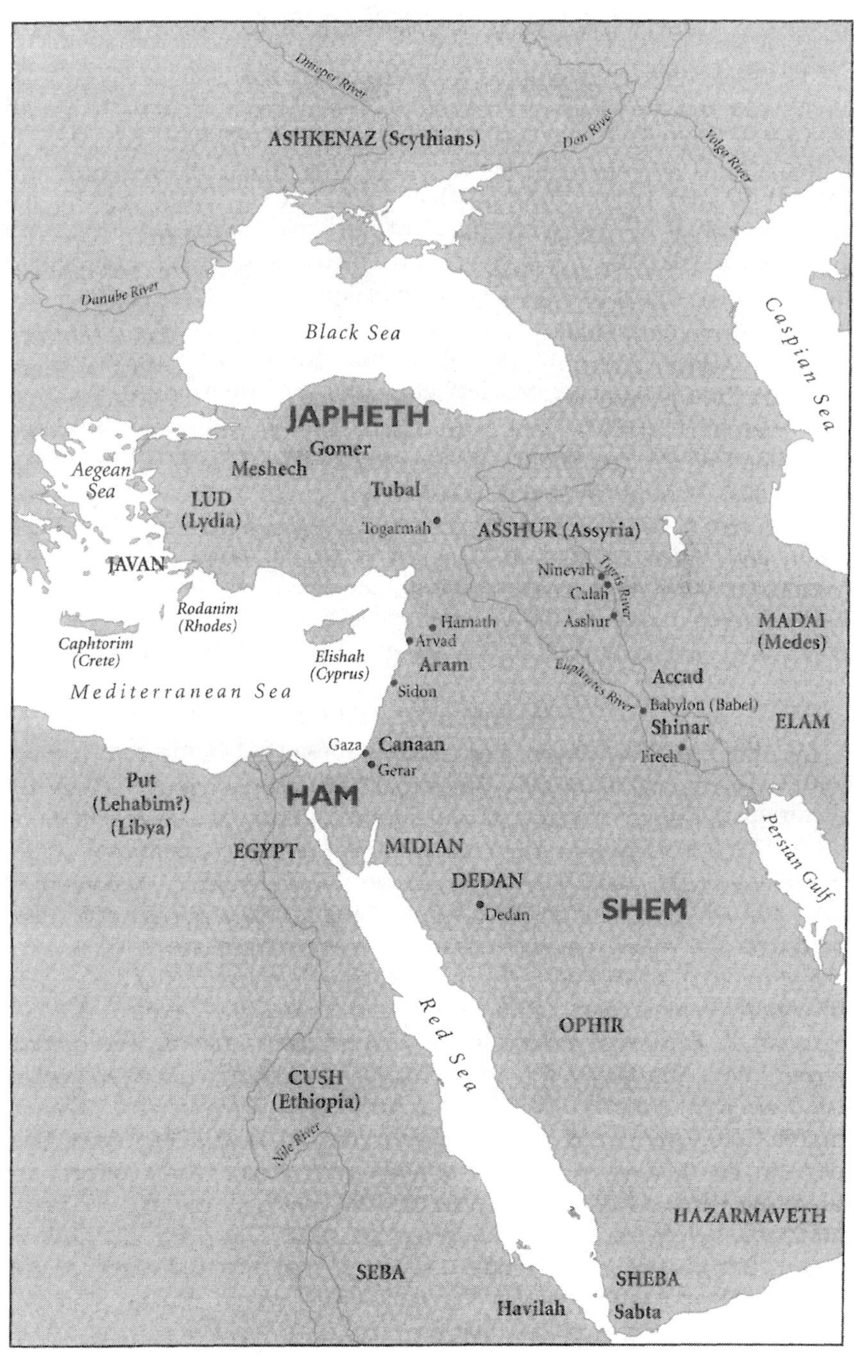

Map of the areas settled by the sons of Noah according to Genesis 10.

The other context, geography, is significant for the "table of nations" in Genesis 10 and the tower of Babel story. The names in Genesis 10 are all peoples or locations in the western Mediterranean and Near East. This is perhaps most obvious with Ham, whose immediate "descendants" are Cush (Ethiopia), Egypt, Put (Libya), and Canaan. Other names in the list are less familiar to modern readers but can be identified from their use elsewhere in the Bible and ancient sources. The "descendants" of Japheth include Javan (Ionia or Greece) and the islands of Cypress (Kittim) and Rhodes (Rodanim). Shem is portrayed as the ancestor of Elam (Persia), Asshur (Assyria), and Aram (Syria). In short, the sons of Noah are identified with three general regions: Japheth with the Mediterranean and western Anatolia (Turkey), Ham with Egypt and its sphere of influence including Canaan, and Shem with the eastern side of the Fertile Crescent, particularly Mesopotamia and its sphere.

The tower of Babel episode is set in Shinar, the southern Mesopotamian plain, and Babel is Babylon. The tower in the story alludes to the Mesopotamian style of temple construction called a *ziggurat*, which was a kind of stepped pyramid. It may refer specifically to the great temple complex known as *Esagila*, dedicated to the god Marduk in the city of Babylon.

INTERPRETATION

Like the first three chapters of Genesis, these next eight are concerned with trying to explain origins. The Babel story is an obvious etiology for the origin of different languages and cultures. There are also explanations offered for the origins of certain occupations—nomadic pastoralists (4:20), musicians (4:21), metalworkers (4:22), and vintners (5:29). The story of Cain and Abel seems to express a preference for the rural life of a shepherd over the settled, perhaps urban life of agriculturalists.

Central to this narrative is the flood story, which was part of the ancient Mesopotamian creation tradition. The texts preceding it explain the reasons for it, and those following explain its repercussions. The biblical writers have moralized the Mesopotamian tradition. The new human creatures do not merely disturb God, but decline into evil and violence, first in Cain's murder of Abel and then in the deeds of all humanity. God destroys his creation and starts over with Noah. Noah's three sons repopulate the earth. Human life spans steadily decline, and the longevity attainable before the flood is no longer possible. This story, like Genesis 1–3, is not history in the modern sense. It was adapted from ancient, mostly Mesopotamian, myths. The table of nations in chapter 10 shows the limited geographical area that the biblical writers have in view. They are concerned not with the world as we know it but with the world known to them.

Interpreting the Primeval History as ancient history writing and, therefore, etiological rather than the reporting of actual events does not disqualify it as scripture. On the contrary, this interpretation is crucial for the proper understanding of scripture and for avoiding oppressive misinterpretations that have sullied the reputation and history of past religious groups and individuals. The tale of the so-called "curse of Ham" (9:20-27) is a fitting case in point. Interpreted as a curse on all black people because one of Ham's sons was Cush (= Ethiopia), this text was commonly used in the nineteenth century to justify slavery and thereafter segregation. Although it is not as widespread today as it once was, this interpretation is still in existence. More common is the myth, upon which this interpretation is based, that there are three great human races (black, Asian, white) stemming from Noah's three sons. This legacy of abusive interpretation of scripture is a compelling argument for the critical study of the Bible.

CHAPTER 4

THE HEBREW PATRIARCHS: ABRAHAM

The second major section of Genesis contains the stories about Abraham, who is renowned in Jewish and Christian tradition as the model of faith. In the biblical stories, though, Abraham does not always live up to this reputation. The reputation comes largely from the famous story of Abraham's willingness to sacrifice his son at God's command. But in most of the stories about him, Abraham is plagued with doubt and mistrust. He prospers less because of who he is than because God blesses him.

CONTENT

Abraham is introduced at the end of the genealogy in chapter 11 as Abram. Linguistically, the two names are dialectal variants of the same name—something like Stephen and Steven—rather than distinct names. Abram or Abiram was likely the original form of the name and meant "the father or my father (relating to a deity) is exalted." However, the biblical author will invest the change from Abram to Abraham with theological significance.

Abram came from Ur of the Chaldeans according to biblical tradition (Gen 11:28). Ur was a city on the shore of the Persian Gulf in southern Mesopotamia (modern Iraq), also known as Babylonia. The reference to it as a Chaldean city is an anachronism, since this region of Mesopotamia came under Chaldean control only in the late seventh and early sixth century B.C.E. The anachronism suggests that this part of the story at least was composed during the Babylonian exile or later (that is, after 586 B.C.E.), long after the setting of the stories (sometime between 2000–1500 B.C.E.).

The stories about Abra(ha)m appear as individual episodes that have been loosely bound together. Although there is no real plot running through them, the stories work together to explain the origins of the Israelites, Abra(ha)m's principal heirs, in the midst of the neighboring peoples, some of whom are also seen as descended from or related to Abra(ha)m. The major theme of these stories, therefore, is the tension between God's promise to Abra(ha)m and his childlessness. Sarai (later Sarah, another dialectal variant), Abram's wife, is unable to bear children (11:30). Yet, when Yahweh calls Abram to move to Canaan, Yahweh promises to make him a great nation (12:1-3).

The promise to the patriarchs in Genesis, considering all its occurrences, is threefold. Besides many descendants, God promises that Abra(ha)m's descendants will possess the land of Canaan and that Abra(ha)m will become a model by which other nations and peoples will bless themselves. This third element occurs in two forms in Genesis, one typically translated as a reflexive (the nations will *bless themselves* by Abra[ha]m) and the other as a passive (the nations will *be blessed* in Abra[ha]m). The Hebrew verb forms are different (hithpa'el and niphal). Since the latter can have a reflexive sense, it is likely that the meaning intended in both cases is reflexive. The promise was not that nations of the world would all be blessed through Abra(ha)m, but that other nations would hold him up as a paradigm of blessing. Despite these promises, Abra(ha)m remains not only childless for most of the story, but landless as well. So much so, that at the end of the story, when Sarah dies, he is forced to pay an exorbitant price for a burial plot, and it is apparently the only portion of the land of Canaan that he owns when he dies. Perhaps the point of the author is that Yahweh fulfills his promises in his own good time.

Another subtheme of the Abra(ha)m story, related to those of the divine promise and the quest for an heir in fulfillment of that promise, consists of Abra(ha)m's responses, faithful or unfaithful, to the promise. At the beginning of the story, following God's directive, Abram goes to Canaan and then continues moving through it toward the south (*negeb*) and on from there to Egypt to escape famine (12:4-10). Egypt is the setting for the first of the "wife-sister stories." There are three of these, two about Abra(ha)m (12:11-20; 20:1-18) and one about Isaac (26:6-11). In each instance, the patriarch lies about his wife, claiming that she is his sister in order to protect himself. In the first version, Pharaoh pays off Abram, making him wealthy on Sarai's account. The story may thus illustrate God's blessing. But it hardly exhibits the faith for which Abra(ha)m is renowned in Jewish and Christian tradition.

Abram's great wealth is shared by his nephew, Lot, and becomes a source of conflict between them. As a result, the two are forced to separate (13:1-13). Abram graciously allows Lot first choice of land, and the younger man opts for the southern end of the (at the time) fertile Jordan Valley, near the city of Sodom. After Lot has separated, however, Yahweh reiterates to Abram the promise of many descendants and adds an explicit promise of the land of Canaan, where he has settled (13:14-18). Abram demonstrates his personal military strength and prowess by defeating the combined forces of four kings who have taken Lot captive (Gen 14). These episodes pave the way for the story of the destruction of Sodom and Gomorrah in Genesis 19–20. That story accounts not only for the desolate area around the Dead Sea but also for the origin of the Moabites and Ammonites, who were neighbors of Israel on the other side of the Jordan and, according to the story, related to them as descendants of Lot. The story may also function to make clear that Lot is not Abram's heir.

There are two accounts of God making a covenant with Abra(ha)m. The first makes use of an ancient treaty-making ceremony in which Yahweh takes upon himself the curses for treaty violation by passing between parts of divided animals (15:7-21). The covenant here is really a promise—the patriarchal promise—particularly those parts relating to descendants and land. The narrator reports that Abram believed Yahweh (15:6). The second covenant text (Gen 17) also reiterates the patriarchal promise. In this case, Abram, who is 100 years old, falls on his face laughing. Abram's name is "changed" to Abraham, and the change is given theological significance as Abraham is taken to mean "father of a multitude." Sarai's name is also changed to Sarah, though the difference in intended meaning between the two names is not clear. God commands Abraham to observe the rite of male circumcision as a sign of the covenant.

Between these two covenant texts is the story of Ishmael's birth (Gen 16). Sarah, desperate to provide Abraham with an heir, volunteers her slave, Hagar, as a surrogate. Hagar's pregnancy causes friction between the two women, and the pregnant Hagar runs away. She returns only after an appearance from a divine messenger ("angel"), who sends her back with a version of the patriarchal promise: her son, too, will become a numerous people. A very similar story is found in Genesis 21, where Sarah insists that Hagar and Ishmael be sent away so that Isaac will not have to share the inheritance. Hagar and Ishmael leave and are about to die of thirst when God shows her a spring and promises that Ishmael will become a great nation.

The climax of the Abra(ha)m story comes in the episode of the near sacrifice of Isaac (Gen 22). After all the struggles to produce an heir that will ensure the fulfillment of the divine promise, God tells Abraham to take Isaac and offer him as a burnt offering. Abraham complies and is only stopped at the last second from killing his son. The divine messenger who stopped the slaying says, "Now I know that you fear God" and reiterates the patriarchal promise to Abraham. Thus, while the various stories about Abraham are hardly a unity, there is a kind of development of Abraham's faith from the fearfulness of the first wife-sister story to his willingness to sacrifice his heir, with episodes of belief and incredulity in between.

GROWTH

The two sources, J and P, that we saw in the Primeval History (Gen 1–11) seem to continue in the Abra(ha)m stories, but the situation is more complicated. The P material is relatively easy to pick out. There are two large P narratives: the second covenant story (Gen 17) and the story of Sarah's burial (Gen 23). The former is widely acknowledged as P because of its concern for chronological detail and the rite of circumcision. It also uses the name El Shaddai (translated "God Almighty" in the NRSV), which is characteristic of P. (But notice that it inexplicably begins with a reference to Yahweh in v. 1!) The story of Sarah's burial is also generally recognized as belonging to P. There are also a few editorial and chronological notices that derive from P, such as those in 12:4b-5; 16:15-16; 21:4-5.

The origin of the non-P material, however, is disputed. Traditionally, scholars discerned a third source behind much of the non-P material. Designated "E" for "Elohist" because it used the name *'elohim*, "God," rather than Yahweh, this source was perceived as independent from but essentially parallel to J. Thus, the second wife-sister story (Gen 20) was assigned to E, and the first covenant story (Gen 15) and story of Isaac's near sacrifice (Gen 22) were viewed as blends of J and E. Some scholars continue to affirm the existence of E. Others have abandoned it altogether, preferring to assign almost all of the non-P material to J and to distinguish between J's sources and J's own compositions. Still others have given up the model of narrative sources in favor of some other paradigm, such as blocks of traditional material that were edited together.

Despite this lack of consensus, there is fairly widespread agreement that P continues from Genesis 1–11 into the Abraham story as a source and perhaps as the final editor/author. P's editorial role may be suggested not only by the organizational rubric "these are the generations of" (see earlier discussion of Gen 2:4a), but also by the fact that the switch from the names Abram and Sarai to Abraham and Sarah is leveled through the stories based on the changes in the P version of the covenant (Gen 17).

There is also general agreement that the J source continues from Genesis 1–11. It is in the Primeval History that J and P as narrative sources appear most clearly. It seems logical, therefore, moving from the known to the unknown, to assume that both sources continue in the Abra(ha)m stories and the rest of the Tetrateuch. At the same time, the detailed treatment of the following two sets of passages will illustrate the complications that arise in attempting to reconstruct the growth of the Abra(ha)m material.

The Wife-Sister Stories (Genesis 12:10-20; 20:1-18; 26:1-11)

The first instance of this story type (12:10-20) lays out the basic plot. The patriarch travels to a foreign land, where he fears for his life because his wife is beautiful. He claims, therefore, that she is his sister. The foreign king discovers the truth and sends the couple away with orders to his subjects not to harm them. This first version of the story takes place in Egypt, where Abram and Sarai have journeyed because of a famine. Sarai is brought into Pharaoh's house, indicating that she is added to his harem, and Pharaoh's payment for her enriches Abram. Yahweh afflicts Pharaoh's house with plagues, but it is not clear how Pharaoh makes the connection that the plagues are because of Sarai.

The second version of the story also involves Abraham and Sarah but takes place at the site of Gerar, in Philistine territory within the land of Canaan. There is no mention of a famine; Abraham merely sojourns in Gerar as a resident alien (Hebrew *ger*, a play on Gerar). Without explaining why, the story reports that Abraham referred to Sarah as his sister. As a result, Abimelech sends for and takes her, again indicating marriage. But while the first version of the story leaves open the possibility that Pharaoh and Sarai consummated the marriage, this second version is quite clear that Abimelech and Sarah did not. God prevented this from happening by warning Abimelech in a dream. The dream also explains how the king discovered the truth about Abraham and Sarah, a facet of the story that is unclear in the first version. When Abimelech confronts Abraham, the latter explains that Sarah is his sister, or half-sister, so that he did not really lie. Abimelech pays compensation to Abraham and gives him permission to settle anywhere within his kingdom. Abraham in turn prays for the healing of Abimelech's household, which God has cursed with infertility.

The third version also takes place in Gerar under King Abimelech, but the couple is now Isaac and Rebekah instead of Abraham and Sarah. It is a famine that drives them to Gerar according to 26:1. But according to 26:6, Isaac simply settled in Gerar. Isaac tells the men of Gerar that Rebekah is his sister, because she, like Sarah, is beautiful, and he is afraid. There is no mention in this version of the king taking Rebekah. Rather, Abimelech finds out about Isaac's lie when he sees Isaac "fondling" his wife. The Hebrew verb translated "fondle" (elsewhere "laugh") is a play on Isaac's name. Abimelech then confronts Isaac. He scolds Isaac about what might have happened and warns his people not to bother Isaac or his wife.

The differences between the three stories may be charted as follows:

12:10-20	20:1-18	26:1-11
Famine	Sojourned	Famine and settled
Abram and Sarai	Abraham and Sarah	Isaac and Rebekah
Egypt	Gerar	Gerar
Pharaoh	King Abimelech	King Abimelech
Explanation for lie	Post-facto explanation, lie defended	Explanation for lie
Unexplained discovery	Discovery in dream	King sees Isaac "fondling"
Plagues on Pharaoh's house	Yahweh closed the wombs of Abimelech's house	Guilt avoided by discovery
Abram enriched by bride price	Abraham paid 1000 pieces of silver as compensation	No payment
Abram and Sarai sent away	Abraham and Sarah allowed to settle in Gerar	King issues order of protection

The literary history of the three versions, however, is harder to discern. The middle version is probably not independent, as it appears to presuppose the first version and to resolve some of the questions it raises. Thus, version two does not explain Abraham's motive for his lie until after it has been discovered. The reader has to be familiar with the explanation given in the initial story that Sarah is beautiful. The second version resolves the ambiguity of the first over whether Sarah had sex with the foreign king. It also does away with the uncertainty about how the king discovered Abraham's lie. And it defends Abraham in a sense by explaining that he did not really lie, since Sarah was his half-sister. The third version is also dependent on the first if the reference to a second famine, beside the one in Abraham's day, is original to this story. However, if the introduction to this story in 26:1-5 is secondary, it might be the earliest of the three.

In short, the version in 20:1-18 seems to be the newest of the three and to have borrowed elements of the other two. The identity of its author (J, E, or a later, independent writer) is uncertain. It is also uncertain which of the other two versions is older (but see below under interpretation).

The Flight of Hagar (Genesis 16:1-14 and 21:8-21)

In the first version of this story, a pregnant Hagar runs away from her abusive mistress (16:1-14). In the second, Hagar and Ishmael are sent away after Isaac has been born (21:8-21). The fact that Hagar casts Ishmael under a bush in the second version suggests that it envisioned him as a much younger boy than the fourteen-year-old indicated by P's chronology in the current narrative (see 16:15-17:1). The two versions, therefore, appear to have been more similar to each other originally than they are now.

Neither of these two versions makes complete sense by itself; it is only together that the full story pattern emerges. Thus, in the second version, the fact that Hagar and Ishmael run out of water in the wilderness creates a crisis situation that is resolved by the appearance of God, or his messenger, and the revelation to Hagar of a water source that saves their lives. The first version also takes place at a water source, a spring, in the wilderness. But here it is a "blind" motif that plays no role in the story. There is no crisis that occasions Yahweh's intervention.

Similarly, both versions have the divine messenger promise to make Hagar's son into a great nation. The first version is more elaborate, describing the rugged lifestyle of the Ishmaelites in the wilderness. But it is only in the second version that one finds the expected fulfillment notice, explaining how God was with Ishmael, as promised, so that he thrived in the wilderness. The first version contains no fulfillment notice at all. Its elaborate description of the Ishmaelites seems premature at this point, since the divine messenger's main task is to get Hagar to return to Sarai.

In view of these features, we might suggest that these two versions represent intentional compositions based on a single, original story, in which Hagar and her unborn or young son were rescued by divine intervention when they nearly died of thirst in the wilderness. As it now stands, the purpose of the divine intervention in the first version is to get Hagar to return to her mistress. The three-fold repetition of the phrase "the angel of Yahweh said to her" (16:9-10) strongly suggests literary reworking, specifically the insertion of the instructions for Hagar to return. The precise reason for composing this first version is probably literary. The author/editor of the Abraham stories simply wished to extend the dramatic tension surrounding the question whether Ishmael was the promised heir. In any case, analysis of these two versions suggests the deliberate artfulness behind the composition of the Abraham stories and the complicated nature of their growth.

CONTEXT

The Abra(ha)m stories are something of an oddity in the context of Genesis. Scholars have noticed that they take place, by and large, in the southern part of Palestine, which is called the Negeb, especially in the area around Beersheba. This observation has led to the suggestion that these stories represent the traditional memories of southern clans or tribes who traced their lineage back to Abra(ha)m and who later joined with the northern "Jacob" tribes to form the nation of Israel. But unlike Jacob/Israel or even Ishmael, there is no people named after Abra(ha)m. To put it another way, there is no nation of Abram or Abraham that might have traced its origin to an ancestor, real or hypothetical, with the same name (what scholars call an "eponymous" tradition). Literarily, the Abraham stories serve to link the primeval genealogies with Jacob/Israel and to introduce the themes of divine promise and blessing and human faith.

The literary function of the Abra(ha)m stories raises the question of their historical veracity. Was Abra(ha)m a historical figure? Fifty years ago, it was commonly held that he was and that the stories in Genesis genuinely reflected the lifestyle of Middle Eastern semi-nomads in the period between 2000–1500 B.C.E. To be sure, they contain widely recognized anachronisms, such as the references to Philistines and domesticated camels, both of which came to Palestine after 1200 B.C.E. (The anachronistic reference to "Ur of the Chaldeans" has already been mentioned.) But by and large, the stories were viewed as genuine artifacts from the first half of the second millennium. Since the 1970s, however, this view has faded. There is a growing consensus that the Abra(ha)m stories were written a thousand years or so after the period in which they are set and that there is little or no reflection of the earlier period in them.

There is no direct archaeological evidence relating to the patriarchs. Nor would one expect to find any, since they were nomads. There is indirect evidence relating, for example, to Beersheba, which archaeology indicates is another anachronism. But the main debate about historicity revolves around Abra(ha)m's social context—the extent to which the customs and practices mentioned in the stories can be documented in the surrounding culture. There are certainly good examples of such parallels. For instance, we have laws and marriage contracts from Mesopotamia that stipulate resort to a female slave in the event that a wife is unable to bear a child. The problem is that such practices are typically not exclusive to any one period. They are documented in the first millennium as well as the earlier, second millennium B.C.E., and the later examples of the custom are often closer to the biblical stories than the earlier ones.

INTERPRETATION

The contextual evidence has led scholars to return to the biblical text, where careful reading has given further suggestion of the late and artificial nature of at least some of the Abraham stories. We will focus on two examples.

Genesis 12:10-20

We have already treated the first wife-sister story for its similarity to the other two such stories. What is worth observing here is its resemblance to the national tradition of Israel's sojourn in and exodus from Egypt. Just as in that tradition, so in the Abram story, there is a famine that induces the characters to move to Egypt. Pharaoh's taking Sarai may mirror the enslavement of the Israelites. As in the exodus story, God afflicts Pharaoh's house with plagues until he releases the Hebrews. In Exod 12:35-36, the children of Israel despoiled the Egyptians by asking for gifts; similarly, Pharaoh enriches Abram on Sarai's behalf. The author of this story has apparently taken the wife-sister motif (borrowed from Isaac in Genesis 26?) and reshaped it using elements of the exodus tradition. It foreshadows the later events in Israel's history and to that extent is a story about Israel rather than about the person of Abram.

Genesis 14

The story of Abram's rescue of Lot begins by recounting a battle between two coalitions, one of four kings (Amraphel of Shinar, Arioch of Ellasar, Chedorlaomer of Elam, and Tidal of Goiim) and the other of five (Bera of Sodom, Birsha of Gomorrah, Shinab of Admah, Shemeber of Zeboiim, and an unnamed king of Bela = Zoar [or perhaps Bela the king of Zoar]). Scholars have struggled to identify these names with historical figures and places. Some are easily recognizable. The domains of the five kings are all cities in the area of the Dead Sea. Shinar is southern Mesopotamia or Babylonia; Elam is Persia; and Goiim means "nations." These identifications alone strongly indicate the literary and artificial nature of this text. Sodom and Gomorrah are drawn from the story about their destruction in Genesis 19. That story is an etiology that seeks to explain the cause for the desolate region around the Dead Sea, as we have seen. It is a legendary explanation rather than a scientific one and can hardly be taken as history. It is dubious whether Sodom and Gomorrah ever really existed as cities. In addition, Babylonia and Persia were, at different times, powerful empires in the ancient Near East. They were rivals and did not band together, especially to oppose the rulers of petty city-states in Palestine.

Further observations only enhance the likelihood of the artificial nature of the story. Bera means "in evil" and Birsha "in wickedness," again bringing to mind the story of the destruction of the evil cities Sodom and Gomorrah. Ellasar may be another name for Assyria, and Tidal is likely a Hittite name, so that they represent two other great empires at different periods of ancient Near Eastern history. The story, then, functions to stress the strength and prowess of Abram by relating his defeat of the kings of four empires. Its purpose is ideological rather than historical.

CHAPTER 5

THE HEBREW PATRIARCHS: JACOB

The story of Abra(ha)m has a strange ending. After the focus on Abraham's and Sarah's quest to have a son, one is surprised to learn that Abraham takes another wife (after Sarah's death?), Keturah, and that she bears him six more sons. These "sons" are actually Arab tribes. (Arabs as well as Jews trace their ancestry to Abraham.) But the biblical writers are interested only in Isaac, the heir to the promise. It is also surprising, therefore, that with the death of Abraham, the attention in the book of Genesis shifts not to Isaac but to Jacob, Abraham's grandson.

CONTENT

The story of Jacob begins in the middle of Genesis 25 with his birth (25:19) and runs through chapter 35. It is often referred to as a "cycle" because the story ends with Jacob back in Canaan, where he started out. The account of Jacob's birth (25:19-26) establishes some of the main themes for the cycle. Jacob and his twin brother, Esau, struggle in the womb. Their mother, Rebekah, uses divination to seek an explanation from Yahweh for the turmoil she feels inside of her. She is told that she carries two nations and that the elder will serve the younger. When she gives birth, Esau comes out first followed by Jacob, who is holding on to Esau's heel. Struggle becomes a theme in the Jacob cycle, as Jacob contends with the other characters he encounters. Another such theme is the competition between older and younger and God's favoring the younger and the "underdog."

This episode about the birth of the twins is also full of wordplays on the names Jacob and Edom, the nation that Esau represents. "Jacob," an abbreviated form of a name meaning "God protects" or "may God protect," ostensibly means "he takes the heel" or "supplants," and Jacob supplants, or replaces, his brother Esau in the subsequent stories by taking first the birthright (25:29-34) and then the blessing (ch. 27) that are properly his. "Edom" means "red." Esau/Edom is red at birth. He is also hairy, and the Hebrew word for hair (*śēʿār*) resembles the name "Seir," which is another name for the country of Edom.

Such wordplays become typical of the Jacob cycle. In the next episode, Jacob trades his "red stuff" for Esau's birthright. The author notes that this is why Esau was called Edom (25:30). The Hebrew words for birthright (*bĕkôrāh*) and blessing (*bĕrēkāh*) are also very similar to each other and form yet another wordplay.

Esau is naturally enraged at Jacob's swindle of his blessing, and he threatens to kill his brother. Jacob flees for his life. His mother sends him to her family for safekeeping. On the way, Jacob has an encounter with God at Bethel (28:10-32). He has a dream in which Yahweh is at the top of a stairway to heaven with angels ascending and descending upon it. Yahweh promises to be with Jacob, to give him many descendants, and to bring him back to the land of Canaan.

Jacob continues on his journey to Haran near the modern border of Turkey and Syria. There he meets and falls in love with Rachel, the younger daughter of his uncle, Laban (29:1-14). He wants to marry Rachel but has nothing to offer as a bride-price for her except his labor. He agrees to work for Laban for seven years in exchange for Rachel (29:15-20). However, at the end of the seven years, Laban deceives Jacob by substituting his older daughter, Leah, for Rachel on their wedding night. Jacob is forced to return to the bargaining table. But he has no leverage. He must agree to work for Laban for another seven years. The only concession he secures is that this time he will marry Rachel up front, only a week after his marriage to Leah (29:21-30).

What follows next is the account of the birth of Jacob's children (29:31–30:24). Yahweh sees that Leah is not loved, so he allows her to bear children, while Rachel is barren. Leah bears four sons: Reuben, Simeon, Levi, and Judah. For each name there is a wordplay that may have nothing to do with the real meaning of the name. These wordplays are somewhat like naming a child "Harry" because he is born with hair on his body. Rachel responds by giving her handmaid, Bilhah, to Jacob for her to serve as a surrogate mother. Bilhah bears Dan and Naphtali. Leah retaliates by giving her handmaid, Zilpah, to Jacob, and she bears Gad and Asher. A brief anecdote is related in which Leah bargains with Rachel for Jacob's "attentions" by using mandrakes that have been found by her son Reuben. The women are interested in the mandrakes because they were reputed to have fertility and aphrodisiac properties. Leah, apparently with the help of the mandrakes, bears two more sons: Issachar and Zebulun. She also has a daughter, Dinah, whose mention (30:21) sets the stage for the story about her in Genesis 34. Finally, God allows Rachel to bear a son—Joseph (30:22-23). Rachel will also bear another son, Benjamin. But since she dies giving birth to him, that episode comes later in the story (35:16-21), following the other stories in which Rachel plays a part.

After recounting the birth of Jacob's children, the narrative relates a new arrangement between Jacob and Laban (30:25-43). Jacob agrees to continue to work for Laban with the understanding that all the black lambs and all the sheep and goats with markings will belong to him. But Laban cheats Jacob again by removing all such animals from his flock. Jacob retaliates with some creative "genetic engineering." He places streaked rods in front of the best animals while they mate so that their offspring are marked with spots and stripes. The result is that Jacob becomes wealthy at Laban's expense. When the rivalry turns bitter, Jacob decides to leave. He takes his family and departs in secret while Laban is away (31:1-21). When Laban finds out, he pursues. He is warned by God against harming Jacob (31:22-24). The two of them make a treaty, or covenant, not to cross the boundary between them to do harm, and Laban invokes God as a witness that Jacob will not mistreat his daughters (31:25-55).

As soon as Laban departs, Jacob learns that Esau is coming to meet him with four hundred men. In another episode full of wordplays and etiologies, Jacob divides his camp (*Mahanaim* means "two camps"), leaving the women and children behind so that they may be able to escape in the event of an attack (32:1-21). He also sends numerous gifts (Hebrew *minhāh*) ahead of him to Esau. As he crosses the river Jabbok (a pun on "Jacob"), he is assaulted by a "man" who turns out to be divine. Jacob's name is changed to Israel (a name whose original sense was most likely "God [El] prevails, rules" but here means "he wrestles with God"), and he names the place Peniel ("face of God").

The encounter prepares Jacob to meet Esau (33:1-14), as is clear from his statement that seeing Esau's face is like seeing the "face of God" (33:10). Jacob and Esau reconcile. But despite Esau's efforts to persuade Jacob to go back with him to Edom, Jacob returns to the land of Canaan from which he originated (33:15-20). The story of the rape of Dinah (Gen 34) provides a reason for Jacob's move to Bethel, where he buries his foreign gods (35:1-8) and receives the promise of land and progeny from God (35:9-15). The cycle ends with the death of Rachel, the list of the sons of Jacob, and the death of Isaac (35:16-29).

The different episodes in the Jacob cycle can be arranged as follows:

- Jacob and Esau (25:19–28:9)
  - Jacob and God (28:10-22)
    - Jacob and Laban (29:23-30)
      - Jacob's sons (29:31–30:24)
    - Jacob and Laban (30:25–31:55)
  - Jacob and God (32:1-32)
- Jacob and Esau (33:1-20)

This kind of structure is known as a chiasm (from the Greek letter *chi* [χ]). Typically, the point of arranging material in such a structure is to emphasize the episode or element that lies at its center or crux. In this case, that central episode is the birth of Jacob's sons.

GROWTH

As with previous sections of Genesis, the Jacob cycle contains both J and P compositions. The P passage in 35:9-15 contains doublets to both the change of Jacob's name to Israel and the naming of Bethel following a divine appearance there. The fact that this passage occurs at the very end of the cycle seems to indicate that the chiastic structure diagrammed above was already present in J.

Of more interest may be the origin of the Jacob story as a whole. Scholars have long suspected that the Jacob cycle was originally independent of the Abra(ha)m stories. This might explain why Isaac is central to the Abra(ha)m story but only peripheral to the Jacob cycle. The theory that scholars sometimes propose is that the Abra(ha)m and Jacob materials represent different "foundation" traditions. That is, they were originally independent versions about where Israel or different elements of it came from. The Jacob stories seem to be related to the city of Shechem in central Israel and may, therefore, have originated among Israelites living in that region. The Abraham stories, in contrast, are mostly set in the area around Beersheba in the south. If this theory is correct, the two groups of stories were linked through Isaac by making him Jacob's father.

CONTEXT

Consideration of the Jacob cycle in its broader literary, historical, and social context makes clear that its stories are eponymous in nature. An eponymous ancestor is a character, usually a hypothetical one, who embodies and represents the group of people (nation, clan, and so on) that bear his name. Hence, Rachel is told that two *nations* are in her womb. The oracle continues, "the one *people* shall be stronger than the other *people*" (so reads the Hebrew; NRSV has omitted the word "people" [Gen 25:23]), making it clear that the nation and the individual are one and the same.

This reveals which nations Jacob and Esau embody by means of the puns on and changes in their names. Jacob's name is changed to Israel (32:28; 35:10). There are also many places in the Bible where the nation is called "Jacob." For instance, Deut 32:9 says, "Yahweh's own portion was his people, Jacob his allotted share." "Jacob" is equated with "Yahweh's people." Esau's depiction as red (*'ĕdôm*) and hairy (*śē'ār*) shows that he represents Edom, also called Seir.

The descriptions and deeds of Jacob and Esau in the Genesis story have been shaped by their function as eponymous figures. Esau is described as being red and hairy at birth because those words pun on the names Edom and Seir. For the same reason, Esau exchanges his birthright for "red" stew. Jacob holds Esau's heel at birth and then supplants his brother by taking his birthright and blessing, because his name resembles the Hebrew root for "heel" and "supplant." Jacob is called a tent-dweller and Esau a hunter (25:27), because the Israelite people were more settled and urbanized, while the Edomites carved out existence in a rugged terrain. The two are twin brothers in the story because the countries of Israel and Edom were neighbors. Their rivalry reflects friction between the two nations. In the story, Esau is older and stronger than Jacob, but he loses his superiority to the latter's trickery. This reflects Edom's subordination to Israel. By means of these eponymous stories, the author of the Jacob cycle attempts to account for the origin of the nations of Israel and Edom and their relationship to one another.

The eponymous nature of the stories also lies behind the structure of the Jacob cycle. It may seem odd at first that of all the episodes in the Jacob cycle, the one about the birth of his sons is at the center. The reason for this is that the sons are the eponymous ancestors of the twelve tribes of Israel. The account of their birth lies at the heart of the Jacob cycle as a kind of self-identification. It is as though the writer is saying, "This is who we, the people of Israel, are as a nation."

The fathering of a child through a handmaid as a surrogate mother occurred in the story of Sarah and Hagar. In that story and in comparative documents from the ancient Near East, the purpose of using the handmaid was exclusively for the production of an heir when the wife was believed to be incapable of bearing children. The situation with Leah and Rachel, however, is completely different. Leah bears four male heirs at the beginning of the story, so there is no need for her or Rachel to resort to their handmaids. Using a handmaid to produce more children when there were already heirs was unheard of in ancient Near Eastern society. Rachel's and Leah's handmaids in the story serve an entirely literary and etiological function. That function is to account for the twelve sons of Jacob, who are, of course, the eponymous ancestors of the twelve tribes of Israel. The story was created to explain the origin of the twelve tribes that had come to compose the nation of Israel in the author's day.

INTERPRETATION

The Jacob cycle is theological as well as etiological in nature. It explains Israel's relationship with Edom and the origin of Israel's twelve tribes. It also explains the character of the nation and people of Israel. It is the story of Israel's corporate identity in relationship to God. This is especially apparent in the story of Jacob's struggle with God leading to the change of his name to "Israel" (32:22-32). The episode identifies Israel as a people who struggled with God and with human adversaries and prevailed. The history of Israel throughout the Bible is one of continuous struggle with God, and God constantly blesses them as God blessed Jacob.

The Jacob cycle, therefore, possesses a certain ambivalence that lent itself to different interpretations at different periods of Israel's history. Jacob's prevailing over human enemies could have been cited in celebration of the dominance of Israel over its national enemies at certain periods. The fact that he and they fought against God might have been used to explain national disasters like the exile. Then again, Jacob's return to Canaan may have been a source of hope for those in exile.

It is ambiguous in the story whether Jacob and his trickery and deceit are to be admired or condemned. It was also apparently ambiguous in later interpretation. This ambiguity is well illustrated by a passage from the eighth-century prophet Hosea. Hosea quotes an older poem praising Jacob and God's revelation to Jacob and his heirs at Bethel (Hos 12:3-4 [Hebrew 4-5]):

> In the womb he seized his brother's heel
> In his manhood he struggled with God.
> He struggled with God and prevailed.
> He wept and entreated him.
> At Bethel he found him/finds us.
> There he spoke with him/speaks with us. (AT)

The poem seems like a proud, even boastful, recitation of Jacob's exploits. But Hosea gives this poem a negative interpretation, accusing the people of Israel of trading in deceit. Thus, he introduces the poem this way:

> Yahweh has a dispute with Israel
> To punish Jacob according to his ways
> According to his deeds he will requite him. (12:2 [Hebrew 3])

Perhaps it is not surprising that the Jacob cycle was open to different interpretations at different times. Jacob, after all, was a multi-faceted character, whose activities reflected the diversity of Israel's experience.

CHAPTER 6

THE HEBREW PATRIARCHS: JOSEPH

The Joseph story, which is found in chapters 37 through 50, is the longest continuous narrative in Genesis. It describes the rags-to-riches life of the older son of Jacob and Rachel in a way that is different from how the lives of most earlier biblical characters are presented. We saw, for example, that the Jacob story is best understood as a cycle comprised of separate and discrete stories that do not have direct sequential relationships to each other. The same might be said about the events of Abraham's life as they are recorded in Genesis. This is not the case with the Joseph story, where each episode builds on the previous one and sets the stage for what is to come. For this reason, most scholars prefer to think of it as a novella or short story, rather than a cycle.

CONTENT

The story opens by calling attention to the tensions that exist among Jacob's sons, a theme that will be picked up again in later chapters. The battle lines between Joseph and his older brothers are drawn in several ways. He is Jacob's favorite son, and he receives preferential treatment when his father gives him a special cloak or robe (37:3). The meaning of the Hebrew word that describes this garment (*passîm*) is not entirely clear, but the Septuagint, or Greek translation of the Hebrew text, identifies it as a cloak of many colors. Their father's favoritism makes the brothers jealous of Joseph, and their anger toward him only increases when he recounts two dreams he had that seem to place him in a position of authority over them (37:5-11).

The brothers are eventually able to act on their resentment when they abandon Joseph in a pit and sell him to some traveling merchants on their way to Egypt (37:12-28). In a final act of family betrayal, the brothers return home to Jacob and show him Joseph's robe, which they have smeared with goat's blood. Thinking his favorite son has been killed by a wild animal, Jacob is overcome with grief while his children try in vain to console him (37:29-36).

The flow of the narrative is abruptly broken in chapter 38, where the focus is on Judah, another son of Jacob. It describes his attempt to deny his daughter-in-law Tamar her right to marry his youngest son after his two other sons die before she is able to conceive a child. By devising a clever plan that involves disguising herself, Tamar tricks her father-in-law into having sexual relations with her, and then forces him to acknowledge his own culpability when her pregnancy is made public. There has been much debate about whether this chapter was originally part of the Joseph story or was a later addition, an issue that will be discussed below.

The thread of the Joseph story is picked up again in Genesis 39, which is the first of three successive chapters that each explain how he is able to rise to a position of authority in Egypt despite his difficult circumstances. The similarities among the three chapters are quite striking and their combined effect underscores one of the central themes of the entire story—Joseph's success is due to God's presence in his life. In chapter 39 Potiphar, Joseph's Egyptian master, recognizes God is with Joseph and consequently puts him in charge of the household. Joseph then rebuffs an attempt by his master's wife to seduce him, and he is thrown into prison when the woman claims that it was he who attempted to seduce her.

A similar pattern is seen in the next episode, when Joseph rises to a position of prominence in prison because the chief jailer sees that the Lord is with him (39:20-23). Among those in prison with him are two servants of the Pharaoh who have disturbing dreams that they are unable to understand. In a scene reminiscent of his own two dreams in chapter 37, Joseph unravels the mystery of the men's dreams and successfully predicts that one of the servants will regain his previous position in Pharaoh's household whereas the other will be put to death (40:9-23).

Some of these same elements are present in the third episode, found in Genesis 41, which describes how Joseph correctly interprets Pharaoh's two dreams after his court officials are unable to do so. Following the pattern of the other two scenes, the Egyptian ruler acknowledges that God is with Joseph and immediately promotes him to the position of second-in-command over the entire country. In the space of just three chapters Joseph has risen from the bottom of a pit to the upper echelons of power, and the text has left no doubt as to the reason for his upward mobility—God is with him.

Pharaoh's dreams were warnings of an impending famine that would devastate Egypt and its neighbors, and Joseph's interpretation offered a plan to meet the challenge this natural disaster would present. With the mention that the entire world came to Joseph to buy grain from Egypt (41:57), the reader anticipates a reunion between Joseph and his brothers. They soon arrive at his doorstep, but he does not reveal his true identity to them for three more chapters. Prior to that, he engages in a cat-and-mouse game with them that includes charging them with being spies, holding one of them in prison, pretending not to understand their language, and accusing them of stealing his personal property (42:1–44:34). Only after they have gone home to Canaan for an extended stay and returned to Egypt does he finally tell them he is their brother (45:1).

At this point Jacob reemerges as a character in the story for the first time since chapter 37. Pharaoh invites him and the rest of the family to settle in Egypt, and Jacob is finally reunited with the son he thought had died many years earlier. Included in the description of their journey to Egypt is a list of the names of the Israelites who make the trek from Canaan (46:8-27).

Chapters 48 and 49 are interesting in that Jacob plays a dominant role throughout them. Some scholars have argued that they are more properly seen as part of the Jacob story rather than part of the Joseph story. In Genesis 48 Jacob blesses Joseph's two sons, Ephraim and Manasseh. This scene is interesting for a couple of reasons. First of all, it explains why the house of Joseph was divided into two tribes. In effect, Jacob adopts Joseph's sons as his own, thereby adding them to his own biological sons so that they, rather than their father Joseph, are the eponymous ancestors of Israelite tribes. Another interesting aspect of the scene is the link it establishes with an earlier moment in Jacob's own life. Here, Joseph disregards the boys' birth order and gives the primary blessing to Ephraim, the younger brother. This is precisely what happened in Jacob's case when he was able to receive the blessing from his father Isaac that should have gone to his older brother Esau in Genesis 27.

The focus remains on Jacob throughout Genesis 49, which is primarily a long poem, presented as a deathbed scene, in which he predicts the destinies of each of his sons and, by extension, each of the tribes of Israel. After he dies, the brothers bury Jacob in Canaan and then return to Egypt, where the others express concern about whether their father's death might signal a change in Joseph's attitude toward them. To ensure their own safety they tell Joseph that one of Jacob's last requests was that Joseph forgive his brothers for what they did to him. Because these words are not found earlier in the text, the brothers might have concocted this as a scheme to protect themselves. Whether or not Jacob actually expressed this wish, it has its desired effect as Joseph reassures the brothers of his commitment to them (50:15-21). The Joseph story ends with a report of his death at 110 years of age and his burial in Egypt. His final words to his brothers are significant because they anticipate the exodus, the next chapter in the history of the Israelites. "When God comes to you, you shall carry up my bones from here" (50:25).

GROWTH

We have noted that there is evidence of sources behind some of the previous sections of Genesis. Although such evidence is not entirely lacking in the Joseph story, it is not as prominent here as it is elsewhere in the book. This story does not contain much material from the P source, but one clear example is found at the beginning of the story in 37:2, which begins "This is the story of the family of Jacob." This sentence contains the same Hebrew word (*tôledôt*) that is usually translated "generations" elsewhere (Gen 5:1; 6:9; 10:1; 11:10, 27; 25:12, 19; 36:1) and is a typical feature of P. The same can be said of the lengthy list of Jacob's relatives and descendants who travel with him to Egypt in 46:8-27; such lists are a common characteristic of the P source. Scholars have also identified material emanating from the Priestly tradition in some of the stories associated with Jacob that are found toward the end of the Joseph story.

This suggests that, as in the rest of Genesis, P has played a role in giving the text its final shape. The Joseph story itself is a cohesive and unified narrative, but the presence of the P material indicates that it underwent a process of redaction, or editing, that attempted to connect it more explicitly with the earlier stories in Genesis. The main body of the Joseph story bears very little direct relationship to the rest of Genesis. Most of the main figures and themes (like covenant, for example) that are central to chapters 1 through 36 are never explicitly mentioned in the Joseph story. This is why some scholars have argued that it originally circulated as an independent story, unattached to the rest of Genesis. But the P material it contains, like the reference to Jacob's "generations" and the list of his descendants, serves as a bridge that establishes a link to the earlier sections and integrates it more fully into the overall story of Genesis.

Another section of the story that has raised the issue of sources is chapter 37, where his brothers sell Joseph into Egypt. This chapter contains quite a few examples of duplications, or doublets (variations of the same story), which are often considered to be an indication of multiple sources. The father is sometimes referred to as Jacob (v. 2), and elsewhere he is called Israel (v. 3). The brother who attempts to rescue Joseph from the others is identified in one place as Reuben (v. 22) and in another as Judah (v. 26). The traveling merchants to whom he is sold are called both Ishmaelites (v. 25) and Midianites (v. 28).

Such discrepancies have caused many scholars to conclude that here, as in the flood story, two separate traditions have been joined together into one account. According to this theory, the J source, which is the dominant one, identifies Judah and the Ishmaelites as the primary characters. At some point the E version, which speaks of Reuben and the Midianites, was joined to the J tradition, resulting in the story that has come down to us.

This understanding of the text's development helps resolve some of its perceived inconsistencies and, consequently, has been accepted by a great many scholars. But it should be noted that this is not the only way to analyze it. In recent times the Documentary Hypothesis has been criticized for a number of reasons, including its overemphasis on the prehistory of the text and consequent lack of attention to the text itself as we have it. Some feel that an argument for sources is one that only a modern person would make and is something that would not enter the mind of an ancient reader. In other words, what appear to us as inconsistencies and duplications would not even be noticed as such by the text's original audience.

Regardless of which side one chooses in this debate, the issue of sources is less relevant for the Joseph story than it is for other sections of Genesis. It is a very well-organized, tightly structured narrative that exhibits cohesiveness and unity rarely seen in other parts of the book.

As we noted, that flow is disrupted somewhat with the story of Judah and Tamar in chapter 38, which seems to come out of nowhere and temporarily sidetrack the Joseph story. Some scholars are of the opinion that it is an intrusion that was not included in the original story of Joseph and his brothers. They see it as more likely a part of the Jacob story because it describes key events in the life of Judah, one of Jacob's most important sons in the biblical tradition. In support of this view is the presence in the chapter of certain themes—like overcoming childlessness, the birth of twins, the rise of the younger son, and difficulties with Canaanites—that are commonly found throughout other stories of the patriarchs.

On the other hand, Genesis 38 contains some interesting connections with the Joseph story that have caused other scholars to view it as an important, if somewhat peculiar, part of it. One of the most intriguing links concerns the role of clothing. Tamar disguises herself by dressing as a prostitute in order to trick her father-in-law into having sexual relations with her. This is related to a central motif throughout the Joseph story in that his clothing often figures prominently in the plot. In chapter 37, the special robe his father gives him is a symbol of his favored status and is the bloody sign of his presumed demise. When fleeing from his master's wife, Joseph leaves his garment in her hand and she uses it as proof of his guilt (39:11-18). Later on, he changes his clothes prior to leaving prison to meet Pharaoh (41:14), and is then given a royal wardrobe when the Egyptian ruler elevates him to a position of authority (41:42). All of these references to Joseph's clothing are found in contexts where he undergoes a change of status, which is similar to the way her clothing functions for Tamar in that it allows for her shift from barrenness to pregnancy.

Because of this common use of the clothing motif, as well as other thematic and vocabulary connections, it is not unreasonable to claim that the

Judah and Tamar episode is part of the Joseph story. Perhaps the most compelling argument for this can be found in the opening verse of the chapter. "It happened at that time that Judah went down from his brothers and settled near a certain Adullamite whose name was Hirah." The phrase "at that time" and the reference to the brothers function as links that bind this chapter to what comes before it, the brothers' betrayal of Joseph. Even if the story was originally a separate tradition, it is now securely tied to the Joseph story. Its disruptive presence therefore plays a vital role in the overall plot. As Joseph makes his way toward Egypt, the Judah and Tamar story is a slight detour that builds tension in the reader's quest to learn what fate awaits him.

CONTEXT

Although there are no perfect parallels to Genesis 37–50 from the ancient Near East, a number of Egyptian texts have been cited as having intriguing connections to certain parts of the Joseph story. One in particular calls to mind a key moment in the biblical account of Joseph's rise to power in Egypt.

The text is called "The Tale of the Two Brothers," and it describes an episode similar to the one in Genesis 39 where his master's wife attempts to seduce Joseph. The tale recounts the story of two brothers, the younger of whom is unmarried and lives with his older brother and his wife. The younger brother, named Bata, is given a position of authority in the household not unlike Joseph's. One day the two brothers are working in the field and the older brother sends Bata back to the house to get some seed. While he is at the house his brother's wife suggests they engage in sexual relations, but Bata rebuffs her advances, citing his loyalty to her and his brother, who are like a mother and a father to him. This rejection causes her to seek revenge and when her husband returns from the fields she claims that Bata has sexually assaulted her. The older brother devises a plan to kill Bata, who, with the help of a talking cow, is able to save himself and convince his older brother of his innocence.

The general outline of this story matches quite closely that of Genesis 39, but it would be a mistake to automatically assume that it is a source for the encounter between Joseph and Potiphar's wife. There are significant differences between the two stories that argue against this. For example, the older brother in the Egyptian story discovers his wife's deception and puts her to death, while the wife in Genesis is not held accountable for what she did. Similarly, the names of the two brothers, Bata and Anubis, are also the names of two Egyptian gods, leading many scholars to assume a mythological background to the narrative. The Joseph story is clearly different in terms of its content and purpose. It is perhaps best to think of "The Tale of the Two Brothers" as part of the literary and cultural milieu the author of the Joseph story drew upon in shaping a distinctively Israelite vision of the scene.

The details of Egyptian history are well known from sources like the royal annals of the Pharaohs and other texts, but none of these documents ever mention Joseph or any of the events described in Genesis 37–50. Nonetheless, scholars have sometimes tried to identify particular phases of that history that would have been more conducive to Joseph's rise to power. One such period is 1700 to 1550 B.C.E., when the Hyksos, a Semitic people who gained political control during a time of internal instability, ruled Egypt. Some have suggested that such a group, as outsiders themselves, would have been more receptive to Joseph and his family. As interesting as such a theory might sound, it is ultimately impossible to prove. The lack of explicit reference to the events in the Egyptian sources and the narrative's inattention to matters of historical detail suggest that any attempt to locate the Joseph story chronologically will remain speculative.

INTERPRETATION

The Egyptian setting of the Joseph story has a significant impact on how we understand its role in the larger biblical context. Egypt is the quintessential foreign land in the Hebrew Bible. Its close proximity to Canaan and their shared border made it a relatively familiar place that was easier to reach than Mesopotamia and other areas that were farther away. At the same time, it is a land that the biblical tradition identifies with hardship and enslavement. This is most clearly seen in the stories about Moses and the exodus that come immediately after the Joseph story. Egypt is a land the Israelites must flee from because Pharaoh and his policies threaten their very existence. It is the place from which they begin their journey to the land promised to them by their God.

The Joseph story plays a pivotal role in this regard because it explains how the Israelites ended up in Egypt. Joseph's brothers sell him into Egypt and then join him there with their father when the famine hits, setting the stage for the dramatic story of their return to Canaan. In this way, the Joseph story functions as a bridge that connects the traditions about Abraham, Isaac, and Jacob with those about Moses and Joshua. As we noted earlier, the sources at our disposal are of no help in determining if the events of the Joseph story actually happened. This is probably the wrong question to be asking of the story anyway. Like many of the traditions found earlier in Genesis, this is not history writing in the way we understand that term. It is, rather, theological writing that presents its message through an imaginative and creative retelling of past events.

Here, too, the Egyptian setting plays a critical role in communicating that theological message. We have seen that a frequently recurring theme throughout the story is that of God's presence with Joseph—his Egyptian master, the chief jailer, even Pharaoh (who was himself a god for the Egyptians) all see that God is with him. Joseph acknowledges the same thing when he discloses his true identity to his brothers and says, "God sent me before you to preserve for you a remnant on earth, and to keep alive for you many survivors. So it was not you who sent me here, but God; he has made me a father to Pharaoh, and lord of all his house and ruler over all the land of Egypt" (45:7-8).

The remarkable thing is that God is with Joseph and does all these things *in Egypt*. In other words, the power of the God of Israel is not limited to the land of Israel. This was a revolutionary idea because it was commonly held in the ancient world that a deity's sphere of influence was tied to a particular place or aspect of nature. This is not the case with the God of Israel, who transcends borders and affects the course of history in a foreign land. The Egyptian setting of the Joseph story helps to establish this unique view of divine power and highlights the fact that the story is as much about God as it is about Joseph.

CHAPTER 7

FROM EGYPT TO THE PROMISED LAND: EXODUS

Cecil B. DeMille's *The Ten Commandments* with Charlton Heston and Yul Brynner and Dreamworks' more recent cartoon version, *The Prince of Egypt,* have made the story of the exodus from Egypt under Moses one of the best known in the Hebrew Bible/Old Testament. These movies help to convey the miraculous nature of the exodus story and to provoke thought about the interactions of the characters. Such movies represent interpretations of the biblical story, especially in their presentation of it as straightforward history. They are primarily for purposes of entertainment rather than instruction and cannot be expected to convey all of the historical, literary, and theological issues associated with the exodus story.

CONTENT

With the book of Exodus, the story of Israel shifts its focus from individuals to a group and from Canaan to Egypt. The story of the exodus has three basic parts: the birth and call of Moses (Exod 1:1–7:13), the ten plagues (7:14–12:36), and the departure from Egypt and crossing of the sea (12:37–15:27).

Birth and Call of Moses

The story begins with the notice that Jacob's descendants who had journeyed to Egypt had multiplied and grown numerous there until a new king, who did not "know" Joseph, that is, did not have a relationship with him or his family, came to power and enslaved them. Afraid that the Hebrews will seize power, Pharaoh orders first the Hebrew midwives and then the Egyptian people to cast newborn Hebrew boys into the Nile. When Moses is born, therefore, his mother hides him as long as she can and then places him in a watertight basket of papyrus reeds and sets him afloat in the Nile, where he is found and adopted by Pharaoh's daughter. In the next episode of the story, Moses is suddenly grown. He is forced to flee Egypt when he kills an Egyptian in defense of a Hebrew. Going to Midian, he meets and marries Zipporah, the daughter of a Midianite priest, and takes up shepherding his father-in-law's sheep. God appears to him one day at the burning bush and calls him to return to Egypt to lead out the Israelites, sending his brother Aaron to accompany him.

The Ten Plagues

Using the miraculous powers that God has given to them, Moses and Aaron confront Pharaoh with God's demand to "let my people go." When he refuses due to his "hardened heart," God sends a series of ten plagues upon Egypt. These are water turned to blood, frogs, gnats, flies, a pestilence on livestock, boils, hail, locusts, darkness, and the deaths of the firstborn. Before the final plague, God gives Moses and Aaron instructions about keeping the Passover as a memorial of the event and as a means for the Israelites to avoid the deaths of their own firstborn.

The Departure and the Sea

As the Israelites depart Egypt, they are given instructions for the feast of unleavened bread and the redemption of the firstborn. Pharaoh's heart is hardened one last time. He changes his mind about letting the Israelites go and decides to pursue them and bring them back. When the Israelites reach the "Reed Sea," therefore, they are trapped between it and the advancing Egyptian army. God answers their cries for help by telling Moses to extend his staff over the sea so that it will divide. After the Israelites have crossed on dry ground with a wall of water on either side, Moses extends his staff again, and the sea returns, killing the entire Egyptian army. The "Song of Moses" in chapter 15 celebrates the victory.

GROWTH

The same literary sources—J and P, and according to some scholars E—that were uncovered in Genesis continue in Exodus. Indeed, one of the best pieces of evidence for such sources is found in the story of the call of Moses. In Exod 6:2, God introduces himself to Moses as Yahweh and tells him that he appeared to Abraham, Isaac, and Jacob as *El Shaddai* ("God Almighty" in the NRSV) but did not use the name Yahweh with them. This statement is flatly contradicted by two texts in Genesis in which Yahweh introduces himself by name first to Abram (Gen 15:7) and then to Jacob (28:13). An angel invokes Yahweh's name in an appearance to Hagar (16:11), and the name occurs repeatedly in the mouths of characters in the patriarchal stories (Gen 15:8; 16:5; 24:3, 7, 12, 27, 35, 40, 42, 44, 48, 51, 56; 27:7, 27; 28:16, 21; 29:35; 32:9; 49:18). Scholars typically explain these contradictions by attributing them to different writers. Exodus 6:2 is the work of P, who prefers the divine name *El Shaddai* and introduces the name Yahweh first with Moses. J, in contrast, as the term "Yahwist" implies, uses the divine name Yahweh from the beginning of its narrative.

A similar passage in Exod 3:13-16 was traditionally viewed by scholars as one of the best examples of an E, or Elohist, text. It also seems to introduce the divine name to Moses by means of a play on the word "I AM" in Hebrew. However, other scholars have recently questioned whether the name Yahweh is intended as new revelation. They contend that this passage serves, rather, to identify the God who is appearing to Moses as the same one worshiped by the patriarchs. It is not that Moses does not know the name Yahweh. He does not know that the God who appears to him is Yahweh, the God of Israel's ancestors, Abraham, Isaac, and Jacob. If the latter interpretation is correct, this passage is probably J's work and links the patriarchal stories in Genesis with those of Moses and the exodus.

P's adoption of the name Yahweh beginning with Moses makes it more difficult to distinguish the sources in the remainder of the Torah, since the divine name is the major distinction between them in Genesis. The literary unevenness caused by the presence of different writers is indicated by such factors as the inconsistent involvement of Moses and Aaron in the plague narrative. Aaron's role seems to have been diminished or absent from the story at an earlier stage of its development. The enhancement of his role is usually seen as P's doing, since Aaron was the ancestor of the priests.

There is also evidence of different traditions about the plagues. Psalms 78 and 105 both contain lists of the plagues upon Egypt that vary in number, order, and content from the Exodus version. Scholars have determined that the list in Ps 78:44-51 is similar to those contained in the J version of the story, which seems to have included the plagues of water to blood, frogs, gnats, flies, pestilence on livestock, hail, locusts, and the death of the firstborn. As in Genesis, the Priestly writer edited and supplemented the J account. In Exodus, P added the other plagues, enhancing Aaron's role, and making other such changes. In addition, the Passover ordinance in Exodus 12 is largely, if not entirely, P's handiwork, while the instructions for keeping the feast of unleavened bread in chapter 13 are J's.

Other signs of the exodus story's growth relate to the accounts of Moses' birth and the crossing of the sea. The story of Moses' birth has affinities with the legend of the birth of King Sargon I, the founder of the Akkadian Empire in middle Mesopotamia around 2300 B.C.E. Sargon recounts his illegitimate birth to a high priestess. Because she was forbidden to bear children, she abandoned him after birth, placing him in a waterproofed basket in the Euphrates. The document goes on to tell how Sargon was found and raised by a gardener and then chosen by the goddess Ishtar to be king and conqueror. The point of the document is to explain how Sargon came from humble beginnings but achieved a position of royalty because of divine agency.

> Sargon, the mighty king, king of Agade, am I.
> My mother was a high priestess, my father I knew not.
> The brothers of my father *loved* the hills.
> My city is Azupiranu, which is situated on the banks of the Euphrates.
> My mother, the high priestess, conceived me, in secret she bore me.
> She set me in a basket of rushes, with bitumen she sealed my lid.
> She cast me into the river which rose not over me.
> The river bore me up and carried me to Akki, the drawer of water.
> Akki, the drawer of water lifted me out as he dipped his ewer.
> Akki, the drawer of water, took me as his son and reared me.

Excerpt of the legend of the birth of Sargon the Great.

The motif in the Sargon legend was reused by other rulers in the region over the millennia for propagandistic purposes. Even the recent despot Saddam Hussein had himself pictured as a baby in a basket in the Euphrates, thereby implicitly promoting his "destiny" to be Iraq's ruler in the tradition going back to Sargon. In much the same way, the biblical writer borrowed this motif for Moses. While there are important differences between the Sargon legend and the Moses tale—Moses' mother acts to save his life rather than herself, and he is found by a princess rather than a gardener—the point of the biblical story is the same: it explains how Moses was saved by God to be the leader of the Israelites. The writer even used this motif as the center of the Moses story and built the rest of the story around it—though not always with complete success. For instance, Pharaoh's goal of reducing the Hebrew population would have been more readily accomplished through the killing of the baby girls rather than boys. The order to kill the boys serves the literary purpose of setting the stage for the story of Moses' birth.

The story of the crossing of the sea also exhibits signs of growth. The poem of victory in Exodus 15 is typically regarded as one of the oldest pieces of literature in the Hebrew Bible/Old Testament. Whatever its date, it seems likely that this poem served as the basis for the narrative account in Exodus 14. The poem seems to envision a naval battle or the like in which the Egyptians are thrown into the sea, sink, and drown (15:1, 4, 5, 10), rather than being covered over by it as they try to follow the Israelites crossing on dry ground. At the same time, the poem makes use of images drawn originally from mythology in which Yahweh defeats the god Sea (Yamm) and divides him. These images are confirmed in mythological texts from ancient Ugarit. The language in the poem about the sea standing up and congealing at the blast from Yahweh (15:8-10) comes from that mythological image of a battle between the two deities. However, the author of the prose narrative in chapter 14 has interpreted this language in such a way as to create the story so well dramatized in *The Ten Commandments* in which Yahweh, through Moses, divides the sea—now a body of water rather than a god—in order for the Israelites to pass over between walls of standing water.

CONTEXT

The most significant issue of context for the exodus story is that of its historical setting, specifically the question of whether the exodus actually happened or at least is based on some historical event. The reconstruction above of the growth of the narrative from the poem in chapter 15 does not preclude the possibility that the poem celebrates some real victory. The problem lies in determining when and under what circumstances such an event may have taken place. In broader perspective, the exodus is the middle event of a series. It is flanked by the stories of Joseph in Genesis and the conquest in Joshua, and the question of its historicity must be treated hand-in-hand with that of these other two episodes.

It should be noted at the outset that it is extremely difficult to determine exactly what historical setting the Bible intends for the exodus and the events surrounding it. The main reason for this difficulty is that the Bible's descriptions do not contain specific references that can be matched with Egyptian records or archaeological evidence. For instance, the king of Egypt throughout the biblical narrative is called Pharaoh, as though it were a proper name. In fact, Pharaoh was a royal title appropriate for every Egyptian monarch. Thus, even though the names of practically every Egyptian ruler are known to modern scholars, the Bible's story cannot be correlated with any of these rulers with certainty, because the Bible does not identify its Pharaohs by name. Conversely, there is no definite reference in any ancient Egyptian document to any of the events surrounding the exodus: not to Joseph, his rise to power, the move of his family to Egypt, their enslavement, Moses, the plagues, or the departure of the Israelites. To be sure, there is ample evidence of people from Syria-Palestine traveling to and living in Egypt from at least 2000 B.C.E. on. But nothing in the biblical story pinpoints a specific time within the next 2000 years. Similarly, there are references in Egyptian documents to disasters at different times, but nothing of the specificity and magnitude of the biblical plagues.

Efforts to date the exodus have focused on the fifteenth and thirteenth centuries. The case for the former is based on chronological references in the Bible, such as 1 Kgs 6:1, which dates the founding of the temple in Solomon's fourth year, 480 years after the exodus. Placing Solomon somewhere in the middle of the tenth century (ca. 950 B.C.E.) and adding 480 to that figure yields a fifteenth-century date for the exodus (ca. 1430 B.C.E.).

The thirteenth-century date relies heavily on the reference to the city of Raamses in Exod 1:11 (cf. Gen 47:11), identifying it with Pi-Ramesses, the capital of Ramesses II, who ruled in the thirteenth century. In this dating scheme, the figure of 480 years is interpreted as a round number for twelve generations of forty years. (The actual length of a generation is closer to twenty or twenty-five years.) Neither date is completely without problems. Indeed, the biblical story may conflate memories of experiences from different people at different periods. At the same time, this story is just that—story and not pure memory. It was composed centuries after the events it describes—whatever the date of their setting—perhaps as late as the seventh century, when the monarchy of Judah was nearing its end, or the sixth century, when much of the population of Judah was in Babylonian exile.

The difficulty of dating the exodus is part of the much larger question of Israel's historical origin. As odd as it may seem, despite the wealth of biblical literature devoted to the exodus and the surrounding episodes, there remains a great deal of uncertainty about where the nation and people of Israel actually came from. Unfortunately, there is very little evidence outside of the Bible to answer this question, and the Bible provides different answers. The primary inscription of relevance is the Merneptah stele, erected ca. 1207 B.C.E. by Merneptah (or Mer-en-Ptah), the son and successor of Ramesses II. The stele contains the earliest mention of Israel outside of the Bible and the only mention of Israel in all of Egyptian literature. It refers to Israel as a group of people, but not a country or nation, in the land of Canaan.

The Merneptah stele does not resolve the issue of the historical setting of the origin of Israel but only adds to the questions about it. Did the Israelites move into Canaan from the outside, as the exodus would have it, or were they indigenous to the land, as recent archaeological evidence seems to indicate? If from the outside, was their entry a peaceful migration, as suggested by the patriarchal stories, or through warfare, as in the conquest narratives of Joshua? Was Israel an ethnic unit, as descent from patriarchal ancestors would dictate, or a "melting pot," as the reference to the "mixed crowd" that came out of Egypt might indicate (Exod 12:38)? Perhaps the answer to these questions is "all of the above." That is, the nation of Israel may have consisted of people of different ethnic and national roots—an even larger "melting pot" than envisioned in the exodus story—with different traditions about their origins. The exodus was one of these and became the primary tradition around which Israel shaped its identity.

INTERPRETATION

Whatever the historical origin of Israel, in the Bible the exodus marks its starting point. The exodus story became the foundation tradition of ancient Israel—the main story the Israelites told about their founding as a nation and a people. More than that, it is the quintessential story of liberation, of God's concern for and rescue of oppressed people. This aspect of the story has been emphasized in recent times by theologians and biblical scholars living in "third world" countries, especially in Latin America and Africa, who see themselves as the victims of oppression by the "pharaohs" of the superpowers. But it is a dimension that is certainly present in the biblical narrative. The exodus story portrays the perennial conflict between slavery and the ideals of freedom and independence, between human arrogance and faithful dependence on God, between raw, abusive power and the power of conscience. This conflict is embodied in Moses, whose sympathies lie with the Hebrews, even though he is raised in the Egyptian court. The very name Moses instantly brings to mind the great Israelite liberator and lawgiver, but it is less well known that the name is Egyptian.

As has long been recognized, Yahweh's competition with Pharaoh in the exodus story is also a competition with Egyptian religion. The pharaoh, or king of Egypt, was deified, as was the Nile. Egyptian gods were typically depicted in the form of animals, including frogs and cattle. The plagues, therefore, demonstrate Yahweh's superiority and control over the gods of Egypt. Magic was also an important element of Egyptian religion, so that the exodus story as it stands with P's editing shows the superiority of Yahweh's agents, Moses and Aaron, over Pharaoh's agents, his magicians. Indeed, as the story itself states, one of the main reasons for sending the plagues was to demonstrate the power of Yahweh. This is the reason given in the text for the motif of the hardening of Pharaoh's heart, whether it is brought about by Yahweh or by Pharaoh himself. Pharaoh's repeated refusal to release the Israelite slaves provides the occasion for Yahweh to "multiply . . . signs and wonders" (Exod 7:3). The demonstration, however, is less for Pharaoh's and the Egyptians' benefit than for Israel's. After all, the Egyptians are drowned in the sea in the final "wonder." The story of the plagues and the exodus, then, and the celebration of Passover are meant to remind the Israelites that they owe their existence to Yahweh and to foster faith in him as their sustainer.

CHAPTER 8

FROM EGYPT TO THE PROMISED LAND: THE LAW

Laws make up nearly one-half of the Torah, so it is not an exaggeration to say that legal material is the heart of the first section of the Hebrew Bible. It is found within the context of a lengthy narrative in which the Israelites flee Egypt and make their way to the land that has been promised to them. That journey is temporarily delayed as God delivers a set of laws to Moses on Mt. Sinai that he passes on to the people.

CONTENT

The units of this section of the biblical story are clearly defined.

1) Exodus 15–18: The Israelites journey through the wilderness and arrive at Mt. Sinai.
2) Exodus 19: God appears on Mt. Sinai.
3) Exodus 20–24: A set of laws, including the Ten Commandments, is given to Moses, and a covenant renewal ceremony follows.
4) Exodus 25–31: Moses is given instructions on how to build the tabernacle and other objects related to the cult.
5) Exodus 32–34: Moses returns from the mountain to find the people worshiping a golden calf. After destroying the calf he leads them in a covenant renewal ceremony.
6) Exodus 35–40: The instructions given in Exodus 25–31 are carried out as the tabernacle and other objects are built.
7) Leviticus 1–7: Moses receives a set of laws related to sacrifices.
8) Leviticus 8–16: Rituals and regulations concerning purity and the priesthood are given.
9) Leviticus 17–26: The Holiness Code
10) Leviticus 27–Numbers 10: The Israelites are instructed on how to prepare for their journey in the wilderness. Included in this section is a set of miscellaneous laws, as well as information on a census, how the Israelite camp should be set up, and the consecration of the Levites.

Monastery of St. Catherine at the foot of Mt. Sinai.
Photograph by Steven L. McKenzie.

Once the people arrive at Mt. Sinai in Exodus 19, they do not depart from it until Numbers 10, some fifty-eight chapters later. This lengthy stopover reflects the important role mountains played as abodes of the gods in the ancient Near East and in the ancient world generally. Many of Israel's neighbors traditionally associated their deities with mountains and other high places. For example, the Canaanite god Baal, who is frequently mentioned in the Bible, resided on Mt. Zaphon in an area of northern Canaan (part of modern-day Syria) known as the city-state of Ugarit. The smoke, lightning, and thunder that the people see and hear upon arriving at Mt. Sinai reinforce the idea that this is no ordinary mountain but is the place where God dwells (Exod 19:16). When he ascends the mount, Moses is quite literally in the presence of God.

But the text goes on to explain that God's presence is not limited to the mountain. Moses is given instructions on how to make the tabernacle, sometimes referred to as the tent of meeting, which the Israelites will take with them on their journey so Moses can continue to communicate with

God. This is how God travels with the people as they make their way to the land (Exod 40:34-38).

The biblical laws cover a wide range of topics and come in a variety of different types. As with other parts of the Bible, scholars study these texts carefully and attempt to discern the forms, functions, and possible sources of the legal material. Certain lists of laws clearly belong together and form what are commonly referred to as codes. The two most prominent ones are found in the section outlined above. The Covenant Code (Exod 20:22–23:19) begins and concludes with legislation related to the ritual life of the community. These laws surround other ones that are concerned with matters of daily life like ownership of property, slavery, personal injury or death, theft, and rape. The Covenant Code is set off from the texts that surround it. It begins with Moses returning to the mountain and God saying, "Thus you shall say to the Israelites," which signals a new section. The next unit begins in Exod 23:20, when the list of laws is concluded and God tells Moses that an angel will go before him.

The laws in the Covenant Code are both casuistic and apodictic. A casuistic law presents a situation in a hypothetical "if . . . then" format. It typically provides a punishment for breaking the law. "When someone delivers to a neighbor money or goods for safekeeping, and they are stolen from the neighbor's house, then the thief, if caught, shall pay double" (Exod 22:7). Apodictic law simply articulates a command or a prohibition with no indication of the punishment. "You shall not oppress a resident alien; you know the heart of an alien, for you were aliens in the land of Egypt" (Exod 23:9). The Covenant Code contains the most well-known example of *lex talionis*, whereby the guilty party experiences the same harm as that suffered by the injured party, commonly abbreviated as "an eye for an eye" (Exod 21:22-25).

The Holiness Code (Lev 17–26) is another collection of laws that is set off from its immediate literary context. The section begins "The LORD spoke to Moses," and it ends with a summary statement that appears to conclude God's communication to Moses on the mountain. "These are the statutes and ordinances and laws that the LORD established between himself and the people of Israel on Mount Sinai through Moses" (Lev 26:46). Unexpectedly, the very next verse resumes God's commands to Moses, showing that the legal material is comprised of discrete pieces that have been collected together. The Holiness Code contains various types of laws and regulations, but it has derived its name from the fact that most of them are concerned with cultic matters and maintaining purity.

An important point to note about many of the laws in the Hebrew Bible is that they reflect a context that is markedly different from the one described in the narrative. As Moses receives the law from God on Mount

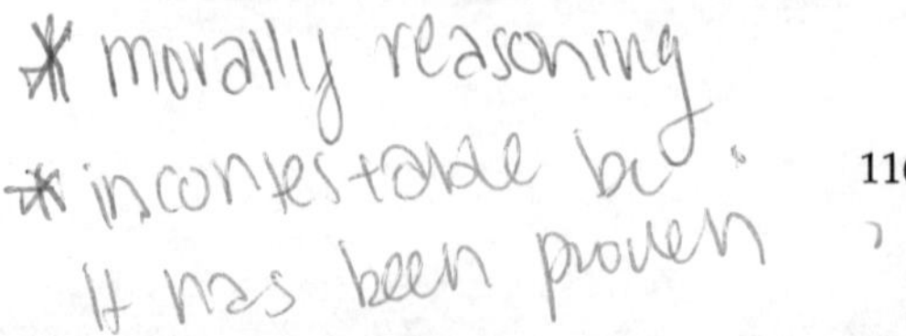

Sinai the Israelites have just begun a period of wandering in the wilderness that will last for forty years and will end only after most of them have died. And yet very little in the legal tradition speaks to that nomadic lifestyle. In fact, much of it presumes a sedentary existence in which the people have settled down and are living in their own land. The mention of houses and aliens in the verses quoted above are examples of this, as are the references to doorposts (Exod 21:6), vineyards (Exod 22:5), and sowing the land (Exod 23:10) elsewhere in the Covenant Code.

GROWTH

The growth of the legal material is best discussed in reference to the book of Leviticus, which scholars have long recognized to have a complex history of development. There is no agreement on what sources are behind the book or when they were written. A debate also continues over when the work reached its final form. Scholarship on Leviticus illustrates the uncertainties that often surround efforts to determine the historical development of biblical books and the necessarily tentative nature of the conclusions that result.

Until fairly recently it was common to assign the entirety of Leviticus to P, the priestly source of the Pentateuch posited by the Documentary Hypothesis. This view is no longer the dominant one, and has been replaced by one that argues for multiple sources that are conceived of in different ways. Even if P never existed and is simply a scholarly construct—a position held by some—there is no denying that Leviticus is written from a "priestly" perspective. A work that focuses almost exclusively on matters like sacrifice, the consecration of priests, impurity, holy days, and blessings could only be the product of those with a deep personal interest and investment in the ritual system. The disagreement arises over where and when these individuals lived and wrote.

As noted earlier, the Holiness Code (Lev 17–26) is usually considered to be a separate collection, and this has led to the common tendency to divide the book into two parts followed by an epilogue in chapter 27. In this model, the material from the priestly tradition (P) in chapters 1–16 precedes that of the holiness tradition (H). Some scholars have imagined that these traditions emerged from different schools, with H offering a more systematic and theologically refined presentation of the material. The division between the two sections is not a hard and fast one, as some H passages are found in the first part of the book. An example of this can be seen in 16:29-34, which adopts a completely different tone to interpret and discuss the ritual of atonement that is described in the first twenty-eight verses of the chapter.

The major point of contention regarding these proposed sources is their dating. Which of the two is the older, and which is later? Some scholars believe P is the older, while others maintain it is H. There have been attempts to place P in the preexilic period due to linguistic factors like vocabulary and grammatical features. If this is correct it is probably the older of the two sources. This is the general approach taken by many scholars, who tend to date P in the preexilic or early exilic period and to place H in later exilic times. Some have even argued that portions of H might reflect a postexilic context, from a time when Israelites had begun to return to the land.

Scholars agree that both P and H contain material that is quite ancient and predates the exile. This raises important questions about the cultic system portrayed in the book and how closely it conforms to actual Israelite practice. There was a time when it was believed that Leviticus and similar writings preserve reliable descriptions of how Israelites worshiped as far back as the time of Moses. Scholars have now abandoned this view, but many still maintain the texts are useful in a more limited way. It is conceivable, perhaps likely, that they are fictitious accounts meant to validate forms of worship from later periods by projecting them back into Moses' time. Nonetheless, they can still offer valuable clues about the forms of worship in later periods of Israelite history.

Which period they reflect depends on when the sources were written, and that is why the issue of dating the material is so important. If they are preexilic, they might be describing the ritual system that was in place prior to the destruction of the temple. If they are exilic, they could be anticipating the rebuilding of the temple and describing how things should be done in the future. If they are postexilic, they may be depicting what went on in the rebuilt temple. How one dates the text has a profound impact on one's understanding of the relationship between text and context.

CONTEXT

No other type of literature from the ancient Near East is more available to us today than are legal writings. Thousands of texts survive from many different periods and cultures that give us a clear sense of how law functioned in antiquity and the various forms it took. In addition to codes of collected laws similar to those in the Hebrew Bible, various legal documents have been discovered that relate to a variety of human activities and interactions like business transactions, real estate contracts, marriage agreements, leases, lawsuits, and adoption records. We even have examples of textbooks like the Sumerian Handbook of Legal Forms, which contains laws and terminology meant to be used in the training of future lawyers.

The major codes come from a wide range of places and times. The laws of the Sumerian kings Ur-Nammu (2112–2095 B.C.E.) and Lipit-Ishtar (1934–1924) are the earliest collections in existence. The famous Code of Hammurabi (1792–1750) is Babylonian, while the Middle Assyrian Laws were compiled in the fourteenth century B.C.E. Also important are the Hittite laws that come from the area of modern-day Turkey and were developed between the seventeenth and twelfth centuries.

Upper portion of the stele of Hammurabi showing the king (left) before the sun god Shamash. Photograph courtesy of Art Resource.

When this body of legal material is compared with biblical law certain similarities and differences are apparent. Among the most notable differences is the larger amount of apodictic law in the Bible. Laws elsewhere in the ancient Near East are usually worded in casuistic form, with a protasis ("if . . .") followed by an apodosis ("then . . ."). Another difference is the presence of laws and regulations related to worship and the cult in the Bible. This area is rarely treated in other ancient codes, which tend to be more concerned with civil and criminal matters.

The Code of Hammurabi has often been compared with the corpus of biblical laws because of the many similarities they share. They both contain examples of *lex talionis,* the law of retribution mentioned earlier. There are a number of striking parallels between Hammurabi's code and the Covenant Code in Exodus. The first of its 282 laws legislates against providing false testimony, something that is also forbidden in Exod 23:1. Some of the other topics treated by both Hammurabi and the Covenant Code are kidnapping (CH 14; Exod 21:16), slavery (CH 117; Exod 21:2-11), striking one's parent (CH 195; Exod 21:15), accidental miscarriage (CH 209; Exod 21:22-23), and damage done by another's ox (CH 250-251; Exod 21:28-36). Echoes of biblical laws can also be seen in the other ancient Near Eastern codes mentioned above.

It is hard to know what to make of the correspondences that exist among these legal traditions. The similarities do not necessarily indicate that the biblical authors were borrowing from neighboring cultures to formulate the Israelite legal system. Some have argued that this may have been the case, particularly when a biblical law bears a strong resemblance to one outside the Bible. But the connections can also be explained by the similar social and economic contexts that gave rise to the laws. It is also plausible that a widespread legal tradition existed throughout much of the ancient Near East that many cultures drew upon as a source. Even if the Israelite legal system was partly influenced by its neighbors, it still has its own distinct features, including the emphasis on cultic matters mentioned above.

The Israelite interest in cult helps to reinforce the link between law and God that is an important element of the Bible's legal system. According to the biblical account, law comes directly from God and is not something of human origin. This adds theological weight to the laws and introduces the notion that whoever violates them is going against God's will and is therefore guilty of sin. No other ancient Near Eastern culture makes this claim as specifically as the Bible does, but there are attempts elsewhere to link law with the divine. For example, the Code of Hammurabi is inscribed on a nine-foot-tall black basalt stele, the top part of which contains an image of the king receiving a scepter from the Babylonian sun god Shamash, a gesture meant to convey the idea that the god is the ultimate source of Hammurabi's legal authority. Here we see how religion can be used as an apologetic tool to serve the political agenda of a ruler. Shamash's endorsement of Hammurabi is a way of validating the latter's status and legitimating the laws he seeks to enact. The same thing might be said about how the close nexus between law and deity functions in the biblical text.

The evidence from the legal material that has been discovered elsewhere in the ancient Near East supports the biblical tradition's description of how legal authority was exercised in Israel. Because he received the law directly from God, Moses was the lawgiver par excellence (Deut 34:10). But law is also identified with other institutions and groups throughout the Hebrew Bible. Kings are associated with legal authority when they are asked to make a ruling on cases brought before them. The best-known example of this is found in 1 Kgs 3:16-28, where two women claim to be the mother of the same child and Solomon must determine who is telling the truth.

Groups of village elders also sometimes play a role in settling disputes and ruling on legal cases. This can be seen in Ruth 4:9-12, when Boaz makes his marriage to Ruth official by soliciting the aid of the elders as they sit at the town gate, the place where many legal transactions took place (see also Deut 21:2-3; 1 Kgs 21:8-11). Another group sometimes associated with legal authority in the Bible is the priests. In those cases that are too difficult to decide, the priests, along with the judge, should be the final arbiter (Deut 17:8-13). These examples from the Bible reflect the situation throughout the rest of the ancient Near East, where the royal court, councils of elders, and the temple were the primary loci of legal authority and justice.

INTERPRETATION

When people think of biblical law one of the first things that usually comes to mind is the collection known as the Ten Commandments, which many consider to be the definitive list of dos and don'ts in the Bible. Also known as the Decalogue, a word from Greek meaning "ten words," the Ten Commandments are a summary of the basic ethical principles upon which biblical morality is based. Although not strictly speaking a law code, the commandments, like all biblical laws, are closely aligned with the covenant as expressions of how God intends humans to behave and interact with one another.

The Ten Commandments do not go back to Moses' time, but took shape over a long period of time. Evidence of this can be seen in the fact that the list is found in two different places in the Bible and the versions do not completely agree (Exod 20:1-17; Deut 5:6-21). The most significant difference is found in the decree to keep holy the Sabbath day. Both texts contain the commandment, but the reason people should observe it is not the same. According to Exod 20:11 one should not work on the Sabbath because after creating the world God rested on that day and blessed it. This is sometimes referred to as the P version of the Ten Commandments because it is the P account of creation that describes God's rest after creation, and Sabbath observance is something that would be of particular interest in priestly circles. The version in Deuteronomy, which is probably the older of the two, links the command to observe the Sabbath with the exodus experience. "Remember that you were a slave in the land of Egypt, and the LORD your God brought you out from there with a mighty hand and an outstretched arm; therefore the LORD your God commanded you to keep the sabbath day" (Deut 5:15). The different versions are most likely due to the different contexts in which they developed and attempted to respond to.

Another discrepancy between the two lists is found in the last commandment. They present a slightly different order of what one should not covet, and the Deuteronomy text adds some things not found in Exodus. In Exod 20:17 the order is your neighbor's house, wife, male or female slave, ox, donkey, or anything that belongs to your neighbor. According to Deut 5:21 you should not covet your neighbor's wife, house, field, male or female slave, ox, donkey, or anything that belongs to your neighbor. In the first version the neighbor's wife is part of what is in his house, whereas in the second she is listed first and therefore is not part of his household possessions.

The reference to the neighbor's wife indicates that the primary audience of the commandments is male, which is reinforced by the fact that the Hebrew words rendered "you" and "your" in English are always male singular forms. This reflects the male-centered nature of the biblical literature generally but is not meant to suggest that women do not have to observe the commandments. It is also worth noting that all ten of the commandments are in apodictic form, without any punishments stated for those who violate them.

Some scholars have argued that the Ten Commandments are a later insertion into the text. This is more apparent in the Exodus version, where the list interrupts the narrative flow of the story. The end of chapter 19 reports that Moses obeys God's order to go down and tell the people to keep their distance from the mountain. The Ten Commandments follow immediately after this, introduced by the words, "Then God spoke all these words." After the commandments are given, the text states that the people were fearful after witnessing the lightning, thunder, and smoke from the mountain (20:18-19). They beg Moses not to let God speak to them because they are afraid they will die. But God has just spoken to them, and they did not die. In fact, the giving of the Ten Commandments is the only time on the mountain when God speaks directly to the people and does not use Moses as an intermediary. The story would flow more smoothly if 20:18 followed immediately after 19:25. The Ten Commandments are an originally independent unit whose presence disrupts the logical and sequential integrity of the text.

The entire list of the Ten Commandments is not found elsewhere in the Hebrew Bible. Similar lists are found in Jer 7:9 and Hos 4:2, and some scholars have suggested the Jeremiah passage might be the origin of the lists of commandments found in Exodus and Deuteronomy. If so, that would give them a relatively late date of just prior to the exile. Interestingly, individual commandments are cited more frequently in the New Testament than in the Hebrew Bible, which is another point in favor of assigning them a late date. Christian communities do not agree on how to count the Ten Commandments. Some denominations take Exod 20:3-6 as one commandment, while others divide it into two. The same thing is done with the tenth commandment on coveting your neighbor's possessions, which some denominations consider to be two separate commandments.

Chapter 9

FROM EGYPT TO THE PROMISED LAND: WILDERNESS TRADITIONS

According to the biblical story, the Israelites' journey from Egypt to the promised land took forty years. During most of this time they wandered about in the desert regions of Sinai, Edom, and Moab. The bulk of these experiences are recorded in the book of Numbers, whose Hebrew title *bĕmidbār* ("in the wilderness") underscores the nomadic nature of Israelite existence in this period. Some of the journey is described in Exodus, but Num 10:11–22:1 recounts the lengthy and theologically significant trek from Mt. Sinai to Moab that will be the focus of this chapter.

CONTENT

The account of the wilderness traditions is episodic in nature. Separate discrete stories have been joined together within the framework of a travel itinerary that serves to organize the various elements. Scholars have noted that this arrangement is quite similar to that of the military itineraries of armies on the march that have come down to us from antiquity. In fact, some of the wilderness stories describe military engagements between Israel and its enemies (21:1-3, 21-31). The largest block of material within the wilderness traditions is the set of laws given at Mt. Sinai that have already been discussed. They are placed in the context of a lengthy stop in the Israelites' journey that disrupts the flow of the overall journey. The larger narrative describes the experiences of the people as they respond to the challenges of living in a desert environment.

Israelite complaints against God are found frequently in this section. The rebellious nature of the people is described in Num 11:1-2, a brief episode that sets the pattern for much of the rest of the journey. "Now when the people complained in the hearing of the LORD about their misfortunes, the LORD heard it and his anger was kindled. Then the fire of the LORD burned against them, and consumed some outlying parts of the camp. But the people cried out to Moses; and Moses prayed to the LORD, and the fire abated."

References to Israelite dissatisfaction, including that directed against

Moses as an authority figure, are found throughout the wilderness stories. Aaron and Miriam, Moses' brother and sister, reject his leadership over them and demand that they be viewed as his equals (12:1-16). A bit later Korah, Dathan, and Abiram complain about how authority is exercised within the community, and they attempt to set themselves up as leaders apart from Moses and Aaron (16:1-35). Elsewhere, the people complain about their bland diet, the lack of meat, and the lack of water (11:4-6; 20:2-5; 21:4-5).

Many of these stories are doublets of others found in Exodus 16 that describe the complaints of the people as they make their way from Egypt to Mt. Sinai. In a number of cases, Moses intervenes on behalf of the Israelites and asks God to respond to their concerns. This appeal is usually successful, but sometimes God ends up punishing the people for their lack of faith (11:33; 21:6). This pattern of complaint, intervention, response, and punishment can be seen in a somewhat different order in the brief passage at 11:1-2 mentioned above. Among the best-known incidents described in the wilderness stories are Moses' producing water from the rock at Meribah (20:1-13) and his construction of a bronze serpent that healed anyone who gazed upon it (21:4-9).

Narrative and legal material alternate throughout the section. Chapters 11–14 contain complaint stories (11), Aaron and Miriam's challenge to Moses' authority (12), and a description of a scouting expedition in which Moses sends out men to spy on the land of Canaan (13–14). This is followed by a set of laws in chapter 15 that are primarily concerned with various kinds of sacrifices and offerings. The narrative resumes in chapters 16–17, which describe the rebellion of Korah, Dathan, and Abiram (16) and a story in which Aaron's rod sprouts buds (17), a divine sign that his priesthood has been approved after the threat posed by Korah's attempt to take over. The priestly theme continues in the legal material that follows in chapters 18–19. Chapter 18 describes the duties of the priests and Levites, as well as offerings and provisions that they are to receive because of the services they perform for the community. Chapter 19 discusses matters related to impurity, particularly as it pertains to coming in contact with corpses.

The narrative returns in the last part of the section, which recounts the water-from-the-rock miracle at Meribah (20:1-13), the making of the bronze serpent (21:4-9), and the difficult relationships the Israelites had with the people of Edom, the Negeb, the land of the Amorites, and Bashan as they made their way through these areas (20:14-21; 21:1-3, 10-35). Also found here is an account of Aaron's death (20:22-29). The travel itinerary ends in 22:1 with the Israelites camped in the plains of Moab across from Jericho, poised to enter the promised land.

The rest of the book of Numbers contains material of different types. Stories about Balaam, a prophet-like figure in Transjordan, are recorded in chapters 22–24. Other themes treated include warnings against intermarriage with foreign women (25), the results of a census of all the Israelites (26), the transfer of leadership from Moses to Joshua (27:12-23), rituals that are to take place throughout the year (28–29), an account of a war against Midian (31), and how land in Transjordan is to be divided up among some of the Israelite tribes (32). A more abbreviated version of the wilderness traditions is found in Numbers 33, which simply lists the stops along the way with a few details included. That chapter will be discussed below in the section on growth.

GROWTH

The alternation of narrative and legal material in the wilderness traditions is an indication of editorial work. The flow of the narrative is disrupted in chapters 15 and 18–19, where the tone suddenly shifts from a reporting of events to a listing of regulations and laws to be observed. This legal material has been inserted into the narrative by a later hand. Some scholars have attempted to argue that there is a thematic or linguistic connection between the legal passages and the surrounding narratives. Even if this is so, the evidence for redactional activity remains strong.

The presence of priestly-related material in the wilderness stories has long been noted. Although the priestly source of the Pentateuch is usually dated to the time of the exile or later, a careful study of the language of these passages shows that some of the words they contain reflect a preexilic context. For example, the Hebrew terms used for "tribe," "clan," and "congregation" in this part of the text were no longer used after the ninth century B.C.E. This suggests that if this material comes from the P source either the priestly tradition is older than many scholars tend to date it or its scribes chose to preserve archaic vocabulary from the sources they were using.

Three places where priestly influence is apparent are in the spy story of chapters 13–14, the account of Korah's rebellion (16), and the description of Moses producing water from the rock (20:2-13). In each case, there is evidence that strong priestly concerns have played a significant role in shaping the central themes that are communicated to the reader.

The spy mission appears to be comprised of two originally separate stories. The first, often attributed to the J source, has the spies visit only the area of Hebron, a city about twenty miles south of Jerusalem. They bring back a positive report of the land ("It flows with milk and honey, and this is its fruit" [Num 13:27]), but they express concern about the strength of its inhabitants and are reluctant to invade it. Caleb, who presses for an invasion, is an important figure in this telling of the story, which is found in 13:17b-20, 22-24, 26b-31; 14:1b, 4, 11-25, 39-45.

In the other version, which traditionally has been associated with P, the spies go all the way up to Lebo-hamath (13:21), in the area of modern-day Lebanon. This discrepancy in the location of the spy mission is one of the strongest arguments in favor of sources. Another difference is that in this account Joshua plays a key role, along with Caleb, in challenging the negative view of the land that is put forward by the spies. This version of the events is found in 13:1-17a, 21, 25-26a, 32; 14:1a, 2-3, 5-10, 26-38. A number of elements in this second account are associated with the P tradition: an interest in the entire land; the presence of Aaron, who is not mentioned in the other version (13:26a; 14:2, 5, 26); and the references to the tent of meeting (14:10) and the census (14:29).

A similar thing can be seen with the rebellion of Korah in chapter 16, which has priestly material within a story that might have originally come from J. The latter tradition—found in verses 1b-2a, 12-15, 25-26, 27b-32a, 33-35—describes how the brothers Dathan and Abiram resent Moses' authority over them and refuse to come when he sends for them. Moses is forced to go to them, and he calls down destruction upon them, which is realized when the earth opens up and swallows them, along with their families and possessions.

This story has been joined with one that features Korah as the antagonist (vv. 1a, 2b, 3-11, 16-24, 27a, 32b). He and 250 other Israelites confront Moses and Aaron, whom they accuse of trying to monopolize the holiness that should be associated with every member of the congregation. A contest is set up between Aaron on one side and Korah with his followers on the other whereby each must present an incense offering to God at the tent of meeting. God accepts the offering of Aaron, leading to the deaths of Korah and his followers, who are referred to as "Levites" by Moses several times in the story (vv. 7, 8, 10). Here, too, the presence of Aaron, the tent of meeting, the incense offering, and the Levites betray the priestly interests of the author, leading many scholars to conclude that the second account probably reflects later tensions between the Levites and the descendants of Aaron over who were the legitimate authorities in cultic matters.

Interestingly, evidence from other parts of the Hebrew Bible supports the idea that these two stories were originally separate and independent. At the end of a list of the many wonderful deeds God has performed for Israel, Deut 11:6 states, "and what he did to Dathan and Abiram, sons of Eliab son of Reuben, how in the midst of all Israel the earth opened its mouth and swallowed them up, along with their households, their tents, and every living being in their company." Psalm 106:16-18 also recalls the event, and adds the reason for their deaths. "They were jealous of Moses in the camp, and of Aaron, the holy one of the LORD. The earth opened and swallowed up Dathan, and covered the faction of Abiram. Fire also broke out in their company; the flame burned up the wicked." Neither of these texts refers to Korah and his destruction, suggesting that the collocation of the two stories in Numbers 16 is the result of editorial activity.

Scholars consider Exod 17:1-17 and Num 20:2-13 to be variations of the same story. The setting of each is a place identified as Meribah, where the people complain about a lack of water. Moses consults God for help, and he is told to take his staff and go to a certain rock. After Moses strikes the rock, water begins to flow from it, and the people are able to quench their thirst. The version in Numbers contains priestly-related elements that are not found in the Exodus account. Aaron, the founder of the Israelite priesthood, plays a vital role as Moses' collaborator, and the references to the tent of meeting and the glory of the "LORD" (v. 6) also give a decidedly priestly spin to the telling of the story. This is an additional way in which the influential role of the priestly tradition in shaping the final form of the wilderness traditions can be seen.

Numbers 33 contains a station-by-station listing of the wilderness wanderings that is presented after the entire journey is complete. It refers to some of the places mentioned in the previous narrative, but it also has information on places and events not found earlier in the book. For example, the eighteen locations listed in verses 18b-35 have no counterparts in Numbers 10–22. It is difficult to interpret what these discrepancies mean. Some scholars have proposed that this itinerary may have served as a source for the author(s) of the narrative, who drew upon it to create a description of the journey. An itinerary frame is clearly discernible throughout that narrative (10:12, 33; 20:1, 22; 21:4, 10-13, 31), but there is no way to know what relationship, if any, it has with chapter 33. Nonetheless, the lengthier itinerary in chapter 33 might imply that there were sources in addition to the narrative in Numbers that contained traditions about the Israelite wanderings in the wilderness.

CONTEXT

Given the nature of this material, with its itinerary framework and emphasis on the Israelites' journey, issues related to the text's geographic context are of importance. Locations are identified throughout the narrative, but not as many place names are specified as one might expect in an account that purports to describe such a lengthy and drawn-out journey. In addition, there are a number of difficulties involved with trying to locate many of the places that are mentioned in the story.

The trip begins in the wilderness of Sinai and the wilderness of Paran

(10:12) as the people set out from Mt. Sinai after Moses receives the law (10:33). The next place mentioned is Taberah (11:3), which means "burning," in reference to God sending fire down upon the people after they complain about their conditions. Another location whose name is derived from an event that occurs there is Kibroth-hataavah ("graves of craving"), marking the burial places of the Israelites who were struck down for greedily consuming the quails sent by God (11:34). From there, the text says they journeyed on to Hazeroth (11:35), where Aaron and Miriam challenge Moses' authority. The precise locations of Hazeroth, Taberah, and Kibroth-hataavah remain unknown.

Returning to the wilderness of Paran (12:16) in the eastern part of the Sinai Peninsula, Moses dispatches the spies to survey the land and bring back a report on its inhabitants (13–14). As already noted, there appear to be two different traditions behind the text as we now have it. In one, the spies go only as far as Hebron; whereas in the other their mission takes them all the way to Lebo-hamath (13:21) in modern-day Lebanon. While the spies explore the land, Moses and the rest of the Israelites wait at Kadesh-barnea, which is located in the wilderness of Paran (13:26). Other than a reference to the Amalekites and Canaanites pursuing the Israelites to Hormah (14:45), a town near Beersheba, the narrative mentions no other place names until chapter 20. There it is reported that the people return to Kadesh-barnea (20:1), this time identified as in the wilderness of Zin, where Miriam dies. Meribah—whose name is an etiology related to the Israelites' quarrel with God over a lack of water—is also placed in this area by many scholars (20:13).

According to 20:22 the people then leave Kadesh-barnea and go to Mount Hor, where Aaron dies. The precise location of this site is unknown, as are the locations of Atharim (21:1) and many of the cities mentioned in 21:10-20, a listing of the places the Israelites passed through as they made their way to Moab. The section ends with a description of Israelite victories over King Sihon of the Amorites, whose main city of Heshbon is near present-day Amman in Jordan (21:21-26), and King Og, whose main city of Bashan is further north near the Sea of Galilee (21:33-35).

The general movement depicted in the narrative is from the Sinai Peninsula to Transjordan, but it is impossible to plot out the exact route described in Numbers. Too many of the places mentioned in the text have not been positively identified, so the locations of key stops along the Israelites' trek remain a mystery. The general area in which much of the story is set had very few inhabitants, and its population continues to be quite low into the present day. Modern Arabic place names often have an etymological connection with their biblical counterparts, and this can be of assistance in establishing the location of a given site. But no such equivalences exist in these cases, which complicates the task of identification. This problem is compounded when the itinerary listed in Numbers 33 is taken into account because many of the place names it contains have not been identified with certainty. For example, the locations of only two (Bene-jakkan and Ezion-geber) of the eighteen places in 33:18b-35 mentioned above have been firmly established.

The details of the journey described in the narrative must remain sketchy, but efforts have been made to trace the general route, and two main alternatives have been put forward. The more traditional is a southern route by which, after leaving Egypt, the Israelites made their way along the western edge of the Sinai Peninsula until they turned inland near its southern tip and headed to modern-day Jebel Musa, the location of Mt. Sinai. From there they journeyed up the east side of the peninsula toward the area of Kadesh-barnea and other places mentioned in the narrative.

The alternative proposes a northern route that does not extend as far down into the Sinai but stays in the wilderness of Shur, which skirts the northern part of the peninsula. This would put Mt. Sinai on a less circuitous route between Egypt and Canaan that would lead more directly to Kadesh-barnea. In general, scholars have tended to favor the northerly journey. One problem with the southern alternative is that the identification of Jebel Musa as Mt. Sinai began only in the fourth century C.E., many centuries after the events purportedly described in the narrative.

The many textual and contextual ambiguities surrounding the wilderness traditions suggest that we should not be too quick to accept the historicity of the narrative. It is primarily a theological document, not a record of history. The precise details regarding what happened cannot be recovered, but the meaning the author ascribes to the events can be discovered through a careful reading of the text.

INTERPRETATION

The wilderness traditions had a profound impact on how the Israelites came to understand themselves and their relationship with God. At Mt. Horeb—another name for Mt. Sinai—God first spoke to Moses in the wilderness from the burning bush (Exod 3:1-6). After leading the Israelites out of Egypt, Moses encountered God again at the same mountain, where he was given the law. In the desert the terms of the relationship between the people and their God were established and tested. The stories describing divinely sent water, manna, and quails set a paradigm for later generations, who should trust that God will provide for them even under the most difficult circumstances. There are benefits for those who are confident and rely on God, but the repeated references to Israelite complaining and backsliding are a reminder of how difficult it is to remain faithful in the desert.

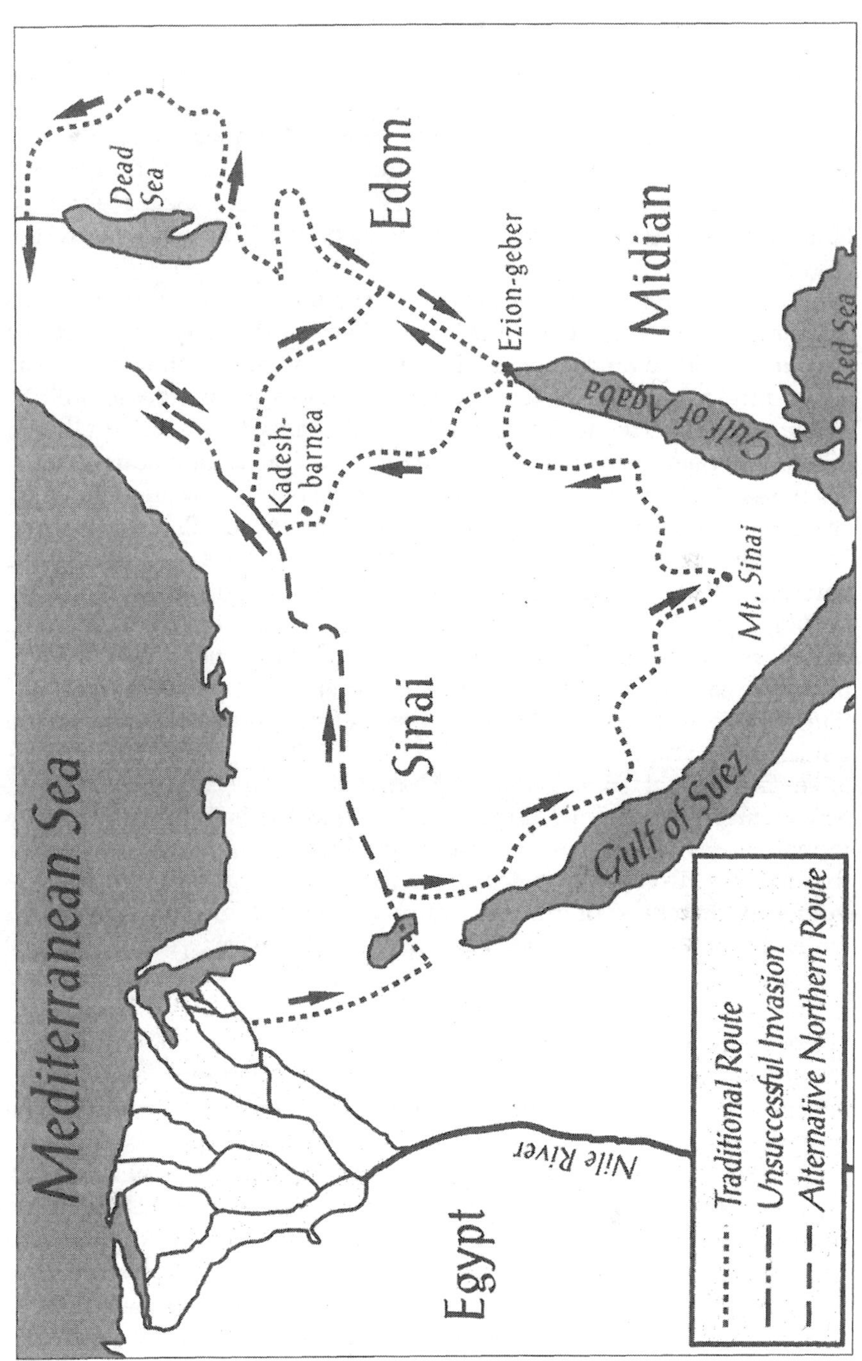

Possible routes of the exodus.

Many scholars believe these traditions took final shape during the exile, a context in which the wilderness stories would have had immediate relevance. The Israelites of the sixth century, who were forced to live as aliens in a strange land, could see their situation reflected in that of their ancestors in the desert, who struggled with what it meant to remain faithful in a foreign environment as they slowly made their way to the land promised to them.

Because of its metaphorical richness the wilderness experience serves as an archetype in other biblical books. Some of the prophetic writings view it as an ideal time when God's care for Israel was manifestly apparent and the people responded in kind. "Therefore, I will now allure her, and bring her into the wilderness, and speak tenderly to her. From there I will give her her vineyards, and make the Valley of Achor a door of hope. There she shall respond as in the days of her youth, as at the time when she came out of the land of Egypt" (Hos 2:14-16; see also Amos 2:10). Elsewhere it is the Israelites' sin and lack of faith that is recalled. "Yet I have been the LORD your God ever since the land of Egypt; you know no God but me, and besides me there is no savior. It was I who fed you in the wilderness, in the land of drought. When I fed them, they were satisfied; they were satisfied, and their heart was proud; therefore they forgot me" (Hos 13:4-5; see also Ezek 20:10-26). Some of the psalms also refer to the wilderness traditions in both positive (Pss 105:37-45; 136:16-22) and negative (Pss 78:17-31; 95:8-11; 106:7-23) terms.

The impression left with the reader is that the Israelites ultimately failed the test of the wilderness. Their lack of trust, constant complaints, and disputes over leadership cause God to deny all but the youngest members of the community entrance into the promised land. "I will do to you the very things I heard you say: your dead bodies shall fall in this very wilderness; and of all your number, included in the census, from twenty years old and upward, who have complained against me, not one of you shall come into the land in which I swore to settle you, except Caleb son of Jephunneh and Joshua son of Nun. . . . But as for you, your dead bodies shall fall in this wilderness" (Num 14:28b-30, 32).

Shockingly, Moses is also denied access to the land. The man chosen by God to lead the people on their forty-year trek through the wilderness, the one who spoke to God face-to-face, also comes up short and is prevented from realizing his final goal. After Moses produces the water from the rock at Meribah, God reprimands him and Aaron. "Because you did not trust in me, to show my holiness before the eyes of the Israelites, therefore you shall not bring this assembly into the land that I have given them" (20:12). Aaron dies later in the same chapter (20:22-29), and the

Pentateuch closes with Moses breathing his last on Mount Nebo, gazing at the expanse of the promised land (Deut 34:1-8).

What did Moses and Aaron do to merit such a harsh penalty? The text does not explicitly tell us, and scholars have long debated the issue. In Num 20:10 Moses says to the people, "Listen, you rebels, shall we bring water for you out of this rock?" Some commentators have argued that he is punished for calling the Israelites rebels, or for claiming that he and Aaron are bringing forth the water when it is actually God's work. A more likely alternative is that they are sanctioned because Moses struck the rock twice with his staff to produce the water, disobeying God's order to command the rock to give up its water (20:8).

The barring of Moses from the promised land sends a powerful message to the reader. No one is exempt from following God's law and all violators will be held accountable. Even the great Moses, who had no peer (Deut 34:10-11), was a flawed person and had to pay the price for his mistake. But the loss of the leader did not lead to the loss of the land. Joshua picks up the mantle and takes Moses' place. The great lesson of the wilderness traditions is that God's promise remains true in the face of human frailty and weakness.

PART TWO

Former Prophets

INTRODUCTION TO THE FORMER PROPHETS

The second section of the Hebrew Bible, the Prophets (Hebrew *nevi'im*) is subdivided into the Former Prophets and the Latter Prophets based on content. The Former Prophets are really historical books and are often so called. The Latter Prophets are books about the lives and oracles of individual prophets.

There are four books in the Former Prophets: Joshua, Judges, Samuel (divided into two volumes designated 1 and 2 Samuel), and Kings (also divided). They relate the story of Israel's entry into the promised land of Canaan under the leadership of Joshua, the period of the judges before Israel was ruled by kings, and the monarchy over Israel united (basically 1–2 Samuel) and then over the separate kingdoms of Israel and Judah (basically 1–2 Kings). As a reminder, the book of Ruth, which is typically placed in English Bibles between Judges and 1 Samuel, is found in the last section of the Hebrew Bible (the Writings) and is not one of the Former Prophets.

Our treatment of Deuteronomy in this section dealing with the Former Prophets is based on scholarly hypothesis rather than canonical arrangement. The book of Deuteronomy has long been recognized as an anomaly among the books of the Hebrew Bible. It is the last book of the Torah and is not included in the Former Prophets in the canon of the Hebrew Bible. However, biblical scholarship tends to regard Deuteronomy plus the Former Prophets as part of a single, extended work known as the Deuteronomistic History.

The theory of the Deuteronomistic History is based on the observation of similarities of theology, language, and structure shared by the books in the Former Prophets. According to this theory, the author(s) of the Deuteronomistic History recounted the history of Israel based on available written and oral sources and evaluated that history according to the religious principles in an older form of Deuteronomy, which they also edited. The date and authorship of the Deuteronomistic History have been debated among scholars. The initial version of the theory construed it as the work of a single individual writing in the Babylonian exile, around or shortly after 562 B.C.E., the date of the last event recorded in 2 Kings, the last book of the Deuteronomistic History. European scholars have generally held to that date for the basic work but have contended that it underwent two or more subsequent editions, which added material reflecting particular interest in, for instance, prophecy or law. North American scholars, in contrast, have tended toward a theory that posits a preexilic, main edition (ca. 618 B.C.E.) that was updated and revised in the exile.

The importance of the Deuteronomistic History lies in its being the only real history of Israel in the Bible. It is thus the only history of Israel that was produced in ancient Israel. The biblical book of 1–2 Chronicles is also a history of Israel, but it is in effect a rewriting of the Deuteronomistic History. It is important to understand, though, that the Deuteronomistic History is a theological history or perhaps a historical theology. That is, it portrays history as the stage for the enactment of its particular theology.

The example of King Omri of Israel well illustrates this statement. Historically, Omri, who ruled ca. 882–871, was a very important king—so much so that Assyrian annals referred to Israel, essentially for the rest of its history, as the "house of Omri." Despite this renown, the Deuteronomistic History devotes only six verses to Omri's reign (1 Kgs 16:23-28), almost all of which is standard, formulaic language. By contrast, there are over six chapters devoted to Omri's son, Ahab. The reason is not that Ahab was a more important king politically or historically than his father. Rather, Ahab received a longer treatment for religious reasons—specifically because of Jezebel, Ahab's wife, and Elijah, the prophet. Jezebel was considered the model of wickedness by the Deuteronomistic Historian(s) because she promoted Baal worship in Israel. Elijah, who opposed her, was the paragon of faithful trust in Yahweh. Their significance for the theological message of the Deuteronomistic History is the reason that the account of Ahab's reign is so long.

The theology of the Deuteronomistic History is basically a prophetic one. It describes national destruction as the result of sin. First Israel and then Judah are invaded, defeated, and lose much of their population to foreign powers because, according to the Deuteronomistic History, they disobeyed Yahweh. This theological viewpoint, in turn, had a significant impact on the composition and theology of much of the rest of the Hebrew Bible.

CHAPTER 10

INTO THE PROMISED LAND: DEUTERONOMY

The title "Deuteronomy" comes from Greek words meaning "second law." The basic setting of the book is Moses' rehearsal of the law given on Mt. Sinai (called Horeb in Deuteronomy) to the people of Israel as they stand poised on the eastern bank of the Jordan River ready to enter the land of Canaan. So it makes sense that canonically Deuteronomy should be part of the Torah, or Pentateuch. But scholars have long recognized that Deuteronomy in some ways shares more with the books that follow it than with those that precede it. That is why we have chosen in this book to treat Deuteronomy with the Former Prophets rather than with the Torah.

CONTENT

There are four headings in the book that divide it into four uneven sections. "The words that Moses spoke to all Israel beyond the Jordan—in the wilderness" (1:1) includes essentially the first four chapters (through 4:43) and incorporates a review of Israel's wilderness journey (1:1–3:29) followed by an admonition to keep the law.

The second section is "the law that Moses set before the Israelites" (4:44). It is by far the longest section of the book, encompassing chapters 5–28. It can be subdivided into three parts. In chapters 5–11 Moses expounds on the importance of faithfulness to Yahweh and the law. This subsection contains two of the most important texts in the Bible: Deuteronomy's version of the Ten Commandments (5:6-21) and the *Shema'* (6:4-9, especially v. 4), the confession of Judaism. Chapters 5–26 then give the law or instruction proper, much of it parallel to laws in Exodus and Leviticus. The lists of blessings (for obedience) and curses (for disobedience) follow in chapters 27–28.

As implied by the heading "the words of the covenant that the LORD commanded Moses to make with the Israelites" (29:1, Hebrew 28:69), the setting of the next section is a covenant-making ceremony between Yahweh and Israel. Chapters 29–30 are another speech by Moses, encouraging obedience of the law and warning about the consequences of disobedience. In chapter 31 Moses bids farewell to Israel and commissions Joshua as his successor to lead the people. He also writes the law down and makes provision for its preservation and occasional reading. Chapter 32 is a lengthy poem, the "Song of Moses," at the end of which Moses again issues a warning and then receives Yahweh's order to ascend Mt. Nebo to die.

Finally, chapters 33–34 are introduced as "the blessing with which Moses, the man of God, blessed the Israelites before his death." Chapter 33 is another poem, the "Blessing of Moses." Chapter 34 recounts Moses' death and Joshua's accession to leadership.

GROWTH

Behind the present outline of the book scholars have perceived another structure—that of an ancient Near Eastern "suzerainty" treaty between a superior king, or suzerain (Yahweh), and a weaker king, or vassal (Israel). Suzerainty treaties typically contained six elements, which have been identified in Deuteronomy: (1) a preamble identifying the parties in the treaty (4:44-49); (2) a historical prologue describing the past relationship of the parties (chs. 5–11); (3) the stipulations or obligations assumed by each party (12:1–26:15); (4) provisions for the deposit and periodic reading of the treaty documents (10:1-5; 31:9-13, 24-26); (5) a list of witnesses—usually gods in treaties, but heaven and earth in Deuteronomy (4:26; 30:19; 31:28)—and the oaths sworn before them (26:16-19; 29:10-29 [Hebrew 9-28]); and (6) a list of blessings and curses for disobedience or obedience of the treaty stipulations (28:1-68).

The curses in Deuteronomy 28 are especially important, as some of them bear a striking resemblance to curses in the vassal treaties of the Assyrian king Esarhaddon (ca. 672 B.C.E.), as the following comparison, originally presented by Moshe Weinfeld (*Deuteronomy and the Deuteronomic School* [Oxford: Oxford University Press, 1972], 117-27), shows:

Deut 28:27: Yahweh will smite you with Egyptian inflammation . . . and with scars from which you will never recover.	VTE 419-20: May Sin . . . clothe you with leprosy.
Deut 28:28-29: Yahweh will smite you with madness, blindness, and confusion of mind, and you will grope at noon as the blind person gropes in darkness.	VTE 422-24: May Shamash . . . not render you a just judgment [not give you a reliable decision]; may he deprive you of the sight of your eyes [so that] they will wander about in darkness.
Deut 28:26: Your corpses will be food for all the birds of heaven and beasts of the earth.	VTE 425-27: May Ninurta . . . fell you with his swift arrow; may he fill the steppe with your corpses; may he feed your flesh to the vulture [and] the jackal.

Deut 28:30a: You will betroth a wife, but another man will lie with her.	VTE 428-29: May Venus, the brightest star, make your wives lie in your enemy's lap while your eyes look.
Deut 28:30b-32: You will build a house, but not dwell in it . . . Your sons and daughters will be given to another people.	VTE 429-30: May your sons not be masters of your house.
Deut 28:33: Another nation which you have not known will devour the fruit of your ground and of your labors.	VTE 430b: May a foreign enemy divide all your goods.

Scholars have noted that the order of curses in the two documents is nearly identical and that some of the curses make sense only in the context of Mesopotamian religion. Thus, the curses in Deuteronomy have been borrowed more or less directly from the Assyrian treaties.

These treaty elements, in turn, suggest that an earlier version of Deuteronomy might have been in the form of a treaty. Indeed, it may have been the "book of the covenant" to which the book refers. However, Deuteronomy as we now have it is not in the form of a treaty or covenant but in that of a series of speeches by Moses. This present form of the book is the work of the author who supplemented the older Deuteronomy and used it as the beginning point for the extended Deuteronomistic History.

CONTEXT

The indications of an older version of Deuteronomy fit well with one of the pillars of biblical scholarship dating back to 1805. In that year, a German scholar named W. M. L. de Wette published a book drawing a correlation between Deuteronomy and the story of King Josiah of Judah in 2 Kings 22–23. According to Kings, in the eighteenth year of his reign (ca. 622 B.C.E.) Josiah ordered some repair work done on the temple in Jerusalem. In the course of the repair work a copy of the book of the law, which had been lost, was discovered. The "book of the law" is also called the "book of the covenant" (2 Kgs 23:2, 21), suggesting a connection with Deuteronomy.

Following the discovery of the book, Josiah ordered a series of reforms to be carried out in Jerusalem and Judah, with special attention to the temple. De Wette pointed out that these reforms matched the regulations in Deuteronomy. The most important of these was the principle of centralization—the idea that the temple in Jerusalem was the only legitimate place for worshiping Yahweh. While Deuteronomy does not explicitly mention Jerusalem, presumably because it would be anachronistic to do so, it does refer to "the place" that Yahweh would choose. In Kings, this place is identified as Jerusalem, and Josiah centralized worship by destroying the shrines outside Jerusalem and bringing their priests to the temple (2 Kgs 23:8-9). Other facets of Josiah's reform match the prescriptions in Deuteronomy, both in the activity and in its description in Kings:

Activity Reformed (2 Kings 23)	Prescription in Deuteronomy
Abolition of the Asherim (23:4, 6, 7, 14)	7:5; 12:3; 16:21
Host of heaven (23:4, 5)	17:3
Destruction of the pillars (23:14)	7:5; 12:3; et al.
Pagan high places (23:13)	7:5; 12:2-3; et al.
Worship of sun and moon (23:5, 11)	17:3
Sacred prostitution (23:7)	23:18
Worship of "Molech" (23:20)	12:31; 18:10
Foreign gods (23:13)	12:13
Necromancy (23:14)	18:11

The identification of Josiah's law book as an early form of Deuteronomy fits well with the evidence for that book being patterned after a seventh-century, Assyrian vassal treaty. It is likely that the book was actually written in or around Josiah's eighteenth year (622) rather than being discovered then. It was a common strategy in the ancient Near East for a king who wanted to undertake some religious or social change that might be considered controversial to produce a document that had supposedly been lost and that mandated exactly the activity in which the king wished to engage. In other words, Josiah probably had the early form of Deuteronomy written to justify the religious and social reforms he wanted to introduce.

INTERPRETATION

In its seventh-century context under King Josiah, the original book of Deuteronomy was probably intended to function as much politically as religiously. Josiah was attempting to consolidate not only Judah but also the remnant of Israel under his rule and in the face of foreign domination. Deuteronomy's call for centralization had sweeping ramifications for society that are the subject of much of the legislation in Deuteronomy. It meant that people could no longer offer sacrifices in their towns and villages, as they had been doing before the seventh century, but only in "the place" chosen by God—Jerusalem (12:2-14). In the ancient world, however, sacrifice was the occasion for eating meat. This would have meant that any time people wanted to eat meat they would have to travel to Jerusalem—an obviously unreasonable requirement. Hence, Deuteronomy makes a distinction between religious slaughter (that is, sacrifice) and secular slaughter for food (12:15-27). The latter could take place anywhere, the former only in Jerusalem. This new practice also meant that the Levites, who had previously officiated at sacrifices throughout the country, could now only work in Jerusalem. They were out of work in the outlying towns and villages, where they had no land, since their allotment in Israel had been portions of sacrifices. As a result, the Levites became a new class of poor, whom Deuteronomy admonishes its readers not to neglect (12:12, 18-19). Since Jerusalem could be far away, and it was impractical to transport animals and produce for sacrifice, Deuteronomy allowed people to exchange livestock and produce for money that could be used to purchase sacrifices in Jerusalem (14:24-26).

These examples illustrate the impact on daily life that Josiah's reforms had, if they were indeed implemented. And it seems likely that they were implemented, since Josiah's aims were not just religious but were political as well. The sense of unity that he sought to instill within his subjects would lend him strength against his Assyrian overlords or their Babylonian rivals. Even the most theological of statements in Deuteronomy was motivated by this concern for political solidarity. The confession that Yahweh is one (6:4) denies that there are other, local manifestations of Yahweh outside the Jerusalem temple.

Whatever its origin, the impact of Deuteronomy on the development of the Hebrew Bible was significant. In this sense, it may be fair to say that Deuteronomy is the most important book in the Hebrew Bible. Its theological significance is most evident in the *Shema'*. The confession that "Yahweh is our God; Yahweh is one" (AT) placed Israel on the threshold of monotheism. Where Israel was concerned, there was to be no other God. "You shall have no other gods before me" (Deut 5:7). Thus, Yahweh is a jealous God who does not permit allegiance to deities. The later additions to Deuteronomy would cross over the threshold into full-blown monotheism by stating explicitly that there was no god besides Yahweh (4:35).

Deuteronomy also launched a trajectory of thought concerning the nature of God with its reference to the place where Yahweh will put his name (12:5, 11). The language of placing the name was used in Assyrian inscriptions for a king laying claim to a particular locale and may have been intended originally to affirm Yahweh's exclusive claim on Jerusalem. Again, though, the later Deuteronomistic History gave new meaning to Yahweh's placement of his name. This became a way of expressing Yahweh's claim or ownership without saying that he was actually limited to a particular location. In theological terms, it guarded God's immanence while asserting his transcendence. As Solomon would later express it, God's true dwelling is in heaven, and he cannot be confined to any earthly space (1 Kgs 8:27). As such, God is spirit and cannot be represented by tangible objects (Deut 4:1-40). Attempts to depict God with images are strictly forbidden (5:8-10). This view of God as spirit and not confined to the temple or any one location enabled Israel's religion to survive the exile when Jerusalem and the temple were destroyed and to evolve into Judaism.

The twin ideas developed in Deuteronomy of Yahweh as the only true God and of Israel as his people gave rise to the theological concept of election. Yahweh, Lord of creation, had chosen Israel as his people (10:14-15), not because they were greater or better than other peoples but because Yahweh loved them (7:7-8). The election forged Israel into a distinct national community. This idea of national unity, which Deuteronomy articulates for the first time, was a central aim of Josiah's political and religious reform movement in resistance to Assyria and Babylon. The tangible sign of this election was the covenant, which Josiah "reaffirmed." Theologically, God's election of Israel is the basis for his ethical prescriptions to Israel, which appear as the covenant stipulations. Among these stipulations, Deuteronomy focuses especially on social justice and on attitude. As immanent deity, Yahweh knows the thoughts of the human heart. The concept of election also underlies the idea of reward and punishment for obedience or disobedience of the law as laid out in the list of covenant blessings and curses near the end of Deuteronomy.

The covenant, according to Deuteronomy, was inscribed in a book, which served as a guide for proper behavior, both religious and social, of individuals as well as the nation. The idea of such a unique, holy, authoritative book containing the comprehensive divine law is the idea of scripture. Deuteronomy introduces this idea, and the Deuteronomistic History furthers it by its use of Deuteronomy as a standard of evaluation for Israel's history. The idea of scripture, like the other concepts discussed above that were introduced by Deuteronomy (monotheism, the nature of God, election, etc.), is fundamental for Judaism and Christianity, as well as Islam—the "religions of the book."

The best example of the significance of scripture in Deuteronomy is the Decalogue, or Ten Commandments, in Deut 5:6-21. This is one of two versions of the Decalogue, the other being in Exod 20:1-17. There are good reasons for thinking that the Deuteronomy version is the older of the two. Above all, the version in Deuteronomy fits its context, while the one in Exodus interrupts the story about God's appearance on Mt. Sinai and the people's fear (19:16-25 continued in 20:18). Also, the form of the Decalogue as a speech from God is appropriate to Deuteronomy but not to the Exodus context. The Exodus version is a P insertion, as indicated by its grounding of the Sabbath in God's resting after creation (Gen 1:1–2:3). In other words, it is Deuteronomy that introduced the Ten Commandments, which have been so formative for Western society and religion.

Deuteronomy also provides an important example of the use and interpretation of scripture. It describes the original covenant on Mt. Horeb not as the entire law but as the Decalogue (4:13; 5:22). The extensive code in Deuteronomy 12–26 is the form of the covenant renewed by the subsequent generation at the end of the wilderness wandering who will enter the promised land. The longer code is the elaboration and interpretation of the original covenant for this later generation. This suggests that the concept of scripture presented in Deuteronomy is not that of a static document, but of one that, from the beginning, required interpretation for each generation.

CHAPTER 11

INTO THE PROMISED LAND: JOSHUA

Joshua is the first book of the Former Prophets, a section of the Hebrew Bible that also includes Judges, 1–2 Samuel, and 1–2 Kings. The book is named after Joshua son of Nun, who succeeded Moses as Israel's leader following Moses' death at the end of Deuteronomy. The name Joshua means "Yahweh saves or gives victory." As we will see, it is quite appropriate to the character of Joshua in his leadership role in this book.

CONTENT

The book of Joshua presents an account of Israel's entry into Canaan under the leadership of Joshua son of Nun, a description of various military battles against the local people, and a record of the portions of the land allotted to each of the tribal entities that comprised Israel. The book is a collection of narratives, summaries, and lists that contains obvious links to the book of Deuteronomy, which precedes it in the canon.

The book's subject matter also ties it to other parts of the Pentateuch. Israel's arrival in Canaan is the realization of the promise God first made to Abraham in Genesis 15 that his offspring would return to the land after experiencing four hundred years of slavery and oppression. Similarly, the book of Joshua relates directly to the Moses tradition and the story of the Exodus, a connection the work clearly underscores in a number of places. Joshua himself was Moses' second in command, and the people's entry into Canaan puts an end to the years of wandering that followed God's freeing them from Egypt and Pharaoh's domination (Exod 14).

Echoes of the Mosaic tradition are most apparent in the way Joshua is presented as a second Moses. Just as the waters of the Reed Sea were parted during the time of Moses, allowing the Israelites to escape Egypt, the Jordan River dries up for Joshua, enabling them to enter Canaan (3:1-17). Joshua sends out spies to view the land just as Moses did before him (2:1). The people are in awe of Joshua as they had been in awe of Moses (4:14). Like Moses, Joshua is told to take off his sandals because he is standing on holy ground (5:15). The similarities between the two figures are repeatedly stressed and recognized by all characters, God included. "No one shall be able to stand against you all the days of your life. As I was with Moses, so I will be with you; I will not fail you or forsake you" (1:5; see also 1:16-17; 3:7).

The book neatly divides into two halves. Chapters 1 through 12 tell the story of the conquest of the land through a series of attacks and skirmishes against the local population. This section can be further divided into two units, with 1:1–5:12 describing the initial entry into the land and preparations for battle and 5:13–12:24 recounting the conquest narratives. Chapters 13 through 24 describe the division of the land among the tribes of Israel and can also be subdivided into two parts. The tribal allotments are listed in 13:1–21:45, and an epilogue and other concluding material are found in 22:1–24:33.

The first half of the book follows a well-defined geographic movement as the Israelites defeat the enemy in stages and extend their control over the area. After crossing the Jordan River and moving from Transjordan to Canaan (chs. 2–5), the central towns of Jericho and Ai are taken (chs. 6–8). From there, Joshua and the Israelite forces go to the south and defeat the local leaders in a series of raids on cities and villages (chs. 9–10). They then venture north, where they crush a coalition of northern kings who have formed an alliance in an effort to overcome Joshua (ch. 11). The first section concludes with a list of all the kings the Israelite forces vanquished in their conquest of Canaan (ch. 12).

Only a few of these battles are described in any detail. Those against Jericho and Ai, for example, are extended narratives with more fully developed plots. But most of the others are nothing more than summary reports of victories that provide no information about the military engagements they mention. The defeat of King Horam of Gezer is a model of brevity. "Then King Horam of Gezer came up to help Lachish; and Joshua struck him and his people, leaving him no survivors" (10:33). Summary statements are also sometimes used to describe the overthrow of entire sections of Canaan, giving the reader only a general sense of the carnage created by Joshua and his followers. "So Joshua defeated the whole land, the hill country and the Negeb and the lowland and the slopes, and all their kings; he left no one remaining, but utterly destroyed all that breathed, as the LORD God of Israel commanded" (10:40).

As the last phrase in the previous quote indicates, credit for the victory over the enemy is given to God alone, who leads the Israelite forces against the enemy. In one of the clearest examples of the divine warrior motif in the Hebrew Bible, the book of Joshua speaks of God guiding the troops and fighting on behalf of Israel. God is the one who drives out the enemies (3:10) and gives them into the hands of the Israelites (8:18; 10:8, 19; 11:6). God controls the outcome of battles by striking fear into the opponents' hearts (10:10) and using hailstones as weapons to decimate the enemy troops (10:11). Even the Canaanites recognize that God is responsible for Israel's success (9:9-10). At one point, it is plainly stated that all of Joshua's success was due to the fact that the "God of Israel fought for Israel" (10:42).

Despite the claim of a total Israelite takeover, the actual conquest covers only six of the book's twenty-four chapters, which are uneven in their treatment of it. Most of the emphasis is placed on the defeat of the central part of Canaan, and the account does not even mention some portions of the land. The second part of the work begins with an acknowledgement that some areas were not conquered. "Now Joshua was old and advanced in years; and the LORD said to him, 'You are old and advanced in years, and very much of the land still remains to be possessed' " (13:1). In the subsequent listing of the allotment of land given to each tribe it is sometimes mentioned that the Israelites were not completely successful in driving out or annihilating the local population (13:13; 15:63; 16:10; 17:12-13; 18:2-3). Such comments are in tension with the summary statements in the first half of the book about a total defeat of the Canaanites at the hands of the Israelites.

The bulk of the second part of the book is made up of boundary descriptions and town lists that map out the territory assigned to each of the tribes, with an occasional brief narrative related here and there (13:1–21:45). The last two chapters of this section identify the locations of the cities of refuge (20:1-9), which were places of asylum to which one who had committed involuntary manslaughter could flee, and the cities of the Levites (21:1-42), the members of the priestly tribe that was not given its own territory. The last chapter of the book describes a covenant renewal ceremony at the city of Shechem in which Joshua reminds the people of all that God has done for them since the days of Abraham, causing them to rededicate themselves to worshiping God alone (24:1-28).

GROWTH

The stories that comprise the book of Joshua are situated in the late thirteenth/early twelfth centuries B.C.E., but they have been edited and shaped with the concerns of a much later period in mind. This can be seen in at least two ways. First, the events describing the conquest of the land are reported from a perspective that has been informed by the ideology of the book of Deuteronomy. In other words, the actions of Joshua and the Israelites are presented and evaluated in light of some of the central themes of Deuteronomy. Second, the book betrays an interest in cultic ritual and other elements that are at the heart of the priestly tradition.

Because both the Deuteronomic and priestly streams developed at a relatively late point in Israelite history, it follows that, regardless of how old some of the individual stories within it might be, the final form of the book as we now have it is the product of a later time.

An earlier generation of scholars sometimes referred to the first six books of the Bible as the Hexateuch because of affinities that exist between Joshua and Deuteronomy, the final book of the Pentateuch. It has now become more common to acknowledge their connection by thinking of Deuteronomy as the introduction to the works that come after it rather than considering Joshua to be the conclusion to the books before it. In many places the material in the former prophets (Joshua through 2 Kings) shows evidence of having been edited with the book of Deuteronomy in mind. In these works the story of Israel, from its emergence in Canaan to its destruction at the hands of Babylon, is retold and appraised by applying the standards that are laid out in Deuteronomy. Because of this influence the record of the rise and fall of Israel that is contained in these writings is often referred to as the Deuteronomistic History, usually abbreviated DH.

One of the hallmarks of Deuteronomy is its focus on the law that was revealed to Moses on Mt. Sinai, or, as Deuteronomy calls it, Mt. Horeb. It frequently urges the Israelites to faithfully follow that law and to obey the statutes and commands that God has placed upon them. This is a central theme in Joshua as well. The book opens after the death of Moses with an appeal from God to the new leader that tells him the law will be the yardstick against which all his actions will be measured.

> Only be strong and very courageous, being careful to act in accordance with all the law that my servant Moses commanded you; do not turn from it to the right hand or to the left, so that you may be successful wherever you go. This book of the law shall not depart out of your mouth; you shall meditate on it day and night, so that you may be careful to act in accordance with all that is written in it. For then you shall make your way prosperous, and then you shall be successful. (1:7-8)

Prior to his own death at the end of the book, within a speech containing many Deuteronomistic elements, Joshua communicates a similar message to the people. "Therefore be very steadfast to observe and do all that is written in the book of the law of Moses, turning aside from it neither to the right nor to the left" (23:6). This bookend arrangement creates an inclusio that identifies the main message of the book, and it is further reinforced by the description in the final chapter of the covenant renewal ceremony centering on obedience and fidelity to God alone.

Deuteronomistic concerns can be seen elsewhere throughout the book. It is stated repeatedly that God has given them the land to possess (1:11; 6:2; 8:1, 18; 11:6). God explains to Joshua that the Israelite defeat at Ai was due to a violation of the covenant (7:10-15). The ark of the covenant containing the tablets of the law plays an important role in some stories (3:7-17; 6:1-21). The Israelites are to pass down from generation to generation the traditions about all that God has done for them (4:21-24).

Some of the most striking examples of Deuteronomy-related language in the book are found on the lips of foreigners. Prior to entering Canaan Joshua sends two men on a spy mission to the land, where a prostitute named Rahab protects them from the local king. At one point the woman acknowledges the power and authority of Israel's God in a statement that contains Deuteronomistic themes similar to those mentioned above.

> I know that the LORD has given you the land, and that dread of you has fallen on us, and that all the inhabitants of the land melt in fear before you. For we have heard how the LORD dried up the water of the Red Sea before you when you came out of Egypt, and what you did to the two kings of the Amorites that were beyond the Jordan, to Sihon and Og, whom you utterly destroyed. As soon as we heard it, our hearts melted, and there was no courage left in any of us because of you. The LORD your God is indeed God in heaven above and on earth below. (2:9-11)

A similar thing occurs in 9:7-11, where the leaders of the Hivites are also aware of all that God has done for Israel.

Turning to texts that reflect a priestly interest, we see that certain scenes are presented in a highly ritualistic way. One of the best examples of this is found in the famous story of the battle of Jericho in chapter 6. It is something of a misnomer to refer to this episode as a battle because there is very little military action in the account. The bulk of the text is a description of how the Israelite forces captured the city because they followed a carefully prescribed seven-day ritual in which priests carrying the ark of the covenant are prominently featured.

The complex of stories in chapters 3 through 5 that describe the Israelites' entry into Canaan is also highly ritualistic. Prior to crossing the Jordan River, Joshua orders the people to purify themselves (3:5) and then, in a scene that echoes the exodus story, the waters part and they are led across by priests who carry the ark of the covenant. Once on the other side, Joshua instructs one man from each of the twelve tribes to pick up a stone from the middle of the Jordan and use it to construct a memorial that will forever commemorate their miraculous passage into Canaan (4:1-24).

The Israelites' final activities prior to claiming the land also reveal the book's priestly agenda. Because none of the men were circumcised during the forty-year period of wandering in the wilderness, they now enact that ritual symbolizing their membership in the covenant community (5:2-9). This is followed by a brief description of the first Passover celebration in the promised land (5:10) and an announcement of a shift in their diet from the manna God provided them in the wilderness to the produce of the land of Canaan. This set of actions purifies the people and establishes their relationship with the land they are about to take as their own.

The strong influence of Deuteronomistic and priestly perspectives on Joshua suggests that the work had a complex process of development. The book may contain some ancient recollections of early Israelite experiences, but those traditions have been shaped and expanded by later editors who were attempting to put their own stamp on the story of the entry into the land. Scholars disagree on precisely when this editorial activity took place and who was responsible for it. The majority view is that the DH of which Joshua is a part does not predate the time of King Josiah of Judah (640–609), during whose reign the book of the law was "discovered" during renovations to the temple in Jerusalem (2 Kgs 22–23). As we have seen, this "discovery" might actually have been the writing of the earliest form of the book of Deuteronomy, which then legitimated Josiah's reform movement. Since faithful observance of the law is also an important theme in Joshua, the book of Joshua likely reached its final shape after Josiah's reign and perhaps even after the beginning of the Babylonian exile just a few years later in 586 B.C.E.

CONTEXT

The time gap between when the book of Joshua reached its present form and the events it purports to describe raises significant questions about its historical reliability. How accurately does the text reflect the events and circumstances related to early Israelite history in Canaan? Evidence from archaeology and the social sciences has assisted attempts to answer such questions by giving us a better sense of the context within which the stories are set. Complete agreement on all the details of that context is lacking and will probably never be achieved, but a general consensus regarding the overall picture has emerged among many scholars.

Excavations during the early and mid-twentieth century appeared to confirm the historicity of many of the stories in Joshua. Archaeologists found evidence of wide-scale destruction during the Late Bronze Age (1550–1200) at many sites that were identified with places mentioned in the book, and this devastation was attributed to Joshua and the Israelites. But later developments and refinements in archaeological methods led others to reexamine the evidence and reach different conclusions. In some cases the destruction levels were dated to earlier periods, and in others the whole idea of an invasion as the cause was dismissed as an attempt to force the archaeological data to fit the biblical text or prove it to be true. It is now generally held that in some places the archaeological evidence coheres with the biblical account, and in other places it does not. In other words, the book's account of a complete and swift conquest of the land by Israelite forces is not tenable in light of what we now know from extra-biblical sources.

The most problematic area is the central part of Canaan, where Joshua locates the initial entry into the land and the first engagements with the local population. Joshua 7:1–8:29 is a lengthy section describing two battles against the town of Ai, but the archeological data suggest that the town was unoccupied in the thirteenth century B.C.E. Some scholars have suggested that the story lacks any historical basis and is simply an etiology that attempts to explain the origin of the name Ai, which means "ruin" (8:28).

The same problem exists in relation to the city of Jericho, whose walls are destroyed by the Israelites in Joshua 6. Jericho is a very old site that was settled in the Neolithic Period, but it was probably not occupied in the thirteenth century B.C.E. It certainly did not possess walls at that time, which directly contradicts the biblical account. Various theories have been put forward to explain the purpose of the story, with one of the more interesting seeing it as some kind of ritualistic conquest that might be connected with the need to purify the area after an outbreak of plague. This would explain the heavy emphasis on ritual in the chapter that was noted above.

The archaeological evidence correlates better with the biblical record in other places, like the more northern cities of Shechem (8:30-35) and Hazor (11:1-15). In both these places, destruction can be dated to the end of the Late Bronze Age, where most scholars date Israel's emergence in Canaan. This does not prove the historicity of the biblical story since it cannot be demonstrated that the Israelites under Joshua's leadership were responsible for destroying the two cities. Nonetheless, the evidence does date the destruction to a time that does not challenge the biblical account, unlike the cases of Jericho and Ai.

An aspect of the archaeological record that is related to the Israelite presence in Canaan is the settlement patterns in the area. The results of both excavations and surface surveys reveal a dramatic increase in the number of settlements in the hill country of the central highlands during the Late Bronze Age. These small, unwalled communities containing architectural features not seen in previous periods emerge rather suddenly and are usually identified by archaeologists as Israelite. The time and location of their appearance make this a logical conclusion, giving some support for an Israelite presence in Canaan around the time indicated by the book of Joshua. Much more contentious is the question of where these people in the highland settlements—and the Israelites more generally—came from.

One of the most hotly debated topics among Hebrew Bible scholars concerns the origin of the people who became the Israelites. Even the biblical text itself is not completely clear on how they entered the land and what happened when they got there. As we will see in the next chapter, the book of Judges presents an account that is somewhat at odds with the description found in Joshua. Three main theories have dominated the discussion over this complicated question.

The first theory is the conquest model, which favors the description of events as recorded in Joshua. In this view the Israelites engaged in a swift and comprehensive series of attacks on the Canaanites that brought virtually the entire land under their control. The evidence of destruction that can be noted at some locations is cited to support this, and the evidence at places like Jericho that seems to contradict it is typically interpreted to bring it more in line with the theory. The second opinion argues for a more peaceful entry that resulted in a gradual settlement in the land. This infiltration model is closer to the events described in Judges, and garners some support from the shifting settlement patterns in the hill country that were mentioned earlier. The third theory, the internal emergence model, sees the Israelites as originating from within the Canaanite population and splitting off from them, perhaps even revolting against the system to free themselves from it. Some who follow this line of thinking say that the group continued to be Canaanite and that we should not speak of a separate entity known as "Israel" until much later.

Many scholars think a combination of these theories might best explain how Israel came to be. According to one possible scenario, a small group of outsiders peacefully entered the land from Egypt, bringing with them traditions about how their god Yahweh had miraculously delivered and guided them. Once in Canaan they encountered natives of the area who were disillusioned by the political authorities or dissatisfied with the social system and their place within it. These Canaanites were attracted to the ideas and beliefs of the newcomers, joining with them as followers of Yahweh. They formed tribal units and settled in the hill country, from which they began to expand their presence and influence throughout the land.

Such a reconstruction of history coheres with the archaeological evidence and presents a plausible picture of how the Israelites entered and spread throughout Canaan. It is, of course, at odds with the events as they are recorded in the book of Joshua and requires a complete rethinking of the origin of the Israelites. In this reading they are not a group of invading outsiders bringing with them a clear sense of who they are and an established set of traditions that they import into the land. They are a mixture of Canaanites and non-Canaanites who all play a role in the development of their shared identity and traditions.

INTERPRETATION

If the results of archaeological study and social scientific analysis indicate we should not accept a literal reading of Joshua, how should we interpret the book? We must keep in mind that the original purpose of the work, like much of the Bible, was not to present an accurate account of events as they happened. Joshua is not history writing in the way we understand that term today. It is a presentation of the past that has been heavily colored by the interests and concerns of a particular theological agenda. In other words, the text recounts past events—whether real or imagined—to interpret what they mean, not simply to inform the reader about what actually happened. In our own efforts at interpretation we must be mindful of the interpretive aims of the authors and editors, or we run the risk of missing the entire point of the text.

The book of Joshua is a theological document and should be read as such. This is seen, for example, when we pay attention to the holy war theme that is found throughout the conquest narratives. The battles are fought at God's command and in God's name, with God or the ark of the covenant leading the way. An important concept associated with the holy war motif is that of *herem,* a term that is related to a Hebrew verb meaning "to destroy completely." The word *herem* can mean "ban" or "doom," and in the stories of the entry into the land it refers to the divine command to kill all the occupants of a town and give the accumulated treasures to God. The *herem* are these treasures, or as the term is often translated into English "devoted things."

Joshua 7 offers a dramatic example of how the *herem* command functions in these stories. A man named Achan violated God's order at Jericho and took some of the devoted things for himself instead of offering them to God, and this led to the defeat of the Israelite forces at Ai. Only after Joshua and the rest of the Israelites had purified themselves and burned Achan—along with his family and all their possessions—were they able to conquer Ai in a second battle. The emphasis on purity, as well as the idea of presenting the spoils of victory as a sacrifice to God, underscores the close association with the priestly tradition in the *herem* requirement.

God's order that the Israelites totally annihilate the native population of Canaan is one of the most troubling aspects of the Hebrew Bible for modern readers. The first half of the book describes how, at God's command, all the inhabitants of various cities and regions are killed (6:21, 24; 8:24-27; 10:28-41; 11:10-11). This is another theme that Joshua shares with the book of Deuteronomy.

> When the LORD your God brings you into the land that you are about to enter and occupy, and he clears away many nations before you—the Hittites, the Girgashites, the Amorites, the Canaanites, the Perizzites, the Hivites, and the Jebusites, seven nations mightier and more numerous than you—and when the LORD your God gives them over to you and you defeat them, then you must utterly destroy them. (Deut 7:1-2)

Many readers find this to be a disturbing image of God that does not resonate with their own belief in a loving and merciful Creator who cares about everything in the world. The idea of a God who prefers some people over others and endorses violence makes sense only within the context of the theological vision out of which the authors and editors of the book are operating. For them God is an all-powerful being who owns the land and can give it to whomever he wishes. God has established a special and exclusive relationship with Israel, and the covenant community needs to be protected from Canaanites, who might tempt or contaminate them.

This notion obviously clashes with the suggestion put forward earlier that the Israelites, or at least a significant portion of them, were Canaanites. Once again, we need to keep in mind the difference between an accurate historical account and a work of theological propaganda that is meant to promote a particular vision or doctrine. The book of Joshua is an example of the latter. It presents an idealized version of Israel's entry into the land that is meant for a much later audience. It was given final shape at a time long after the period it is describing, after King Josiah initiated his reform that encouraged Israel to return to strict observance of the law. The stories in Joshua announce the benefits for those who follow the law and warn of the consequences for those who fail to do so.

CHAPTER 12

INTO THE PROMISED LAND: JUDGES

The book of Judges purports to describe what occurred between the time the Israelites entered Canaan and the establishment of the monarchy. The account presents these events in an orderly, sequential manner that addresses how authority was exercised in Israel after the deaths of Moses and Joshua, the two leaders who dominate the previous complex of stories that recall the exodus, wandering in the wilderness, and entry into the promised land.

CONTENT

Like much of the biblical tradition, Judges is a theological work rather than an accurate portrayal of history. This becomes clear when we recognize the rather limited scope of the book. It does not contain a comprehensive report of everything that occurred, and it is quite selective in what it chooses to describe. Long stretches of time are sometimes summarized in a few words like "And the land had rest eighty years" (3:30). Particular towns and areas are highlighted, while others are not mentioned at all. In addition, evidence from archaeological excavations and other sources has raised questions about whether some of the events described in the book ever occurred.

This lack of attention to historical detail indicates that the theological agenda of Judges is the primary focus of the book. It is more interested in why things happened than in what actually happened. Its explanation of how Israel's successes and failures were directly tied to its obedience to God's will is, at the same time, an evaluation of the faith and commitment of the people. It adopts this perspective because Judges is part of the Deuteronomistic History. All events in the book are viewed and assessed in light of how closely the law of God is followed.

There are three sections to the book: (1) an introduction that summarizes the conquest of the land and establishes the pattern that will be the framework of the rest of the book (1:1–3:6); (2) a main section that contains stories related to the various judges (3:7–16:31); and (3) a conclusion comprising a number of traditions that do not directly refer to judges but describe the civil strife that existed prior to the rise of the monarchy (17:1–21:25).

The introduction begins by recounting the circumstances the Israelites had to confront in the land after Joshua's death. They are successful at defeating the enemy in some cases (1:4-7), but elsewhere they are not able to drive them out and so they must coexist with the local population (1:27-33). This background helps to explain later events in the book when the Israelites, under the leadership of a judge, will engage in military campaigns against Canaanites in different parts of the land.

The theological focus comes to the fore in chapter 2, which captures the essence of the entire book. After a brief message from an angel of the Lord (perhaps a human messenger) that urges the people to keep the covenant (2:1-5) and an announcement of Joshua's death (2:6-10), verses 11-23 give an overview of the pattern that will dominate the next fourteen chapters of the book. This section explains how the people abandoned God and did what was evil, how God became angry and gave them over to their enemies, how the Lord raised up judges to deliver them, and how, once each judge died, the people reverted to their old sinful ways. This entire history is presented as a divine trial meant to determine Israel's faithfulness. "In order to test Israel, whether or not they would take care to walk in the way of the LORD as their ancestors did, the LORD had left those nations, not driving them out at once, and had not handed them over to Joshua" (2:22-23).

Some of the information found in the introduction has raised issues of historicity for scholars. This version of events sometimes disagrees with the account of the entry into the land found in the book of Joshua, leading to questions about which, if either, is a more accurate account. Elsewhere there appear to be conflicting reports about the fate of Jerusalem (1:8, 21). Similarly, there is no archaeological evidence to support the story that Judah took Gaza, Ashkelon, and Ekron, which remained Philistine cities into the period of the monarchy (1:18).

The main section of the book is a set of cycles, each treating the career of a particular judge. Six of these deal with the "minor judges," so called because the information provided about them includes little more than the person's name, place of origin or father's name, number of years as judge, and burial place. Their names are Shamgar (3:31), Tola (10:1-2), Jair (10:3-5), Ibzan (12:8-10), Elon (12:11-12), and Abdon (12:13-15). The account of Elon's judgeship provides a good example of the brevity of these reports. "After him Elon the Zebulunite judged Israel; and he judged Israel ten years. Then Elon the Zebulunite died, and was buried at Aijalon in the land of Zebulun."

The other six cycles are lengthier descriptions of the "major judges": Othniel (3:7-11), Ehud (3:12-20), Deborah (4:1–5:31), Gideon (6:1–8:35), Jephthah (10:6–12:7), and Samson (13:1–16:31). This part of the book also contains a collection of stories about Gideon's son, Abimelech (9:1-57). Each of the six cycles is built on a pattern that contains the following eight elements:

1) Israel does evil in the Lord's sight
2) The Lord gives them into the hand of the enemy
3) Israel serves the enemy for a certain number of years
4) Israel cries out to the Lord for help
5) The Lord raises up a judge
6) The Lord's spirit comes upon the judge
7) The enemy is defeated
8) The land rests for a certain number of years

With the death of each judge, the pattern begins anew. The same basic structure can be observed in each cycle, although most of them insert stories in different places within the overall framework. The pattern is preserved in its most basic form in the first cycle, which discusses the career of Othniel.

> The Israelites did what was evil in the sight of the LORD, forgetting the LORD their God, and worshiping the Baals and the Asherahs. Therefore the anger of the LORD was kindled against Israel, and he sold them into the hand of King Cushan-rishathaim of Aram-naharaim; and the Israelites served Cushan-rishathaim eight years. But when the Israelites cried out to the LORD, the LORD raised up a deliverer for the Israelites, who delivered them, Othniel son of Kenaz, Caleb's younger brother. The spirit of the LORD came upon him, and he judged Israel; he went out to war, and the LORD gave King Cushan-rishathaim of Aram into his hand; and his hand prevailed over Cushan-rishathaim. So the land had rest forty years. Then Othniel son of Kenaz died.

The other five cycles are noted for their richly drawn narratives, some of which are among the most interesting and memorable stories in the Hebrew Bible. The account of how the left-handed Ehud is able to infiltrate the palace, kill King Eglon of Moab, and slip away before he can be discovered is a marvelous tale that is full of clever wordplays and coarse images. The story of Deborah—the only female judge—contains the equally gripping scene of Jael hammering a tent peg into Sisera's head as he attempts to flee from the Israelites. The traditions about Samson, the best known of all the judges, include the famous description of his love affair with Delilah that resulted in his demise. These and many other stories captivate the reader and are all part of the repeated pattern centering on Israel's sin and God's response that organizes the book of Judges.

That pattern begins to unravel as the cycles move along until it is hardly discernible in the Samson cycle. It is as if the book as a whole is describing the downward spiral of the Israelite community as it continues to come up short in its efforts to remain faithful to God. The sense of moral breakdown is effectively conveyed in the concluding section of Judges, which describes idol worship (17–18), lack of hospitality, and a brutal gang rape (19) among the Israelites. The latter offense leads to a civil war between the tribe of Benjamin and the rest of Israel (20–21).

As already noted, this final section of the book does not make a single reference to judges. But it does repeatedly refer to another office that will soon come to dominate Israelite society. In four places (17:6; 18:1; 19:1; 21:25) the reader is reminded that "in those days there was no king in Israel." The first and final occurrences also mention that "all the people did what was right in their own eyes," creating a chiastic pattern throughout the book's conclusion.

These four references to kingship point both forward and backward. They anticipate the anointing of Saul as king by Samuel, the last of the judges of Israel (1 Sam 9:1–10:27). This suggests a positive view of kingship—what Israel needs is the stability and authority that a king provides so that people will not do whatever they want. But the statements also recall an earlier scene in Judges that adopts a more critical attitude toward kingship. In 8:22, when the Israelites ask Gideon to rule over them he replies, "I will not rule over you, and my son will not rule over you; the LORD will rule over you" (8:23). According to Gideon, a human king would usurp the role that is reserved for God alone. This lends an ominous air to the references to kingship at the end of Judges, where it is seen as a solution to the community's difficulties. As Samuel himself will note later on, having a human king might solve some problems, but it will also create a set of new ones.

A final point to mention is that the book's title "Judges" is something of a misnomer since hardly any of these individuals ever actually judge in a juridical sense. Deborah, the lone female judge, is the only one the text refers to as judging Israel (4:4). For the most part, their skills and talents are manifested on the battlefield and in armed conflicts. They are therefore more like military leaders than judges in the way we normally define that term. The other unique aspect that sets them apart is that there is a spiritual or charismatic dimension to their office by virtue of the fact that they have been appointed and empowered by God.

GROWTH

The book of Judges as it has come down to us is the result of significant editorial activity. Traditions of various types, each focusing on a particular judge and area, were pieced together into a running narrative that describes the chaotic transition from a tribal-based society to a monarchy. The compilers of the book drew upon local legends, folktales, battlefield stories, and hymns to construct a history of the period that is presented from a decidedly Deuteronomistic perspective.

The resulting text describes a series of ongoing wars between the Israelites and their hostile neighbors, including Edom, Moab, and Midian. Only the judges, who form a chain of divinely chosen leaders, are able to rally the Israelites and guide them to (temporary) victory over their enemies. The sequential ordering of these events is something that is imposed on it by its editors. The repetitive cycle of Israelite sin followed by divine punishment, followed by the people crying out, followed by God sending a judge suggests that the period of the judges lasted an extended period of time. In fact, if we add up the number of years the text makes reference to, the total amount of time the judges ruled is more than four hundred years. This is much longer than the period of time between the emergence of Israel in the land and the rise of the kingship. Consequently, the book of Judges cannot be an accurate historical account of what happened. Many scholars believe that, contrary to the sequential ordering of the text, some of these events had to be occurring at the same time.

The book avoids such overlap in order to convey the idea that the military and theological challenges posed by neighboring cultures were an ongoing struggle for the Israelites. The repetition of the cycle of sin helps to reinforce this idea, as does the text's suggestion that this was a problem experienced by all of Israel. Numbers often matter in the Bible, and this is a case in point. The twelve judges mirror the twelve tribes of Israel, perhaps indicating the pervasive nature of the people's sin and their need for deliverance. In the same way, the geographic movement of the action reinforces this notion. The stories about the earlier judges are located principally in the south and the subsequent ones gradually move north until the book ends with an account of the Benjaminite war, which took place in the central part of the land. No part of Israel is immune from sin, and all are in need of deliverance.

The occasional repetition of information suggests there may be sources behind the book of Judges. There is a double reference to Joshua's death in 1:1 and 2:8, which might reflect a joining of separate traditions. Similarly, there appear to be two endings to the Samson story (15:20; 16:31) that both state he judged Israel twenty years, information that typically comes at the end of the description of a judge's career.

It might also be the case that the material about the minor judges has a different history of transmission than that of the major judges. As we have seen, the information given about them is much briefer, to the point that all we really have is a list with none of the narrative features that typify the cycles related to the major judges. In addition, the numbers of years the minor judges ruled are less formulaic than what we see for the major judges, virtually all of whom (Jephthah is the lone exception) hold office for a time period that is a multiple of twenty. The lengths of tenure for the minor judges, on the other hand, are more "realistic": twenty-three years (Tola), twenty-two years (Jair), seven years (Ibzan), ten years (Elon), and eight years (Abdon). In other words, the traditions about the minor judges were not edited with the same patterns in mind that we find for the major judges.

In chapters 4 and 5 the narrative account of the defeat of King Jabin of Canaan by Deborah, Barak, and Jael is followed immediately by a poetic composition that celebrates the event. Many scholars consider the poem in chapter 5 to be among the oldest writings in the Hebrew Bible, perhaps going back to as early as the twelfth century B.C.E. Regardless of its precise dating, the poem is certainly much older than the prose version of the story. The juxtaposition therefore provides a unique opportunity to study how texts written in two genres at two different times attempt to convey the same tradition.

Certain differences between the two texts can be attributed to the characteristics and conventions typical of these two forms of communication. The prose account exhibits features like characterization, plot development, and a narrator that one expects in that style of writing. The poem, meanwhile, is set apart by the use of meter, rich imagery, and symbolic language, some of the chief qualities associated with poetry. It is, rather, when we examine who the actors are and how they are described that we find some of the most intriguing divergences between the two texts.

Both versions present Jael's killing of Sisera, which is described in a similar way in each, as the climax of the battle (4:17-22; 5:24-27). However, the two texts treat the other principals involved in the story in somewhat different ways. The prose account names Jabin as the main antagonist and leader of the Canaanites (4:2), and identifies only Naphtali and Zebulun among the tribes of Israel, presumably because of their proximity to the battle, which is located in the north (4:6). The poem, on the other hand, speaks of a coalition of Canaanite kings and never mentions Jabin by name (5:19), while also speaking of other Israelite tribes. Zebulun and Naphtali, along with Benjamin and Issachar, are again praised for their involvement in the military engagement (5:14-15a, 18). But this time Reuben, Gilead, Dan, and Asher are chastised for not coming to the aid of their fellow Israelites (5:15b-17). This difference has a significant impact on how the reader views the events. What is, in the prose story, a relatively localized battle involving one Canaanite leader and two Israelite tribes is, in the poem, a larger military engagement pitting Canaan against Israel.

Perhaps the most striking difference between the two is the presence of Sisera's mother in the poem (5:28-30). She is portrayed peering out her window, anticipating her son's return from war. His delay causes her and the ladies with her to speculate on the reason why his chariot has not yet returned. Their supposition that he is dividing the spoils of war indicates they assume he has had a successful campaign and will soon arrive home as the conquering hero. Little do they know he has been murdered by a woman, his head crushed by a hammer and pierced with a tent peg. The scene adds an element of pathos to the poem that is missing entirely from the narrative account, where he is nothing more than an enemy of Israel. Here, he is a son whose untimely death is about to break his mother's heart.

CONTEXT

According to the most widely accepted view of the biblical chronology, the events described in Judges should be located in the period approximately 1200 to 1020 B.C.E., called Iron Age I by archaeologists. This is not to say that the stories reflect what actually happened in pre-monarchic Israel. It simply means that the phase of Israel's history that is described in this book can be dated to the late thirteenth through the late eleventh centuries B.C.E. The issue of historicity is another matter entirely. It could well be that the traditions in Judges preserve some reliable recollections of events that took place in the period between the emergence of Israel in the land and the rise of the kingship. But, as has been noted above, these traditions have been heavily edited to serve the purposes of the book's compilers, and so any attempt to find authentic material within them must proceed cautiously.

Even if it is next to impossible to match up elements of the stories with historical facts, it can be said with confidence that the overall image of the early Israelite community that emerges from the pages of Judges is an accurate one. This is particularly true regarding the lack of political, military, and religious centralization that is evident in the book. Studies of the development of societies indicate that the period prior to centralization is characterized by the absence of a standing army and bureaucracy, and this is clearly the situation in Judges. In addition, leadership in this phase tends to emerge in an unpredictable way that favors more charismatic individuals who are appointed by popular acclaim rather than formally elected. This perfectly fits the circumstances described in the book, where the judges assume power to respond to particular threats.

The Merneptah Stela, which was mentioned in the chapter on the exodus, is a stone plaque that was commissioned by the pharaoh Merneptah, son of the famous Ramesses the Great, in order to commemorate his military victories. Among the vanquished enemies mentioned in the inscription are Ashkelon, Gezer, Yanoam, and Israel. The stela dates from around 1207 B.C.E., and this is the earliest reference to Israel outside the Bible. Of particular interest is the fact that the first three names on the list are accompanied by markers in the Egyptian language that indicate they are cities, while Israel is designated as a people rather than a place. This suggests that Merneptah considered Israel to be nomadic wanderers rather than a sedentary group that had settled in one place. In other words, just as the book of Judges describes, they were lacking the structure and centralization that typified places like Ashkelon, Gezer, and other Canaanite cities.

Further support for this interpretation comes from a series of four battle scenes from the temple at Karnak, in southern Egypt, that have been attributed to Merneptah. Each scene depicts a different subdued enemy, and one is clearly identified as Ashkelon. Of the other three battles, two, like that against Ashkelon, are presented as taking place in cities. The fourth, however, is situated in an open field. It is quite possible that these three unidentified scenes refer to the defeat of the other three enemies listed after Ashkelon in the Merneptah Stela. The setting of an open field for the fourth argues in favor of this because it is the most obvious way to make a distinction between people who are settled in towns and those, like Israel, who are unattached to a particular place.

A further interesting aspect of these scenes is that the people in the open field, the Israelites, are portrayed in a way that is identical to the people in the other three scenes. In other words, they are Canaanites. This suggests that at the beginning of the period of the judges, Merneptah considered the Israelites to be a group of Canaanites even if they didn't have their own territory in Canaan. This is an argument in favor of the theory about Israelite origins, mentioned in the previous chapter, postulating that at least some of them were native Canaanites.

INTERPRETATION

The book of Judges is a good example of a style of writing that is called historiography. Simply put, historiography attempts to write *about* history rather than give a strict reporting *of* history. It doesn't limit itself to a description of events; it offers a way of understanding and making sense of those events. In other words, there is an element of analysis and interpretation in historiography. The author doesn't just stick to the facts of what happened but tries to persuade the reader as to the meaning of what happened.

In a sense, any attempt to write about the past is bound to be historiography. The process of recording an event always involves subjective decisions that have a bearing on how the story is told. Certain things are highlighted while others are left out. In addition, the author's personal background and motivation for writing exert a great deal of influence on how the events are reported. Because of these and other factors, what we usually call history writing might more properly be labeled historiography.

The historiographic quality of some writings is more apparent than in others, and that is the case with a work like Judges. We have noted how the same pattern is repeatedly used throughout the book to describe the careers of the judges. This framework is a way of giving literary organization to the story, but it also allows the editor to influence the reader's opinion on the meaning of the events being narrated. It imposes a structure on the account that forces the reader to interpret what happened in a particular way—Israel's lack of obedience to the law led to a cycle of sin that was broken only when God sent judges.

The historiography of Judges also reinforces a critical point about Israelite unity. Many of the stories in the book probably originated as independent traditions that were important to particular tribes or smaller groups. Collecting all these traditions and organizing them into a whole helped create a communal identity that enabled the various entities within Israel to see themselves as part of the larger whole. This editorial work did not take place until centuries after the events described in the book, perhaps during the time of King Josiah in the late seventh century B.C.E. or later. The organization of these disparate traditions into a cohesive story then became part of Israelite national history and identity. Such is the purpose and power of historiography.

CHAPTER 13

THE UNITED KINGDOM: THE BEGINNING OF MONARCHY IN ISRAEL (1 SAMUEL 1–15)

Following the order of the Former Prophets in the Hebrew Bible, the book of 1 Samuel follows Judges. The book of Judges ended with the observation that there was no king in Israel at that time, so it is no surprise that 1 Samuel recounts the origin of kingship in Israel. It is perhaps no surprise either that the leading character at the beginning of 1 Samuel is the prophet Samuel, though that will change in short order. To refer to Samuel merely as a prophet is to shortchange him, for Samuel is a transitional figure who combines the roles of prophet, priest, and judge.

CONTENT

The book of 1 Samuel begins with the story of Samuel's birth. The motif of the barren wife found in Genesis resurfaces here. Samuel's mother, Hannah, is unable to have children until she visits the temple at Shiloh and vows that if Yahweh will give her a son she will dedicate him to Yahweh's service. Yahweh answers her prayer, and she fulfills her vow by bringing the boy to Shiloh when he is weaned and entrusting him to the priest there whose name is Eli.

Following a poem exhibiting Hannah's gratitude (2:1-10), the story continues by relating Eli's failure as a father. His two sons, Hophni and Phinehas, abuse their position as priests by, in effect, stealing sacrifices to God. Eli does not discipline them. A nameless man of God brings him an oracle announcing the death of his sons and the fall of his house (2:11-36). The oracle is confirmed in a sense by another one given to Samuel—the first of many that he will receive in his career (3:1–4:1). Both oracles are then fulfilled when the Philistines defeat Israel in battle and seize the ark of the covenant. Eli's sons are killed in battle, and Eli himself dies from a fall when he learns the news (4:2-22). The Philistines place the ark in the temple of their god, Dagon, as a trophy but wake to find the image of Dagon first fallen before the ark and then dismembered. Then a plague accompanying the ark sweeps through their cities until they return it to Israel, where plague breaks out again until the ark receives proper handling (5:1–7:1).

In an episode reminiscent of the stories of the judges, after a twenty-year interval Samuel convenes the people of Israel for fasting, sacrifice, and prayer. In the midst of these activities, Yahweh defeats the Philistines, who have launched an attack (7:1-14). There is a notice about Samuel's judgeship (7:15-17), and then the narrative reports that Samuel has grown old and that his sons, like Eli's, are unfaithful. The Israelites ask for a king, much to Samuel's displeasure. Yahweh tells Samuel that it is he, not the prophet, whom the people have rejected by their request and instructs him, nevertheless, to comply with the request. He warns the people about the ways in which a king will take advantage of them (ch. 8).

What follows are three distinct episodes about how Saul became Israel's first king. In the first, he is secretly anointed by Samuel, whom he has come to consult about some lost donkeys belonging to his father (9:1–10:16). In the second, he is chosen by public lottery (10:17-27a). In the third, he is made king by acclamation after he leads Israel to victory against the Ammonites (10:27b–11:15). A kind of farewell speech from Samuel follows, in which he warns the people to remain faithful to Yahweh (ch. 12).

While Samuel does not yet die, the focus of the narrative clearly changes to Saul and especially his battles against the Philistines. There are two accounts of sins committed by Saul that lead to his rejection. In the first he fails to wait until Samuel comes to offer a sacrifice before battle (13:1-15a). In the second, he fails to execute the annihilation of the Amalekites, as commanded (ch. 15). Even when Israel has success, it is Jonathan's doing rather than Saul's and comes despite a foolish vow made by Saul that nearly brings disaster (13:15b–14:52).

GROWTH

Saul's Search for Lost Donkeys (1 Samuel 9:1–10:16)

First Samuel 9:9 contains the following statement: "Formerly in Israel, anyone who went to inquire of God would say, 'Come, let us go to the seer'; for the one who is now called a prophet was formerly called a seer." This verse is an indisputable instance of editorial intervention. The person who wrote this verse sought to update and define the term "seer" for the readers. The intervention suggests several things about the literary growth of the story. First of all, it indicates at least two levels of composition in this story. As indicated by other evidence of editing, 9:9 is not an isolated insertion by a later scribe but is rather the work of the author of the story, who is recording and reworking an older tradition. Second, this author is writing some time later than the tradition that he records. Exactly how much later is hard to say, but it is far enough removed from the older story that this verse twice uses the term "formerly," referring to an earlier period in Israel, and the author feels that the term "seer" has become archaic enough to require definition for the readers. Finally, though, the author of 9:9 remains faithful to the tradition at least to the extent that he reproduces the term "seer" rather than replacing it throughout the story with the word "prophet."

The other hints of revision in this story suggest that the older tradition has been transformed and refocused. Thus, in the first part of the story the seer or man of God is nameless. It is not until 9:14 that he is identified as Samuel. What makes this identification even stranger is that Saul's servant does not name him as Samuel in 9:6. He simply observes that there is a reputable man of God in the town to which they come. Yet Samuel is much more than a man of God; he is Israel's national leader. Scholars therefore think that the older tradition concerned an unidentified man of God and that the identification of him as Samuel was part of the revision.

Perhaps the best example of the refocusing of the story occurs in 9:19-20. Samuel invites Saul to come home with him and promises to tell him "all that is on your mind" the next morning (9:19). What is on Saul's mind is the location of the lost donkeys that he and his servant are seeking; this is the entire reason for their journey. Hence, it is very odd that Samuel goes on in the very next verse to tell Saul that the donkeys have been found. This is exactly what is on Saul's mind! Why, then, does Samuel tell Saul to wait until morning? And what is the meaning of Samuel's statement that Israel's desire is focused on Saul and his house?

The answers to these questions lie in the literary growth of this story. The older tradition had to do with Saul's search for some lost donkeys and his encounter with a nameless seer who told him where they were after consulting God and receiving a nocturnal revelation. That is why Samuel answers Saul's questions in the morning. Indeed, that is what he does in 10:2-4, along with filling the need for food that Saul and his servant have before the encounter (9:7). However, this older tale has been refocused into a story of Saul's anointing as king, as indicated in Samuel's message about the desire of Israel being for Saul (9:20). Unfortunately, we cannot retrieve all the details of the older tale. It did not originally involve Samuel. Perhaps it did not originally involve Saul either but was simply a story about the needs for food and information being supplied by a man of God. Whatever its contours, the author of the present story, perhaps the Deuteronomistic Historian, used it as a starting place for a story about Saul's private anointing by Samuel.

The Making of Israel's First King (1 Samuel 9–11)

As noted earlier, the story in 9:1–10:16 is the first of three about how Saul became Israel's first king. The way in which the three stories have been bound together also illustrates the literary development of this material. The story in 9:1–10:16 ends with an interview between Saul and his uncle (10:14-16). The uncle is not named, and he plays no role in the story, in contrast, for example, to Saul's father, who sent him on the search for the lost donkeys. These observations suggest that the uncle is merely a functional character. He is introduced to play a specific role. In this case, that role is to make or reinforce the point that Saul's anointing was a private matter between Saul and Samuel, not even witnessed by anyone else. This observation raises doubt about the story's historicity, for how could it have come to be known to the author? Historical or not, the interview has the literary function of preparing the reader for the next story (10:17-27a) in which Saul's election as king is public. The second and third stories also conclude with notices that function as links between them. The question of the scoundrels who doubt Saul's suitability to rule in 10:27a ("How can this man save us?") is answered by the third story when Saul exhibits his military leadership. After the victory, there is a call, which Saul graciously declines, for those who doubted his capability to be put to death (11:12-13). This anecdote simply binds the third story all the closer to the second one.

The story of Saul's victory in chapter 11, like the one in 9:1–10:16, contains evidence of an older story that has been revised. The story actually begins at 10:27b. This half verse is not in all English translations. It was accidentally lost from the manuscripts underlying printed editions of the Hebrew Bible but is included in the NRSV and a few other versions based on a Dead Sea Scroll fragment of Samuel. It shows that the story had an independent beginning that was unconnected to the story in 10:17-27a. According to the story, Nahash the Ammonite king allows the elders of the town of Jabesh-Gilead to send messengers to Israel looking for help. Why he agrees to this is unclear; perhaps he is confident that none will be forthcoming. What is important for our purposes is that the elders do not mention King Saul, and the messengers are not sent specifically to Saul or to Gibeah, his hometown. The messengers simply happen to pass through Gibeah, and Saul only happens to find out about the predicament of Jabesh-Gilead when he overhears the people weeping at the news. In fact, Saul is coming home from plowing in the field when he learns about Jabesh-Gilead. In other words, this story does not assume that Saul is yet king of Israel and therefore is independent of and does not presuppose the previous two stories about Saul becoming king. Indeed, at the very end of the story, the people go to Gilgal to make Saul king (11:15). However, this statement has been modified by the addition of Samuel's summons of the people to Gilgal to *renew* the kingship (11:14).

Once again, then, an older, independent story has been revised for purposes of incorporation into the larger narrative about Israel's first king. The three stories now work together to paint a picture of Saul becoming king in three stages: private anointing, public designation, and then confirmation by military victory.

The Birth of Samuel (1 Samuel 1)

Scholars often point to two other texts in these chapters as containing evidence of literary reworking. One of these is the story of Samuel's birth, which, it has been suggested, was originally about Saul rather than Samuel. The reason for this suggestion is that the wordplays on the name of Hannah's son make use of the Hebrew verb "to request" and therefore fit with the name Saul (Hebrew *shā'ûl*) rather than the name Samuel. Thus, as it now stands, 1:20 makes no sense when it says that Hannah named her son Samuel because she *requested* him from Yahweh. The reader expects to find the name Saul. Even clearer in Hebrew is 1:28 where the word translated "given" in the NRSV is a form of the verb *shā'al* that is identical to the name Saul (*shā'ûl*).

The Ark Narrative (1 Samuel 4:2–7:1)

Another older document that has been posited beneath the current narrative has even been given the title "Ark Narrative." Unlike the texts just treated, there is no internal evidence of revision supporting the existence of an independent document here. The evidence is primarily circumstantial. It lies in the fact that Samuel, who is the focus of the stories before 4:2 and after 7:1, disappears from the intervening narrative. The original dimensions of this theoretical source are uncertain. It presupposes that the reader knows who Eli is and thus seems dependent on the foregoing material. On the other hand, it seems unlikely to have ended with 7:1, so some scholars believe that it was continued in the story of David's moving the ark to Jerusalem (2 Sam 6). In short, it seems clear that the author of 1 Samuel 1–15 made use of sources that he revised in conformity to his goals in the larger narrative; it is less certain whether an independent Ark Narrative was one of these sources.

CONTEXT

The historical and social context of the stories about Samuel and Saul is indicated by the geographical references they contain. The stories about both men are set within a limited area encompassing basically the highlands of Benjamin and southern Ephraim. There is no reason to believe that Saul's "kingdom" was any larger. It probably did not include all of the tribal areas of Israel. Israel was at best a loose confederation of tribes at this point, certainly not a true nation. Parallels to Saul's status in other cultures suggest that he is best considered a tribal chief rather than a real king, as social-scientific scholars observed in the 1980s. Still, there were inter-tribal connections. The tie between Saul and the people of Jabesh-Gilead may be one example. According to Judges 21, the Benjaminites intermarried with the people of Jabesh, so it may be no coincidence that the messengers sent from Jabesh went to Benjamin. The connection between Saul and Jabesh will prove significant in later stories as well.

While the traditions of Samuel and Saul are set in the eleventh century B.C.E. and may well emanate at least partly from that time, they were written in their present form much later. Unfortunately, it is not easy to tell when the stories preserve genuine ancient traditions and when they reflect much later circumstances. An example of the latter, however, may be the prominence of the town of Mizpah as a place of national assembly and worship (7:7-17; 10:17-27a). This prominence is especially intriguing in view of the fact that Mizpah essentially replaced Jerusalem as the administrative capital of Judah following the latter's destruction in 586 B.C.E. The prominence of Mizpah in these stories may be an anachronism betraying the historical context of the author. What is even more intriguing is the fact that the Benjaminite highlands in which so many of the Saul stories are set largely escaped the ravages of the Babylonian invasion that led to the exile of 586. The impact of that much later context of the author on these stories, therefore, may be much greater than is generally recognized.

In terms of literary context, both Samuel and Saul are transitional figures. We have already seen how this is so for Samuel, who is presented as the last of the judges, as well as a prophet and a priest. It is no less true for Saul. While he may have been a chieftain historically, he is presented as the first king of Israel. He provides a transition and a contrast to Israel's greatest king, David. It is in this contrast that the story of Saul presents some thorny interpretive issues.

INTERPRETATION

Saul is a foil for David—a contrast to David's success and highly positive evaluation. Saul is a tragic figure. David, it will seem, can do nothing wrong; Saul can do nothing right. Saul is barely king before he is rejected in favor of a man after Yahweh's own heart—David (13:14). And it is hard to escape the impression that the reason for Saul's rejection is little more than a pretext. He follows Samuel's order to go to Gilgal and wait for seven days. Samuel is late, and the army begins to desert, so Saul offers the sacrifice himself (13:8-9). The story raises more questions than it answers. Why is this Saul's fault and not Samuel's? And what, exactly, did

Saul do wrong? Kings in the ancient Near East often functioned as priests; David will eat holy bread (21:5) and will dress as a priest and offer sacrifices (2 Sam 6:14, 17). The point seems to be simply that Yahweh does not like Saul and wants to replace him with David, whom he favors, as soon as possible.

The second story of Saul's sin in chapter 15 yields a similar impression. He is commanded to annihilate the Amalekites, and he does so except for the king, Agag, and the best of the animals, which he preserves for sacrifice (15:21). Since the annihilation is a form of sacrifice to Yahweh, what is the difference? As for Agag, it is not clear why Saul kept him alive, partly because of difficulties with the text. One translation of 15:32 is that Agag was brought in bonds and said, "Is death as bitter as this?" This reading might indicate that Saul kept Agag alive not as a favor to his royal status but for some sort of special execution, which is what he receives from Samuel anyway (15:33). If this interpretation is correct, then again one must ask, "What did Saul do wrong?" The point of the story is not so much to answer this question as it is simply to say that Yahweh rejected Saul for David. One is left to wonder, if Saul was rejected so quickly, why God chose him in the first place.

Saul's rapid rejection in favor of David touches on another difficult interpretive issue raised by these chapters. Is monarchy viewed as a good thing or a bad thing? The people's cry for a king is viewed as a rejection of God (8:7). Yet Yahweh permits a king and even guides Samuel to anoint him. The force of Samuel's departing speech (1 Sam 12) is that Yahweh can work with a king if the king and the people will remain faithful. Here, it seems that the institution of monarchy per se is neither good nor evil but can be used for both depending on an individual king's loyalty to Yahweh. Perhaps Saul and David are meant to be contrasting examples of the exercise of kingship. The problem is that for the modern reader the points of contrast between them are not entirely clear.

Chapter 14

THE UNITED KINGDOM: THE RISE OF DAVID (1 SAMUEL 16–2 SAMUEL 5)

Since Saul was really a kind of local chieftain, David was Israel's first true king. Surprisingly, there is more literature devoted to David in the Bible than to any other character, including Moses and Jesus. His story and character have fascinated readers throughout history, as evidenced in the myriad of art and literary works devoted to him. This fascination with David comes, in large measure, from the fact that he is a study in contrasts, even contradictions—capable of great piety and humility but also of ruthlessness. His portrait, in short, is a very human one.

CONTENT

The account of David's rise to kingship can be divided into four sections.

David's Origins (1 Samuel 16–17)

There are three texts in this section. The first (16:1-13) recounts David's anointing by Samuel in Bethlehem. At Yahweh's command, Samuel travels to Bethlehem to anoint one of Jesse's sons as Saul's replacement. The sons of Jesse are presented to Samuel and rejected one by one until the youngest, David, is called from the flock and chosen. In the second text (16:14-23), Saul hears of David's skill as a musician and a warrior and has him brought to court to relieve his episodes of torment caused by an evil spirit from Yahweh. David becomes Saul's armor bearer. The third text (chapter 17) is the famous story of David's victory over Goliath.

David's Conflict with Saul (1 Samuel 18–20)

The second section tells of David's career in Saul's army and the friction between them that erupts into conflict. Saul's jealousy is aroused at David's acclaimed military success, so that he makes several attempts, subtle and overt, on David's life. Despite Saul's animosity, David is close to Saul's children. He is married to Saul's daughter, Michal, and has a covenant of friendship with Jonathan, the crown prince.

David in the Judean Wilderness (1 Samuel 21–2 Samuel 1)

David flees from Saul into the wilderness, where he gathers a small army of outcasts and ruffians around him. Saul is insane with jealousy and annihilates an entire village of priests who give assistance to David. David and his men survive by pillaging non-Israelite villages and by serving as mercenaries to the Philistines. After a couple of narrow escapes from Saul, David has a couple of chances to kill Saul, but he refuses to do so. He nearly annihilates the household of a wealthy rancher named Nabal but is kept from it by the man's wife, Abigail, whom David marries after Nabal's untimely demise at Yahweh's hands. When the Philistines go to war against Saul, David and his men are sent away from the Philistine ranks and find their town (Ziklag) razed and their families gone. While they pursue the Amalekite raiding party that is responsible, Saul and Jonathan are killed in battle on distant Mt. Gilboa, as foreseen by a necromancer whom Saul consulted on the eve of the battle.

2 Samuel 2:1–5:5

David's anointing as king over Judah and his overture to Jabesh-Gilead spark a war with Saul's successor, Ishbaal. The murders of Saul's general, Abner, and of Ishbaal bring an end to the civil war, and David is anointed king over Israel, replacing Saul.

GROWTH

The growth of this material has been traced at two different levels. First, in terms of the basic story, some scholars have posited the existence of an older, independent document known as the "Story or History of David's Rise." This document remains hypothetical, and there is no clear evidence for it. It is just as possible that the Deuteronomistic Historian simply composed the story of David's rise on the basis of traditions available to him that had not previously been collected.

Another theory holds that two extended sources about David were edited together to form the present narrative. Those who hold to this theory point to instances of doublets in the narrative. Thus, there are two versions each of Saul attempting to kill David with his spear (18:10-11; 19:8-10), of David's marriage or near marriage to a daughter of Saul (18:17-19, 20-29), of chances David had to kill Saul (1 Sam 24; 26), and of Saul's death (1 Sam 31; 2 Sam 1). However, other explanations—textual and literary—for these doublets have limited the popularity of this theory.

The second level of development is much less theoretical since it is based on textual evidence. There is strong evidence that at least certain parts of the David story were still undergoing change even at the stage when it was being transmitted by copyists. The best example is the famous David and Goliath story (1 Sam 17). The Hebrew text of this story, which is translated in English versions of the Bible, is essentially twice as long as the version preserved in the Greek Septuagint (LXX). This is because the Hebrew either conflates two distinct versions of the story or contains substantial supplementation of the original story. The LXX basically contains the story in 17:1-11, 32-49, 51-54. The rest of the Hebrew version was added some time after the LXX translation was produced (ca. 200 B.C.E.). The additions have caused some tensions in the text of the story that can be seen in English translations. For instance, in the story as it now stands, David kills Goliath twice—once with the sling stone, when the text says explicitly that there was no sword in David's hand (17:50), and a second time by beheading him with his own sword (17:51). Again, at the end of the end of the present story Saul does not know who David is (17:55-58), an obvious contradiction to the scene in which Saul interviews David and has him try on armor (17:32-39).

Similar tensions continue into chapter 18, where verses 1-5 obviously interrupt the continuation of what happened when the Israelites returned from the battle in which David killed Goliath (18:6). These five verses are not found in the LXX. The LXX also lacks one of the versions of Saul's attempt to kill David with a spear (18:10-11) and the account of David's near marriage to Merab (18:17-19). All three of these are late scribal additions, probably associated with the variant Goliath story. This does not mean that there existed a variant version of the entire story of David's rise.

CONTEXT

In the context of the Deuteronomistic History, David is clearly the single most important character. Not only is there more space by far devoted to David than to any other character, but the David story is at the center of the History. David is also of continuing importance in the History as the standard against which other kings are measured. In that sense, he is the model of kingship for Israel. His reputation has only been enhanced in post-biblical Jewish and Christian interpretation, where he is revered as the shepherd boy whose faith and piety helped him to slay a giant and as a man after God's own heart.

The extent to which these stories reflect genuine history is disputed. This is partly because there is virtually no mention of David outside of the Bible. Before 1993, in fact, no reference to David had ever been found in any ancient document independent of the Bible. This changed somewhat in 1993 and 1994 with the discovery of fragments of a ninth-century Aramaic stele at Tel Dan, which contained a reference to the "house of David." Even so, this was a reference to the nation of Judah ruled by the Davidic dynasty rather than to David the person. Still, this inscription has tipped the scales in favor of the position that David was a historical figure. Nevertheless, admitting that David really existed is a far cry from viewing all the Bible's stories about him as historical. After all, the story of David's rise in its present form was written hundreds of years after the events it purports to report. As with the Saul stories, therefore, there may be anachronisms that fit better with the author's time than with David's.

The geographical and topographical context of ancient Israel is important for understanding the stories of David's rise. It is helpful to know, for instance, that the Judean wilderness was rugged territory, full of caves and rocky terrain that readily lent themselves as hideouts for outlaws and other social outcasts and fugitives. It makes sense in such a setting that David would gather a band of ruffians and mercenaries about him, all the more since this was territory that Saul may never have claimed, much less controlled. Several of the stories, such as those about David's chances to kill Saul, take place in caves or on craggy hills.

In certain instances, geographical knowledge casts new light on a story. For example, David's flight from Saul to Ramah (19:18-24) seems historically implausible, since one would expect him to go south toward Bethlehem or the Judean wilderness rather than north and deeper into Saul's domain. The story makes good literary sense, though, because Ramah is Samuel's home. It therefore confirms the prophet's support of David over against Saul. Similarly, Saul's death on Mt. Gilboa, far north of the anticipated battleground between Saul and the Philistines, is historically questionable. Gilboa serves the literary function of placing as much distance as possible between the site of Saul's death and David's location, thereby furthering the claim that David was completely uninvolved in felling Saul. A final example is that of Jabesh-Gilead, the city that Saul rescued from the Ammonites (1 Sam 10:27b–11:15). Its citizens returned the favor by rescuing Saul's corpse and those of his sons from Philistine abuse (1 Sam 31:11-13). David's letter to them, thanking them for their loyalty to Saul and inviting them to support him, threatened to take away the last enclave of support for Saul's son and successor, Ishbaal—all the more so since Ishbaal had been driven by the Philistines' victory over Israel to Mahanaim, which was not far south of Jabesh. Ishbaal was left with no choice but to attack David and thus to fight on David's terms.

Several items of cultural context are also crucial for understanding these stories. There is, first of all, the institution of hereditary monarchy, in which a king's successor will normally be his firstborn son. When it is not—and especially when the successor is not even a blood relative of the king—an explanation is in order. Similarly, the connection between marriage and politics is an important cultural assumption behind this material. Almost all of David's marriages about which anything can be surmised are political in nature. Michal was the king's daughter and brought David into the royal family. Abigail brought the wealth and status of her deceased husband to her marriage with David, giving him an important boost on his ascent to the throne of Judah. David's marriage to a princess of Geshur suggests that he had a treaty with that small kingdom just east of the Sea of Galilee, which would have added to the pressure on Jabesh-Gilead to support him and to Ishbaal's sense of being hemmed in.

INTERPRETATION

The story of David's rise is sophisticated literature with themes that run throughout it, frequent use of wordplays, and complex characterizations. It also seems to be history with descriptions of actual events and deeds by real persons of the past. Readers of the story struggle to balance historical and literary concerns—to uncover the history while also appreciating the literature.

A scholarly approach that seeks to do both begins with the recognition of the David story as apologetic in nature. The function of apology as a literary genre or tool is to offer a defense—in the case of the story of David's rise, to defend David against the charge that he usurped the throne from Saul. Such a defense would be called for because David was not Saul's heir or blood relative. The apology would also defend the Davidic dynasty, which after all derived its legitimacy from its founder. In addition to the principal charge of usurpation, there were likely other charges, such as that David betrayed Israel by serving the Philistines as a mercenary.

The apology worked not by denying the facts in such matters, which may have been widely known, but by explaining the circumstances. We might think of the apologist as an ancient "spin doctor," seeking to justify David's actions and motives. Thus, the story admits that David did not have a hereditary right to the throne (though it casts him as Saul's son-in-law), but explains that he was divinely chosen to succeed Saul. Thus, the apology reflects literary skill and creativity. At the same time, the critical reader can perceive the historical facts for which the literature seeks justification. In order to discern such facts, the reader must be skeptical of the legitimating claims made by the apologist and suspect that David behaved according to natural human inclinations in much the same way as other Middle Eastern potentates, ancient and modern. This means reading contrary to the apologist's intentions, or "against the grain," of the apology. Such a reading reveals some of the techniques used by the author in shaping the apology.

In the story, David's path to kingship is littered with corpses, those of Nabal, Saul and Jonathan, Abner, and Ishbaal. A kind of pattern emerges: a prominent man dies, usually violently and under suspicious circumstances, and David is the clear benefactor. The story admits as much, but consistently denies that David was in any way involved. Nevertheless, circumstantial evidence in each case leads the critical reader to suspect that David orchestrated each of these deaths to further his career. In the case of Saul and Jonathan, the author goes to great lengths to deny David's involvement, devoting all of 1 Samuel 24–2 Samuel 1 to this purpose.

In the stories in 1 Samuel 24 and 26, the text shows that David did not kill Saul on two occasions when he had the chance. The point they seem to be making is that David would surely not have killed Saul later on if he could have easily disposed of him on these occasions. In chapter 25, David is prevented from killing Nabal, who is a Saul-like figure. It is Yahweh who takes Nabal's life, just as it is Yahweh who ordains Saul's death in battle, as announced by Samuel's ghost in chapter 28.

In chapters 29–30, David is dismissed by the Philistines, so that he does not go to war against Saul and Israel. The author makes clear in David's clever remark to the gullible Achish about the "enemies of my lord the king" (29:8) that David remained loyal to Saul and would have turned against the Philistines had he gone to battle. Indeed, the author suggests here that David might have prevented Saul's death. As we have seen, when Saul dies on Mt. Gilboa in the north, David is far away in the south chasing the Amalekites who raided Ziklag (and whom, incidentally, Saul failed to annihilate!). The story includes the extraordinary admission that David gained possession of Saul's crown and royal insignia. But it explains that David executed the Amalekite who brought them to him because the man claimed to have finished Saul off on the battlefield. The amount of effort that the author devotes to the denial that David was involved in Saul's death is a case of "protesting too much" that leads one to suspect just the opposite.

The circumstantial evidence in the cases of Abner and Ishbaal is equally damning. The story admits that both men were assassinated. Since both were prominent leaders in Saul's succession, David benefited enormously from their deaths. Abner was killed by David's own right-hand man, Joab. The story does not deny this, but does deny that David had any knowledge beforehand of Joab's plans or deed. David laments profusely over Abner and curses Joab. But David does not punish him. Ishbaal is also assassinated. Similar to the narrative about Saul's death, there is the extraordinary admission that David ends up in possession of Ishbaal's head. Yet the apology explains that David in no way endorsed the deed and that he in fact had the assassins executed for it.

These examples illustrate the apologetic nature of the story of David's rise. The stories are well narrated; portions of them may be whole-cloth inventions. David's innocence is consistently maintained. But the basic facts of what happened surface. As apology, the story of David's rise represents a strong argument in favor of the historicity of King David, for it is difficult to imagine anyone inventing such allegations against a fictional character merely for the purpose of trying to explain them away.

CHAPTER 15

THE UNITED KINGDOM: THE REIGNS OF DAVID AND SOLOMON (2 SAMUEL 5–1 KINGS 11)

The reigns of David and Solomon are typically viewed together as a kind of "Golden Age" for Israel. The two reigns do go together, as Solomon continues and enhances many of the policies established by David. As is typical for so-called "Golden Ages," a great deal of legendary material has accrued around the stories of David and Solomon, and it is not always easy to distinguish the legendary elements from the historical ones.

CONTENT

The account of David's reign in 2 Samuel has three main sections. The first (5:6–12:31) in effect lists activities undertaken by David as king. These include the conquest of Jerusalem and moving the capital there (5:6-10), building a royal residence (5:11-12), a list of sons born to David in Jerusalem (5:13-16), victories over the Philistines (5:17-25), installing the ark in Jerusalem (6:1-23), God's promise to build David a dynasty (7:1-29), victories over surrounding peoples (8:1-18), David's treatment of Jonathan's son Mephibosheth (9:1-13), and the defeat of an Ammonite-Aramean coalition (10:1-19; 12:26-31). The story of David's adultery with Bathsheba and the oracle of the prophet Nathan in response (2 Sam 11:1–12:25) interrupt this last battle story.

The second section (2 Sam 13–20) is the story of Absalom's revolt, precipitated by Amnon's rape of Tamar and Absalom's murder of Amnon (13) and followed by a secondary revolt led by Sheba (20).

The third section is a collection of miscellaneous materials: two narratives about David's execution of Saul's heirs (21:1-14) and David's sin of taking a census (24:1-25), encompassing two lists of David's war heroes and their exploits (21:15-22; 23:8-39), which in turn surround two poems (22:1-51; 23:1-7).

The story of David continues into 1 Kings, with the report of his death, summary of his reign, and notice of his succession by Solomon coming in 2:10-12. But the focus of 1 Kings 1–11 is Solomon's reign. The first two chapters deal with his succession of David, the next three with his wisdom, wealth, and power. The centerpiece is the account of the construction and dedication of the temple (1 Kgs 5–8). This is followed by further anecdotes about the magnificence of his kingdom, including the visit of the queen of Sheba (1 Kgs 9–10) and the troubles caused by his apostasy (1 Kgs 11).

GROWTH

There is a long-standing theory that the story of David's reign is based on an older, independent document known as the "Succession Narrative," so called because it was purported to be an explanation of why Solomon succeeded David as king. Further examination has convinced most scholars that the concern for succession is limited to the first two chapters of 1 Kings, so that the designation "Succession Narrative" for all of this material is a misnomer. The term "Court History," referring primarily to the story of Absalom's revolt, is more appropriate. However, if such a document existed it must have included other materials presupposed in the story of the revolt, especially the stories of the deaths of Asahel, Abner, and Ishbaal (2 Sam 2:12–4:12), the introduction of Mephibosheth (2 Sam 9), and the account of the deaths of Saul's heirs (2 Sam 21:1-14). The beginning and ending of this document cannot be determined, so that as with the postulated Ark Narrative and History of David's Rise, the Court History remains hypothetical as one of the Deuteronomistic Historian's sources.

Internal clues in these stories may put us on firmer ground in tracing their growth. For instance, the story of David's execution of Saul's heirs must have stood at an earlier stage of the narrative before David's dealings with Mephibosheth. This is because the latter begins with David asking whether there are any heirs left to Saul's line (9:1). The very similar lists of David's cabinet members immediately preceding each text (8:15-18; 20:23-26) are likely a remnant of the original order. The removal of 21:1-14 from its original place before chapter 9 was probably deliberate, since the current arrangement of the miscellaneous texts in chapters 21–24 is intentionally ordered. The reference in 24:1 to Yahweh being angry *again* alludes to the famine in 21:1 and suggests that the two narratives were once together. They were probably separated by the insertion of the list of David's war heroes, which was in turn divided by the insertion of the poems.

Another text that may be a secondary insertion, though this is not widely accepted by scholars, is the one about Bathsheba. As noted above, the story in 11:1–12:2 obviously interrupts the battle account that surrounds it. The Bathsheba episode also differs from the rest of the David story in 1–2 Samuel in that it is not apologetic. David's offense is openly admitted without any attempt to justify it or to defend him. One might contrast this story with the one about David's marriage to Abigail (1 Sam 25). The end result is similar in both—David ends up with another man's wife, and her former husband dies. The Abigail story, though, assures the reader that David has nothing to do with Nabal's death, while the Bathsheba account leaves no doubt about David's guilt.

In the account of Solomon's reign, the allusions to exile and destruction of the temple (e.g., 8:46-51; 9:6-9) have been taken as later additions by those who posit a preexilic, primary edition of the Deuteronomistic History. The contention is that these texts are in tension with the promise to David that there would always be an heir of his on the throne of Judah and that his son might be disciplined but would not lose the kingdom (2 Sam 7:12-16).

CONTEXT

It is illuminating to consider the account of David's reign in the context of the surrounding accounts of Saul and Solomon and in the even broader context of ancient Near Eastern monarchy. A fairly obvious trajectory develops from Saul through David to Solomon of typical characteristics of ancient Near Eastern kings and states. This trajectory indicates that David was the first true king of Israel—or at least he is portrayed as such; it was he who brought Israel to national status.

One of the most obvious and most important items in this trajectory concerns the establishment of a *capital*. Whereas Saul ruled from his hometown, Gibeah, David established a new capital in Jerusalem and named it after himself, "city of David." It has long been recognized that David's establishment of Jerusalem as his capital was an astute political move designed to unite Israel (at least Benjamin and Ephraim) and Judah. Jerusalem was not only geographically neutral, located roughly between Benjamin and Judah, it was also politically neutral as well, since it belonged to the Jebusites until David conquered it and set up his administrative center there.

Within his new capital David had a royal residence built—a palace. Solomon enlarged it or built a new one for himself. Neither of these houses probably was comparable to the expansive palaces of ancient Egyptian or Mesopotamian monarchs. But they were more than what Saul had, since he remained in his family home. The Bible ascribes no building projects to Saul, a handful to David, mostly in Jerusalem, and extensive building to Solomon. It is remarkable in this respect that David is not credited with building the *temple*, all the more so since he was the founder of the dynasty. In the ancient Near East the connection between palace and temple was meaningful. The two usually stood next to each other as a way of representing the king's devotion to the god and the god's support of the king. There was no tradition about David building the temple. The Deuteronomistic Historian sought to correct this absence by having David express the intent to build a temple, to which Yahweh responded by promising him a dynasty (2 Sam 7).

How did Solomon build the temple? The answer, in part, is by compelling the Israelites to serve in his *labor force* (1 Kgs 5:13). Judah, the tribe of David and Solomon, was exempt. This would prove to be one of the main reasons that the kingdom divided after Solomon's death. But it was David rather than Solomon who instituted the labor force, as is clear from the inclusion of an officer over the labor force in the list of David's cabinet (2 Sam 20:24). Saul did no building and therefore had no need of a labor force.

The labor force was part of a system of *taxation*. Solomon changed Israel's tribal system by dividing it into provinces, each of which was responsible for supplying provisions for the royal household one month out of the year (1 Kgs 4:7-19). Since it was David who conquered Israel and who began the labor force, it was probably he as well who started the tax system.

In addition to a labor force, Solomon's conscription also enlisted soldiers for his *army*. Again, this practice likely began with David, who carried out a census of the young men of military age (2 Sam 24:9). David's army, and probably Solomon's, boasted different divisions—an honor guard of "mighty men," as well as a bodyguard, and a contingent of Philistine mercenaries (2 Sam 15:18-22). This was an extensive, significant change from the situation under Saul, whose army, at least at the beginning, was a militia called up to face the Ammonites (1 Sam 11). His army consisted mainly of men from his own tribe of Benjamin (1 Sam 22:7), though he was constantly on the lookout for other worthy volunteers (1 Sam 14:52).

Another area of clear development among the three kings was the *harem*. The Bible names only one wife and one concubine of Saul's. David had at least ten times as many—the Bible mentions twenty wives and concubines. Solomon is reputed to have had seven hundred wives and three hundred concubines (1 Kgs 11:1-3). These numbers may well be exaggerated, but they illustrate the ideal of monarchy imagined for Solomon. Also, as we have seen, David's marriages, by and large, were political.

They ratified treaties—a common practice in the ancient Near East—and so represented alliances with other countries. Similarly, Solomon's many marriages represent his extensive diplomatic relationships.

One of the primary expectations of an ancient Near Eastern king was that he would enforce *justice* in his country. Solomon is renowned for the wisdom of his judgments (1 Kgs 3). There are stories of two occasions when David was approached to render a legal decision (2 Sam 12:1-6; 14:4-11), and Absalom garnered support for his rebellion by claiming that those who brought suits before the king would not receive a fair hearing (2 Sam 15:2-6). There is no such story about Saul; unlike David and Solomon, he is not envisioned as trying to implement a centralized justice system.

As we have seen, Saul's domain was basically limited to the territory of his home tribe, Benjamin, and perhaps part of Ephraim. David's claim and probably his control were more extensive—including all of Israel. David also gave and rescinded land grants (2 Sam 9:7; 16:4). Solomon, as we have seen, carried this further, redividing Israel into districts or provinces. In anthropological terms, Saul is depicted as ruling over a chiefdom. The Bible portrays David, followed by Solomon, as the first true kings of Israel, who developed it into a nation.

INTERPRETATION

The apologetic nature of the David story described in the last chapter continues in the account of David's reign. The clearest example is the narrative of David's dealings with Saul's heirs (2 Sam 21:1-14). The story begins with a three-year famine during David's reign. When David inquired of Yahweh about the reason for the famine, he was told that it was retribution for Saul's having violated a treaty with the people of the Canaanite city of Gibeon by trying to annihilate them. It is worth noting that there is no account of Saul's assault on the Gibeonites anywhere else in the Bible. David then asks the Gibeonites how he might appease them for Saul's crime. They reply that it is a matter of blood vengeance and that seven of Saul's sons and grandsons should be handed over to them for execution. David complies, with the result that Saul's line is effectively wiped out except for Jonathan's lame son, Mephibosheth.

It was typical in the ancient Near East for new kings, especially the founders of new dynasties, to kill off all potential rivals—especially the male heirs of the previous dynasty. This strategy was employed repeatedly by the kings of Israel, as we will see. David also had Saul's heirs executed. The text does not deny this, but it justifies his actions by explaining that he was compelled by the Gibeonites and moved to save Israel from famine. Historically, David probably acted in typical monarchical fashion for political reasons. The apology itself offers a sort of confirmation of this elsewhere. In the story of Absalom's revolt, as David flees from Jerusalem, he encounters a Benjaminite named Shimei, who jeers and throws stones at him, calling him a murderer and saying that Yahweh is avenging the blood of Saul's house (2 Sam 16:5-8). Where did Shimei get this idea? The very fact that the text has him say this is a good indication that the suspicion that David had Saul's heirs, if not Saul himself, assassinated for political reasons was widespread and probably well founded.

Related to David's treatment of Saul's male heirs were his dealings with Saul's daughter, Michal. As we saw in 1 Samuel, there is a story about David's marriage to Michal. It is at least curious that there is no mention of David ever trying to contact Michal or bring her with him during the time he was a fugitive in the wilderness. The next time she is mentioned is when Abner proposes to bring the kingdom to David (2 Sam 3:12-16). David refuses to meet with him unless he brings Michal, who we learn has since been married to someone else. The reason is that she represents his claim, however indirect, to Saul's throne.

The next time Michal is mentioned is after David brings the ark to Jerusalem (2 Sam 6:20-23). She scolds him for his behavior, and the episode ends by saying that she had no children. The text leaves the reason ambiguous: Is it because God punished her for speaking against David or because David had her isolated? David would have had a political motive for isolating Michal, since any children she bore would be heirs of Saul. To take this line of thought a step further, it may be that the entire account of David's marriage to Michal is apologetic and serves both to supply him a hereditary claim, through marriage, to the throne and to justify his taking her from her husband and placing her in isolation, resulting in her childlessness.

The major apologetic interests in the account of David's reign concern the deaths of his sons, Amnon and Absalom. Each of them at the time of his death appears to have been the oldest living son and hence a potential threat to David's power. Abṣalom was in revolt. Their deaths were similar to those of others of David's rivals. The two sons both died violently, and the story seems to show a concern for explaining David's innocence. This is especially so for Absalom, who was killed by Joab, who is also blamed for the "hits" on others of David's enemies. David is consistently cast in this story as gentle and meek—someone who deplores the violence of Joab and his brothers, the "sons of Zeruiah." David does not discipline his sons because he loves them too much, and he weeps profusely over Absalom's death, as he did over Abner's. Again, the historical critic suspects that David was responsible for the ends of both sons.

Finally, there may be apology behind the account of Solomon's accession as well. There is a clear rivalry between Solomon and Adonijah over who will succeed David. Adonijah is the expected successor because he is the oldest surviving son. Since it was Solomon rather than Adonijah who ultimately succeeded David, some explanation is needed. The explanation is that David, on his deathbed, designated Solomon to succeed him because of a promise he had made to Solomon's mother, Bathsheba. David then ordered Solomon to do away with individuals who had caused him trouble, which included some prominent supporters of Adonijah. Solomon, then, was simply following David's dying wishes rather than acting in his own political interests. The apology here is so thin that some scholars have taken the view that the story is not written to legitimate Solomon but to denigrate him and his kingship by showing the violence in which he engaged and which was typical of hereditary monarchy.

CHAPTER 16

THE DIVIDED KINGDOM: THE DIVISION AND ITS CONSEQUENCES (1 KINGS 12–22)

A radical change in the story of Israel occurs with the death of Solomon and the subsequent division of the kingdom. From this point on, the story of Israel is the story of two kingdoms, Israel in the north and Judah in the south. This chapter will treat the second half of 1 Kings. The break between 1 Kings and 2 Kings is artificial, but it provides a convenient dividing point for our survey.

CONTENT

This section begins by recounting the division of Solomon's kingdom between Israel and Judah. As the narrator describes it, the division was caused by the secession of the northern tribes from the "house of David." The secession was led by Jeroboam, who became the first king of the new, divided kingdom of Israel. Solomon's son, Rehoboam, continued to rule over the new kingdom of Judah, which consisted of the tribes of Judah, Benjamin, and Levi, at least those Levites serving in Jerusalem.

Following the story of the division, the account of the history of the two kingdoms is organized according to their kings. The following list gives the names of the kings, with their approximate dates, whose reigns are narrated in 1 Kings 12–22.

ISRAEL	JUDAH
Jeroboam (922–901)	Rehoboam (922–915)
	Abijam (915–913)
Nadab son of Jeroboam (901–900)	Asa (913–873)
Baasha (900–877)	

Elah son of Baasha (877–876)	
Zimri (876)	
Omri (876–869)	Jehoshaphat (873–849)
Ahab son of Omri (869–850)	

The kings of Judah are all descendants of David, while Israel goes through a series of royal houses or dynasties. The histories of the two countries are integrated in the narrative, such that the reigns of the kings of Israel are dated according to the reigns of their contemporaries in Judah and vice versa. For instance, the account of King Abijam of Judah begins, "Now in the eighteenth year of King Jeroboam son of Nebat, Abijam began to reign over Judah" (1 Kgs 15:1). Similarly, the account of Nadab begins, "Nadab son of Jeroboam began to reign over Israel in the second year of King Asa of Judah" (1 Kgs 15:25).

The account of each king's reign typically consists of introductory and concluding formulas, between which are found whatever events or episodes about the king that the narrator recounts. The introductory formula for the Kings of Israel has three components: the dating formula as just explained, the length of the reign, and an evaluation. In addition to these same three components, the introductory formulas of the kings of Judah in 1 Kings list the name of the king's mother. Also, Jehoshaphat's age at accession is included in his introduction.

The concluding formulas typically begin by referring to "the rest of the acts" of the king and then asking, "Are they not written in the Book of the Annals of the kings of Israel/Judah?" These concluding notices often synthesize a king's reign or allude to other events not narrated in detail. Then they end with a statement that the king "slept with his ancestors"—an idiom for death—and a mention of his successor. For the kings of Judah there is an additional note about their burial with their forebears in the city of David.

Incorporated within the accounts of the northern kings are a number of stories about prophets. Thus, 1 Kings 13 narrates a tale about two prophets or "men of God," one older and one younger, that deals only tangentially with King Jeroboam. In 1 Kings 14, the prophet Ahijah, who had announced the division of the kingdom to Jeroboam (11:26-40), now announces the fall of Jeroboam's own house. The prophet Jehu does the same for the ruling house of Baasha (16:1-4). Above all, several stories about Elijah—his miracles, his defeat of the prophets of Baal, and his condemnation of Ahab and Jezebel—are narrated within the context of Ahab's reign. Ahab's reign is also the setting for other stories about nameless prophets (1 Kgs 20) and about Micaiah, who predicts the king's death from a wound sustained in battle (1 Kgs 22).

GROWTH

The literature in 1 Kings seems to have developed in at least three stages. The first of these might be loosely termed "sources." As the foregoing discussion suggests, the two main sources were some kind of official record or records about the kings of Israel and Judah and stories about prophets. Some scholars think that the citations of the "annals" or "chronicles" of the kings of Israel and Judah are an invention of the author of Kings, but most see them as genuine. Even though official records from other ancient kingdoms are attested, none has ever been found for Israel or Judah. Hence, it is unclear exactly what information they might have contained. But at least the chronological figures for such matters as the length of kings' reigns are generally considered to have some historical base. As for the prophetic stories, these may have been oral or written. They most likely had their origin in Israel and may have come to the author of Kings already in collected form, probably some time after the fall of the northern kingdom in 721 B.C.E.

The second stage was the primary one for the writing of the book of Kings. This was the work of the Deuteronomistic Historian (or Dtr), who gathered the sources and composed them into a running narrative. Dtr was responsible for giving Kings its structure. Following the division of the kingdom, the history of Israel is a series of royal houses (Jeroboam, Baasha, Omri) that rise and fall according to prophetic word. A prophet predicts the downfall of each house (1 Kgs 14:1-14; 16:1-6; 21:20-24). The oracles use similar language such as making the royal house like that of Jeroboam by ostracizing all its males, bond or free, and threatening that their corpses will be eaten by dogs or birds. The threat of non-burial is probably borrowed from curses associated with the violation of treaties. For each oracle there is then a notice detailing how it was fulfilled in the overthrow of the ruling dynasty and establishment of a new royal line by a military commander (1 Kgs 15:27-30; 16:9-13; 2 Kgs 9–\10). As with the oracles themselves, these notices use similar language.

An illustration of the distinction between these first two stages is the story in 14:1-14. In the original story, Jeroboam sends his wife in disguise to inquire whether their sick son will recover from his illness. Though blind, Ahijah knows who she is when he hears the sound of her feet. He tells her to go home, that when her feet enter the city the boy will die. Dtr used this story as the setting for the oracle against the house of Jeroboam that he inserted (14:7-11), thus changing it from a tale about Ahijah's powers as a "man of God" to a prediction of the destruction of Jeroboam's royal line.

A third stage is represented by certain texts and stories that scholars have seen as additions to the Deuteronomistic History. The story about the young and old prophets in chapter 13 (actually 12:33–13:33) has long been considered secondary by many scholars. The prophetic stories in chapters 17–19, 20, and 22:1-38 are also suspect in the minds of some scholars because they lack Deuteronomistic language and conflict with Deuteronomistic ideology, as when Elijah offers an acceptable sacrifice to Yahweh on an altar outside of Jerusalem (18:30-35). Some of these stories may have originated earlier than Dtr but were not included by him in his History and were only inserted at a later date.

CONTEXT

Another illustration of the growth of this material may be seen in the reasons given for the division of the kingdom. Dtr explained it theologically as God's punishment for Solomon's sin of worshiping the gods of his foreign wives (1 Kgs 11). But the story in chapter 12 locates the cause for the secession of the northern tribes elsewhere, namely in Rehoboam's failure to heed the people's request that he lighten their workload. This request and the people's reaction to Rehoboam's refusal can only be understood in the context, which goes back to David, of the forced labor of the northern tribes.

One of the members of David's cabinet was an officer named Adoram, who was in charge of the forced labor (2 Sam 20:24). He was apparently the same man who served Solomon in the same capacity, though his name occurs in a slightly different form as Adoniram (1 Kgs 4:6). At any rate, 1 Kgs 5:13-14 makes clear that Solomon conscripted the people of the northern tribes ("Israel") in monthly rotations to build his royal projects, including the temple and his palace. Judah, as Solomon's own tribe, was not part of his provincial system and was probably exempted from the conscription. That is why the northerners demanded that Rehoboam lighten the heavy "yoke" of work that Solomon had placed upon them before they would confirm him as their king (1 Kgs 12:4). When he refused, they seceded.

It is intriguing that the passage about Solomon's conscription already uses the name "Israel" for the northern tribes alone. In the broader historical context Israel and Judah may always have been distinct. They are often referred to separately in the David story, and David ruled as king over Judah alone before coming to the throne of Israel. Historically, David and Solomon may have been first and foremost kings over Judah who dominated and in effect enslaved the Israelites. If so, then Israel's "secession" was actually a return to political independence. Judah was the smaller kingdom and in a sense the real splinter state.

Further historical context for the account of the divided monarchy is supplied by inscriptional evidence from ancient Egypt. Carved on the temple to Amun in Thebes is a relief commissioned by Pharaoh Sheshonq, which celebrates his raid into Canaan with a list of places that he claims to have captured. The Bible refers to Sheshonq as Shishak and reports this raid detailing some of the plunder seized from Jerusalem (1 Kgs 14:25-28). The raid is an important fixed point for the Bible's chronology, since it can be dated archaeologically to about the year 925 B.C.E., which Kings reports as the fifth year of King Rehoboam.

Further archaeological and inscriptional evidence for this period is available. Sometimes it appears to confirm the biblical record, but at other times it raises questions about the historical validity of the Bible's account. Thus, excavations at the site of Tel Dan in northern Israel have discovered the remains of what appears to be a sizeable temple or cultic site in agreement with the report that Jeroboam set up a royal shrine at Dan (1 Kgs 12:29-31). On the other hand, Assyrian annals describe warfare between the Assyrians and a powerful Israelite army under Ahab in alliance with the Arameans (Syrians). This description contradicts the Bible's portrayal in 1 Kgs 20 and 22:1-38 of Ahab as being subservient to a much stronger Aramean adversary, and it has led many biblical scholars to suggest that these stories in the Bible are out of historical order. (Note that Ahab is rarely called by name in these chapters but is generally referred to by the generic term "the king of Israel.")

INTERPRETATION

The evaluations of the kings of Israel and Judah in their introductory formulas are especially important for indicating the nature of the history in Kings as a theological history or even a historical theology. The kings are not evaluated for their leadership qualities or military prowess but on religious grounds. Specifically, all the kings of Israel are condemned for doing evil in Yahweh's sight by "walking in the way of Jeroboam, who caused Israel to sin" (16:19). In Judah, Rehoboam and Abijam are condemned for doing evil in the sight of Yahweh, while Asa did what was right in Yahweh's eyes, and Jehoshaphat followed suit.

Perhaps the clearest example of the overriding theological interest of the book of Kings lies in the contrast between the portraits of Omri and his son Ahab. As noted in the introduction to this section, from a strictly historical perspective Omri was a very significant king, such that the Assyrian annals mentioned above refer to Israel from his time on as the "house of Omri." Yet 1 Kings devotes a mere six verses in total to his reign (16:23-28). In contrast, 16:29-34 and all of chapters 17–22 concern the reign of Ahab. Ahab was probably also an important king historically—but certainly no more important than his father. The disparity in the treatment that each of them receives in 1 Kings is not the result of historical considerations but of theological ones. More space is devoted to Ahab's reign because of two people who were religiously significant—Jezebel, Ahab's foreign wife, who is depicted as trying to lead Israel astray into the worship of her native god Baal, and Elijah, the great prophet of Yahweh who opposed her. This contrast illustrates that the real interest of the book of Kings has more to do with theology than with history.

The story in the book of Kings, then, is intended not primarily to report history but to explain it theologically. In that sense it is etiological. Specifically, the author of the book of Kings, Dtr, seeks to offer theological explanations for the division of the kingdom and the subsequent histories of Israel and Judah. As we have already seen, Dtr accounted for the division as the result of Solomon's sin, without camouflaging the fact that there were major social causes—namely the oppression of the northern tribes by the Davidic rulers.

Dtr also accounts etiologically for the series of royal houses in the North. Historically, the leader of a coup d'etat would typically kill not only the previous king but all his male heirs and even the male members of his extended family in order to do away with potential rivals to the new king and royal house. This is what Baasha did to the male members of the house of Jeroboam and what Omri did to the males of the house of Baasha. Similarly, the house of Omri will be overthrown, as reported in 2 Kings, and all of its male members executed. Dtr ignores the political reasons for this series of events and explains them theologically as the fulfillment of prophecies. The reason for the overthrow of each royal house in turn is also theological. As explained by each of the prophets who predict the overthrows, each of the founders, and indeed all of the kings of Israel, persisted in the sin of Jeroboam.

Dtr explains the sin of Jeroboam in 1 Kgs 12:25-33. Concerned that his subjects would return to Jerusalem to worship and that he might lose his kingdom as a result, Jeroboam undertook to build two royal shrines at the northern and southern ends of his kingdom. This violated the principle of centralization, according to which Yahweh was to be worshiped only in Jerusalem. This principle is central to Dtr's history and theology, which is based on divine election: God chose Israel from among the nations as his people, David and his descendants among the citizens of Israel as its rulers, and Jerusalem among the cities of Israel as its capital. However, as we have seen, the principle of centralization likely originated with the community of scribes and officials who produced the book of Deuteronomy in the context of the reign of King Josiah of Judah in the seventh century B.C.E. Its application to Jeroboam, therefore, is anachronistic. Jeroboam's construction of royal shrines was perfectly in keeping with the activities of ancient Near Eastern kings, who typically built temples for the gods whom they credited with installing them on their thrones. Dtr evaluates Jeroboam, and all the kings of Israel for that matter, according to a criterion that did not exist in their day and that was tied, anyway, to the social and political circumstances of the kingdom of Judah, not of Israel. Just as history is told by the victors and the survivors, so the account of the monarchy in Kings, like the Deuteronomistic History as a whole, is narrated by an author from Judah, which had outlasted its northern neighbor and sought an explanation in its theology and political ideology.

CHAPTER 17

THE DIVIDED KINGDOM: FROM AHAB TO THE FALL OF ISRAEL (2 KINGS 1–17)

The division between 1 Kings and 2 Kings is artificial; they are really the same book. Thus, 2 Kings continues recounting the history of Israel and Judah simultaneously as begun in 1 Kings. The first seventeen chapters, which we will treat in this chapter, cover the period until 721 B.C.E., when the kingdom of Israel fell to the Assyrian Empire. The rest of 2 Kings then describes the history of Judah alone down to 586 B.C.E., when Judah experienced a similar fall to the Babylonians.

CONTENT

Because 2 Kings is the continuation of 1 Kings, it begins in the middle of the dynasty founded by Omri in Israel. Indeed, 1 Kings ends with the introductory formula for Ahaziah, and 2 Kings takes up the account of his reign. The following chart of kings and their approximate dates continues the one provided in the previous chapter.

ISRAEL	JUDAH
Ahaziah (850–849)	Jehoram (849–843)
J(eh)oram (849–843/2)	Ahaziah (843/2)
Jehu (843/2–815)	Athaliah (843/2–837)
Je(ho)ahaz (815–802) son of Jehu	Joash (837–800)
Joash (802–786)	Amaziah (800–783)
Jeroboam II (786–746)	
Zechariah (746–745)	Azariah/Uzziah (783–742)
Shallum (745)	

Menahem (745–737)	Jotham (742–735)
Pekahiah (737–736)	
Pekah (736–732)	
Hoshea (732–724)	
Fall of Israel (722/1)	Ahaz (735–715)

However, the first eight chapters of 2 Kings are dominated by stories not about kings but about prophets, particularly Elisha, who becomes Elijah's replacement in 2 Kings 2 after his master ascends into heaven. Even more than Elijah, Elisha is a miracle worker. He purifies poisonous food and undrinkable water, multiplies oil and meal, heals leprosy, makes an axe head float, and even raises a child from the dead. He also consults with kings and predicts if not determines political and military events.

A second major unit in the book well illustrates this prophetic control over political events. It is the story of the overthrow of the Omride dynasty by the usurper, Jehu, in 2 Kings 9–10. The story is remarkable for its grisly account of Jezebel's death. Her death and the fall of the Omrides takes place in fulfillment of prophecy as part of the structural framework described in the previous chapter on 1 Kings. Jehu is commissioned in his coup by Elisha through one of his disciples. The story also appears to establish a chronological fixed point in the essentially simultaneous deaths of the kings of both Israel and Judah.

The annihilation of Omri's male heirs did not do away with the dynasty's influence. Athaliah, the daughter of Ahab and Jezebel, replaced her own son as monarch of Judah after Jehu had assassinated him. The conspiracy against her, the restoration of the Davidic line in King Joash, and his repair of the temple are the subjects of 2 Kings 11–12.

The next four chapters "seesaw" back and forth between Israel and Judah, with chapter 13 treating kings Jehoahaz and Jehoash of Israel, 14 Amaziah of Judah and Jeroboam II of Israel, 15 Azariah and Jotham of Judah and the rest of the kings of Israel up to Hoshea, and 16 Ahaz of Judah. Chapter 17 briefly describes the reign of Hoshea, the last king of Israel, followed by an account of the Assyrian invasion and its aftermath with an extensive explanation of the theological reasons for them.

GROWTH

The same three stages discussed in the literary growth of 1 Kings are found also in 2 Kings. These are (1) the sources used by Dtr,

(2) Dtr's own composition, and (3) later additions to Dtr's work. As in 1 Kings, the sources appear to be principally of two types—some kind of official records about the kings of Israel and Judah and some prophetic stories. The former is generally perceived to be behind such specifics as the ages of the kings when they were crowned and the lengths of their reigns.

Dtr's use of a prophetic story is well illustrated in the story of Jehu's revolt. In 2 Kgs 9:1-3 Elisha commissions one of his trainees to go to the town of Ramoth-gilead where the Israelite army is camped for war against the Syrians. The young prophet is to take one of the generals, Jehu, into a private room, anoint him as king, and then leave immediately. As the stories about prophets elsewhere in Kings show, precise obedience to such orders is crucial; disobedience even in seemingly minor details can bring death. So it is surprising that in this story, the disciple diverges considerably from Elisha's instructions without consequence. He finds Jehu and takes him aside. He anoints him king, speaking the words Elisha has told him. But then instead of fleeing immediately, he supplements those words with an oracle commanding Jehu to annihilate the house of Ahab. Only then does he follow Elisha's directive to run away.

The oracle uses terminology common to the prophecies against the Israelite dynasties in 1 Kings, such as the idiom for males ("one who urinates on the wall"), the expression "bond or free in Israel," and the threat of making Ahab's house like Jeroboam's. Those prophecies, as we saw, were the handiwork of Dtr and were used by him to structure his history of the Israelite monarchy. There is good reason to believe, therefore, that the trainee's oracle in 2 Kgs 9:7-10a is also Dtr's composition, which he inserted into an older prophetic story, which originally had Elisha's disciple doing exactly as he had been told and fleeing as soon as he had anointed Jehu king. This example, therefore, illustrates two of the three levels of development: the prophetic story, which provided the basic story, and Dtr's composition, which he effected through revision of that story.

The third level can be illustrated by another example involving the relationship between prophetic stories and Dtr's composition. The story of Elisha's succession of his mentor, Elijah, is told in 2 Kings 2. Elijah is taken up to heaven by a chariot and horses of fire. Elisha takes up his mantle and then shows himself to be very much a miracle-working man of God in the tradition of Elijah. Elisha parts the Jordan River, as Elijah had done. He also purifies the water of Jericho and then curses some boys who ridicule him so that forty-two of them are killed by bears.

This chapter falls in the "crack" between the concluding regnal formula for Ahaziah of Israel and the introductory formula of Jehoram his successor. This is unusual for Dtr, who elsewhere narrates events within the reigns of kings, that is, between the introductory and concluding formulas of a given king. The placement of 2 Kings 2 in "limbo" outside the regnal formulas for any king suggests that its contents were added later to Dtr's composition.

In addition to the placement of the stories in 2 Kings 2, their content also seems foreign to Dtr. They do not deal at all with kings, nor do they display any of the same religious interests of Dtr. Rather, they seem concerned only to exalt the prophets as miracle workers, who are to be feared rather than loved. The Elisha who causes the violent deaths of forty-two young boys merely because they made fun of his baldness is powerful but not especially moral. Because most of the stories about Elisha and the other prophets in 2 Kings 1–17 share this perspective on prophets mainly as wonder workers, it may be that more of these stories belong to the post-Dtr stage of development rather than being Dtr's sources.

CONTEXT

Literary

The present literary context of 2 Kings 1–17 is, of course, the Deuteronomistic History and its account of the monarchies of Israel and Judah. However, scholars tend to identify the stories about Elisha in 2 Kgs 2; 3:4-27; 4:1–8:15; 13:14-21 as a once-separate collection. These stories as a whole do not contain any Deuteronomistic language or reflect the same interests as Dtr's work. Their focus is the prophet Elisha as an awesome, wonder-working "man of God" rather than the kingship. In fact, the king of Israel, if he is mentioned at all in these stories, is usually referred to by title rather than by name. He is secondary to the prophet. As mentioned previously, these stories are also not integrated into Dtr's political history but appear to have been inserted more or less as a block into it.

The prophetic stories, especially those about Elisha, have been compared to the legends that developed about early Christian saints as miracle workers. They are not really designed to teach theological lessons but to inspire awe and perhaps to entertain with their accounts of the legendary exploits of these figures.

The stories about Elisha may have furnished the core of an even larger collection of prophetic tales. They certainly influenced other such stories. This influence can be seen in a comparison of certain of the Elisha stories with similar ones about Elijah. For instance, there are stories about both Elijah and Elisha multiplying oil for a widow. The stories are similar enough to lead one to suspect some relationship between them, and close analysis shows that the direction of influence is from the Elisha story to the Elijah one. The widow with whom Elijah deals is a foreigner, from the

Phoenician town of Zarephath, whom Elijah meets for the first time. Yet his commands to her to fetch him water and to prepare her last morsel of food for him (1 Kgs 17:10, 13) and then her obedience of them seem to presuppose that the two of them have a prior relationship. While that is not the case in the Elijah story, it is so in the Elisha tale (2 Kgs 4:1-7), where the widow was married to one of the "sons of the prophets." Also, the reference to the widow's household in the Elijah story (1 Kgs 17:15) seems out of place, since she is so poor that she is preparing what she anticipates will be the last meal for her and her son. It has probably come into the Elijah story from the Elisha version, where the prophetic widow is being hounded by a creditor but is not destitute.

There are also two stories—one for Elijah and one for Elisha—about the prophet raising a boy from the dead. In the Elijah story, the boy is the son of the destitute Phoenician widow. Hence, the reference to her as the "mistress of the house" (17:17) does not fit. Neither does the detail that Elijah took the boy to the upper room of the house (17:23). Both items, however, fit well in the Elisha tale (2 Kgs 4:8-37), where the woman is wealthy and builds a small roof chamber for Elisha. Again, therefore, the Elisha story has influenced the one about Elijah, suggesting that they may have been part of a larger group of stories that circulated together. In even broader literary context, some have suggested that the miracle stories of Elijah and Elisha may have played a role in shaping stories of Jesus in the New Testament, such as the multiplication of the loaves and fishes.

Historical

The most significant circumstance in the historical context surrounding the narrative in 2 Kings 1–17 was the rise and expansion of the Assyrian Empire in the ninth and eighth centuries and the interrelationships between Assyria, Israel, and Aram (Syria). As is reflected in the prophetic stories, Israel and Aram were rivals. However, they joined forces to oppose Assyria's invasions. As a result, inscriptions from both the Arameans and the Assyrians mention Israel. These inscriptions help to establish chronological dates for the kings of Israel and Judah. They confirm the historical veracity of certain details in the Bible, while calling others into question. Among the best known of extra-biblical inscriptions are the following.

The *Tel Dan stele* was mentioned previously because of the occurrence on it of King David's name in the expression "house of David." It is important for the events described in 2 Kings 9–10 because it appears to contradict them. The author of the stele's inscription, presumably an Aramean king, claims that it was he who killed the kings of Israel and Judah, Ahaziah and Jehoram, rather than Jehu.

The *Black Obelisk* is the name given to an inscribed monument of black limestone erected by the Assyrian king Shalmaneser III in ca. 841 B.C.E. and discovered in modern Iraq in 1846. Standing about two meters high, it contains 190 lines of writing describing Shalmaneser's military campaigns and the tribute he exacted from his conquests. There are also five registers of captioned reliefs, one of which depicts a figure identified as "Yahua, son of Omri" bowing down before the Assyrian king. This is usually interpreted as a depiction of Jehu. Since Jehu was not a descendant of Omri, the inscription indicates the international prestige that Omri attained.

The Black Obelisk showing King Jehu of Israel bowing before King Shalmaneser III of Assyria. Photograph courtesy of Art Resource.

In addition to the Black Obelisk, annals from many others of the Assyrian kings confirm the threat they represented especially to Israel but also to Judah. There are also numerous references and allusions to the Assyrian threat in the eighth-century prophetic books of Isaiah, Hosea, and Amos.

A particularly significant event for these prophets and for the history of Israel and Judah was the Syro-Ephraimitic Crisis of 734 B.C.E., which is recounted from the perspective of Judah's king, Ahaz, in 2 Kings 16 and provides the context for Isaiah 7–8 and probably Hosea 1–3, as well as other parts of these prophetic books. Basically, Israel and Aram formed an alliance in opposition to the advance of the Assyrian king Tiglath-pileser III and tried to force Judah to join the alliance. King Ahaz chose instead to seek the protection of Tiglath-pileser, against the advice of Isaiah. In so doing, he established a costly relationship for Judah as Assyria's vassal. The consequences were worse for Aram and Israel. Damascus was destroyed by the Assyrians in 732. Israel's capital, Samaria, survived because of a change in regime but lost much of its northern territory to Assyrian annexation. The rump state lasted another ten years until Hoshea foolishly revolted and the Assyrians brought an end to the independent kingdom of Israel. The description in 2 Kings of the siege of Samaria by Shalmaneser V in ca. 724 B.C.E. and the city's fall to his successor Sargon II in 722/1 fits with Assyrian records.

This historical context hints at the cultural or social context from which not only the Deuteronomistic History but also some of the prophetic books were written. For the people of Israel and Judah in the eighth and seventh centuries, the terrors associated with the destruction wrought by an invading army were a real fear. Such terrors involved the destruction of crops, livestock, and homes, capture of wives and children, exile to a foreign land, torture, and death. Such realistic terrors were the source of the threats made by prophets in their oracles and of the experiences that the author of Kings explained as the result of divine wrath.

INTERPRETATION

As in 1 Kings, the author (Dtr) offers a theological interpretation of historical events. Jehu's revolt and overthrow of the Omride dynasty is explained as the fulfillment of prophecy as with the previous royal houses in 1 Kings. At the same time, Dtr adapts the prophecy and fulfillment somewhat in order to incorporate the gruesome death of Jezebel. Jehu receives a special word of commendation because of his purge of Baal worship linked to Jezebel, and Dtr explains the fact that the Jehu dynasty lasted through five generations as a reward for its founder's good deed (2 Kgs 10:30). Notably, Hosea offers an entirely different interpretation of these events when he prophesies punishment on Jehu's house for its bloody beginning (Hos 1:4-5).

As in 1 Kings, all the kings of Israel are seen as wicked because they all maintain the royal shrines erected by Jeroboam. Even Jehu perpetuates this "sin of Jeroboam." The climax to this theme comes in 2 Kgs 17:21-23, where Dtr explains that Yahweh removed Israel because of its kings' failure to abandon Jeroboam's great sin. The verses before this (17:7b-20) are often regarded as a later addition. They offer a different explanation for Israel's demise, namely the idolatry of the people rather than the "sin of Jeroboam." The sins they list are more typically associated with Judah than with Israel. Thus, these verses were probably added after the destruction of Jerusalem and the Babylonian exile of 586 B.C.E. The chapter, therefore, reflects reinterpretation and reapplication of its basic principle to Judah. That principle is that disaster, specifically in the form of national destruction, is divine punishment for sin. This theological doctrine, which explains catastrophe as the result of sin and prosperity as blessing for righteousness, is typically associated in the Bible with prophets. It will be clear from other books, especially Job, that there were other possible explanations for Israel's and Judah's demise. But the exile as divine punishment was the explanation adopted by Dtr in the book of Kings.

CHAPTER 18

THE DIVIDED KINGDOM: THE END OF JUDAH (2 KINGS 18–25)

The final segment of Kings deals, of course, only with the kingdom of Judah, since Israel as an independent kingdom is no more. It is arguably the most significant section of the book for discerning such matters as the date and authorship of the entire book of Kings.

CONTENT

The list below completes the charts of kings begun in the previous chapters.

Hezekiah (715–687)
Manasseh (687–642)
Amon (642–640)
Josiah (640–609)
Jehoahaz (609)
Jehoiakim (609–598)
Jehoiachin (598/7)
Zedekiah (597–586)

Included in this section are those kings ranked best (Hezekiah, Josiah) and worst (Manasseh) by Dtr among the kings of Judah. The interest in Hezekiah and Josiah is suggested by the amount of space devoted to each of them. The account of Hezekiah's reign covers three chapters (18–20), and the account of Josiah's most of two (22:1–23:30). In the case of Hezekiah, the focus is on the invasion of the Assyrian king Sennacherib in 701 B.C.E., which occupies most of 2 Kings 18–19. For Josiah, it is on his religious reforms sparked by the discovery of the book of the law in his eighteenth year (622 B.C.E.). Both Hezekiah and Josiah are described as incomparable in some way. For Hezekiah, it was his trust in God that set him apart: "He trusted in the LORD the God of Israel; so that there was no one like him among all the kings of Judah after him, or among those who were before him" (2 Kgs 18:5). In Josiah's case, it was his adherence to the law: "Before him there was no king like him, who turned to the LORD with all his heart, with all his soul, and with all his might, according to all the law of Moses; nor did any like him arise after him" (2 Kgs 23:25). These statements of incomparability set the themes for the accounts of these two kings.

Sandwiched between them are the accounts of Manasseh and Amon. Manasseh is accused of committing worse offenses than Israel, which had already been destroyed for its sins, and even more than the nations that God drove out before the Israelites. As a result, the destruction of Judah and Jerusalem is promised. Amon continues his father's practices, but he is insignificant. Judah's die was cast with Manasseh. Even Josiah, whose reforms correct Manasseh's apostasies, cannot stem the tide of divine wrath incited by Manasseh. Josiah dies unexpectedly in battle, and the kingdom quickly declines.

Josiah is succeeded by his son Jehoahaz, but he reigns only three months before being deposed by Pharaoh Neco, who killed Josiah. Neco replaces Jehoahaz with his brother, Jehoiakim, whose reign lasts eleven years. He apparently dies during the Babylonian siege of Jerusalem in 598–597, and his death may have prevented the city's destruction at that time. But 2 Kgs 24:13-16 reports that the Babylonians stripped the temple of its treasures and took the upper classes and artisans captive to Babylon, leaving only the peasants in the land. The young king, Jehoiachin, Jehoahaz's son and successor, bore the brunt of the Babylonian siege after his father's death and was among those taken captive to Babylon following a brief, three-month reign.

Nebuchadnezzar, the Babylonian king, replaced Jehoiachin with his uncle and even changed his name from Mattaniah ("Yahweh's gift") to Zedekiah ("Yahweh's justice"), perhaps as a way of reminding Zedekiah that he had sworn an oath of loyalty by Yahweh to the Babylonian king. The reminder proved ineffective, and when he rebelled against Babylon, Jerusalem felt the full force of the Babylonian army. In 586 following a brief siege, the city was destroyed, the temple and palace pillaged and burned. Most of the population was deported to Babylon. This included Zedekiah, who was first forced to witness the executions of his sons and then blinded. Judah no longer existed as an independent kingdom, and there was no longer a king ruling in the Davidic line. A certain Gedaliah was appointed governor over the Babylonian province that had been Judah, and the administrative capital was moved from Jerusalem a few miles north to the town of Mizpah. The book of Kings ends with an update on Jehoiachin, reporting that his status was elevated by the Babylonian king Evil-merodach, who released him from prison and allowed him to dine at the royal table with other captive kings.

GROWTH

Martin Noth, the scholar who initially formulated the theory of the Deuteronomistic History, dated the history to 562 B.C.E., or shortly thereafter, because that was the approximate date of the last event reported in Kings, namely Jehoiachin's release. An alternative to Noth's view that has proven especially influential in North America argues that the present ending of Kings is a second edition or extension of an earlier work that was originally written during the reign of Josiah. As noted previously in our treatment of Deuteronomy, there is a correspondence between the reform measures undertaken by Josiah in 2 Kings 23 and the prescriptions in Deuteronomy. This correspondence, long observed by scholars, has led to the widely accepted dating of the original version of Deuteronomy in the context of the purported discovery of the book of the law in Josiah's eighteenth year (ca. 622). Scholars who favor the view that the original edition of the Deuteronomistic History (Dtr[1]) was written under Josiah point out how favorably he is presented in 2 Kings. He is the only king who is said to have walked perfectly in the way of David and the only king, including David, about whom nothing negative is reported. The suggestion, therefore, is that Dtr[1] was written to support Josiah and promote his reforms.

Another argument for this "double edition" theory has to do with the unexpectedness of Josiah's death and the blaming of the exile on Manasseh in the last two and one-half chapters of 2 Kings. Since Josiah is depicted as thoroughly righteous, nothing in the narrative prepares the reader for his death in battle (2 Kgs 23:29). What makes this report even more unexpected is that the prophetess Huldah had predicted Josiah's death "in peace" (22:20). According to the "double edition" theory, an original version of Huldah's oracle upon the finding of the law book praised Josiah but threatened destruction on the basis of the law if its prescriptions were not followed. This oracle did not foresee Josiah's violent death. It served, rather, to impel Josiah to execute the religious reforms detailed in 2 Kings 23. In the second edition, written after the start of the Babylonian captivity, Huldah's dire predictions were augmented, perhaps with the addition of 22:16-18a, in light of the destruction of Jerusalem that had since taken place. The prediction of Josiah's death "in peace," perhaps reinterpreted, remained as a clue to the original version of the oracle.

Another such clue to the two editions may be the blaming of the exile on Manasseh. As noted, Josiah's reforms in 2 Kings 23 actually correct most if not all of the crimes Manasseh is accused of committing. How, then, could Manasseh's misdeeds be responsible for causing the exile? "Double edition" scholars propose that blaming the exile on Manasseh was a strategy of the second, exilic editor (Dtr[2]). Dtr[1] praised Josiah for correcting Manasseh's misdeeds and saw him as the hope for Judah's future. After his sudden death, however, the Dtr[1] edition promoting him could not be completed. Dtr[2] updated the work of Dtr[1] by recounting what happened after Josiah. It was Dtr[2] who laid the blame for the exile on Manasseh's shoulders. In spite of Josiah's reforms, Manasseh had so angered God that the exile was inevitable.

The "double edition" theory, though widely held, is not universally accepted. Clearly the book of Kings and the Deuteronomistic History as they now stand blame the exile on Manasseh for wickedness so bad that even Josiah's good deeds could not prevent it. It is less certain, though, that this requires an earlier edition of these works. It may be that the single author, Dtr, writing in the exile, made use of available sources, such as reports about individual kings and the story of Huldah, in an effort to find an explanation for Judah's demise.

> As to Hezekiah, the Jew, he did not submit to my yoke, I laid siege to 46 of his strong cities, walled forts and the countless small villages in their vicinity, and conquered them by means of well-stamped earth-ramps, and battering-rams brought thus near to the walls combined with the attack by foot soldiers, using mines, breeches as well as sapper work. I drove out of them 200,150 people, young and old, male and female, horses, mules, donkeys, camels, big and small cattle beyond counting, and considered them booty. Himself I made a prisoner in Jerusalem, his royal residence, like a bird in a cage. I surrounded him with earthwork in order to molest those who were leaving his city's gate.

Excerpt of the annals of King Sennacherib of Assyria.

The existence of such sources is affirmed by scholarly analysis of the account about Hezekiah, which contains two accounts of invasions by Sennacherib, a brief one in 2 Kgs 18:13-16 and a much longer one in 18:17–19:37. Despite attempts by a few to argue for two distinct invasions, scholars have, by and large, long viewed these as variant versions of the same event. The first, or A version, is a straightforward historical account without theological elaboration that was probably drawn from official sources. The second, or B version, is itself composite and is typically subdivided between one narrative consisting of 18:17–19:9a and 19:36-37 (B^1) and another including 19:9b-35 (B^2). Both of these latter two accounts display strong theological interests. The B^2 version consists largely of speeches by the Assyrian official known as the Rabshakeh that revolve around the theme of trust. Specifically, the Rabshakeh ridicules Hezekiah and the people of Jerusalem for trusting in Yahweh, whom he reproaches as powerless against the Assyrian king. The B^2 version (apart from verses 21-31, which were probably inserted later) reports a prayer of Hezekiah's that contrasts Yahweh with idols and an oracle of salvation delivered through Isaiah. The B^2 version contains typical Deuteronomistic language and motifs (especially the reference to the Davidic promise in v. 34), indicating that Dtr was its author. In short, Dtr borrowed an official account (A) wholesale, retouched another version with an emphasis on trusting in God (B^1), and combined both in his own account focused on Hezekiah's prayer (B^2). Dtr, therefore, probably authored these materials, just as he did other portions of the Deuteronomistic History that we have treated, on the basis of sources that he borrowed and adapted to suit his purposes.

CONTEXT

The historical context, especially the activities of other ancient Near Eastern nations, is paramount for understanding these historical narratives about Judah's last days. For the reign of Hezekiah, in particular, there are several extra-biblical sources. The best known are probably those that relate to Sennacherib's invasion of 701 B.C.E. These sources are both written and pictorial. They include Sennacherib's annals, which are inscribed on a hexagonal clay prism about a meter high discovered in the ruins of ancient Nineveh in 1830 and a famous relief found on the walls of his palace in the same city. The annals are primarily a list of Sennacherib's military campaigns, in the third of which he boasts of confining Hezekiah in Jerusalem "like a bird in a cage." Sennacherib lists tribute paid to him by Hezekiah but never actually claims to have conquered Jerusalem. On his palace wall Sennacherib had depicted his conquest not of Jerusalem but of Lachish, a heavily fortified outpost of Hezekiah's about twenty-five miles southwest of Jerusalem. It is one of the most vivid depictions of the kind of siege warfare practiced in the ancient Near East. These two sources help establish the context of the account(s) in 2 Kings 18–19 relating Sennacherib's invasion. The Assyrians likely devastated the countryside of Judah and exacted costly tribute from Hezekiah, but did not conquer Jerusalem. Dtr interpreted this as a miraculous deliverance brought about by Hezekiah's faith and piety.

Another well-known source that may also relate to the Assyrian invasion is the Siloam Inscription. The Siloam tunnel, also known since the nineteenth century, runs about 1750 feet from the Gihon Spring, ancient Jerusalem's water source, to the Siloam Pool. Its purpose was to bring water from the spring, which was outside the city wall and camouflaged, into the city so as to enable its residents to survive a siege. The inscription, found at a curve in the tunnel, explains that it was cut from both ends. Although the inscription does not mention Hezekiah, 2 Kgs 20:20 mentions that he constructed a pool and a conduit to bring water into the city. He was, therefore, the builder of the tunnel and may have commissioned the inscription. Furthermore, since ensuring the city's water supply by means of such a tunnel was a defensive strategy, it is likely that Hezekiah undertook this project as part of his preparation against an anticipated invasion by the Assyrians.

International activities are also important background for the reigns of Manasseh and Josiah. Manasseh is mentioned in Assyrian annals as a loyal vassal. Josiah's involvement in international affairs cost him his life. In 609 B.C.E., the Assyrian Empire was quickly being devoured by the Babylonians. The Egyptian king, Neco, was on his way to try to aid the Assyrians and halt the Babylonian advance when Josiah went out to challenge him.

Josiah's death in the ensuing battle in a real sense marked the end of Judah as an independent nation, and the remainder of the history narrated in 2 Kings was dependent on power struggles in the ancient Near East. Neco replaced Josiah's successor, Jehoahaz, with his own puppet ruler, Jehoiakim. But four years later, in 605 B.C.E., Neco was soundly defeated by the Babylonians, and Judah, which had been an Egyptian satellite, now made a treaty with Babylon. A few years after that, the Egyptians succeeded in driving the Babylonians back, and Jehoiakim changed allegiance—a serious mistake that led to the Babylonian incursion of 598–597. The official record of Babylonian kings known as the Babylonian Chronicle confirms the fall of Jerusalem on March 16, 597. Zedekiah faced the same problem of indecision between Babylonia and Egypt as did his predecessors. Jerusalem paid the price in 586 for his eventual choice of Egypt.

INTERPRETATION

Martin Noth, who originated the theory of the Deuteronomistic History, referred to it as "an etiology of the end." According to Noth, Dtr sought to explain the fall first of Israel, then of Judah. The explanation that he offers for Judah's demise in the last section of Kings is primarily theological and is essentially the same as his explanation for the end of Israel. Judah was destroyed because of sin, just as Israel had been before it. In much the same way as Dtr blamed Israel's fall primarily on Jeroboam, so he blamed Judah's end primarily on Manasseh.

The main difference between Israel and Judah was the Davidic monarchy, and Dtr used the promise to David to explain why all the kings of Judah were in the Davidic line and why Judah outlasted Israel. It should be noted, however, that scholars who favor the "double edition" theory hold that the Davidic promise was a theme only in the first edition written at the time of Josiah. They believe that Dtr^1 viewed Josiah as a kind of new David who would restore the united kingdom of Israel but that those hopes were dashed when Josiah died suddenly in battle. They point out further that there is no mention of the promise to David in the final two and one-half chapters of 2 Kings dealing with the kings following Josiah.

The question of the interpretation of the Davidic promise figures especially prominently in the very last episode in 2 Kings, the release of Jehoiachin from prison. This notice may offer a measure of hope for the future by its subtle observation that the Davidic line still survives so that God can renew the kingdom and reactivate the promise to David. In other words, this passage may indicate that Dtr wished to offer more than a simple explanation for Israel's and Judah's demise in his History. He may have tried to indicate a place where God could begin again with his people to restore them to national status. If so, however, it must be admitted that Dtr's hope is only suggestive and therefore faint.

PART THREE

Latter Prophets

INTRODUCTION TO THE LATTER PROPHETS

The second part of the section of the Hebrew Bible known as the Prophets (Hebrew *nevi'im*) is the Latter Prophets. It is made up of fifteen books, each identified with a particular prophetic figure. In almost every case (Jonah is the lone exception) oracles and messages from the prophet comprise the bulk of the book, with some biographical or autobiographical material also sometimes included.

A distinction based solely on the lengths of the books is made between the three Major Prophets—Isaiah, Jeremiah, and Ezekiel—and the twelve Minor Prophets. The latter group, also known as the Book of the Twelve because they could be copied on a single scroll, includes the following books: Hosea, Joel, Amos, Obadiah, Jonah, Micah, Nahum, Habakkuk, Zephaniah, Haggai, Zechariah, and Malachi. The placement—and even the number—of the Latter Prophets varies depending on what kind of Bible one is reading. The Jewish order places them before the Writings, the third section of the Hebrew Bible, while in Christian Bibles they are the last books of the Old Testament. In addition, the Christian arrangement includes the book of Daniel among the Latter Prophets.

Until the rise of critical scholarship in the nineteenth century, it was commonly believed that each of the prophetic books accurately preserves the utterances of the man whose name is attached to it. This view is no longer held by scholars. All of these works are the result of a process of development and expansion that often lasted many decades. This is most easily seen in Isaiah, which was one of the first prophetic books to be critically studied. There are clear indications in the text that the book is responding to a number of different historical contexts that cover almost two centuries, so there is no way the entire work originated with the eighth-century B.C.E. prophet. As with the other prophetic writings, a core group of original sayings can be traced back to Isaiah himself, but these have been supplemented and augmented by material from later times.

This means that the issue of context is particularly important when studying this part of the Hebrew Bible. This is true on both the communal and the individual levels. International relations, national interests, and social practices and attitudes all played a role in shaping the prophetic books. The works are in constant dialogue with the political, cultural, and socioeconomic contexts in which they were produced. In the same way, the personal backgrounds and life experiences of those who wrote this material provide the lens through which they view the world and interpret what they are seeing. In many places, what is going on in the prophet's personal life is as important as what is happening in the world around him.

The theological concerns of the Latter Prophets mirror those found in the two previous sections of the Hebrew Bible. Obedience to God's will, as most fully expressed in the law, is the centerpiece of the Torah. When the Israelites fail to hold up their end of the covenantal agreement, they suffer the consequences and experience divine wrath. The prophets draw upon this view of the relationship between God and the people, and they interpret tragedies like the invasions by Assyria and Babylon as being the direct result of a violation of the covenant. Similarly, the Former Prophets present what we have termed a theological history of the Israelites that interprets events in light of how well the various kings and their subjects lived up to their obligation to obey God. The Latter Prophets, too, treat the course of history from this perspective, and they provide a more theologically nuanced interpretation of many of the same figures and events that are described in the Deuteronomistic History.

It is important to note that prophecy is not a distinctly Israelite phenomenon. There are many examples of prophetic figures from other parts of the ancient Near East, so Israelite prophecy should be seen as just one manifestation of a broad development that was also present in neighboring cultures. Similarly, Israelite prophecy was not limited to the fifteen individuals associated with these books. Figures like Elijah and Elisha, as well as the many unnamed prophets who are mentioned elsewhere in the Hebrew Bible, testify to the widespread and diverse nature of Israelite prophecy. Women, too, were counted among the prophets, as evidenced by prophetesses like Huldah (2 Kgs 22:14) and Deborah (Judg 4:4). For reasons that are still not fully understood, from the eighth century B.C.E. on, the oracles and traditions associated with these prophetic figures were written down and collected to form the basis of the biblical books known as the Latter Prophets.

Many modern people labor under a misunderstanding of the role and function of prophets in the ancient world. When we hear the word *prophet*, we often tend to think of someone who possesses some preternatural ability to peer into the future and predict what will happen. This is not what the biblical prophets did. They often did speak about the future, but it was always tied to the present. Their message was typically, "In light of what I see happening today, here is what will happen in the future." For the prophets, the present had implications for the future, and this highlighted the importance of human responsibility and free will in shaping coming events. If their audience heeded the warning and changed their lives, the future would be different. If we keep this in mind we gain a fuller understanding of how prophets functioned in Israelite society. It also puts us in a better position to determine who the prophetic voices of our own day might be.

Chapter 19

THE PREEXILIC PROPHETS: FIRST ISAIAH AND MICAH

The earliest prophetic books originated with prophets who lived in the eighth century B.C.E. Two of these prophets worked in Israel and two in Judah. In this chapter, we treat the two who worked in Judah—Isaiah and Micah.

FIRST ISAIAH

Since the late nineteenth century Bible scholars have recognized that the book of Isaiah is a complex work with a long and complicated history. It is composed of material that comes from the mid-eighth through the mid-sixth centuries B.C.E., a period of time during which the following key developments and events had a major impact on Israelite society.

744	Rise of the Late Assyrian Empire
734	Syro-Ephraimite Crisis
721	Fall of the northern kingdom to Assyria
701	Assyrian attack on Judah
612	Rise of the Neo-Babylonian Empire
586	Fall of Judah to Babylon and beginning of the exile
539	Rise of the Persian Empire and end of the exile

The references to particular kings in several places in the book (1:1; 6:1; 36:1) allow us to date Isaiah's prophetic career to the period 742–700 B.C.E. Many sections of the earlier part of the book reflect this context in which Assyria was the dominant power in the Near East. But there is a noticeable shift later on in the book when Assyria in its role as the enemy is replaced by Babylon, which indicates these texts are responding to later circumstances.

Chapter 40 is the division point of the book. Much of the material prior to it appears to stem from the earlier period, and the material after it comes from the later exilic context. This has led to the view that there are two distinct sections to the book: First Isaiah (chs. 1–39), much of which comes from around the time of the eighth-century prophet, and Second

Isaiah (chs. 40–66). Some scholars suggest a further subdivision of the latter part into Second Isaiah (chs. 40–55) and Third Isaiah (chs. 56–66), an issue that will be discussed in a later chapter.

CONTENT

There is no obvious organizational framework to First Isaiah, but clear divisions exist in the text, allowing us to break it into six sections. Within these sections the movement often appears to be haphazard and random, but structural, thematic, and vocabulary connections among the various parts indicate the text is not as disorganized as it might appear. The somewhat chaotic impression it leaves on the reader is the effect of a process of expansion and editing over centuries as the compilers of the book attempted to address and reflect upon ever-changing circumstances.

Chapters 1–12

Much of the material in this first section goes back to the time of the prophet Isaiah. The first two chapters begin in a similar way, which suggests that the first chapter is meant to be an introduction to the entire book, whereas the second chapter introduces the message to Jerusalem and Judah that follows immediately. The song of the vineyard (5:1-7) is a well-known composition in the form of a parable that identifies some of the central themes of the book. It equates the relationship between Israel and God to that between a vineyard and its owner. God loves Israel, but it has not yielded fruit so it will be abandoned and destroyed. This message about Israel's need to remain faithful to God and bear fruit or suffer the consequences is a common refrain throughout the book.

Most of Isaiah is written in poetry but there are narrative sections throughout the book. One of the most important of these is found in chapters 6 through 8, which provide descriptions of key moments in the prophet's life. Chapter 6 recounts an unusual vision Isaiah has in the temple, where he encounters God and receives a commission to go and speak to the people even though they will not heed him. Many refer to this as the call of Isaiah and believe it is a description of the start of his prophetic career. But its placement in chapter 6 is somewhat odd since other prophetic calls, like those of Jeremiah and Ezekiel, are located at the beginning of their books. More likely, this is not his inaugural call but a call for Isaiah to do a specific task. That task is to meet with King Ahaz of Judah to give him advice on how to respond to a looming international crisis known as the Syro-Ephraimite Crisis. That meeting, during which the famous Immanuel oracle is given, is described in chapter 7 and will be discussed later in this chapter.

Chapters 13–23

This section contains a series of warnings directed toward foreign nations. It is organized around a set of nine oracles of judgment against Israel's neighbors, including Moab (15:1–16:14), Damascus (17:1-3), Egypt (19:1-15), and Tyre (23:1-18). In each case, the addressee is found guilty of certain offenses and its punishments are graphically described. The presence of similar taunts against foreign nations in other books (Amos 1–2; Obad 1-4; Joel 3:4-8) suggests this was a standard feature of prophetic works that is probably meant to build up Israel at the expense of its neighbors.

Some of this material, like the oracle against Babylon (13:1-23), comes from long after Isaiah's lifetime. The reference in 13:17 to God stirring up the Medes against Babylon is particularly interesting in this regard. They are the group who defeated the Babylonians and ushered in the Persian Empire in 539, some two hundred years after the prophet lived.

Chapters 24–27

These chapters have been the subject of much scholarly discussion. The section is sometimes called the apocalypse of Isaiah because of certain features it appears to share with apocalyptic literature, like the repetition of the phrase "on that day" (24:21; 25:9; 26:1; 27:1, 2, 12). Likewise, the description of the future destruction of an unnamed city (24:10-13; 25:2; 26:5-6; 27:10-11) is presented in ways that can be associated with apocalyptic. Despite these echoes, it is a mistake to categorize these chapters as apocalyptic. They describe events in the near future rather than things that will occur at the end-time as is standard in apocalyptic writing. There has been some debate regarding whether this section circulated independently prior to being placed in First Isaiah. Even if it was originally a separate composition that was added at a later point, it is well integrated into its literary context. In particular, its descriptions of future destruction fit well on the heels of the previous section containing oracles of doom against the nations.

Chapters 28–33

The focus returns to Israel and Judah in this section, which is a set of long oracles that speak of the people's blindness and arrogance in the face of God's anger and coming judgment. Much of this material can be traced to the eighth century and therefore is a response to certain challenges faced by the prophet, including King Hezekiah's association with Egypt despite Isaiah's objections (30:1-7; 31:1-3). An interesting literary feature is that each chapter but one (32) begins with the word "alas" (*hôy* in Hebrew), which serves to unify the entire section.

Some parts of the section reassure the Israelites rather than condemn them. An example of this is seen in 31:4-5:

For thus the LORD said to me,
As a lion or a young lion growls over its prey,
  and—when a band of shepherds is called out against it—
is not terrified by their shouting
  or daunted at their noise,
so the LORD of hosts will come down
  to fight upon Mount Zion [Jerusalem] and upon its hill.
Like birds hovering overhead, so the LORD of hosts
  will protect Jerusalem;
he will protect and deliver it,
  he will spare and rescue it.

This is a good example of Isaiah's "Zion theology," a recurring motif in the book. As the place associated with God's presence and the king's throne, Mount Zion became a symbol of the people of Israel and their special relationship with God. The prophet frequently refers to it as a way of expressing God's protection of Israel, and the text cited above assures them that they need not fear the Assyrians because God will guard them from harm.

Chapters 34–35

These chapters present two conflicting scenes that are best situated in the period of Babylonian domination and the exile. Chapter 34 describes the punishment of Edom, the quintessential enemy, who was able to invade and exploit Judah after the Babylonian attack. In language somewhat reminiscent of that found in chapters 24–27, the destruction and desolation of Edom is depicted in graphic terms. In contrast to this, chapter 35 offers a hopeful and idyllic portrayal of the fate that awaits Judah after the exile. The land will be transformed from a wilderness to a garden, waters will flow, and the people will return on a highway called "the Holy Way." These images are remarkably similar to what is found in Second Isaiah beginning in chapter 40, and it is likely that this chapter was originally meant to conclude First Isaiah and serve as a bridge to the rest of the book.

Chapters 36–39

The final section of First Isaiah, almost all of which is written in narrative form, presents an account of events that occurred during the rule of Hezekiah, who was on the throne of Judah during the Assyrian invasion. It describes how he followed Isaiah's advice to remain faithful to God in the face of Assyrian pressure to surrender and become a vassal. In this way, he is the antithesis of his predecessor King Ahaz, who rejected Isaiah's counsel and became subservient to Assyria in chapter 7. The Deuteronomistic History contains a version of these same events in 2 Kgs 18:13–20:21.

GROWTH

This overview of the content of First Isaiah shows that the work underwent a long process of growth and development. Some of the material is from the time of the eighth-century prophet whose name is attached to the book, while other texts are more properly placed in much later contexts like the Babylonian invasion or the exile.

This means it would be a mistake to assume that all of First Isaiah was written prior to Second Isaiah. The first section of the book is a very complex collection of traditions that cannot be that easily categorized. This is perhaps best seen in chapters 13–23, the second section of First Isaiah, where we find eighth-century material on Assyria (14:24-27), Philistine (14:28-31), and Egypt (18–19) alongside sixth-century texts that mention Babylon (13:1-16) and Persia (13:17-22).

This raises important questions about the connection between First Isaiah and the actual words of the prophet himself. The work has its origin in his message, and it is quite likely that it contains some of the words he spoke. But those original words have been heavily reworked and expanded in light of subsequent events as later editors tried to apply them to new circumstances like the rise of Babylon. This explains, for example, the presence in First Isaiah of a passage like chapter 35, whose message of return from exile would be much more at home in Second Isaiah. It responds to a context centuries after the life of the prophet, but it continues to draw upon many of the themes and motifs that have their roots in his original message, like the reference to the returnees going to Mount Zion in 35:10. Many such connections can be noted between the earlier and later parts of the book.

It is impossible to reconstruct the precise history of development of First Isaiah throughout its various stages from an eighth-century origin to the postexilic period. But the evidence of that development is undeniable, and the work—as does the entire book of Isaiah—stands as a paramount example of the evolving nature of the Hebrew Bible.

CONTEXT

The history of the period in which Isaiah lived and preached is well documented by sources from Assyria and elsewhere in the ancient Near East. The numerous inscriptions, royal annals, letters, and other forms of communication that have come down to us provide a wealth of information about his context and the circumstances to which his message was directed. Not every passage in the book can be precisely located at a given moment in time, but the evidence from the extra-biblical sources gives us a fairly accurate and detailed picture of the overall state of affairs.

At times, the text and other sources allow us to pinpoint the context more sharply, and that is the case with the events of Isaiah 7. The chapter describes an encounter between Isaiah and King Ahaz of Judah, who was facing a serious international crisis. The meeting can be dated to 734, when the kingdoms of Israel and Syria decided to form an alliance to hold off the growing threat posed by the Assyrian Empire. The resulting crisis is referred to as the Syro-Ephraimite Crisis, taking part of its name from Ephraim, the most prominent tribe of Israel at the time.

The alliance leaders, King Rezin of Damascus, the capital of Aram, and King Pekah of Israel, approached King Ahaz about joining them in their effort to hold off the Assyrians. Ahaz had a number of options. He could join forces with Syria and Israel in the hope that their combined armies would be sufficiently strong to turn back the enemy. Otherwise, he could inform the Assyrian leader Tiglath-pileser III about the plot against him, thereby setting himself up as a likely beneficiary if the Syro-Ephraimite plan did not succeed. A third option was that Ahaz could adopt a position of neutrality and do nothing by not aligning himself with either side.

After receiving a message from God, Isaiah advises Ahaz to pursue the third option and not involve Judah in the conflict. The prophet explains to the king that he has nothing to fear since Rezin and Pekah will not be successful in their attempt to remove Ahaz from the throne and replace him with a puppet ruler (v. 6). Quoting God's words, Isaiah reminds the king that it is ultimately a matter of having trust and confidence. "If you do not stand firm in faith, you shall not stand at all" (v. 9).

King Ahaz did not heed Isaiah's advice but chose instead to inform Tiglath-pileser III of the coalition's intention to fight against him. He did so in order to receive Assyria's protection from Kings Rezin and Pekah, who were angered by Ahaz's refusal to join the coalition. The results were disastrous for Judah. Ahaz did receive Tiglath-pileser's protection in exchange for the information he provided, but he was also forced to become a vassal of Assyria, a situation that lasted for more than a century. In this way, he became the personification of the unfaithful leader who does not listen to God's word as communicated through a prophetic intermediary.

This background is vital to a proper understanding of Isaiah's next words, which are among the most well known in the entire book. When Ahaz refuses God's invitation to ask for a sign verifying the truth of the message he has heard, Isaiah tells him what sign God will offer.

> Therefore the LORD himself will give you a sign. Look, the young woman is with child and shall bear a son, and shall name him Immanuel. He shall eat curds and honey by the time he knows how to refuse the evil and choose the good. For before the child knows how to refuse the evil and choose the good, the land before whose two kings you are in dread will be deserted.

> The LORD will bring on you and on your people and on your ancestral house such days as have not come since the day that Ephraim departed from Judah—the king of Assyria. (7:14-17)

The prediction of the birth of the child named Immanuel is clearly in response to the dilemma Ahaz is experiencing during the Syro-Ephraimite Crisis. Its location immediately after the prophet's demand that Ahaz stand firm in faith indicates this, as do the references to the two kings and Assyria that are found in the oracle.

The identity of the child has been a topic of debate and fascination. A common Christian reading of the text sees it as a prediction of the birth of Jesus, something that will be discussed in the next section on interpretation. Keeping in mind the original eighth-century context, it is more likely that the passage is describing a more imminent birth. How can it be a sign for Ahaz unless it is something that he can witness and verify?

Various solutions have been proposed regarding the identities of this young woman and her mystery child. Some have said it is a reference to Ahaz's wife and her son, who would be the heir to the throne, and others have claimed it is pointing forward to King Hezekiah, who will be on the throne when Judah is attacked by the Assyrians in 701. The most intriguing theory suggests that the woman is Isaiah's wife, and the child in question will be his son. The symbolic meaning of the name Immanuel ("God is with us") is an argument in favor of this because elsewhere in the book the prophet's children have symbolic names like his son Shearjashub ("a remnant shall return") earlier in this chapter (7:3). Despite the uncertainty surrounding who these figures are, there is no doubt they are cited by Isaiah in response to the particular context he and Ahaz find themselves in.

The reference to the coming of the king of Assyria at the end of the Immanuel oracle is followed in verses 18-25 by four brief texts that all describe the unpleasant effects of the imminent Assyrian invasion. It is unclear if this is meant to be the Assyrian destruction of the kingdom of Israel in 721 or the Assyrian attack on Judah in 701, which devastated the area although Jerusalem survived. The latter invasion is commemorated in a lengthy inscription that proclaims the military victories of Sennacherib, who was emperor of Assyria in 704–681 B.C.E. In the inscription he brags that his attack on Jerusalem left King Hezekiah "trapped like a bird in a cage."

INTERPRETATION

Knowledge of its context can play an important role in how a biblical text is interpreted. This is especially true for the prophetic books of the

Bible, which present some unique challenges in this regard. Because the words of the prophets are often future-oriented, there is a tendency on the part of many to understand the message as a prediction about some far-off time, sometimes even that of the present-day reader. For modern people prophecy is often about foretelling the future, and a prophet is someone who can predict what will happen long before it occurs.

To apply this view to biblical prophecy is to misunderstand what it is. Prophets like Isaiah often did speak about the future, but it was always in relation to the present. They were able to tell their audience what was going to happen only because they were aware of what was happening here and now. Their capacity to peer into the future and inform their contemporaries of what awaited them was tied to their ability to look around themselves and interpret the signs of the times. The message of the prophets was "Here is what is going to happen to you because of what you're doing now."

In other words, a prophetic message is all about context because it is directed to a particular audience at a particular moment in time. Sometimes people forget that and believe the prophet is speaking to a later audience and context. One of the classic examples of this is the Immanuel passage in Isaiah 7. There is a long history of reading this chapter as a prediction of the birth of Jesus that can be traced back to the New Testament itself. In the course of explaining how Mary, the mother of Jesus, could have become pregnant without having sexual relations, the Gospel of Matthew cites the Isaiah passage. "All this took place to fulfill what had been spoken by the Lord through the prophet: 'Look, the virgin shall conceive and bear a son, and they shall name him Emmanuel'" (1:22-23).

The alert reader will notice that the Isaiah passage quoted by Matthew is slightly different from the one quoted earlier. The "young woman" in Isaiah has become a "virgin" in Matthew. This change is due to Matthew's use of the Greek translation of the Hebrew Bible, called the Septuagint, which he frequently cites to understand the events of Jesus' life. The Greek version supports his claim that Jesus was virginally conceived, but the same cannot be said for the Hebrew one. The word there is *'almāh*, which refers to a young woman of marriageable age but does not specify that she is a virgin. There is a common Hebrew word for virgin that Isaiah could have used to describe the sign for King Ahaz, but he chose not to do so.

The New Testament frequently quotes or alludes to the Hebrew Bible, especially the prophets, in order to explain or support certain aspects of Christian faith. Sometimes, as in this case, the New Testament writers even claim that the earlier scriptures were predicting later events. Such an approach may be common and acceptable within the framework of a community of faith, but it runs the risk of putting forward a distorted view of the prior writings. It is inaccurate to say that Isaiah 7 is predicting the virginal conception of Jesus and leave it at that. Such an interpretation ignores the original context of the passage, which, as we have seen, was a very real crisis that Ahaz had to confront. The child of whom Isaiah spoke would be born in his time, not seven hundred years in the future. The historical situation that gave rise to the text should be acknowledged and recognized before attempting to explain the text's relevance for the later Christian community.

Ahaz plays an important role in First Isaiah because through him the prophet is able to address some of the major themes of the book. One of those themes is the need for the people to have faith and trust in order to experience God's protection. Ahaz rejects Isaiah's advice and looks instead to Tiglath-pileser III for protection, ushering in a century of foreign domination. In this way, he is the opposite of his successor King Hezekiah, who will heed Isaiah's words when the Assyrians attack in 701.

Another central theme of the book is the idea that the foreign nations, even mighty Assyria, are ultimately powerless and must do God's bidding. "Ah Assyria, the rod of my anger— /the club in their hands is my fury" (10:5). Isaiah reminds Ahaz that God is the supreme authority to whose will all nations must bend. Ironically, the king of God's people is incapable of believing that message and, unlike the prophet, he cannot read the signs of the times.

MICAH

Micah was an eighth-century prophet of the south who was probably a contemporary of Isaiah. According to the first verse of the book bearing his name, he was active during the reigns of kings Jotham, Ahaz, and Hezekiah, who ruled approximately 760–687 B.C.E. The opening verse also identifies his hometown as Moresheth, a small village southwest of Jerusalem. Like Isaiah and the other eighth-century prophets, Micah warns the people that they will be attacked by a foreign power as a result of their sin. He chastises Judah as a place devoid of social justice whose leaders are corrupt. "Its rulers give judgment for a bribe, its priests teach for a price, its prophets give oracles for money; yet they lean upon the LORD and say, 'Surely the LORD is with us! No harm shall come upon us'" (3:11).

CONTENT

The book of Micah is a combination of oracles of doom and oracles of hope. The oracles of doom are found mostly in chapters 1–3, 6, and the first part of 7. The oracles of hope are primarily in chapters 4 and 5, which speak of the rebirth of the community through a faithful remnant not unlike the one mentioned in Isaiah. "The lame I will make the remnant, and those who were cast off, a strong nation; and the LORD will reign over them in Mount Zion now and forevermore" (4:7).

The individual units and poems that make up the book of Micah are well defined, but they do not flow smoothly because they lack thematic and linguistic connections that would link them together. A well-known passage in 4:1-4 that speaks of the people beating their swords into plowshares and their spears into pruning hooks is virtually identical to what is found in Isa 2:2-4, but there is still no satisfactory explanation for why it is found in both books.

GROWTH

Some scholars have tried to defend the textual unity of the book by claiming that it all comes from the hand of the eighth-century prophet, but this position is difficult to support. The final section of the book (7:8-20) is often referred to as a liturgy, and it should be dated to a time after the prophet Micah, perhaps as late as the postexilic period. This composition is a blend of lament, petition, and prayer that might have functioned in a worship setting. The opening words of verse 18—"Who is a God like you?"—are probably an allusion to the prophet's name, which is a shortened form of Micaiah, meaning "Who is like Yahweh?"

Many scholars believe much of the material in chapters 4 and 5 was added to the prophet's original message. The more positive tone adopted in this section better reflects a later time when it was too late to warn the people and an attitude of hope and confidence was more appropriate. It is also possible that certain passages may come from an earlier time in the prophet's career prior to 721 B.C.E., when the Assyrians overran the north. This would help explain the reference to the coming destruction of Samaria, the northern capital, in 1:6. "Therefore I will make Samaria a heap in the open country, a place for planting vineyards. I will pour down her stones into the valley, and uncover her foundations."

CONTEXT

The sociopolitical context of the book of Micah mirrors that of Isaiah described earlier in this chapter. The prophet recognized the growing challenge Assyria posed for Judah, and he issued a warning to repent before it was too late. This fits best with the earlier part of Hezekiah's reign (715–687), when the Assyrian threat was most keenly felt. That setting is supported by the list of towns mentioned in 1:10-16, which were all along the route taken by the Assyrian ruler Sennacherib during his campaign through Judah in 701 B.C.E. The final verse of that passage makes a direct reference to the horror of exile. "Make yourselves bald and cut off your hair for your pampered children; make yourselves as bald as the eagle, for they have gone from you into exile."

As noted earlier, the first three chapters are generally believed to come from the prophet's time. In this part of the book only 2:12-13 offers a message of hope in the midst of the warnings of imminent destruction, and it is likely a later insertion. The first section ends on a note of despair in anticipation of the annihilation of the holy city and the temple it contains. "Therefore because of you Zion shall be plowed as a field; Jerusalem shall become a heap of ruins, and the mountain of the house a wooded height" (3:12). It is difficult to determine the precise dating of the material in chapters 4–7, but it addresses a later context when the people will be restored to the land. Some texts, like 4:10, are products of the Babylonian exile of the sixth century. "Writhe and groan, O daughter Zion, like a woman in labor; for now you shall go forth from the city and camp in the open country; you shall go to Babylon. There you shall be rescued, there the LORD will redeem you from the hands of your enemies."

INTERPRETATION

In a very rare case of a prophet being mentioned and quoted in another prophetic book, Micah is referred to in Jer 26:17-19. This is a second version of the Temple Sermon, a speech given by Jeremiah that is also found in chapter 7 of the book that bears his name. As Jeremiah is about to be sentenced to death, people rise to his defense and say that he does not deserve to be punished because he has spoken in God's name. They cite as a precedent "Micah of Moresheth, who prophesied during the days of King Hezekiah of Judah," and they then quote Mic 3:12. Hezekiah took to heart Micah's warning about the destruction of Jerusalem, and tragedy was averted. The implication is that if his audience responds in the same way to Jeremiah, all will be well for them.

The book of Micah does not contain an account of a meeting between the prophet and King Hezekiah similar to the one that is alluded to in Jeremiah. This has led some scholars to posit the existence of an unknown narrative about such a meeting that was used by the author of Jeremiah. This is a highly speculative theory that lacks evidence and should be viewed cautiously. More revealing is what the Jeremiah text tells us about Micah's reputation and status. He is held up as a model prophet who spoke on God's behalf and warned his contemporaries about the painful consequences of disobedience to the divine will. This fits very well with the image of him that emerges from the book with which he is associated. According to the book of Jeremiah, long after his death Micah was so highly regarded by later Israelites that the mere mention of his name was able to save the life of one of his prophetic successors.

CHAPTER 20

THE PREEXILIC PROPHETS: HOSEA AND AMOS

Like Isaiah and Micah, Hosea and Amos were prophets who lived in the eighth century B.C.E. Also like Micah, Hosea and Amos are in the book or scroll of the twelve "minor" prophets, so designated because they are not as lengthy as the "major" prophetic books of Isaiah, Jeremiah, and Ezekiel. But unlike Isaiah and Micah, the prophets who lent their names to Hosea and Amos directed their oracles to the people of the northern kingdom (Israel). Hosea, son of Beeri, was a native of that area, whereas Amos was originally from Judah (the village of Tekoa) but prophesied in Israel. Despite living in the same century, the careers of Amos and Hosea do not appear to have overlapped; they do not mention one another. Amos evidently preceded Hosea. The book of Amos is dated to the first half of the eighth century, whereas Hosea is said to have worked in the mid-to-latter half of the same century.

HOSEA

The central theme of the book is the deterioration of the relationship between God and the people of Israel. Hosea uses a wide variety of arresting images to explain how a union once built on trust and fidelity is now marked by betrayal and uncertainty. The people bear the responsibility for this changed state of affairs because of their ignorance and stupidity. They have forgotten what God did for them in establishing the covenant (2:19; 8:1) and leading them through the wilderness after the exodus (2:15; 13:5-6), and they must now suffer the consequences. The book is a warning to them about the dangers of a lack of knowledge of these things and a reminder never to forget the obligations that come along with being God's chosen people.

CONTENT

The book of Hosea is divided into two parts. Chapters 1–3 are a prologue that discusses the relationship between God and Israel within the context of the prophet Hosea's marriage to a promiscuous woman. Two prose accounts of that marriage (1:2-9; 3:1-3) are sandwiched around a mostly poetic speech (2:1-23) that centers on the faithlessness of the people and the mercy of God. Just as Hosea's wife is a whore who wanders from partner to partner, the people of Israel follow other deities and violate the relationship they have with their God. But the situation is not as dire as it might seem because Hosea often follows a message of judgment (1:2-9; 2:1-13) with a note of hope (1:10-11; 2:14-15). If the people reject their faithless ways and return to God, they can be saved. This alternation of negative and positive oracles is found throughout the entire book.

There are no further references to the personal life of the prophet in the second part of the book, chapters 4–14, which elaborate on the relationship between Israel and God. Throughout this section the people are guilty of a variety of offenses that signal their break from the Lord. Some of these, like giving in to the temptation to follow other gods (13:2), are theological. Others, like becoming smugly confident in their wealthy lifestyles (10:12-15), are social. Still others, like their aligning with Assyria for protection and security (5:13), are political. References to Israel as a whore frequently appear in these condemnations.

In chapters 9–11 Hosea uses a series of four striking metaphors to describe God's view of Israel. The first (9:10-17) compares the people to grapes that have grown in the wild that, because of their idolatry, will wither away. The second (10:1-10) speaks of Israel as a fertile vine that embraces other gods and rejects the Lord, leading to its defeat at the hands of its enemies. In the third metaphor, God refers to Israel as a trained heifer (10:11-15) that goes against its master's wishes by plowing injustice and relying on itself. This will result in its ruin and destruction.

There is an interesting development among these three images as each conveys a more intimate and personal relationship between God and Israel than its predecessor. A vine requires more long-term care than grapes in order to ensure its survival, and a heifer requires even more attention than the other two. It is as if the prophet is attempting to convey the idea that God's commitment to Israel has continued to deepen and grow over time. That progression reaches its culmination in the metaphor of Israel as a child (11:1-11) that concludes the series. In one of the more memorable passages of the Hebrew Bible, Hosea describes Israel as a son whom God calls, teaches to walk, carries, leads, and feeds. This parent/child relationship expresses a union that is deeper than any of the other three, but the result is the same—Israel turns from God and is defeated by its foes. Only this time the oracle ends on a positive note as God acknowledges the deep bond that exists between them and refuses to allow Israel, here called by its other name Ephraim, to suffer the same fate as Admah and Zeboiim, two cities destroyed with Sodom and Gomorrah.

How can I give you up, Ephraim?
  How can I hand you over, O Israel?
How can I make you like Admah?
  How can I treat you like Zeboiim?
My heart recoils within me;
  my compassion grows warm and tender.
I will not execute my fierce anger;
  I will not again destroy Ephraim;
for I am God and no mortal,
  the Holy One in your midst,
  and I will not come in wrath. (11:8-9)

It is this continued presence of divine compassion despite human transgression that dominates the book of Hosea and makes it such a forceful work. The references to the calves set up by King Jeroboam I of Israel in Beth-El and Dan (1 Kgs 12:25-33) are meant to represent the lure of idolatry (8:5-6; 10:5; 13:2). The temptation to follow other gods, especially the Canaanite deities Baal and Asherah, is a constant danger for Israel (2:8, 13; 4:12-13, 17). At one point God's ultimate victory over Baal is expressed through a nice wordplay on the latter's name, which can mean "husband" in Hebrew. "On that day, says the LORD, you will call me, 'My husband,' and you will no longer call me, 'My Baal' " (2:16).

Even if the people give in to false worship, they can recover. All they need to do is repent and return to God. Sounding one of his favorite themes, Hosea reminds the people repeatedly that, if they have knowledge and if they remember, they can experience God's steadfast love (4:6; 6:3, 6; 10:12; 11:3-4). Fittingly, the book ends with a verse that explains the implications of the choice the people must make between knowledge and ignorance.

Those who are wise understand these things;
  those who are discerning know them.
For the ways of the LORD are right,
  and the upright walk in them,
  but transgressors stumble in them. (14:9)

GROWTH

Scholars generally agree that much of the book has its origin in the late eighth-century context of the prophet Hosea. But many also see evidence of a later redaction of the work that was done either in Judah during the time of King Josiah, who ruled in 640–609, or during the exile. Such a redaction would help explain the presence of Deuteronomistic concerns in Hosea like the importance of obeying the covenant, which are characteristic of literature of the later time period.

The unusual nature of the book's superscription is a point in favor of a later southern editor. "The word of the LORD that came to Hosea son of Beeri, in the days of Kings Uzziah, Jotham, Ahaz, and Hezekiah of Judah, and in the days of King Jeroboam son of Joash of Israel" (1:1). Jeroboam II ruled in Israel until 747, some twenty-five years before the northern kingdom was taken over by the Assyrians. The dates of the four Judean kings mentioned in the superscription extend well beyond that, with Hezekiah's reign coming to an end in the early seventh century B.C.E. Listing four southern kings and only one northern ruler is a somewhat strange way to begin a work that purports to be written by a northerner for a northern audience, and it suggests the hand of a Judean editor who was working sometime after the fall of the north in 721.

A later southern redaction would also explain the inconsistent way Judah is portrayed in the book of Hosea. Certain references to the southern kingdom suggest that Judah, unlike Israel, will remain faithful to God and the covenant. "Ephraim has surrounded me with lies, and the house of Israel with deceit; but Judah still walks with God, and is faithful to the Holy One" (11:12; see also 1:7). Such texts must be dated to the late eighth or early seventh centuries when Judah's situation was stable, prior to the time Assyria began to pose a serious threat in the south.

Other passages, however, indicate that Judah is as guilty as Israel and would be punished for its sins. "Israel's pride testifies against him; Ephraim stumbles in his guilt; Judah also stumbles with them" (5:5; see also 12:2). Texts like this would only make sense in a later time period when the situation in Judah was not as comfortable and secure as it had been earlier. Some of them might even be later than the Babylonian invasion of Jerusalem in 586. The presence of these conflicting views of Judah within the same book is best explained by a later redaction of the work that expanded the prophet's original message in light of subsequent events.

The first three chapters of Hosea also show evidence of editorial activity. In the first place, the two narrative accounts of the prophet's marriage are quite different. The first one (1:2-9) is told in the third person and is the longer of the two. His wife is Gomer, who is a harlot, and God symbolically names their three children. The oldest (1:4-5) is their son Jezreel ("God sows"), whose name refers to the place where King Jehu (842–814) staged a coup d'etat that began a dynasty that lasted until the end of the reign of Jeroboam II. God tells Hosea that the child's name means that Israel is about to be punished for what the house of Jehu did. Gomer's second child (1:6) is a daughter named Lo-ruhamah ("not pitied"), symbolizing God's lack of concern and compassion for Israel. Immediately following this is a statement that God *will* have pity on Judah (1:7), a verse that is probably a later insertion because the prophet's message was originally addressed to the north. The couple's last child is another son (1:8-9), named Lo-ammi ("not my people"), signaling the end of the relationship between God and Israel.

The second account is presented in the first person as the prophet describes his relationship with the woman (3:1-3). Here she has no name, and no children are mentioned. God commands Hosea to love a woman who is an adulteress, and so the prophet purchases her for some money, grain, and wine. He then informs her that she is not to have sexual relations with any man, including him, for a set period of time. As in the first account, the relationship between Hosea and the woman symbolically represents that between God and Israel. It might be that this autobiographical passage of chapter 3 goes back to the prophet himself, although the relationship between the two accounts is a subject of debate that will be discussed more fully later in this chapter.

Between the two texts on Hosea's marriage is a section that contains an oracle of judgment followed by an oracle of hope. This alternation sets the tone for the rest of the book, which often puts contrasting messages like these side by side. The first passage (2:1-13) is a scathing condemnation of Israel that accuses the people of whoring after other gods and not remembering the God who has provided them with all they need. The consequences will be swift and painful. "I will punish her for the festival days of the Baals, when she offered incense to them and decked herself with her ring and jewelry, and went after her lovers, and forgot me, says the LORD" (2:13). The entire oracle is presented as a plea to Jezreel that he should tell his siblings, here named Ammi ("my people") and Ruhamah ("pitied"), to convince their mother to turn from her evil ways.

The next section offers a message of hope that draws on language and imagery from the creation and exodus traditions (2:14-23). God will draw Israel out into the wilderness where they will establish a covenant with all the animals. Israel will become God's wife, and they will live together in perfect love. God again refers to the children of Gomer and Hosea, this time reversing the symbolic meanings of their names.

> On that day I will answer, says the LORD,
>   I will answer the heavens
>   and they shall answer the earth;
> and the earth shall answer the grain, the wine, and the oil,
>   and they shall answer Jezreel;
>   and I will sow him for myself in the land.
> And I will have pity on Lo-ruhamah,
>   and I will say to Lo-ammi, "You are my people";
>   and he shall say, "You are my God." (2:21-23)

The first three chapters of Hosea reveal the hand of the work's final editor. The two accounts of the prophet's marriage have been placed on either side of a middle section that contains messages of judgment and hope that will be juxtaposed often throughout the remainder of the book. There are many thematic and vocabulary links between that middle section and the two marriage accounts that help to unite all three chapters. In addition, the entire section helps to set the agenda for the rest of the work by introducing topics and images that are found throughout the entirety of the book.

CONTEXT

It has already been noted that Hosea is the only prophetic work written by a northerner for a northern audience. Other than the references to his marriage, the book provides no information on his origin or personal history, but virtually all scholars consider him to be a northerner. The superscription (1:1) locates the beginning of his ministry during the time of King Jeroboam II of Israel (788–747 B.C.E.), most likely during the latter part of his reign. According to 1:4, the end of Jehu's dynasty is imminent, which suggests that Hosea's career began sometime around 750. He probably ceased prophesying by 721 because the book anticipates Assyria's invasion and takeover of Israel but does not actually describe the event.

Beyond that, it is somewhat difficult to determine Hosea's precise context because there are not many clues given in the text. Still, although most passages cannot be dated with certainty, the reader is left with a clear sense of the problems in Israelite society that the prophet was trying to address. The challenges presented by the worship of Baal and other Canaanite deities have already been mentioned (4:12-14). In addition, the text indicates that this was a time of relative wealth and prosperity for the Israelites.

> Ephraim has said, "Ah, I am rich,
> I have gained wealth for myself;
> in all of my gain
> no offense has been found in me
> that would be sin." (12:8)

Such complacent and self-righteous attitudes reflect a lack of knowledge that Hosea warned against.

Despite Ephraim's claims to the contrary, corruption and sin are rampant throughout the community, leading to oppression and the breakdown of society. "Swearing, lying, and murder, and stealing and adultery break out; bloodshed follows bloodshed" (4:2). The priests are singled out for special blame because they have forgotten the law of

God and are leading the people to ruin (4:4-6). Acts of worship have become nothing but empty rituals. The people have developed a blind trust in cultic activity as a way of staying in God's favor. They have forgotten that true faith is a matter of inner commitment, not external actions. "For I desire steadfast love and not sacrifice, the knowledge of God rather than burnt offerings" (6:6).

Elsewhere, the prophet chastises the people of Israel for placing too much trust in their military leaders' ability to respond to the Assyrian threat and other international crises. "Ephraim has become like a dove, silly and without sense; they call upon Egypt, they go to Assyria" (7:11). This is yet another example of Hosea identifying the problem as one of ignorance. Israel, the "silly dove," is guilty of a lack of knowledge of what God has done for it in the past and a lack of trust that the same can be done in the present, which leads it to turn to foreign powers for assistance.

All these passages describe a situation that sounds quite similar to that portrayed by Amos, who directed his own prophetic message to the northern kingdom. The general context is one in which Israel has wandered far from God, and that rejection has affected its social, political, and religious life.

More specifically, it is likely that some passages attempt to address the aftermath of the Syro-Ephraimite Crisis, which took place in 734. As an Assyrian invasion became more probable, King Pekah of Israel (735–32) joined forces with King Rezin of Aram to hold off the enemy. We have already seen that the book of Isaiah addresses this situation as it affected the southern kingdom of Judah. The northern kingdom decided at first to submit to Assyria and become its vassal, a situation that is reflected in Hos 5:8–6:6. Hoshea, the last king of Israel (732–22), disagreed with this policy and killed Pekah. He then refused to pay the tribute due to Assyria and tried to align himself with Egypt, which ultimately led to Israel's ruin. Hosea speaks out strongly against these shifting allegiances, which he views as a rejection of God and a return to the way things were prior to the exodus. "They shall return to the land of Egypt, and Assyria shall be their king, because they have refused to return to me" (11:5; see also 9:3; 12:1).

The Assyrian ruler Shalmaneser V destroyed the northern kingdom in 721 because of Hoshea's refusal to render tribute. Some scholars have claimed there is a reference to him in 10:14, but the identity of the Shalman mentioned in that verse is far from certain. There are no accounts of the final days of Israel, although some texts indicate that the end is imminent. As noted earlier, this suggests that Hosea's career ended just prior to the fall of the northern kingdom. Like many of the other prophets, Hosea does not see these events as in any way undermining the power and authority of Israel's God. Shalmaneser and the Assyrian forces are merely instruments that fulfill God's will. "Where now is your king, that he may save you? Where in all your cities are your rulers, of whom you said, 'Give me a king and rulers'? I gave you a king in my anger, and I took him away in my wrath" (13:10-11).

INTERPRETATION

The passages treating Hosea's marriage present some interesting interpretive issues that have been discussed throughout the history of scholarship on the book. Jewish and Christian commentators in the early and medieval periods often spoke of Hosea's wife as a symbolic figure and preferred not to view the texts as describing an actual marriage. This was due in part to the seemingly immoral nature of what God is asking the prophet to do by marrying a prostitute. The symbolic meanings of the children's names have also been cited as a point in favor of understanding the marriage itself in symbolic terms. In such readings the woman merely represents a faithless, evil person who is the personification of the people of Israel.

Another common approach has been to understand the texts as referring to a real marriage, but interpreting it as a prophetic act performed by Hosea. There is support for this in that some of the prophets, particularly Jeremiah and Ezekiel, engaged in such prophetic acts on occasion (Jer 13:1-11; 18:1-12; Ezek 12:1-16, 17-20; 37:15-28). Similar to what we see in the case of Ezekiel's marriage, these actions were commanded by God and were meant to represent some aspect of the prophet's message. It is particularly noteworthy that the marital statuses of Jeremiah (16:1-2) and Ezekiel (24:15-27) had a strong symbolic content. Both Jeremiah's celibacy and Ezekiel's lack of outward expression of grief at his wife's death were symbolically associated with the effects of the destruction of Jerusalem and the exile.

The passages themselves indicate that there is a symbolic dimension to Hosea's marriage by connecting it to the infidelity of the Israelite people (1:2; 3:1). But there is no reason to assume that the marriage did not take place. The fact that there are two commands from God to the prophet to take the woman has sometimes led to the suggestion that chapters 1 and 3 describe the same event in Hosea's life. In other words, they present two accounts—one autobiographical and the other in the third person—of the divine order to marry Gomer. An argument against this is the presence of the word "again" in 3:1. This verse presents a translation problem because it can be rendered as either "The LORD said to me again, 'Go, love a woman who has a lover and is an adulteress,'" or "The LORD said to me, 'Go, love again a woman who has a lover and is an adulteress.'" However the verse is translated, it is clear that the passages are describing two separate moments rather than the same event.

A sequential reading of the texts fits better with the prophet's reason for using the marriage metaphor. The union between Hosea and Gomer is meant to represent the one between God and Israel. The latter two already had a relationship of love and trust prior to Israel's violation of the covenant. According to Hosea, that prior relationship—as expressed in all the things God did for Israel—is precisely what the people have forgotten. God is ready to forgive that offense and invite them back to resume their earlier bond. The double reference to Hosea and Gomer's marriage mirrors this perfectly. The first passage establishes the union between them, and the second one anticipates its resumption or restoration after Gomer has violated the relationship. The word "again" in chapter 3 makes apparent the chronological development. Just as Hosea takes back Gomer, God will take back Israel.

AMOS

Amos's central concern is social justice. With scathing rebukes, often laced with sarcasm, he condemns the oppression of the poor by Israel's upper class. He threatens the nation of Israel, especially its wealthy urbanites, with destruction at the hands of an invading army. While Amos never mentions the invader by name, it seems likely that he had in mind the rising Assyrian Empire, which would indeed bring an end to the northern kingdom in the last quarter of the eighth century.

CONTENT

The book of Amos may be divided into three sections consisting of chapters 1–2, 3–6, and 7–9.

Amos 1–2

The first section contains a series of oracles against the nations. The nations dealt with are, in order, Aram/Syria (1:3-5), Philistia (1:6-8), Phoenicia (1:9-10), Edom (1:11-12), Ammon (1:13-15), Moab (2:1-3), Judah (2:4-5), and Israel (2:6-16). It is not unusual for prophetic books to have a collection of oracles against foreign nations. However, several features make Amos's collection unique. For one thing, the oracles in Amos all begin the same way: "For three transgressions of *x* and for four, I will not restore it" or possibly "I will not revoke [the punishment]." The similar beginning suggests that these were not separate oracles but were delivered together on the same occasion. The second difference is that there are oracles against first Judah and then Israel included among the collection. Third, this set of oracles stands at the beginning of Amos rather than later in the book.

These three features work together to illustrate the artful and sarcastic character of the book of Amos. The ancient audience would have hailed

Amos's condemnations of the surrounding nations, all of which were neighbors of Israel, mainly for treaty violations and war crimes. They probably saw the promised overthrow of those nations as the "Day of the LORD" when Yahweh would intervene on behalf of his people. But Amos's message is that the real target of God's wrath is Israel itself, especially the upper class, who "sell . . . the needy for a pair of sandals" and "trample the head of the poor into the dust" (2:6-7).

Amos 3–6

The second section of Amos contains a variety of other oracles directed against Israel. Here the themes of oppression of the poor by the rich and the abuse of justice continue. For instance, 4:1-3 is directed against the upper-class women of Samaria, called "cows of Bashan," after Israel's choicest pastureland. Their luxurious lifestyle not only ignores the plight of the poor but is actually exploitative. Similarly, 6:1-8 condemns the wealthy in Samaria, who have the best of everything and are oblivious to the inequities of their society.

These oracles threaten disaster for Israel, especially its upper class. Israel was Yahweh's chosen people and should have known better than to commit its offenses, so its punishment is assured (3:1-2). It is Amos's job as a prophet to proclaim the impending devastation (3:3-8). The main threat that he envisions is invasion by a foreign army (3:11; 6:14). The "cows of Bashan" will be hauled, whether dead or alive is not clear, through the breaches in the city wall made by the invaders (4:2-3), and the upper class in general will be the first taken into exile (6:7). This time of devastation is portrayed as the "day of the LORD" (5:18-20), when the wicked will encounter God (4:12). It can still be avoided if they will reform their ways and follow the path of justice and fair treatment of the poor (5:14-15, 24).

Amos's artfulness and sarcasm come through in these oracles. In 4:4-5 he makes use of a call to worship at shrines at Bethel and Gilgal. But he calls people instead to sin at those sites. It is important to recognize that Amos does not adopt the principle of centralization, which will not appear until Deuteronomy, over a century later. He does not condemn the fact that they go to Bethel and Gilgal for worship nor their cultic activities per se at those places. His condemnation, rather, concerns the emptiness of their religion; they follow cultic details precisely but neglect broader matters of justice and equity. In 5:4-5, he mentions Bethel and Gilgal again, this time making plays in Hebrew on the names (Gilgal and "exile" and Bethel and "nothing"). One of the most sarcastic texts in Amos is 6:4-7, which describes the elite of Samaria as fancying themselves great musicians like David, with whom they really have nothing in common. They also drink wine from "bowls," referring to large vessels designated elsewhere for cultic use. Their offense, therefore, is twofold. They profane the sacred and get drunk, callously ignoring the social problems that plague their nation.

Amos 7–9

The third major section of Amos consists mainly of a set of visions relating to Israel's impending destruction. These include visions of locusts (7:1-3), fire (7:4-6), a plumb line (7:7-9), a basket of summer fruit (8:1-3), and Yahweh standing beside an altar (9:1-4). The series of visions is interrupted by an account of Amos's encounter with Amaziah, the priest at the royal shrine of Bethel (7:10-17) and by oracles condemning wealthy merchants for their deceptive and oppressive business practices (8:4-6) and depicting future judgment (8:7-14). The final vision on the inescapability of punishment is extended by a doxology (9:5-6) and a declaration of Israel's destruction and exile (9:7-10). The book concludes with a brief oracle envisioning Israel's restoration (9:11-15).

GROWTH

As we have seen in other instances, Isaiah especially, prophetic books often reflect reinterpretation and reapplication of their oracles to later periods. The same is true for the book of Amos. Two passages in particular—one at the beginning and one at the end of the book—reflect this kind of reapplication. Amos addressed his oracles to Israel, so the few references to Judah in the book have often been considered additions that reapply his original message(s) to Judah. The oracle against Judah in 2:4-5 may be one of these. It is shorter than the surrounding oracles and also bears some similarity in language to Deuteronomistic phraseology. For these reasons, many scholars regard this oracle as a later addition to the book. The brief oracles against Tyre (2:9-11) and Edom (2:11-12) may be secondary as well, since they seem to reflect hatred of Edom for its collaboration with the Babylonians after they destroyed Jerusalem in 586 B.C.E.

The other secondary text is the oracle of restoration that closes the book. It is clear from the first verse of this oracle (9:10) that it differs radically from the rest of Amos. In the first place, its orientation is positive—prophesying restoration rather than destruction like the rest of the book. It concerns the "booth of David," an allusion to the Davidic dynasty that ruled in Judah rather than in Israel, which is the concern of the rest of Amos. Moreover, the "booth of David" is already fallen according to this text, and it looks forward to its rebuilding. Therefore, it is no longer called a "house" but only a "booth"; the dynasty is weakened. The passage thus presupposes the situation after 586 B.C.E. when Jerusalem was destroyed and the Babylonian exile inaugurated, rather than the eighth century when Amos prophesied. This text, therefore, indicates that the book of Amos reached its present form over 200 years after Amos. The destruction of Israel in 721 B.C.E. lent credibility to Amos's threats. His oracles were probably transported to Judah, where they were read and reinterpreted as referring to Judah's destruction, since Judah was the remnant of Israel. Judah's devastation in 586 was seen as a further fulfillment of the prophet's words.

CONTEXT

The historical context of the prophet Amos can be discerned from the book's heading (1:1) and from his encounter with Amaziah (7:10-17). Amos is introduced as a sheep rancher (not the common word for shepherd) from Tekoa, which was a small village south of Jerusalem. Amos, therefore, was from Judah but prophesied in Israel. The priest Amaziah warned Amos, telling him to return home to Judah and earn his living as a prophet there. Amos responded that he was not a prophet by profession but a herdsman (or perhaps sheep rancher again) and a pruner of sycamore trees whom God had called to prophesy. He was probably not among the poor or lower class but was likely a landowner. The literary sophistication of his oracles and his familiarity with international politics (chs. 1–2) also indicates that he was a well-to-do sheep owner rather than a lowly shepherd or laborer. He nevertheless championed the cause of the poor and downtrodden.

According to the book's opening, Amos worked during the reigns of Jeroboam II of Israel (ca. 788–747) and Uzziah of Judah (ca. 785–733). A strict interpretation of this verse would place his career between 785–747. More important than the precise dates is what we know of Jeroboam II's reign. It was a time of territorial expansion and perhaps the greatest prosperity Israel had ever experienced. To judge from Amos, however, the prosperity seemed to be enjoyed only by the wealthy and indeed to further separate the upper and lower classes. It may be as well that the growing class distinction Amos observed was a division between rural and urban life, with the well-to-do urbanites perverting the court system and deceitfully acquiring the hereditary land of poor farmers. Certainly, it is the elite of Samaria who bear the brunt of Amos's indictments. Amaziah even accused Amos to King Jeroboam of treason for prophesying the king's demise. Amaziah quotes Amos as saying,

> Jeroboam shall die by the sword,
>   and Israel must go into exile
> away from his land. (7:11)

There is no such saying elsewhere in Amos, and Amaziah may be paraphrasing. But Amos does not deny that this is the sense of his message.

INTERPRETATION

The enduring legacy of Amos is its concern for social justice and fair treatment of the poor and disadvantaged in society. To be sure, Amos addressed problems in eighth-century Israel, and the language and images he used must be interpreted in that context in order to be understood. For instance, his demand to establish justice *in the gate* (5:15) makes no sense in a modern context where courthouses are the locus for dispensing justice. In ancient Israel, though, the city gate was the place where legal and business transactions took place.

The principles of fairness and justice, however, are applicable to all societies. It is for this reason that Martin Luther King, Jr. invoked Amos in his call for equal treatment for African Americans during the civil rights movement: "Let justice roll down like waters, and righteousness like an ever-flowing stream" (Amos 5:24). The passage of which this verse is a part is one of the most powerful in Amos in this regard.

> I hate, I despise your festivals,
>   and I take no delight in your solemn assemblies.
> Even though you offer me your burnt offerings and grain offerings,
>   I will not accept them;
> and the offerings of well-being of your fatted animals
>   I will not look upon.
> Take away from me the noise of your songs;
>   I will not listen to the melody of your harps.
> But let justice roll down like waters,
>   and righteousness like an ever-flowing stream. (5:21-24)

In order to grasp the force of this oracle, we can transpose it into a modern setting by envisioning a church or synagogue setting in which a respected member of the community stands up and rails against its worship activities in the name of God.

> I hate and detest your worship services.
> I will not accept your prayers or offerings.
> Take the noise of your hymns and organs away from me,
> Until you replace them with justice and fair treatment of other people.

Again, it is not the liturgical activities per se with which Amos finds fault, nor does he object to the locations of those activities. As we have noted, Amos does not presuppose the principle of centralization. What Amos is saying, rather, is that the Israelites' worship activities are meaningless and even offensive to God because they neglect the right treatment of others. They have missed the point of religion, because they have not allowed it to affect their attitudes or their daily lives.

CHAPTER 21

THE PREEXILIC PROPHETS: NAHUM, HABAKKUK, ZEPHANIAH

The seventh, eighth, and ninth writings in the scroll of the twelve prophets are those of Nahum, Habakkuk, and Zephaniah. The three have in common that they come from the same basic time period—the latter half of the seventh century B.C.E.

NAHUM

Nahum is unique in that it is the only prophetic work actually to call itself a "book" or "scroll" (1:1). Like many of the prophets, virtually nothing is known about Nahum's life. Even the location of the place that the first verse of the book calls his hometown, Elkosh, is a mystery. His name, Nahum, though attested outside of the Bible, might seem tailored to the book's message. It means "comforted," and Nahum finds comfort and delight in the destruction of Nineveh, one of Israel's great enemies, and in Yahweh's control of human history.

CONTENT

The book of Nahum has three main parts following the introduction in its first verse: (1) 1:2-8 is a poem praising Yahweh in the role of the divine warrior who marches against his enemies and those of his people. Scholars have perceived evidence that this poem is based on an older acrostic in which each line began with the successive letter of the Hebrew alphabet. The present poem extends only through the first half of the alphabet, and even then some letters are not represented, so that the older version of the poem cannot be reconstructed. The poem sets the stage for the parts of the book that follow in its depiction of Yahweh's power as warrior and sovereignty as king.

(2) 1:9–2:2 (Hebrew 2:3) presents a series of brief oracles alternating in audience between Nineveh and Judah, as the following chart shows.

Verses	Addressee
1:9-11	Nineveh
1:12-13	Judah
1:14	Nineveh
1:15 (Hebrew 2:1)	Judah
2:1 (Hebrew 2:2)	Nineveh
2:2 (Hebrew 2:3)	Judah

The addresses to Nineveh are threats, while those to Judah are promises that they will no longer be oppressed. The contrast between 1:15 and 2:1 is particularly striking. For Judah, the arrival of a messenger bringing good news is announced:

> Look! On the mountains the feet of one
> who brings good tidings,
> who proclaims peace!

Then this messenger tells Judah,

> Celebrate your festivals, O Judah,
> fulfill your vows;
> for never again shall the wicked invade you;
> they are utterly cut off.

Nineveh anticipates a very different figure:

> A shatterer has come up against you.
> Guard the ramparts;
> watch the road;
> gird your loins;
> collect all your strength.

Following these verses, 2:2 (Hebrew 2:3) reveals Yahweh's objective in attacking Nineveh and the Assyrians—to restore his people to their former glory:

> For the LORD is restoring the majesty of Jacob,
> as well as the majesty of Israel,
> though ravagers have ravaged them
> and ruined their branches.

(3) The third part of Nahum, 2:3 (Hebrew 2:4)–3:19, describes the fall of Nineveh in the third person (2:3-12 [Hebrew 2:4-13]; 3:1-3), supplemented with taunts (2:13 [Hebrew 2:14]; 3:4-19). The book ends with a question addressed by God to the Assyrian king: "For who has ever escaped your endless cruelty?" (3:19). The ending is nearly unique, since Jonah—which

also deals with Nineveh—is the only other book in the Bible that ends with a question.

GROWTH

The primary issues relating to the growth of Nahum concern the divine warrior poem in the book's first section (1:2-8). The incomplete acrostic underlying the present poem suggests that an older piece has been modified for the book. Even as it stands, this poem does not reflect any particular historical situation. It describes Yahweh in typical storm-god language and imagery as marching forth in tempest and earthquake. Verse 9 then serves the editorial function of linking the poem with the following oracles by asking, in effect, how Nineveh can dare to oppose Yahweh with his power.

CONTEXT

The city of Nineveh was destroyed by the Persians and Babylonians in 612 B.C.E. Nahum either looks forward to or celebrates Nineveh's demise, and so was written either before or shortly after 612. The book also mentions the fall of the Egyptian city of Thebes (Nah 3:8), which took place in 663 B.C.E. Thus, Nahum was written sometime after 663 but before or immediately after 612.

Other historical facts make it possible to narrow down an even more specific, probable date for Nahum's prophecies. The Assyrian Empire, of which Nineveh was the capital, began to disintegrate after the death of King Ashurbanipal in 627. Assyria's closest rival, Babylon, produced a new, aggressive ruler in the form of Nabopolassar in 625. Then Assyria's older capital, Asshur, fell in 614. With each of these events, the hope and expectation of Nineveh's fall would have become more intense. While it is impossible to know for certain, it seems likely that Nahum would have been written quite close to Nineveh's fall, maybe after the demise of Asshur, when it became apparent that Nineveh's end was imminent.

Perhaps more important than the precise date of Nahum are the background and environment that occasioned it. The Assyrian Empire had dominated the ancient Near East for nearly a century and a half. The measures that the Assyrians employed in warfare and in the deportation of captives were ruthlessly and cruelly oppressive. Among their victims, the Assyrians counted the kingdom of Israel, which was destroyed in 721 B.C.E. Many of those fortunate enough to escape capture fled to Judah, which survived in part because of its proximity to Egypt. Even Judah, however, was forced to be a vassal to Assyria for about a century. The oracles in prophetic books like Amos that describe destruction by a foreign invader illustrate the level of fear inspired by the Assyrians. Nineveh's fall, therefore, meant the end of a long-dreaded oppressor and must have been celebrated throughout the ancient Near East.

INTERPRETATION

Although it does not use the expression, the book of Nahum epitomizes the idea behind the "Day of Yahweh." Its opening chapter depicts the coming of Yahweh as the divine warrior. As in the oracles against the nations in other prophetic books, Yahweh's coming is against Israel's enemies. He comes as an "avenging God" (Nah 1:2), taking vengeance on Assyria for its oppression of Israel and Judah. Unlike other prophetic books, Nahum contains no condemnation of Israel or Judah. The Day of Yahweh in Nahum is a day of punishment for Nineveh but a day of salvation for Judah.

Nahum offers a theological explanation of historical events. Its main theological principle is that Yahweh is in control of world history. The book also seems to espouse the idea that Yahweh punishes cruelty and oppression, at least against his own people. Yahweh acts through human agency. Thus, the attacks on Nineveh, though carried out by humans, were actually Yahweh's. Yahweh is sovereign; whatever happens in the world is according to his will and is actually his doing.

HABAKKUK

Less is known about Habakkuk than about any other prophet in the Bible. The barest details, such as his father's name or the place where he was from, which are supplied for most other prophets, are lacking for Habakkuk. Even the meaning of his name remains uncertain. It has been related to the Hebrew word for "embrace" as well as to the Akkadian name of a kind of plant. Plenty of other unknowns also surround the prophetic book that bears his name, making Habakkuk one of the most challenging books in the Bible to study.

CONTENT

The book of Habakkuk may be (and has been) divided in different ways. The headings in the book divide it into two large sections: an oracle (1:1), which encompasses the first two chapters, and a prayer (3:1) in the third chapter. However, the first two chapters contain two distinct sections: a dialogue between the prophet and God (1:2–2:4) and a series of woes (2:5-20).

The dialogue consists of two complaints about injustice and oppression (1:2-4, 12-17), each followed by a divine response (1:5-11; 2:1-4). The first response refers to God's rousing the Chaldeans, or Babylonians, as the instrument of his retribution. The second complaint seems to protest God's response by pointing out that the Babylonians themselves are oppressive and thus part of the problem rather than the solution. The woes emanate from the nations and people subjected by the Babylonians and taunt them.

The prayer of Habakkuk is a psalm that uses divine warrior imagery to praise God's great deeds in the past. It begins with a plea that God exhibit his power on behalf of his people as in the past (3:2). This is followed by descriptions of the march of the divine warrior (3:3-6) and of his victory over enemies, especially the mythical god Sea (7-15).

GROWTH

While there are certain themes shared by the different parts of Habakkuk, those parts are distinct enough to suggest that the book may not originally have been written as a unit. The poem in chapter 3, in particular, may have been added to the materials in the first two chapters. That does not necessarily mean that the poem was written later than the "oracle." It may be an older poem that was attached because it seemed to supply an appropriate response to the issues raised in the foregoing material, especially the complaints. The poem expresses confidence that Yahweh will save his people (v. 13), thereby confirming the trust of the righteous in God's power to execute justice.

CONTEXT

The general historical context of Habakkuk is evident from Yahweh's statement in 1:6: "For I am rousing the Chaldeans." "Chaldea" is a term used in the Bible for Babylonia. More precisely, "Chaldeans" refers to the Neo-Babylonian Empire, which arose with the fall of Nineveh in 612 B.C.E. and lasted until its conquest by the Persians in 539. Habakkuk's reference to God "rousing" the Chaldeans indicates that its oracles were delivered near the time of the rise of the Neo-Babylonians, roughly in the last quarter of the seventh century B.C.E. Habakkuk, therefore, was a contemporary of Nahum's, and their books were apparently compiled at around the same time.

Nevertheless, the exact setting of Habakkuk is uncertain. The different sections of the book may have been occasioned by different circumstances. The rise of Babylon may have initially been viewed with hope and gratitude by people in Judah, since it meant the end of Assyrian oppression. But the hope soon faded. King Josiah of Judah was killed in battle in 609 when he tried to prevent the Egyptians from coming to the aid of Assyria against the Babylonians. Babylon defeated Egypt in 605 and shortly thereafter became Judah's overlord. When the king of Judah (Jehoiakim) later rebelled against Babylon, the Babylonians captured Jerusalem (597) and a decade later destroyed it (586). The book of

Habakkuk was written in the context of these events and both raises and responds to questions about God's justice and the role of the Babylonians in the divine plan.

INTERPRETATION

The major concern of Habakkuk is the question of God's justice in the light of the events of the late seventh and early sixth centuries in Judah. The book's overall message is most clearly expressed by the psalm in chapter 3. It is that the people of Judah should place their hope and trust in the power of Yahweh, who has saved and guided Israel in the past. This message is also summed up nicely in Hab 2:4: "The righteous live by their faith."

The major interpretive question in the book has to do with the function of the Chaldeans. Are they the oppressors of Judah, as they appear to be in most of the book, or are they the agent through whom God punishes the oppressors, as the statement about God rousing them (1:6) implies? Most interpreters do indeed see the Chaldeans as the problem—that is, the oppressors. The reference to God rousing them may be explained as part of an intensification of the complaint about the nations in 1:2-4. The Chaldeans may defeat other oppressors, but then they themselves become the epitome of oppression. The series of woes against people who accumulate wealth at the expense of others (2:5-20), then, is probably not concerned with evildoers within Judah but with Babylon, as suggested by the international context. Judah as a nation is the righteous victim.

ZEPHANIAH

While nothing is known about Zephaniah outside of the genealogy for him (1:1), that genealogy is suggestive because of two features: it is unusually long for the introduction to a prophetic book, and it traces Zephaniah's roots back to Hezekiah. Although it is not specified, this Hezekiah may have been the king who ruled Judah at the transition from the eighth to the seventh century (714–687). This possibility is all the more likely since Hezekiah is not a common name in the Bible. Zephaniah, then, may have been a member of the royal family. The fact that he was clearly from Jerusalem and criticized the political and religious status quo in the city fits well with this possible background.

CONTENT

The book of Zephaniah follows a typical pattern in prophetic books with a series of judgment oracles (1:2–3:8) followed by salvation oracles (3:9-20). The judgment oracles begin with an apocalyptic vision of universal judgment, which is reminiscent of the flood story in Genesis in its reversal of creation (1:2-3). These oracles then focus on the Day of Yahweh as a day of punishment, especially for Judah and Jerusalem because of the worship of other gods (1:4–2:3). Next comes a collection of oracles against other nations (Philistines, Moab, Ethiopia, and Assyria) in 2:4-15, followed by another oracle against Jerusalem (3:1-8). In much the same way, the salvation oracles begin with the nations (3:9-10) and then focus on Jerusalem (Zion).

GROWTH

Most of the book of Zephaniah fits with the late seventh century, near the end of Judah's existence as an independent kingdom. As indicated by its content, the book complains about the behavior of officials and priests. There are, however, some portions of the book that reflect a setting at least a century later, after the Babylonian exile.

This is especially true of the book's last passage (3:14-20). The statement that Yahweh has taken away Jerusalem's judgments (3:15) suggests that the exile is over. The statement is similar to Second Isaiah's declaration that Jerusalem has served its term and paid its penalty (Isa 40:2), and the cry to Jerusalem to sing and exult is similar to those of other postexilic prophets and may have been borrowed from them (Zech 2:10 [Hebrew 2:15]; 9:9; Isa 65:18). The final verse in the book (3:20) speaks of restoring the people of Judah and bringing them home from exile, presupposing at least the beginning of the exile and anticipating its end. Thus, much like the book of Amos, the concluding passage of Zephaniah is a later addition to the oracles that make up the developing book.

CONTEXT

According to the first verse, Zephaniah prophesied during the reign of King Josiah of Judah (640–609). The book of 2 Kings depicts Josiah as one of the best kings of Judah and describes in detail the religious reforms that he carried out after the finding of the book of the law in his eighteenth year (2 Kgs 22–23). As we have seen, this book of the law was some form of Deuteronomy. Also, the supposed finding of a piece of writing prescribing a particular deed or course of action was a typical strategy among ancient Near Eastern kings for legitimating something that a king wished to do. Thus, Josiah's eighteenth year (622) was probably the date when an early form of Deuteronomy, written under him, was made known.

Deuteronomy was a work produced by a fairly broad coalition of the Jerusalem nobility—priests, prophets, officials, and landowners. Zephaniah may have been part of this coalition. The book sometimes uses language consistent with that in Deuteronomy and the Deuteronomistic History (e.g., "host of the heavens" in Zeph 1:5; cf. Deut 4:19; 17:3; 2 Kgs 17:16; 21:3; Jer 8:2). Zephaniah's condemnation of the

Jerusalemite hierarchy, especially in regard to such practices as the worship of the "host of the heavens" (sun, moon, stars), which are prohibited by Deuteronomy, suggests that he may have prophesied early in Josiah's reign before the king's reforms were fully developed or executed. Zephaniah may have been one of the leading proponents of reform whose oracles led to this watershed moment.

INTERPRETATION

As a member of the Jerusalem nobility, Zephaniah demonstrates familiarity with previous prophets and with other literary traditions, biblical and nonbiblical. As noted, the book's content—judgment followed by salvation oracles—is typical of prophets. The focus on the ills of Judah's society is in line with the concerns of eighth-century prophets like Isaiah (cf. Zeph 3:1-3; Isa 1:21-23), Micah (cf. Zeph 3:3-5; Mic 3:1-12), and Amos. Zephaniah also shares several themes with these earlier prophets, such as the Day of Yahweh as a day of punishment for Judah/Israel (especially in Amos) and the righteous remnant as the grounds for hope (especially in Isaiah, cf. Zeph 2:7, 9; 3:12-13).

Zephaniah's oracles against the nations seem to make use of treaty curses and thus suggest the prophet's familiarity with the language of international treaties. We have already seen how Zeph 1:2-3 plays upon the story of the flood as it describes all creation being "swept away." These verses represent the reversal of creation, as the destruction of humans, animals, birds, and fish is the opposite of the created order in Gen 1:20-26.

We have also seen that the final oracles of Zephaniah, which are likely secondary, make use of motifs from Second Isaiah, such as the rejoicing of Judah and Jerusalem (Zion) and the conversion of the Gentiles to acceptance of Yahweh's supremacy. It is worth pointing out that Zephaniah's oracles may have served as a source and model for later prophets. For instance, Ezekiel (22:25-28) appears to develop Zephaniah's metaphor of the officials in Jerusalem as lions and wolves (Zeph 3:1-5) and of Yahweh's wrath and indignation being poured out like fire on the nations (Ezek 22:31; Zeph 3:8).

In short, Zephaniah stands firmly in the stream of prophetic tradition within the Bible both in its interpretation of previous prophetic works and in serving as a model for later prophets. Zephaniah was well suited for this dual role because of its setting in the latter half of the seventh century, between "classical" eighth-century prophecy and later exilic and postexilic prophecy. The prophet Zephaniah may be one of the most overlooked and unheralded characters of the Bible. If he did help to spark Josiah's reform and the composition of Deuteronomy by his oracles, he was an important figure indeed, and his contribution can hardly be overestimated.

CHAPTER 22

THE EXILIC PROPHETS: JEREMIAH

Jeremiah is the second of the Major Prophets, following Isaiah. But Jeremiah prophesied over a century later than the original Isaiah. Jeremiah's career coincided with and was focused on the tumultuous final years of the kingdom of Judah and the beginning of the Babylonian exile in 586 B.C.E.

CONTENT

The book of the prophet Jeremiah has posed some unique challenges to commentators. Many have called attention to the disorganized nature of its contents and the lack of a clear structure. The chronological relationships among the various sections are often not apparent, creating the impression of a random, haphazard collection of disparate traditions. Scholars have proposed many different ways of trying to make sense of the book's organization and impose order on its seeming chaos. Some of these efforts have been more widely accepted than others, but all agree that one should not read Jeremiah expecting to find an orderly, cohesive work that logically flows from point to point. It is a book whose perspective, mood, and message are constantly shifting.

A wide range of writing styles and genres are found within the fifty-two chapters of Jeremiah. Like the other prophetic books, it contains many oracles communicating God's message to particular individuals and groups. Other literary forms commonly found in the text include biography, autobiography, sermons, and liturgical compositions that are similar to the psalms found in the Hebrew Bible. Because much of this material relates directly to the prophet Jeremiah, we know more about his personal life than we do about any of the other writing prophets. But scholars disagree over how these biographical sections should be interpreted and what they can tell us about the man himself.

Particular passages in Jeremiah are directed to different audiences: kings, priests, the people of Judah, foreign powers, prophets, even God. The book as a whole is addressed to a people who are confronting the exile. One cannot understand the book of Jeremiah without an appreciation of the significance and import of the events leading up to and following 586 B.C.E., when the Babylonians destroyed Jerusalem and the kingdom of Judah came to an end. The text clearly indicates that Jeremiah began his prophetic career during the last quarter of the seventh century B.C.E. and that he was among those who fled to Egypt after the Babylonian invasion, so that crisis point is the background against which the book should be read and interpreted.

It is impossible to briefly summarize the message of a book as complex as Jeremiah. The prophet attempts to explain that the coming destruction is a necessary result of the sin of Judah, but because there is some cause for hope it is not the final word on God's relationship with the people. He draws on Israelite traditions that are associated with creation, the patriarchs, Moses, kingship, Deuteronomy, Psalms, and Wisdom literature to both warn and encourage his audience.

The poetry makes rich use of standard conventions like metaphor and simile. Israel is described as a choice vine (2:21), an animal in heat (2:23-24), and a woman in childbirth (4:30-31). The enemy is like the roaring sea (6:23) and "their quiver is like an open tomb" (5:16). This rich imagery, combined with an effective use of such techniques as repetition, hyperbole, irony, and wordplay, enhance and strengthen the poetry of Jeremiah.

As noted above, the prose sections often give information about the prophet's life. Sometimes this personal information is presented in the first person, as when Jeremiah describes a vision he receives of two baskets of figs, one representing the people who go into exile and the other symbolizing those who stay (24:1-10). Elsewhere, it is given in the third person, and many scholars think this material may come from Baruch, who served as Jeremiah's assistant and scribe (36:4-8). The passage about Baruch's recording activity in chapter 36 has sometimes been cited as a report of how the book of Jeremiah first came to be written down. This is far from certain and many scholars question whether the book contains any accurate information on the prophet's life and work.

In studying Jeremiah, scholars have often preferred to treat the material in blocks of chapters that appear to form thematic or structural units. One such unit is chapters 1–20, which are set off by the phrases "before I formed you in the womb I knew you" (1:5) and "why did I come forth from the womb to see toil and sorrow" (20:18), an inclusio that unites this part of the book. This first section, like the rest of Jeremiah a combination of poetry and prose, begins with the prophet's call (1:4-19) and introduces some of the central themes of the book like the need to return to following the covenant and warnings about the coming destruction. Even though the enemy from the north (1:14) is never identified, there is no doubt that Babylon is meant.

Chapters 24–45 are a section of primarily prose material that comes from a variety of times and contexts, reinforcing the impression that the book lacks structure and organization. The biographical information on the prophet in this section covers the years 609–604, 597–594, and the period right around the fall of Jerusalem in 586. Many believe Baruch is the source of this material. One of the most frequently studied units of this section is chapters 30–32, sometimes referred to as the "Book of Consolation," in which Jeremiah addresses the themes of hope and the eventual restoration of the land. It contains the description of the new covenant God will make with Judah and Israel, one of the most famous passages in the book of Jeremiah (31:31-34).

Another very important part of this section is the Temple Sermon of 26:1-24, which is reported in a somewhat different form in 7:1-15. At God's command, the prophet goes to the temple in Jerusalem and urges the people of Judah to follow the law of God if they wish to avoid destruction at the hands of the Babylonians. A hearing ensues in which the priests and prophets call for Jeremiah's death, but he is eventually found innocent because he was merely following God's command to prophesy. The text raises some important questions about the nature of true prophecy and the role of prophets in Israelite society.

A series of oracles against nine foreign nations, similar to those in Isaiah 13–23 and Amos 1–2, is found in chapters 46–51. These oracles probably circulated independently prior to being added to the book, and scholars disagree over whether Jeremiah is their author.

A final group of passages that deserve some mention are the "confessions of Jeremiah." In six places that are unique in the prophetic writings Jeremiah complains about some aspect of his work as a spokesperson for God or about how he is being treated by his contemporaries (11:18–12:6; 15:10-21; 17:14-18; 18:18-23; 20:7-13; 20:14-18). The language of these laments is quite personal and full of raw emotion, leading some commentators to conclude that the confessions can serve as an entrée into the mind of the prophet. Others are uncertain of the passages' authorship and therefore less convinced that they give us any insight into Jeremiah's psyche or personality. Regardless of their origin, they offer a rare example in the Hebrew Bible of a glimpse into the personal anguish that is part of a prophet's life.

> Heal me, O LORD, and I shall be healed;
> save me, and I shall be saved;
> for you are my praise.

See how they say to me,
  "Where is the word of the LORD?
  Let it come!"
But I have not run away from being a shepherd in your service,
  nor have I desired the fatal day.
You know what came from my lips;
  it was before your face.
Do not become a terror to me;
  you are my refuge in the day of disaster;
Let my persecutors be shamed,
  but do not let me be shamed;
let them be dismayed,
  but do not let me be dismayed;
bring on them the day of disaster;
  destroy them with double destruction! (17:14-18)

GROWTH

The variety of literary forms contained in Jeremiah reminds us that, like most other books of the Hebrew Bible, the work evolved and developed over time. Remarkably, the book contains a reference to this growth and expansion when it describes what Jeremiah has Baruch do after King Jehoiakim destroys a scroll upon which God's message to Jeremiah has been written. "Then Jeremiah took another scroll and gave it to the secretary Baruch son of Neriah, who wrote on it at Jeremiah's dictation all the words of the scroll that King Jehoiakim of Judah had burned in the fire; and many similar words were added to them" (36:32). We should not identify this scroll with the current book of Jeremiah, but the reference to Baruch adding to its contents is an acknowledgement of the evolving nature of the prophetic message.

A more stunning indication of the growth of the Jeremiah tradition is given when the Hebrew version of the book, the Masoretic Text (MT), is compared to the Greek Septuagint (LXX). The usual trend is for the LXX to be longer than the MT, but in the case of Jeremiah it is about one-eighth shorter than the Hebrew text. In addition, after 25:13 the order of the two versions differs in some significant ways. This has led to many questions regarding the possible reasons for these differences and which of the two textual traditions is the older or superior.

Many of the differences are minor changes. For example, the MT has certain words or phrases like "thus says the LORD" that are not found in the LXX. Elsewhere, the Hebrew text attaches the designation "the prophet" to Jeremiah's name and gives titles to other people like "the king" that are missing in the Greek translation. In other places longer passages contained in the MT are not present in the LXX. Although they are much less common, a few passages in the LXX do not have equivalents in the Hebrew.

A significant shift occurs in the order of the contents of the two versions. The most important difference is seen with the oracles against the foreign nations that are found in chapters 46–51 of the MT. The LXX places these oracles right after 25:13a so that they run from 25:14 to 31:44. For a number of reasons, most scholars believe the LXX preserves the original order. Referring to Babylon in 25:13a, God says, "I will bring upon that land all the words that I have uttered against it, everything written in this book." But up to this point nothing has been stated about Babylon's punishment. In the LXX order, the oracles against the foreign nations—including Babylon—come right after this, indicating what the punishment will entail. In the MT this information is still more than twenty chapters away.

The second half of 25:13 in the MT reads, "which Jeremiah prophesied against all the nations," a phrase that also does not fit the context since the prophet has not yet spoken against the nations. These words are found in chapter 32 of the LXX, after the oracles against the nations, an arrangement that flows more smoothly and is therefore the likely original. The MT also adds 25:14, which introduces the theme of punishing the nations, as a way of smoothing the transition to what follows. This verse is not present in the Greek version because the oracles against the nations follow immediately upon 25:13a and there is no abrupt shift of topic.

The order of the oracles is also somewhat different in the two texts, with the placement of the one against Babylon being the most interesting variation. In the LXX Babylon is located at the center of the list, whereas in the MT, which adopts a western movement from nation to nation, it is last in the series. In either ordering an argument can be made for Babylon being the focal point as either the central element of the Greek version or the culminating point of the Hebrew text.

When confronted with differences like these between the LXX and the MT, it used to be that the common tendency among Hebrew Bible scholars was to view the Hebrew text as the more trustworthy and reliable version of the two. There has been a rethinking of this position in recent times, and the book of Jeremiah has played an important role in this shift of attitudes. Scholars are now more cautious about assuming that the MT is the more original version by default. In this case, as we have seen, a consideration of the literary advantages of the LXX's placement of the oracles against the nations suggests it preserves the original order.

Evidence from the Dead Sea Scrolls has also confirmed the importance of the LXX Jeremiah text. Three partial manuscripts of Jeremiah were among the finds in cave 4. Of the two oldest of these manuscripts, one reflects the MT version and the other agrees with the LXX. In other words, two different forms of the book of Jeremiah were available to the community at Qumran. This has led to the theory that by the second century B.C.E. a shorter Hebrew text (different from the Hebrew text that led to the MT) existed that was translated into Greek to be used by some Jewish communities.

The two forms of the book of Jeremiah that are reflected in the MT and the LXX developed in separate areas independently of each other. It would therefore not be correct to give primacy to the MT and say that the LXX is nothing more than a shortened version of it that rearranged the order in places. The relationship between the two is something that must be studied carefully, and their coexistence is a clear indicator of the complex way the Hebrew Bible evolved and took shape.

CONTEXT

Two critical aspects of the context within which Jeremiah functioned as a prophet were the rise of Babylon and the religious reform of King Josiah of Judah (640–609 B.C.E.). Babylon became the major power in the ancient Near East in the late seventh/early sixth centuries B.C.E. Assyria and Babylon had been battling for dominance for the twenty years prior to the latter's emergence as victor in 609. This situation of international rivalry and instability allowed Josiah to introduce and implement a policy that was meant to bring the people of Judah back to proper worship of God.

According to 1:2, Jeremiah was called to be a prophet in 627, the thirteenth year of Josiah's reign. He became an ardent supporter of the reform the king was calling for, and even after Josiah's untimely death in 609 Jeremiah continued to urge the people to return to God. Egypt tried to come to Assyria's assistance against Babylon in 609, but Pharaoh Neco was delayed when he met the forces of Josiah at Megiddo. Josiah lost his life in the battle, and Egypt took control of Judah until 605, when King Nebuchadnezzar of Babylon defeated Egypt at Carchemish on the Euphrates River, a battle that is mentioned in 46:2.

Egypt regained control of Judah in 601, when it forced Babylon to retreat. This caused Jehoiakim son of Josiah (608–598) to declare independence from Babylon, who then returned in force with a coalition of Judah's neighbors that defeated it in 598. Zedekiah (597–586) was then set up as a puppet ruler for a ten-year period full of internal problems and corruption.

Many in Judah considered Jehoiachin, who ruled briefly in 597 before being exiled to Babylon, to be the legitimate king who should have been on the throne in Zedekiah's place. This led to public unrest and the return of Babylon in 589 to maintain control over the situation. In 586 the kingdom of Judah came to an end when the Babylonians returned one final time to take over Jerusalem, destroy the temple, and deport the leading citizens to Babylon. The tragic outcome is revealed to Zedekiah in the form of a message from God. "I am going to give this city into the hand of the king of Babylon, and he shall burn it with fire. And you yourself shall not escape from his hand, but shall surely be captured and handed over to him; you shall see the king of Babylon eye to eye and speak with him face to face; and you shall go to Babylon" (34:2-3).

The Lachish letters, found in the ruins of a Judean military installation, offer another perspective on these events. The letters record a series of exchanges between personnel at the fort and their superiors that were written while Jerusalem and the surrounding area were under attack by the Babylonians for the final time. The letters refer to the signal fires of Lachish and Azekah as being the only ones still burning, indicating that all the other military installations had been abandoned or destroyed by the advancing Babylonians. The references to these two military posts are a poignant corroboration of the information given in 34:6-7. "Then the prophet Jeremiah spoke all these words to Zedekiah king of Judah, in Jerusalem, when the army of the king of Babylon was fighting against Jerusalem and against all the cities of Judah that were left, Lachish and Azekah, for these were the only fortified cities of Judah that remained." Soon after the destruction of Jerusalem Jeremiah fled to Egypt, never to be heard from again.

> May Yahweh cause my lord to hear this very day tidings of good! And now according to everything that my lord hath written, so hath thy servant done; I have written on the door according to all that my lord hath written to me. And with respect to what my lord hath written about the matter of Beth-haraphid, there is no one there.
>
> And as for Semachiah, Shemaiah hath taken him and hath brought him up to the city. And as for thy servant, I am not sending anyone thither [today(?), but I will send] tomorrow morning.
>
> And let (my lord) know that we are watching for the signals of Lachish, according to all the indications which my lord hath given, for we cannot see Azekah.

Excerpt from Lachish letter 4.

The second element of context important for understanding the book of Jeremiah concerns King Josiah's rule. A description of the religious reform initiated by Josiah, discussed in an earlier chapter, is found in 2 Kings 22–23. According to that account, in the course of a temple renovation that had been ordered by the king a copy of the book of the law was found. The identity of this book has been a subject of interest among Hebrew

Bible scholars for a long time, and many have argued that it may have been some portion or form of the book of Deuteronomy. Upon hearing its contents and realizing that their ancestors had strayed from God, Josiah tore his garments and requested that members of his court consult the Lord. They went to Huldah, a prophetess in Jerusalem, who confirmed Josiah's fears. She announced that because they had followed other gods the people would be destroyed and their land would be taken from them.

Josiah immediately went about the task of removing every vestige of false worship. He ordered the destruction of all altars to Baal and other gods, dismantled the shrines known as the "high places" and the cultic systems associated with them, and banished their religious personnel from Judah and Samaria. Among the places Josiah destroyed was the altar at Bethel that had been set up by his predecessor Jeroboam after the kingdom was divided. Josiah urged the people to rededicate themselves to God and led them in the most successful celebration of Passover since the days of the judges. The Deuteronomistic History evaluates his reign in glowing terms and considers him to be the most pious king to ever rule. "Before him there was no king like him, who turned to the LORD with all his heart, with all his soul, and with all his might, according to all the law of Moses; nor did any like him arise after him" (2 Kgs 23:25).

Another account of Josiah's reign is found in 2 Chronicles 34–35, which presents the same overall story but changes the order of events and consequently spreads the reform over a longer period of time. Both versions agree that the Passover he celebrated took place in the eighteenth year of his rule, which would be 622, or five years after Jeremiah's call to be a prophet. Jeremiah is never mentioned in connection with Josiah's reform in either 2 Kings or 2 Chronicles, but the dominant message of his book leaves no doubt that he and Josiah were trying to achieve the same thing. Their shared vision on matters like idolatry indicates that the king's program of renewal was a crucial part of the prophet's context. "Has a nation changed its gods, even though they are no gods? But my people have changed their glory for something that does not profit. Be appalled, O heavens, at this, be shocked, be utterly desolate, says the LORD, for my people have committed two evils: they have forsaken me, the fountain of living water, and dug out cisterns for themselves, cracked cisterns that can hold no water" (2:11-13).

INTERPRETATION

It has already been noted that the thirteenth year of King Josiah's reign is considered to be the starting point of Jeremiah's career as a prophet. The first two verses of the book support this view. "The words of Jeremiah son of Hilkiah, of the priests who were in Anathoth in the land of Benjamin, to whom the word of the LORD came in the days of King Josiah son of Amon of Judah, in the thirteenth year of his reign." This would place Jeremiah's call to be a prophet, which follows immediately after these verses, in the year 627.

It would also mean that Jeremiah had a career that spanned some forty years, until the destruction of Jerusalem in 586. By the fifth year of that career Josiah's reform was in full swing. In 622 the book of the law had already been rediscovered in the temple and Josiah led the people in a major celebration of Passover. The king would live for another thirteen years after that, meaning he was alive and actively promoting a return to Yahweh during the first eighteen years of Jeremiah's prophetic career.

Curiously, there are no references to these events in the book of Jeremiah. In quite a few places Josiah's name is mentioned, but most of these are part of a formulaic way of referring to kings like "Jehoiakim, son of Josiah." In 3:6 a revelation from God to the prophet is dated to the days of Josiah, but there are no descriptions, accounts, or even oblique references to the king's reform. Many scholars believe the first six chapters of the book are from the earlier part of Jeremiah's career, and yet none of this material can be unambiguously assigned to Josiah's reign. Even the passage dated to Josiah's days in 3:6-10 does not necessarily relate to his period because it is a general condemnation of the idolatry of Israel and Judah.

The lack of any mention of Josiah is strange in light of the fact that the message Jeremiah preached was very much in line with the king's agenda. Many of the themes about which the prophet is most passionate—like keeping the covenant and obeying God's laws and statutes—are central to the message of Deuteronomy that was at the heart of Josiah's program. A description of Josiah's efforts at reform or some comments on their common interests to reestablish proper worship would do much to validate Jeremiah's message and strengthen its credibility. But such things are missing. This is in marked contrast to later sections of the book, where many messages are dated to the reign of a particular ruler, and there are reports of the prophet's personal interactions with kings (25:1; 27:1; 28:1; 38:14). Why does Jeremiah fail to mention Josiah and his reform?

It has been suggested that the reason for this is that Jeremiah was not functioning as a prophet when Josiah was king. According to this theory, the mention of the thirteenth year of Josiah's reign in 1:2 is a reference to the birth of the prophet, not his call. By that reckoning, Jeremiah was only five years old during the Passover celebrated by Josiah and eighteen years old when the king died. The first words from God to the prophet that are recorded in the book state, "Before I formed you in the womb I knew you, and before you were born I consecrated you; I appointed you a prophet to the nations" (1:5). This can be interpreted to mean that Jeremiah had been chosen to be a prophet prior to his birth and the statement in 1:2 that the word of the Lord came to him in the thirteenth year of Josiah's rule is in reference to that divine choice. The comment that the word of the Lord came to him again during the time of Josiah's son Jehoiakim until the exile is then taken as a reference to his "official" call and acceptance of that role.

An advantage of this reading is that it explains why Jeremiah does not mention Josiah's reform or interact with him—the king had died by the time he began his prophetic career. It also makes sense of the curious juxtaposition of the word of the Lord coming to Jeremiah in verse 2 during Josiah's time and then coming again immediately after it in verse 3 during the reign of his son. But there are some shortcomings to this interpretation. The text does not explicitly state that Jeremiah's birth is what is meant, and so one has to read more into the text than is there. Another difficulty is the other reference to Josiah's thirteenth year in 25:3, which indicates that Jeremiah has been speaking as a prophet since that time, something that would require him to be functioning as a prophet even as a young child. "For twenty-three years, from the thirteenth year of King Josiah son of Amon of Judah, to this day, the word of the LORD has come to me, and I have spoken persistently to you, but you have not listened."

Given these problems with the alternative interpretation, it is best to take the position that Jeremiah's prophetic career began in 627 while Josiah was king and, for unknown reasons, the book does not make explicit mention of the religious reform endorsed by the king during the first eighteen years of Jeremiah's prophetic career. The absence of such detail might have been a choice of the prophet himself, or it could be the result of later editorial work on the book. Despite the lack of explicit mention of it, though, there is no doubt that Jeremiah agreed with and was influenced by the reform work undertaken by King Josiah in the first half of his prophetic career.

CHAPTER 23

THE EXILIC PROPHETS: EZEKIEL

Ezekiel, son of Buzi, was a priest and prophet who lived during the time of the Babylonian exile. The work bearing his name is the last of the three major prophetic books, and it possesses a clearer organizational structure than either Isaiah or Jeremiah.

CONTENT

The book of Ezekiel is neatly divided into three sections that are chronologically ordered and trace the development of Ezekiel's prophetic career as his message shifted from one of warning about the impending disaster to one of hope for the future.

Chapters 1 through 24 contain oracles of judgment against Israel that explain why God brought an end to Jerusalem and the kingship. Oracles against the foreign nations follow in chapters 25 through 32, which offer a hopeful message by predicting the downfall of Israel's enemies in anticipation of its restoration. The third section, chapters 33 through 48, comprises oracles of salvation directed toward Israel. These texts describe the reestablishment of Israel, including the redistribution of the land and the rebuilding of the temple in Jerusalem (chs. 40–48). The movement from oracles of judgment to oracles of restoration communicates an unambiguous message to the people of Israel: the destruction of their temple and the loss of their land is only a temporary punishment for their sins against God. These oracles are frequently supplemented by poems, proverbs, and parables that combine to create a unique style of preaching and prophecy.

One of the distinctive features of the book of Ezekiel is a series of precise dates throughout the work that identify when oracles were delivered and events occurred. The one found at 24:1 is typical of the pattern. "In the ninth year, in the tenth month, on the tenth day of the month, the word of the LORD came to me" (see also 1:2; 3:16; 8:1; 20:1; 33:21; 40:1). There is a similar set of dates in the second section of the book containing the oracles against foreign nations (26:1; 29:1; 29:17; 30:20; 31:1; 32:1; 32:17). Ezekiel states that the year designations are in reference to the exile of King Jehoiachin in 598 B.C.E. (1:2), so these time indicators allow us to date sections of the work with great precision. For example, his call to be a prophet is dated to the fifth year of Jehoiachin's exile, or 593. The dating formulas throughout the book are listed in chronological order except for the one in 29:17, which is an oracle against Egypt that is dated to the twenty-seventh year, or 571. Because this is the latest date given in the book, it is commonly held that Ezekiel's prophetic career spanned the years 593 to 571.

As a priest Ezekiel insisted that the people remain faithful to God and the covenant whether they were in Israel or, like him, in exile. Priestly concerns can be seen in a number of the themes that the prophet returns to throughout the book. He stresses the need for them to remain pure and free of defilement. "Thus says the Lord GOD: Will you defile yourselves after the manner of your ancestors and go astray after their detestable things?" (20:30). He warns them about the dangers of idol worship. "Thus says the Lord GOD: Any of those of the house of Israel who take their idols into their hearts and place their iniquity as a stumbling block before them, and yet come to the prophet—I the LORD will answer those who come with the multitude of their idols" (14:4). Ezekiel urges them to instead follow the law and keep the Sabbath. "Its priests have done violence to my teaching and have profaned my holy things; they have made no distinction between the holy and the common, neither have they taught the difference between the unclean and the clean, and they have disregarded my sabbaths, so that I am profaned among them" (22:26).

In addition to his interest in these themes, Ezekiel's concern for the temple—most dramatically seen in his detailed vision of it being rebuilt in chapters 40 to 47—is evidence of his priestly identity. No other prophet spends as much time addressing cultic issues or comforting his audience with the prospect of a new temple every bit as grand as its predecessor. Ezekiel's familiarity with the priestly tradition also accounts for the similarities that have been noted between his book and the Holiness Code of Leviticus 17–26. This collection of legal material that centers on sacrifice and cultic worship was not written down until the end of the exile, but the connections between it and Ezekiel's book show his acquaintance with priestly circles.

A set of visions that the prophet receives is found throughout the book and, like the dating formulas, give a sense of structure and unity to the work. Some of these are visions of the presence of God, which helps to underscore the close personal relationship Ezekiel has as a priest with God. The first of these is found in the book's first three chapters, which describe his call to be a prophet. Similar call narratives are found in Isaiah 6 and Jeremiah 1, but Ezekiel's is unique due to its length and the very unusual, even bizarre, nature of the vision he receives. This text will be discussed more fully below, but for now it should be noted that it establishes a level of intimacy between the prophet and God that continues throughout the book. Chapters 8 through 11 describe a series of visions Ezekiel receives at the temple in Jerusalem when he is miraculously transported from Babylon by "the hand of the Lord GOD." He witnesses the idolatry of the people and an enactment of the punishment they will receive for their sins, culminating in the departure of the glory of the Lord from the temple.

A third vision of the presence of God—one that reverses the previous one—is found in chapter 43. The Lord's glory returns through the same gate it left from and once again takes up residence in the newly rebuilt temple. God will remain with them as long as the people have learned from their mistakes and reject their sinful ways. "Now let them put away their idolatry and the corpses of their kings far from me, and I will reside among them forever" (43:9). Ezekiel receives other visions like the famous description in chapter 37 of the dry bones coming back to life, symbolizing the return of the people from exile. But these three visions of the divine presence capture the three-part message of the entire book: (1) a relationship with God has been established and violated; (2) God rejects the people, symbolized by the empty, destroyed temple; (3) God reclaims the people, symbolized by the rebuilt, occupied temple.

Some of the other characteristic features of Ezekiel help to reinforce the book's central themes. The prophet is typically addressed by God as "mortal" (literally, "son of man"), a title that stresses his humanity and total dependence on the deity. Certain formulaic sayings like "I, the LORD, have spoken . . . ," "as I live . . . ," and "the oracle of the LORD . . ." appear with great frequency. This is unique within the prophetic corpus and serves to highlight the ongoing and intimate communication that is taking place between God and Ezekiel. The expression "that (or then) you (or they) many shall know that I am the LORD" is found more than seventy times in the book (see, for example, 6:7, 10, 14). This formula conveys God's self-revelation and supreme authority. Finally, the references to the "glory of the LORD" (1:28; 3:23; 8:4; 10:4; 11:22-23; 43:1-5) express the power and majesty of God that fills the temple and invigorates the people.

GROWTH

The book's tight organization and its consistent use of the dating formulas led many early scholars to conclude that Ezekiel is a unified whole that does not show evidence of editorial activity. That view changed dramatically in the first half of the twentieth century when there were many attempts to argue that very little of the work comes from the prophet Ezekiel himself. Some claimed that as little as twenty percent of the book should be traced directly to him. Various dates were given for sections of the book, some as early as the late eighth/early seventh centuries B.C.E. and some as late as the third century B.C.E.

By World War II opinions began to swing the other way as more of the book was dated to the prophet's time. The current consensus sees it as a product of Ezekiel's exilic context that shows signs of later editorial work. For example, it is likely that the material in chapters 40–48 describing the redistribution of the land and the rebuilding of the temple comes from a later time and was added to the prophet's original message.

The identity of those responsible for this editorial activity has been often discussed, and the issue has not been fully resolved. It could be that, as has been proposed for other prophets, a group of Ezekiel's disciples expanded and added to the work he passed on to them, resulting in the text we now have. Such a school would have been composed of others like him who were familiar with the priestly tradition and interpreted their context from that perspective.

The literary activity that shaped it is more obvious in the book of Ezekiel than in most other prophetic books. The clear three-part structure that organizes the work is the result of editorial work, not oral performance. In other words, the design of the book reflects the efforts of those who wrote it and is not due to the way the prophet Ezekiel went about delivering his message. Its form derives from its identity as a written work, not from the actual way the prophet communicated to his audience. At the same time, however, certain aspects of the book call attention to the oral deliverance upon which the written work is based. The frequent references to specific dates function in this way. Some oracles and events can be tied to an exact day in history. For example, Ezekiel's call occurred on the fifth day of the fourth month of the fifth year of King Jehoiachin's exile (1:1-2), which was July 31, 593 B.C.E. This ability to locate the text in specific moments grounds it in the prophet's daily life and is a constant reminder that his message is always linked to a particular context.

The same can be said of the many prophetic actions performed by Ezekiel throughout the book. God frequently commands him to engage in certain activities that are meant to symbolize some aspect of his teaching. At his call he is told to eat a scroll as a way of internalizing the message he will preach (3:2). He is to lie on his left side for 390 days and then lie on his right side for 40 days to represent the numbers of years Israel and Judah will be punished (4:4-8). He is told to go out in public with his baggage and simulate the experience of a person in exile (12:1-7). These and his many other symbolic actions are an alternative way of conveying his message and warning the people. Scholars debate whether Ezekiel actually performed all these actions or if they are literary conventions. Either way, they add a representational aspect to the book that allows the reader to visualize the prophet's message in action.

Ezekiel's relationship to earlier prophetic traditions is an important issue, and certain connections between him and Elijah and Elisha (1 Kgs 17–19:21; 2 Kgs 1–8) can be noted. Parallels between his symbolic actions and some of the feats attributed to them can be overstated because their works typically have an element of the miraculous that is missing from his prophetic acts. More intriguing are the similarities that can be observed in how the "hand of the LORD" comes upon all three at key moments (1 Kgs 18:46; 2 Kgs 3:15; Ezek 1:3; 3:22; 37:1) and how they can be suddenly transported from one place to another (1 Kgs 18:12; 2 Kgs 2:11; Ezek 3:12-14; 8:1-3; 37:1).

His resemblance in these ways to the earlier ninth-century prophets is due to the fact that Ezekiel is the most charismatic and spirit-filled of all the writing prophets. But while certain aspects of his life share similarities with Elijah and Elisha, his message and life most closely cohere with those of the latter prophets, especially Jeremiah. Just as Ezekiel eats a scroll God gives him (Ezek 3:1-3), Jeremiah eats the words of God (Jer 15:16). Each prophet is strengthened and hardened to face the challenges to his authority that he will have to confront (Jer 1:18-19; Ezek 3:8-9). Both texts refer to Judah and Samaria as whoring sisters who chase after false gods (Jer 3:6-10; Ezek 23). Babylon is described in both as a foe from the north (Jer 1:13; Ezek 1:4). The two books even quote the same proverb about the children's teeth being set on edge because their parents ate sour grapes (Jer 31:29; Ezek 18:2).

It is unclear why these and other connections exist between Ezekiel and Jeremiah. They were contemporaries who were responding to many of the same issues and concerns, and it is conceivable that some form of Jeremiah's book might have been available to Ezekiel in Babylon. Ezekiel never acknowledges Jeremiah's existence, let alone claims familiarity with his message, but we know from the writings themselves that there was communication between the exiles in Babylon and those who remained behind in Jerusalem (Jer 29:24-32).

CONTEXT

Ezekiel was an exile in Babylon, where he spent his entire prophetic career. He probably lived in the Jewish settlement of Tel-abib, which was on a canal called the Chebar near the city of Nippur (3:5). The Babylonian king Nebuchadnezzar first invaded Jerusalem in 598 B.C.E., when the initial group of Judeans was taken into exile (2 Kgs 24:10-17). Because Ezekiel was already there in 593 (1:2), he was probably among the people who were sent to

Babylon in that first deportation. This suggests he may have been an important priest or the member of a prominent family, since these were among the first people the Babylonians would remove from conquered areas.

The book begins with a mention of "the thirtieth year" (1:1), which is generally held to be a reference to Ezekiel's age when he was called to be prophet. If that is the case, he was born sometime around 623 B.C.E., so he would have been a young boy when Babylon came to power, Josiah's reform efforts were introduced, and Jeremiah began his prophetic career.

Other than the fact that he was married and his wife died (24:15-18), virtually nothing is known about Ezekiel's personal life. His wife's death provided the opportunity for another of the prophet's symbolic actions. Ezekiel obeys God's order to not engage in any of the usual outward expressions of grief after his wife dies. When people ask him what his lack of mourning means, he explains to them that this will be their response to the invasion of Jerusalem and the death of their loved ones. They will "pine away in [their] iniquities and groan to one another" (24:23) and come to learn that God is the Lord. On this note of personal loss the first part of the book comes to an end. God tells Ezekiel to remain silent until Jerusalem falls, at which point he is to begin to preach a message of hope. The road to restoration begins immediately after this with the oracles against the nations in chapters 25–32.

Most of the book is dated to the years 593–585 B.C.E. During this period Zedekiah, the puppet king appointed by Babylon, was on the throne in Jerusalem, but events are consistently dated from the beginning of King Jehoiachin's exile in 598 (1:2). This suggests that Ezekiel considered Jehoiachin to be the legitimate king who might one day return to reclaim his rightful place.

With the possible exception of chapters 40–48, it does not seem likely that any sections of the book were composed toward the end of the exile. There are in fact some clues in the book that its final redaction took place quite some time before the return to the land. Babylon is never criticized or condemned for its actions, which suggests it was still firmly in power and not in danger of losing control as it eventually did with the shift to Persian rule in 539. In chapters 36 and 37 the prophet envisions the return from exile of not just Judah but also the northern kingdom of Israel. Such a development was considered possible in earlier periods but was most unlikely by the time of the return from exile. Contrary to what is predicted in 29:19-20, Egypt was never captured by Babylon, and the odds of such a thing happening would have grown more remote as time went on.

The conditions of life in exile continue to be debated by scholars. Forced relocation to another land undoubtedly resulted in deep psychological and emotional trauma. The spiritual and theological effects of the destruction of the temple in Jerusalem would have been equally devastating for some, and one of the main purposes of a work like Ezekiel was to respond to some of these concerns. Many people would have been tempted to assimilate into Babylonian culture, particularly as time went on and a return to Judah seemed less likely. Ezekiel urged the people to not forget who they were and where they came from. The vision of a restored Jerusalem and a new temple that closes the book provided them with a blueprint of what awaited them if they remained faithful.

Babylonian policy did not require that all deportees fully assimilate since exiled communities were allowed to keep their own language and religious practices. They were also permitted to establish a limited form of governance among themselves, and the book of Ezekiel contains evidence of this among the Jewish community at Tel-abib. In a number of places the prophet mentions that he received visits from the elders of Israel, who came to seek his advice. "In the seventh year, in the fifth month, on the tenth day of the month, certain elders of Israel came to consult the LORD, and sat down before me" (20:1; cf. 8:1; 14:1; 33:30-31). These occasional gatherings with the elders indicate that Ezekiel was an influential leader of the exile community whose input was sought out and valued.

INTERPRETATION

It has already been noted that the book contains descriptions of a number of visions received by Ezekiel (chs. 1–3; 8–11; 37; 40–47). These vision accounts comprise approximately one-third of the book, and the somewhat mystical, otherworldly effect they produce leaves its mark on the work as a whole. In each case, the prophet is transported to some other place by "the hand of the LORD" (1:3; 3:22; 8:1; 37:1; 40:1) and is allowed to witness something beyond the normal limits of human experience. At times these appear to be actual physical relocations—one even describes him being grabbed by the hair and carried through the air (8:3)—but the language of the accounts suggests it is better to view them as spiritual experiences that give the prophet supernatural insight and knowledge.

These ecstatic visions that seize Ezekiel contain very unusual and peculiar elements that caused some earlier commentators to question the prophet's physical health and mental stability. The combination of the "symptoms" described in the visions along with the muteness (3:24-27), paralysis (4:4-8), and other physiological irregularities that are associated with some of his prophetic actions led some to diagnose him as suffering from a physical ailment that resulted in seizures and hallucinations. Such interpretations do not pay sufficient attention to the literary nature of the work. As mentioned earlier, it was the process of writing and editing—

rather than the prophet's actual experiences—that shaped the form and content of the book. The use of strange and bizarre images and language was the author's way of trying to convey the uniqueness of the prophet's experiences and should not be taken as an accurate historical account.

The call narrative in chapters 1–3 typifies the complex, surreal nature of the visions. Whereas the call narratives of Isaiah (6:1-13) and Jeremiah (1:4-10) are brief, Ezekiel's extends over three chapters. All three prophetic calls contain the standard elements that are found in texts of this type: (1) a divine encounter in which God or a messenger appears to the prophet, (2) an introductory word to the prophet, (3) a commission in which the prophet's task or responsibility is identified, (4) an objection raised by the prophet about the commission, (5) a reassurance from God that responds to the objection, and (6) a sign to the prophet as proof of the legitimacy of the call. Sometimes, as in Isaiah's case, all six elements of the pattern are found, but it is not uncommon to have one or more of them missing. Ezekiel's call appears to lack a clear-cut objection from the prophet about the commission.

What distinguishes Ezekiel's call narrative is its length, which is due to the detailed description of the vision he receives prior to the call. Chapter 1 is a vision of God's presence that is mostly taken up with describing the four living creatures with four faces that are the attendants at God's throne. They move about by the spirit, and the prophet makes use of wind, cloud, and fire imagery to portray their appearance and the effect it has on him. Also in the vision are eye-filled wheels, similarly propelled by the spirit and able to move in any direction. Above is a dome, and above that is God's throne. Ezekiel describes what he sees as the appearance of the likeness of the glory of the Lord. His priestly identity is to the fore with this description because the phrase "the glory of the LORD" is a technical term to speak of God's presence in the temple. Many other aspects of the description of the vision recall other elements of the priestly accoutrements in the temple and the rituals that took place in it.

In this vision Ezekiel sees the throne chariot that will transport God from the temple when it is destroyed and will bring God back when the temple is rebuilt. It is a completely overwhelming experience that leaves him speechless. Unlike Isaiah and Jeremiah before him, Ezekiel makes no objection to the prophetic mission God has entrusted to him. In fact, he never says a single word throughout the entire vision. Perhaps the lack of an objection is the author's way of conveying the idea that Ezekiel was completely convinced that he was in the presence of God and it would be impossible for him to resist what he was being asked to do.

Ezekiel's location when he receives this initial vision is very important. He is in Babylon, a member of the exiled community at Tel-abib on the

Chebar canal (1:1). What he sees is a sign of God's ongoing presence outside the land of Israel that is meant to give hope to the people. This is a mobile God not limited to one land or one building, who can be with the community wherever they are. Later in the book the prophet envisions a day when the temple will be rebuilt (chs. 40–48), but until that happens God continues to be active and present for them.

At the same time God remains totally transcendent, beyond human experience and understanding. Even Ezekiel, a priest, is at a loss for words as he tries to comprehend what he has seen. The constant repetition of the word "like" and terms related to it throughout the first chapter reinforces the ineffable nature of the vision. In the space of twenty-four verses (1:4-28), the word "like" appears twenty-five times as Ezekiel attempts to describe what he sees in language that his audience will understand. The frequency intensifies as his gaze moves toward the throne and he tries to portray God's presence.

> And above the dome over their heads there was something like a throne, in appearance like sapphire; and seated above the likeness of a throne was something that seemed like a human form. Upward from what appeared like the loins I saw something like gleaming amber, something that looked like fire enclosed all around; and downward from what looked like the loins I saw something that looked like fire, and there was a splendor all around. Like the bow in a cloud on a rainy day, such was the appearance of the splendor all around. This was the appearance of the likeness of the glory of the LORD. (1:26-28)

The book of Ezekiel is quite different from the other prophetic works in content and tone. It has a unique vocabulary that includes phrases like "son of man" and "glory of the LORD," a series of dates and visions that unify the work, a plethora of symbolic prophetic actions, and an interest in priestly matters that set it apart from its counterparts in the prophetic corpus. Some scholars have suggested that it might be a form of early or proto-apocalyptic, a style of writing that is best seen in the Hebrew Bible in Daniel 7–12. There are some connections between the book and apocalyptic works, especially in the visions, and so there is a sense in which Ezekiel is anticipating that genre, which develops a few centuries later. But it would not be correct to label it as an apocalyptic writing. Its style and message are most similar to the other prophetic books, and it should be counted among them.

CHAPTER 24

THE EXILIC PROPHETS: SECOND ISAIAH

An earlier chapter discussed the complex nature of the book of Isaiah, which contains material from the period extending from the mid-eighth to the late sixth centuries B.C.E. Chapter 40 is the dividing point of the book. Much of the material in the first thirty-nine chapters can be traced back to the time of the prophet Isaiah, who was responding to the growing threat Assyria posed to Judah. A noticeable shift occurs in chapter 40, as everything from that point on appears to come from a much later time. For this reason, a distinction is commonly made between First Isaiah (chs. 1–39) and Second Isaiah (chs. 40–66), also sometimes called Deutero-Isaiah. Some scholars have also argued for the presence of a Third Isaiah, a topic that will be treated later in this chapter.

CONTENT

The striking difference between the two sections is obvious from the first words of Second Isaiah. "Comfort, O comfort my people, says your God. Speak tenderly to Jerusalem, and cry to her that she has served her term, that her penalty is paid, that she has received from the LORD's hand double for all her sins" (40:1-2). Such a message of hope and consolation would seem out of place in First Isaiah, which is dominated by threats of punishment and condemnation. The tone has completely changed, and when we compare the two sections of the book it is as if we are looking at "before" and "after" photographs. The first part of the book is a warning to the people of the impending punishment God is about to send upon them for their sin. The second part is a reassurance that is meant to give them solace and strength after that punishment has been administered.

The punishment was the series of invasions by foreign powers that began in the time of the prophet Isaiah with the Assyrian attacks on Judah and Jerusalem, events that form the backdrop of many of the passages in chapters 1–39. The culminating point was the Babylonian assault on Jerusalem in 586 that began the period of time known as the exile, when large numbers of people were deported from Judah and sent to live in

Babylon. The Neo-Babylonian Empire (626–539 B.C.E.) had replaced Assyria as the dominant force in the ancient Near East, and it remained in power until its demise at the hands of the Persians, who toppled Babylon in 539. It was the Persians, under their leader Cyrus, who ended the period of the exile by allowing the Judahites, along with all other conquered peoples, to return to their homeland.

Explicit references to this context are found throughout Second Isaiah. Babylon (sometimes referred to by its other name, Chaldea) and its gods are mentioned in a number of texts (46:1-2; 47; 48:20-21). Cyrus, the king of the Persians who defeated Babylon, is acknowledged, sometimes indirectly (41:2-3; 48:14) and elsewhere by name (44:24–45:8). At the same time, nothing in chapters 40–66 directly links them back to the eighth-century context of the prophet Isaiah. For example, nothing suggests the Israelites are currently living under Assyrian domination. In fact, that appears to be a thing of the past (52:4). The community to whom this part of the book is addressed is certainly living in Babylon, not Jerusalem.

Structurally, Second Isaiah is similar to First Isaiah because there is no clear, overarching organization to the work. The two are different in that Second Isaiah does not contain any narrative sections like those found in the first part of the book, where events from the prophet's life are sometimes recounted. Second Isaiah is comprised almost entirely of poetic speeches, but scholars have long differed on how to analyze this material. Some believe the work is a collection of a relatively few long speeches that have been joined together. Others prefer to see it as a compilation of many short speeches, some of which are only partial fragments of originally longer pieces. In addition, there are questions concerning who brought together the various elements to create the work as we now have it and when this was done. Was the redactor a single individual or a group? Was the work created during the exile or sometime after it? Scholars continue to wrestle with these and related questions as they study the text of Second Isaiah.

A major theme of the work is that no individual, group, or foreign power can prevent God from doing whatever God wants. These had to be encouraging words for a people who had been forced to move far from their land and whose temple, the focal point of their faith, had been destroyed in the Babylonian invasion of Jerusalem. What God wants most, according to Second Isaiah, is for the people of Judah to return home renewed in their faith. The book uses a wide variety of different genres and styles of writing—including laments, hymns of salvation, victory songs, and trial speeches—to convey this point.

Break forth into singing,
  you ruins of Jerusalem;
for the LORD has comforted his people,
  he has redeemed Jerusalem.
The LORD has bared his holy arm
  before the eyes of all the nations;
and the ends of the earth shall see
  the salvation of our God.
Depart, depart, go out from there!
  Touch no unclean thing;
go out from the midst of it, purify yourselves,
  you who carry the vessels of the LORD.
For you shall not go out in haste,
  and you shall not go in flight;
for the LORD will go before you,
  and the God of Israel will be your rear guard. (52:9-12)

It is God who makes the return from exile possible, as this text indicates. Drawing upon images and language that would be familiar to his hearers, Second Isaiah explains that this is not the first time God has done such a thing. Just as God led the people through the wilderness after the exodus during the days of Moses, so will he now guide them back to the land.

When you pass through the waters, I will be with you;
  and through the rivers, they shall not overwhelm you;
when you walk through fire you shall not be burned,
  and the flame shall not consume you.
For I am the LORD your God,
  the Holy One of Israel, your Savior. (43:2-3a)

The title "Holy One of Israel" is one that is used of God frequently in Second Isaiah. It underscores the special relationship that exists between God and the people, and it establishes God's authority above the other gods, particularly the Babylonian deities the Judahites might be tempted to worship while they are in exile. Some texts make an outright mockery of the attempt to follow other gods, like the condemnation against idolatry that includes a satirical description of a man who cooks food with half his wood and then uses the other half to make a god to whom he prays for salvation (44:9-20).

Elsewhere, Second Isaiah uses themes and ideas that are commonly found in First Isaiah. One that will be considered below is the notion that the actions of foreign rulers help to fulfill God's purposes. Just as the

Assyrian king was an instrument of God in the first part of the book, here Cyrus the Persian leader serves a similar purpose. Another of First Isaiah's characteristics that is found frequently in the latter part of the book is Zion theology. This language is often used in passages that describe the restoration of Jerusalem to its former glory and holiness. "Awake, awake, put on your strength, O Zion! Put on your beautiful garments, O Jerusalem, the holy city; for the uncircumcised and the unclean shall enter you no more. Shake yourself from the dust, rise up, O captive Jerusalem; loose the bonds from your neck, O captive daughter Zion!" (52:1-2). Such reuse of prior motifs forms a nice bridge between the two sections of the book and shows how Second Isaiah was modifying and adapting First Isaiah's concepts to fit its own context.

GROWTH

Despite the obvious changes in tone and content between First Isaiah and Second Isaiah, there are no clues in the text informing the reader that a new section has begun. There is no break, introduction, or superscription at the beginning of chapter 40 that serves this purpose, which suggests that, despite the shift, the final editor wanted to create the impression that the two parts are intimately connected and meant to be read together.

Many scholars have argued that the same thing can be observed within Second Isaiah. According to this view, chapters 56 through 66 form a distinct unit that should be identified as Third Isaiah. This section lacks markers that help to fix its context like the references to Assyria in First Isaiah and Babylon in Second Isaiah. Neither does it mention historical figures like King Ahaz and Cyrus the Persian leader, which can aid in the dating of a text. Even if it cannot be contextualized with confidence, it is claimed that there are certain indications that the material in these eleven chapters differs from what is found prior to it. Those scholars who posit a Third Isaiah commonly date it to sometime after the exile (post-539 B.C.E.), and the majority of them see most of the material as a product of the late sixth or early fifth centuries B.C.E.

One of the most important pieces of evidence cited in favor of a Third Isaiah is the references to the Jerusalem temple that appear throughout this part of the book (56:7; 60:13; 63:18; 64:11). Because the building had been destroyed by the Babylonians in 586, some have argued that these texts are describing the temple that was rebuilt after the return from exile. A problem with this argument is that the passages do not require that the rebuilt temple already exists. Some of them, like 64:11, refer to the earlier temple the Babylonians destroyed. "Our holy and beautiful house, where our ancestors praised you, has been burned by fire, and all our pleasant places have become ruins." Other passages are future-oriented texts and anticipate what will happen when the temple is rebuilt. "The glory of Lebanon shall come to you, the cypress, the plane, and the pine, to beautify the place of my sanctuary; and I will glorify where my feet rest" (60:13). These temple references, which are an interesting feature of the last part of Isaiah, do not offer conclusive proof for a postexilic date for these texts.

When we compare chapters 56–66 with the rest of Isaiah we see a more detailed emphasis on the future restoration of the community. Chapters 60–62, which are often referred to as the core of Third Isaiah, are a glorious vision of what awaits those who will return from Babylon. Jerusalem will be repopulated and become the envy of other nations (ch. 60). Its inhabitants will live in peace and justice, free of the suffering they have endured in the past (ch. 61). The city and its people will take on new identities by virtue of the special relationship they have with God (ch. 62). Another highly idealized view of Jerusalem, containing some of the richest imagery in the Bible to describe the relationship between God and the people, presents the city as simultaneously a mother who will nurse those who mourn and a child who will itself be comforted by God, its mother (66:7-16).

Another noteworthy difference between what has been called Third Isaiah and other sections of Isaiah is its greater interest in what might be termed "priestly" matters like covenant, cultic purity, sacrifice, and the Sabbath (56:2; 58:13-14). This reflects a concern with holiness and proper worship that is greater than what is found in chapters 1–55. Interestingly, this is not just limited to the members of the community, but also includes foreigners and other outsiders.

> And the foreigners who join themselves to the LORD,
>   to minister to him, to love the name of the LORD,
>   and to be his servants,
> all who keep the sabbath, and do not profane it,
>   and hold fast to my covenant—
> these I will bring to my holy mountain,
>   and make them joyful in my house of prayer;
> their burnt offerings and their sacrifices
>   will be accepted on my altar;
> for my house shall be called a house of prayer
>   for all peoples. Thus says the Lord GOD,
>   who gathers the outcasts of Israel,
> I will gather others to them
>   besides those already gathered. (56:6-8)

Such an inclusive view best fits a diverse environment like the exile and is a point in favor of a late date for the text.

It is quite likely that Isaiah 56–66 is the work of more than one author. Approximately twelve different literary units can be identified throughout the chapters, and they appear to come from different hands. Some sections, like chapters 60–62, have similarities with other parts of the book. In particular, the use of Zion imagery is reminiscent of earlier passages (60:14; 61:3; 62:1, 11). Also, the allusion to Moses and the use of exodus imagery in 63:10-14 recalls the same style of writing that was noted previously in Second Isaiah. On the other hand, sections like chapters 65–66 and its idealized, almost apocalyptic, vision of the future are quite different from other parts of the book of Isaiah. Similarly, these latter chapters do not speak of God using foreign rulers and powers to achieve the divine will as was the case in First and Second Isaiah. Here, God acts alone to return the exiles to Jerusalem and rebuild the city (57:17-18; 59:15b-19). A further difficulty, noted above, that complicates any attempt to get at the possible sources behind Third Isaiah is the lack of references to historical events or figures that would facilitate determining its possible context(s).

Given these problems, we should avoid speaking of a Third Isaiah, which gives the impression of a cohesive, well-organized work that might stem from a single individual. It is better to take the view that, like First Isaiah, Second Isaiah shows evidence of being redacted and expanded, reserving judgment on the precise nature of that editorial work and who was responsible for it. It appears that chapters 40–66 are the work of two or more prophets, working within the Isaiah tradition, who attempted to respond to their unique contexts in the sixth century B.C.E. or later.

It is possible that the individuals responsible for chapters 40–55 and 56–66 were contemporaries who were concerned with the same things—the restoration of Zion and membership in the community of faith—but they chose to treat different aspects of these issues. In other words, they shared the same context, but their perspectives differed. Second Isaiah attempted to explain how it was that current events like the fall of Babylon and rise of Persia fit into the divine plan. Those responsible for chapters 56–66—traditionally referred to as Third Isaiah—wrote at the same time but chose to look to the future to envision the imminent return to Judah.

CONTEXT

The references to Cyrus of Persia help to establish the context of Second Isaiah. His rise to power, defeat of the Medes in 550 B.C.E., and consolidation of territory are well documented in ancient sources like the Babylonian Chronicle and Herodotus's *Persian Wars.* Virtually the entire ancient Near East, with the exception of Egypt, eventually came under his control. It was his conquest of Babylon in 539 that had the most impact on the history of the Israelite people because it led to the end of the exile and their return to the land.

The Cylinder of Cyrus is a baked tablet upon which is a cuneiform inscription written soon after Cyrus's defeat of Babylon. In the inscription Cyrus explains how he was able to achieve victory due to the help of Marduk, the chief god of Babylon, who chose him for the task and guided him in battle. This divine endorsement of a foreigner came about because Nabonidus, king of Babylon, was a faithless and corrupt ruler. Cyrus goes on to describe how, with Marduk's assistance, he was able to improve the social conditions in Babylon and was warmly embraced by the local population and foreign leaders. He then recounts how he allowed all conquered peoples to return to their homelands and gave them permission to rebuild their sanctuaries. The latter policy was an extraordinary one in light of the standard Assyrian and Babylonian practice of deporting the most prominent members of vanquished areas and forcing them to spend the rest of their lives far from their native lands.

There is a striking connection between the inscription on the Cylinder of Cyrus and the biblical tradition in that Second Isaiah also attributes Cyrus's rise and success to divine approval. The key text is Isa 45:1-3.

> Thus says the LORD to his anointed, to Cyrus,
> whose right hand I have grasped
> to subdue the nations before him
> and strip kings of their robes,
> to open doors before him—
> and the gates shall not be closed:
> I will go before you
> and level the mountains,
> I will break in pieces the doors of bronze
> and cut through the bars of iron,
> I will give you the treasures of darkness
> and riches hidden in secret places,
> so that you may know that it is I, the LORD,
> the God of Israel, who call you by your name.

This is a remarkable text for a number of reasons. In the first place, it describes a level of intimacy and closeness between God and Cyrus that is usually reserved for Israelites. God grabs Cyrus's right hand, calls him by name, and guides his actions—these are all expressions of divine approval that are typically directed toward prophets and other leaders within the covenant community.

> But Marduk who does care for . . . on account of the fact that the sanctuaries of all their settlements were in ruins and the inhabitants of Sumer and Akkad had become like living dead, turned back his countenance his anger abated and he had mercy upon them. He scanned and looked through all the countries, searching for a righteous ruler willing to lead him (i.e. Marduk) in the annual procession. Then he pronounced the name of Cyrus, king of Anshan, declared him to become the ruler of all the world.

Excerpt of the Cyrus Cylinder.

The most arresting aspect of the text is the description of Cyrus as God's "anointed." This term *māšîaḥ* in Hebrew, from which the English word "messiah" is derived, is most commonly used to refer to a leader like a king or a priest who is designated, or anointed, by God to play an important role. This is the only time in the Hebrew Bible that the term is used in reference to a non-Israelite, which highlights the uniqueness of Cyrus's role in defeating the Babylonians and allowing the Israelites to return to Judah. This stamp of divine approval is particularly fascinating in light of the fact that Cyrus himself makes the same claim about his relationship with Marduk on his cylinder.

INTERPRETATION

The "Servant Songs" are four passages in Second Isaiah that are often studied together because of certain themes and language they have in common. The first describes a figure referred to as God's servant, whose purpose is to bring justice to the world.

> Here is my servant, whom I uphold,
>   my chosen, in whom my soul delights;
> I have put my spirit upon him;
>   he will bring forth justice to the nations.
> He will not cry or lift up his voice,
>   or make it heard in the street;
> a bruised reed he will not break,
>   and a dimly burning wick he will not quench;
>   he will faithfully bring forth justice.
> He will not grow faint or be crushed
>   until he has established justice in the earth;
>   and the coastlands wait for his teaching. (42:1-4)

The second passage (49:1-6) is a partly first-person account in which the servant explains that he was called by God before he was born. The text also contains words from God to the servant. At one point, God says to him, "You are my servant, Israel, in whom I will be glorified" (49:3). It shares with the first passage a universal understanding of the servant's role that will extend well beyond Israel. "I will give you as a light to the nations, that my salvation may reach to the end of the earth" (49:6b).

The third Servant Song (50:4-9) is written entirely in the first person, and it describes someone who is taught and assisted by God while suffering at the hands of his enemies. "I gave my back to those who struck me, and my cheeks to those who pulled out the beard; I did not hide my face from insult and spitting" (50:6). Despite such mistreatment, the servant remains confident that God will vindicate and protect him.

The fourth text (52:13–53:12), the longest of the group, further develops the themes of pain and suffering. It speaks of the servant anonymously growing up among his people like a small plant until he is mistreated and put to death, all the while not saying a word. The passage is remarkable because it describes the ultimate vindication of the servant in terms that understand his death as atonement for the sins of others. "Therefore I will allot him a portion with the great, and he shall divide the spoil with the strong; because he poured out himself to death, and was numbered with the transgressors; yet he bore the sin of many, and made intercession for the transgressors" (53:12).

Opinions vary on how to understand this enigmatic figure. Nowhere in them does it state that the four servant songs refer to the same individual, but this has been the standard way of reading the texts. Some scholars believe he should be identified with some historical figure like the prophet responsible for Second Isaiah or Cyrus, the Persian ruler who allowed the Israelites to return from exile. Others prefer to see him as a symbolic figure representing the people of Israel, who have proved their fidelity to God by enduring the suffering imposed upon them. The reference to the servant as "Israel" is a point in favor of this interpretation.

Christianity has traditionally identified the Suffering Servant with Jesus. The references to the servant's willingness to bear innocent suffering in faithful obedience to God's will match the image of Jesus that emerges from the Passion Narrative found in the four Gospels. Excerpts from the Servant Songs are read in churches each year in the week before Easter, and this helps to forge the link between the two figures. Similar to the Immanuel text discussed earlier, many Christians believe that Second Isaiah is actually speaking about Jesus in these passages. But here, too, it is a mistake to hold that view. The author is writing about his own day, not some time in the distant future. The servant's message is directed primarily to those in exile, not those in the church. Christians might see him as a prototype or symbol of the founder of their faith, but they should remember that they were not the author's original audience.

CHAPTER 25

THE POSTEXILIC PROPHETS: JOEL AND OBADIAH

The books of Joel and Obadiah display different reactions to Judah's devastating experience of destruction and exile. Joel focuses on lamentation followed by an apocalyptic vision of restoration; Obadiah's focus is on the devastation coming to Judah's enemy, Edom, for the part it played in Judah's demise. The two books have in common that they play upon and reinterpret the notion of a coming "Day of Yahweh" found in earlier prophetic books, notably Amos. They also share with each other and with "classical" prophecy the expressed hope in Judah's restoration.

JOEL

Like several of the "minor" prophets, virtually nothing is known about the prophet Joel. The name "Joel" is common in the OT. The fact that it occurs primarily in the book of Chronicles may indicate something of Joel's date and historical setting (see Context below). However, it is also possible, as may be the case with Obadiah and Malachi, that there was no individual prophet named Joel. The name has the same meaning as "Elijah": "Yahweh is God." It could have been invented for the purported author of the book as a way of encapsulating its message that Yahweh is in control.

CONTENT

There are six relatively distinct parts to the book of Joel:

Part 1: (Joel 1:1-20)

Following the book's heading (1:1) and a summons to the people of the land to listen (1:2-4), there is a series of addresses to different segments of society: "drunkards" and "wine drinkers" (= consumers?, 1:5-10), farmers and vinedressers (1:11-12), and priests (1:13-18). Each address begins with a call to lament or "wail" because of the devastation wrought by a plague of locusts.

Part 2: (Joel 2:1-11)

This is a poem likening the devastation caused by the locusts to that of an invading army. It is set apart by an inclusio (vv. 1-2, 10-11), which refers to the disaster associated with the "Day of Yahweh" as darkness.

Part 3: (Joel 2:12-17)

The call to repentance in this section draws on both prophetic (vv. 12-14) and priestly language and images (vv. 15-17).

Part 4: (Joel 2:18-27)

God's response to the lamentation and repentance promises the reversal of the disasters described in the first three parts: the grain, wine, and oil will be replenished (1:10; 2:19); Judah will no longer be a mockery (2:17; 2:19); the locusts will be driven out (2:3; 2:20); the land that mourned will rejoice (1:10; 2:21); animals will again graze (1:19-20; 2:22); orchards, trees, and vineyards will flourish (1:12; 2:22); all that the locusts ate will be restored (1:4; 2:25); and the people once told to wail are now told that they will praise Yahweh (1:5, 11, 13; 2:26).

Part 5: (Joel 2:28-32 [Hebrew 3:1-5])

The phrase "afterward" in 2:28 (Hebrew 3:1) signals the beginning of a new section of the book. This section is apocalyptic-like and promises the salvation of Jerusalem in the earth's final crisis.

Part 6: (Joel 3:1-21 [Hebrew 4:1-21])

The last segment of the book is also apocalyptic in orientation. It promises Yahweh's judgment on the nations and the ultimate vindication of Judah and Jerusalem.

As suggested by the survey of its content, the book of Joel can be construed as having two main divisions: the first four parts (1:1–2:27), which deal in some way with the plague of locusts, and the final two parts (2:28–3:21 [Hebrew 3:1–4:21]), which are apocalyptic.

GROWTH

The main question in the study of the book of Joel is how the two major divisions of the book relate to each other. There are two leading views on this question. Traditionally, Joel has been understood as a unit consisting, as is typical of prophetic books, of judgment oracles followed by salvation oracles. The judgment oracles are the first three parts of the book surveyed above (1:1–2:17) and the salvation oracles the last three (2:18–3:21). The response in 2:18-27 begins the salvation oracles, which are continued in the apocalyptic passages (2:28-32; 3:1-21 [Hebrew 3:1-5; 4:1-21]). Thus, the locust plague in the first half of the book somehow signifies the approaching apocalypse. A difficulty with this perspective is that it does not fully account for the contrast in nature between the first four sections of the book and the last two apocalyptic sections.

An alternative view, therefore, is that the book is the combination of two phases of writing represented in (a) the first four sections dealing with the locust plague and (b) the apocalyptic sections (5 and 6 above). The phrases that begin each of the apocalyptic sections ("afterward," 2:28 [Hebrew 3:1], and "in those days and at that time," 3:1 [Hebrew 4:1]) would then represent editorial efforts to add those sections to the previous book. In this view, the original book of Joel (sections 1-4 above) consisted of the lament (1:1-20) at the devastating locust plague (2:1-11) and the call to repent because of it (2:12-17), followed by God's response promising restoration (2:18-27), which provided a fitting conclusion. This original book was supplemented by two apocalyptic oracles (2:28-32; 3:1-21 [Hebrew 3:1-5; 4:1-21]) that reinterpreted the passages about the locust plague from an apocalyptic orientation.

CONTEXT

The book of Joel contains no clear reference to any political or historical event that would indicate the context in which it was written. Hence, our understanding of the date and historical setting of the book depends to some extent on the interpretation of it—in particular whether one views it as an original unit or as a composite with two distinct phases of writing.

The first division of the book, the first four parts listed above, fits the concerns of preexilic prophecy in its depiction of disaster, call for repentance, and promise of future restoration. At the same time, the absence of any reference to a king or political circumstance, the attention given to priests, and the positive view of ritual activities all suggest a theocratic perspective similar to those of Haggai, Zechariah, and Malachi, and therefore might indicate a postexilic date. If the locusts are a metaphor for a foreign invasion (see Interpretation below), it would suggest a setting after the destruction of Jerusalem at the hands of the Babylonians in 586.

The apocalyptic section of Joel (parts 5 and 6 above) is easier to date, not only because apocalyptic literature is essentially a product of the postexilic period but also because of allusions in this section to Judah's dispersion, exile, and return. For instance, Joel 3:2, 7 (Hebrew 4:2, 7) look forward to God gathering the people of Judah from the nations where they have been scattered and bringing them back to their homeland. In the same context, the mention of the Greeks in 3:6 suggests a postexilic date, perhaps as late as the fourth century.

Joel's quotation and reinterpretation of an earlier prophecy shared by Isaiah and Micah also indicates a late date. In a famous vision of peace, Isaiah (2:4) and Micah (4:3) both prophesied that nations would turn their weapons into farm implements.

> He shall judge between nations, and shall arbitrate for many peoples; they shall beat their swords into plowshares, and their spears into pruning hooks; nation shall not lift up sword against nation, neither shall they learn war any more. (Isa 2:4)

You may recognize this quotation from its inscription on the United Nations building in New York. Most scholars think that it is actually a later, postexilic addition to both Isaiah and Micah because of its utopian vision of universal peace and Yahweh's concern for all peoples. Joel's description of apocalyptic warfare reinterprets and reverses the vision of peace from Isaiah and Micah:

> Proclaim this among the nations:
> Prepare war, stir up the warriors.
> Let all the soldiers draw near, let them come up.
> Beat your plowshares into swords,
>   and your pruning hooks into spears;
>   let the weakling say, "I am a warrior." (Joel 3:9-10 [Hebrew 4:9-10])

All of these pieces of evidence, then, indicate that the book of Joel as we have it was written late in the postexilic period. The first major section of the book (1:1–2:27) may come from the early part of the postexilic period, perhaps in the late sixth century. The apocalyptic section (2:28–3:21 [Hebrew 3:1–4:21]) arose later, perhaps in the fourth century.

Joel's literary context is varied, as its different parts use an assortment of genres and forms. Chapter 1, as we have seen, borrows from the form of a communal lament. Joel 2:1-11 is a poem about the Day of Yahweh. The call for repentance (2:12-17, part 3 above) begins with a typical prophetic form—a plea to return to Yahweh with a whole heart (vv. 12-15). It also uses a description of Yahweh shared by other prophets as well as psalms and legal material:

> Return to the LORD, your God,
>   for he is gracious and merciful,
> slow to anger, and abounding in steadfast love,
>   and relents from punishing. (2:13)

Then verses 15-18 use priestly forms to call a solemn assembly and sanctify the congregation for a liturgy of community repentance. The apocalyptic material in the book, especially chapter 3 (Hebrew 4), uses divine warrior imagery to describe Yahweh's judgment on the nations and vindication of Judah. The variety of forms in Joel illustrates the book's rich heritage in Israel's religion, literature, and culture.

INTERPRETATION

The major interpretive issue in Joel concerns the "Day of Yahweh," which is referred to five times in the book (1:15; 2:1, 11; 2:31 [Hebrew 3:4]; 3:14 [Hebrew 4:14]). This is a theme that we have seen already in the book of Amos. In essence, it anticipates God's intervention into human affairs. God can intervene for purposes of judgment or of salvation. Thus, in Amos, the people anticipate that God will intervene to destroy their enemies in the other nations. Amos interprets the Day of Yahweh differently than the people. He informs them that the Day of Yahweh is indeed coming, but it will be a day of judgment against them rather than a day of their salvation and judgment against their enemies.

Joel inherits the idea of the Day of Yahweh from Amos. Joel borrows and reinterprets Amos's language about the coming of Yahweh as a warrior (Joel 3:16 [Hebrew 4:16]; Amos 1:2). The question is whether Joel interprets the Day of Yahweh as a day of judgment or a day of salvation. This question relates to the matter of whether the book of Joel is an original unit or consists of two distinct divisions. If a unit, then the locust plague in the book's first four parts is a prelude to the apocalyptic visions in its last two parts. If so, then the Day of Yahweh throughout the book has to be a day of salvation for the people of Judah and of judgment for the surrounding nations, because this is its sense in the apocalyptic material.

On the other hand, if the first four parts of the book originally treated the locust plague as a crisis of its own, distinct from the apocalyptic visions, then there are two different understandings of the Day of Yahweh. In the portions of the book dealing with the locust plague, the Day of Yahweh was seen as a day of judgment against Judah—judgment in the form of the devastation caused by the locusts. In the apocalyptic portions, in contrast, the Day of Yahweh is a day of salvation for Judah—not in terms of political institutions or natural phenomena (like locusts), but in terms of God's direct intervention.

The likelihood that the Day of Yahweh was originally understood in Joel 1:1–2:27 as a day of judgment against Judah raises the further question about the meaning of the locusts. The detailed description of the devastation wrought by the locusts suggests that the writer had in mind an actual infestation, perhaps one that he had witnessed.

Nevertheless, the reference to different kinds of locusts all at once (1:4) and the image of an invading army (2:1-11) raise the possibility that the locusts are intended as a metaphor for invaders. This interpretation seems all the more likely in view of Amos's use of the Day of Yahweh motif precisely for foreign invasion. The author may be depicting the destruction associated with the Babylonian exile or giving a general description of such invasions, perhaps even conflating the experiences suffered by Israel and Judah.

The Day of Yahweh theme has an extensive history in the Bible—one that extends long before Amos and long after Joel. As noted earlier, the apocalyptic portions of Joel make use of the divine warrior motif. Yahweh's coming is envisioned as the marching out of a soldier to war. Yahweh fights on behalf of the chosen people and against their shared enemies. This motif of a divine warrior is one that is drawn originally from mythology, in which the storm and fertility god takes up his weapons such as the lightning bolt and marches to battle against the forces of sterility, death, or chaos. In Joel and other postexilic writings, this ancient motif is reused to depict Yahweh's final vindication of Judah against its enemies. It is a motif that becomes particularly popular in apocalyptic literature. Beyond this, the Day of Yahweh theme surfaces again in the New Testament, where God's intervention for purposes of salvation is emphasized. Thus, in the story of the day of Pentecost, Peter's sermon quotes extensively from Joel (Acts 2:17-21; Joel 2:28-32 [Hebrew 3:1-5]).

OBADIAH

Obadiah is the shortest book in the Old Testament, consisting of a single chapter. Like Joel, the prophet Obadiah is unknown outside of the book. A prophet of the same name in the story of Elijah (1 Kgs 18) may have lent his name to the book's author, though the two prophets are not to be identified. Since "Obadiah" means "servant of Yahweh" it may even be an epithet for the book's author, as is possible also for Joel and Malachi, rather than a proper name.

CONTENT

The book of Obadiah falls easily into two parts. The first fourteen verses contain an oracle against Edom, Judah's neighbor to the southeast. Edom is condemned for its participation in Judah's downfall through gloating, looting, and handing over fugitives (vv. 10-14). Then, the second part of the book (vv. 15-21) presents a vision of the Day of Yahweh as a day of judgment against Judah's enemies, especially Edom, and salvation for Judah itself.

GROWTH

The oracle against Edom in Obadiah resembles oracles against foreign nations in other prophetic books. It bears special similarity to an oracle against Edom found in the book of Jeremiah (49:7-22). Compare, in particular, the following texts:

Obadiah 1-4	Jeremiah 49:14-16
The vision of Obadiah. Thus says the Lord GOD concerning Edom: We have heard a report from the LORD, and a messenger has been sent among the nations "Rise up! Let us rise against it for battle!" I will surely make you least among the nations; you shall be utterly despised. Your proud heart has deceived you, you that live in the clefts of the rock, whose dwelling is in the heights. You say in your heart, "Who will bring me down to the ground?" Though you soar aloft like the eagle, though your nest is set among the stars, from there I will bring you down, says the LORD.	I have heard tidings from the LORD, and a messenger has been sent among the nations: "Gather yourselves together and come against her, and rise up for battle!" For I will make you least among the nations, despised by humankind. The terror you inspire and the pride of your heart have deceived you, you who live in the clefts of the rock, who hold the height of the hill. Although you make your nest as high as the eagle's, from there I will bring you down, says the LORD.

Obadiah 5-6	Jeremiah 49:9-10a
If thieves came to you, if plunderers by night— how you would have been destroyed!— would they not steal only what they wanted? If grape-gatherers came to you, would they not leave gleanings? How Esau has been pillaged, his treasures searched out!	If grape-gatherers came to you, would they not leave gleanings? If thieves came by night, even they would pillage only what they wanted. But as for me, I have stripped Esau bare, I have uncovered his hiding places, and he is not able to conceal himself.

There is clearly a relationship of some kind between these two texts, but the exact nature of their relationship is difficult to determine. Did one of them borrow from the other or did they both make use of a common document or set of sayings? Still, the oracle against Edom in Obadiah 1-14 functions differently from the usual oracles against nations like the one in Jeremiah. That is, the point of Obadiah's oracle is not just to condemn Edom but to lead up to the vision of Judah's future dominion over Edom and its other enemies (vv. 15-21). This difference may suggest that the first part of Obadiah made use of already existing oracles against Edom, like the one in Jeremiah, and reshaped them to its own purpose. If so, then the book of Obadiah was composed in part by borrowing and integrating elements of older oracles against Edom in its first part in order to set the stage for its primary message about the coming Day of Yahweh in its second part.

CONTEXT

As indicated by the discussion thus far, Obadiah emerged from a particular literary and historical context. The literary context is the oracles against the nations, which are a relatively common section of prophetic books (Isa 13–23; Jer 46–51; Ezek 26–32; Amos 1–2), representing apparently a significant element in the activity of these prophets. The difference in Obadiah is its essentially exclusive focus on one nation—Edom—and then its use of the oracle against Edom not just for condemnation but to lead to the vision of Judah's vindication over all its rivals.

The focus on Edom suggests a particular historical context for Obadiah. Edom's cooperation with the Babylonians in Judah's downfall is mentioned elsewhere in the Old Testament.

> Remember, O LORD, against the Edomites
>   the day of Jerusalem's fall,
> how they said, "Tear it down! Tear it down!
>   Down to its foundations!" (Ps 137:7)

> Because you cherished an ancient enmity, and gave over the people of Israel to the power of the sword at the time of their calamity, at the time of their final punishment . . . (Ezek 35:5)

Thus, although Obadiah does not explicitly mention the Babylonian exile of 586 as the context for Edom's activities against Judah, it seems likely that this event lies in the background of its first oracle (Obad 1-14).

The second part of the book (vv. 15-21), however, seems to come from a later context. These verses resemble the second part of the book of Joel in their focus on the Day of Yahweh as a day of salvation for Judah and vindication over all of its enemies. They do not describe a return from exile—perhaps that has already happened. On the other hand, they are not fully apocalyptic, as they do not envision Yahweh's direct intervention into history. These verses, then, and the present form of the book of Obadiah, should probably be dated a little before the final form of Joel—after the exile, perhaps in the late fifth or early fourth century.

INTERPRETATION

As in Joel, the main interpretive theme in Obadiah is the Day of Yahweh. Obadiah illustrates the development of that theme from classical prophecy. The oracle against Edom (vv. 1-14), as we have seen, is typical of prophetic oracles against the nations found in preexilic prophetic books as early as Amos. Thus, the allusions to the Day of Yahweh in this part of Obadiah ("on that day" in vv. 8, 11) refer to Yahweh's punishment of Edom. Yahweh's judgment is limited in the first part of Obadiah to Edom, rather than all nations, because of historical circumstances, namely the role played by Edom in Judah's destruction in 586 B.C.E.

The second part of Obadiah begins with a specific reference to the Day of Yahweh (v. 15). Yahweh's judgment is expanded to all the nations. It may be that the second part of Obadiah reinterprets the first part such that Edom stands for all foreign nations. Along with judgment on Edom and the nations, the Day of Yahweh brings ultimate salvation for Judah. This final, or "eschatological," vindication of Yahweh's people and the judgment of their enemies is an important ingredient of apocalyptic literature. Hence, although Obadiah itself is not apocalyptic, like Joel, it illustrates a stage in the development from prophecy to apocalyptic.

CHAPTER 26

THE POSTEXILIC PROPHETS: JONAH

The story of Jonah is one of the best known in the Bible. But it is also one of the most poorly understood. At the very least it is fair to say that there is a lot more to the story than the simple fish tale of Jonah and the whale.

CONTENT

The book of Jonah presents its story in four distinct scenes. The book has two halves, each introduced by the statement that Jonah received a message or "word" from Yahweh (1:1; 3:1). Then, the references to Jonah's prayers (2:1; 4:2) further divide each half in two. As a result, the book's four scenes correspond roughly to its present chapter divisions.

Scene 1, Chapter 1: Jonah's Call and Flight

Yahweh tells Jonah to go to the city of Nineveh and "cry out" against it because of its wickedness. Jonah, however, flees in the opposite direction, boarding a ship sailing across the Mediterranean Sea. Yahweh "hurls" a strong wind against the ship, so that it is on the verge of sinking. The crew of the ship begins to panic. They cast the cargo overboard and call on their gods for help. Jonah, meanwhile, is asleep in the hold of the ship and must be awakened. The sailors cast lots to determine whose fault it is that the storm has come upon them, and the lot falls on Jonah. He explains (boasts?) that he is Hebrew and that Yahweh, whom he worships but from whom he is fleeing, is the God of sea and land. He further tells the sailors to throw him overboard and the storm will calm. The sailors are reluctant to do this and only follow through after exhausting every effort to row ashore. The storm immediately stops when Jonah is thrown into the sea, and the sailors worship Yahweh. Yahweh appoints a large fish to swallow Jonah, who remains inside the fish for three days and nights.

Scene 2, Chapter 2: The Psalm of Jonah

Inside the fish, Jonah prays to Yahweh in the form of a poem or psalm. The gist of the psalm is thanksgiving for its author's survival of a "near death" experience. "Sheol" (v. 2) is the Hebrew name for the underworld or place of the dead, also called the "Pit" later in the poem. The metaphor used for death in the poem is drowning, which is similar to Jonah's situation in the sea.

Scene 3, Chapter 3: Jonah's Mission to Nineveh

Having learned that he cannot run away from Yahweh, Jonah goes to Nineveh when he is told for the second time to do so. Nineveh is described as an enormous city—a three days' walk across. Jonah proceeds a day's walk into the city and then delivers his oracle. In forty days, he says, Nineveh will be overturned. This is usually taken to mean that the city will be destroyed, but the word might mean that it will be changed. His threat throws the city into an uproar, as everyone in it believes and repents with fasting and sackcloth (a traditional sign of mourning). The king of Nineveh issues an edict requiring all the people and animals in the city to fast, wear sackcloth, and pray for forgiveness in hopes of changing God's mind about destroying the city. And it works.

Scene 4, Chapter 4: God's Lesson to Jonah

Far from being pleased at the success of his message, Jonah is angry. He tells Yahweh that this was the reason he ran away in the first place—because he knew God was merciful. He even asks God to take his life. He goes out and sits opposite the city, apparently hoping that it will still be destroyed. Yahweh offers Jonah an object lesson, designating a plant to grow up and provide him with shade and then sending a worm to attack the plant so that it dies as quickly as it grew up. Jonah is miserable and again asks God to take his life. The book ends with a question as God asks Jonah if it is not appropriate for him to show the same kind of concern and compassion for the people and animals in Nineveh that Jonah felt for the plant that briefly shaded him.

GROWTH

The main issue relating to the growth of the book of Jonah is the question of the origin of the psalm in chapter 2. The content of the psalm is not entirely appropriate to the story of Jonah. For one thing, it seems odd that Jonah would express thanksgiving at this point in the story. Although he has not drowned in the sea, he still does not know whether he will survive his ordeal in the fish. Indeed, thanksgiving does not fit entirely well with the obstinate character of Jonah elsewhere in the story. Other differences include the fact that it is Yahweh in the psalm, rather than the sailors, who throws the psalmist into the sea. In fact, the psalm does not mention the fish at all or, for that matter, any of the events leading up to Jonah's being swallowed by it.

The references to Yahweh's "house" or "temple" in the psalm are also inappropriate to Jonah's situation; the temple was in Jerusalem, the capital of Judah, while Jonah was from the kingdom of Israel. The condemnation of idol worshipers as forsaking their loyalty fits ill with the story in Jonah, since the foreigners, who presumably worship idols, are more faithful and obedient to Yahweh than Jonah. The mention of sacrifice at the temple also presupposes a setting on land rather than in the fish's belly. The vow mentioned at the end of the poem was probably made by the psalmist during his ordeal. There is no reference to any vow on Jonah's part in the story. The promise to fulfill the vow indicates that the psalmist has been restored, which has not yet happened to Jonah at this point.

These differences indicate that the poem was originally composed for another occasion and has been secondarily borrowed for Jonah's situation. It is impossible to determine whether this was done by the author of Jonah or by a later editor of the book. The psalm does not materially alter the story and may even contribute to the characterization of Jonah by what it does not say. There is no indication of any regret on Jonah's part for his disobedience and failure to carry out God's order. He may be thankful to have survived, but his experience in the fish has not made him any less stubborn or hateful.

CONTEXT

Literary

The book of Jonah is one of the Latter Prophets in the Hebrew Bible, though it never actually calls Jonah a prophet. Jonah is clearly not a typical prophet, and the book of Jonah is not a typical prophetic book. Most prophetic books are dominated by prophetic sayings or oracles, but Jonah has only one, very brief oracle: "Forty days more, and Nineveh shall be overthrown" (3:4). The book is a narrative. As the outline above indicates, its central character is the prophet Jonah, and it deals with his interaction with the book's other characters. But the story is also not biography. The book launches into its story with very few details about Jonah and, unlike other prophetic books, there is no attempt to supply a precise date for the events it describes. As we will see below, it also contains a number of historical problems. Because the exact nature of the book is a key interpretive question, it is best compared not with other prophetic works in the Bible but with short stories or "novellas," such as Ruth, Esther, and the Joseph story in Genesis.

Historical

The prophet Jonah is mentioned in one other place in the Hebrew Bible, in 2 Kgs 14:25. There it says that Jonah, the son of Amittai, was a prophet who lived during the time of King Jeroboam II of Israel (ca. 786–746 B.C.E.). It adds that he was from a town called Gath-Hepher in Israel, and that he prophesied the enlargement of a portion of Israel's northern border under Jeroboam. The story in the book of Jonah, therefore, is set in the eighth century.

However, biblical scholars have pointed out several serious historical problems with Jonah. For instance, the city of Nineveh came to prominence as the capital of the Assyrian Empire only in the seventh century B.C.E., a hundred years or so after the Jonah of 2 Kgs 14:25. In fact, by the time Nineveh became the capital, the nation of Israel had ceased to exist. The Assyrians themselves brought an end to the kingdom of Israel by destroying its capital, Samaria, in 721 B.C.E. and taking many of its citizens into captivity. Thus, the role of Nineveh in the book of Jonah appears to be an anachronism. In addition, the title "king of Nineveh" is not attested in any of the vast literature from ancient Assyria. What is more, the location of ancient Nineveh has long been known, and its ruins long ago excavated. At its height, the city had a *circumference* of only about 7.75 miles; at its widest point it was about three miles across. It was, therefore, nowhere near the size of three days' walk across as described in the book of Jonah.

These historical problems have suggested to most scholars that the book of Jonah was written much later than the time in which it is set. Scholars typically place the book in the context of the postexilic period, perhaps around 400 B.C.E. Part of the reason for this date is linguistic. The text of Jonah uses certain words that appear to be Aramaic in origin. Another reason for this date is the themes of Yahweh's universal dominion and concern for all people, which became especially pointed issues of debate in the postexilic period. These themes surface in Jonah in God's sending the prophet to non-Israelites, the people of Nineveh. The debate over Yahweh's concern for non-Israelites looms large in other biblical books from this period, such as Chronicles and Ezra–Nehemiah.

INTERPRETATION

The key to the interpretation of Jonah lies in understanding the nature of the story as satire or parody. This understanding of the book would account for the historical problems noted above. Indeed, the story is full of comic features that become apparent upon close reading. To begin with, there are many instances of hyperbole and exaggeration. The book uses the word "great" a lot. It refers to a "great" wind, a "great" storm, and a "great" fish. Nineveh is called the "great" city, and its size—three days' walk across—is greatly exaggerated, as we have seen. This hyperbole figures in other portions of the story. Thus, the entire city repents at

Jonah's single announcement. No prophet ever experienced such success as Jonah.

Jonah's startling success points out another comic strain in the book. There are statements and images in it that can only be described as ridiculous. Above all is the fact that it is not just the people of Nineveh who repent. The animals in the city also repent, fast, pray, and don sackcloth. The idea of a man spending three days inside the belly of a large fish is another of these ridiculous images. Then there are other, more subtle images. For example, the Hebrew text literally reads that the ship on which Jonah sailed "considered breaking up" (1:4), ascribing thought to an inanimate object. Similarly, the fish that swallows Jonah changes gender. When it is first mentioned, the Hebrew text uses a masculine form. But when Jonah prays from the fish's belly, the Hebrew uses a feminine form.

The portrait of God in Jonah is another comical element. Yahweh in Jonah is a real micromanager. He personally hurls the storm and appoints the large fish, to which he speaks. He also appoints the bush that shades Jonah and even the worm that kills it. Although the idea of God being in control of creation is a serious theological concept, the image of the Almighty addressing a fish and then personally appointing a worm carries this idea to a ludicrous extreme.

Of all the ridiculous features in Jonah, the most ridiculous ones concern the prophet himself. Jonah's behavior is the opposite of what one expects from a prophet. He is the only character in the book who disobeys God. He tries to run away from his commission, for reasons that he does not explain until later. If he truly believes in Yahweh as the God of sea and dry land, as he boasts to the sailors, then his actions make no sense. When the storm hits the ship, Jonah is the only one who does not respond by calling on his God. He is asleep in the hold. (The ancient Greek translation of Jonah even says that he was snoring!) Even after he is roused by the ship's captain, the text does not say anything about him praying—until he is swallowed by the fish. As we have seen, his prayer at this point is not entirely appropriate to the story, so that it fits with his nonsensical character. He never repents of his disobedience and only goes to Nineveh because he has no choice. His mission to Nineveh is successful beyond any prophet's wildest imagination. But far from being pleased, as any other prophet would be, Jonah is angry. He finally explains why he ran from God in the first place. It is because God is merciful—and this makes Jonah angry. He does not want the Ninevites to be saved but wants to see them destroyed. He asks God to take his life, saying, in effect, that life is not worth living if God is going to be merciful to everyone. Yahweh's object lesson shows that Jonah cares more about his plant than he does about a city full of people and animals. In short, Jonah is disobedient to God and hateful toward other people.

Despite its comic nature, the book of Jonah was probably intended to convey a serious message. That is the function of satire—to paint a ridiculous picture of a particular attitude or viewpoint in order to combat it and lure readers away from it. Most scholars think that Jonah was written to promote universalism—the idea that God cares for all people—and to ridicule the attitudes of bigotry, prejudice, and hatred toward non-Israelites. Jonah's name means "dove," and the dove is sometimes used in the Bible as a symbol for Israel (Hos 7:11). In a similar way, Ninevites represented the quintessential evil foreigners in Jonah because Nineveh was the capital of the Assyrian Empire, which had destroyed the kingdom of Israel in 722 B.C.E.

Jonah was probably intended, therefore, as a symbol of Israel or a representative of a certain attitude prevalent among Israelites and Nineveh as the symbol of non-Israelites. In the story, Jonah's attitude toward non-Israelites blinds him from appreciating God's mercy and causes him to do foolish and irrational things, such as trying to run from God. Furthermore, the non-Israelites in Jonah are all righteous; they all come to believe in Yahweh as the true God, and they act obediently. Only Jonah is stubbornly disobedient. Jonah's priorities are so confused that he even values a plant more than people and vengeance more than life. Through the use of humor, the book of Jonah offers a powerful lesson about the ridiculousness of racial and religious prejudice and hatred toward other people.

CHAPTER 27

THE POSTEXILIC PROPHETS: HAGGAI, ZECHARIAH, MALACHI

Haggai, Zechariah, and Malachi are the final three prophetic writings among the "minor" prophets, or Book of the Twelve. These works are all written in the period after the Babylonian exile. The Babylonian Empire had been conquered by the Persians, and the kingdom of Judah was now the Persian province of Yehud. Persian policy mandated the return of foreign captives to their native lands and the support of local religious and political traditions in order to maintain peace at the fringes of the empire and easy Persian access to trade routes. Haggai, Zechariah, and Malachi share a concern for proper worship in the rebuilt temple, which will result in prosperity and blessing for the people. These works also exhibit some interesting literary relationships among themselves.

HAGGAI

Haggai's name means "one of (born on) a pilgrimage festival." It is an appropriate name for a prophet who promoted the rebuilding of the temple in Jerusalem, where pilgrimage festivals were held. Haggai's prophetic activity is mentioned in Ezra (5:1; 6:14), but there is no other biographical information about him in the Bible.

CONTENT

The book of Haggai has two main parts: first, an oracle calling for the temple to be rebuilt (1:1-11) followed by a report of the positive response by the leaders and the people (1:12-15a) and, second, three oracles of encouragement (1:15b–2:9, 10-19, 20-23). All four oracles in the book are marked by chronological notices (1:1; 1:15b–2:1, 10, 20).

Each of the oracles in the second part of the book makes a different point related to the temple. The first recalls Yahweh's presence with his people at the exodus and reaffirms it for the future, promising that the rebuilt temple will be more splendid than the one it replaces. The second oracle of encouragement begins with an inquiry of priests regarding the contagiousness of ritual holiness and uncleanness. The point is that the people did not prosper as long as the temple was in ruins because everything they touched became unclean. With the founding of the temple, however, the oracle promises that things will turn around as a result of Yahweh's blessing. The final oracle envisions Yahweh's defeat of the nations and restoration of Judah as an international power. The three oracles, then, are bound together by their flow from past to present to future.

GROWTH

The flow of the oracles indicates the overall unity of the book of Haggai. However, there is some indication that Haggai is a component of an even larger editorial unit. There are strong similarities between Haggai and Zechariah 1–8. The two men were contemporaries and must have known each other (Ezra 5:1; 6:14), despite the fact that they do not mention one another. Both books were written within a close time frame (see below), and both deal with the same cast of characters (notably Zerubbabel and Joshua) as well as the same problems and questions. In addition, Haggai and Zechariah 7–8 share forms of expression, language, vocabulary, and themes that mark them as the frame of a single literary work.

CONTEXT

The chronological notices in Haggai help to date its oracles precisely. All four oracles are ascribed to the second year of the Persian king Darius I, who reigned 522–485 B.C.E., hence 520, specifically August 29 (1:1), October 17 (1:15b–2:1), and December 18 (2:10, 20) of that year. This means that the oracle in 1:15b–2:9 was delivered during the Jewish festival of *Sukkoth*, or booths (Lev 23:33-36, 39-42), making Haggai's reference to the exodus (2:5) quite apropos. December 18, on which both of the last two oracles are dated, was evidently the day on which the temple foundation was laid, as indicated by the promise of blessing "from this day on" (2:19).

Efforts to rebuild the temple may have begun with the first wave of returnees from exile in 538 B.C.E. under the leadership of Sheshbazzar (Ezra 1:1-4, 8; 2:68; 5:14-16; 5:17–6:5). But for reasons that remain obscure, the work slowed to a standstill. It was Haggai's prophecy that sparked the renewal of the building effort. Haggai noted that the people were struggling economically, a situation that existed, he said, because of the failure to rebuild the temple. He promised that prosperity would come with its construction. Haggai's principal addressees were Zerubbabel, the governor and royal heir, and Joshua, the high priest, as corulers (1:1, 12, 14; 2:2, 21). This dual leadership, or diarchy, was apparently fostered by the Persians and is one of the similarities between Haggai and Zechariah 1–8. Haggai's strategy proved effective. The temple construction began in 520 at Haggai's urging and was completed some five years later. Zechariah 1–8, as we will see, presupposes that work on the temple has begun and thus must be dated slightly later than Haggai, in 518. The edited book of Haggai plus Zechariah 1–8 was probably compiled shortly after that date and presented at the temple's dedication in 516–515.

INTERPRETATION

The book of Haggai shows both continuity with and new interpretation of earlier prophecy. Like earlier prophets, Haggai is an intermediary between God and the people. Also like many other prophets, Haggai's message is directed primarily toward the leaders and nobility. Obviously, the temple was central to Haggai's message and thought. In delivering his message, Haggai made use of imagery borrowed from earlier prophets. For instance, his reference to plagues sent by God before the building of the temple (2:17) is very similar to an oracle in Amos (4:9).

In general, Haggai is more positive than most prophetic books. This is because of the positive response to his warning in chapter 1 that prosperity depends on the temple being rebuilt. Haggai's eschatological vision in the book's final oracle (2:20-23) also bears similarity to visions of an idealized future in other prophets, for example, Second Isaiah. The role of Zerubbabel, who is the addressee of this oracle, is especially interesting. His status as the heir to the throne of David receives no emphasis in this passage. Rather, it is the kingship of Yahweh that is stressed; Zerubbabel is simply Yahweh's "signet" (2:23)—the instrument and symbol of God's power and authority. This apparent downplaying of the hope in the restoration of the Davidic kingdom may betray the Persian dominance felt by the remnant of Judah, now the province of Yehud. However, it also reflects the prophet's belief in Yahweh's universal control over history.

ZECHARIAH

Zechariah, son of Berechiah, son of Iddo, was a priest (Neh 12:16) as well as a prophet. His career as a prophet overlapped with that of Haggai, and his mission was similar, as it related to the rebuilding of the temple and the benefits that he saw stemming from that project. The book of Zechariah, at least in the first eight chapters, is also closely tied with Haggai. Nevertheless, the tone and presentation of the two works are markedly different.

CONTENT

Zechariah consists of two main parts: chapters 1–8 and 9–14. Zechariah 1–8, like Haggai, advocates the rebuilding of the temple. Even more than

Haggai, Zechariah portrayed the benefit resulting from the temple in terms of a transformation of Judah and the world into a kind of utopia. Zechariah described this transformation by means of a series of symbolic visions that resemble apocalyptic literature. In fact, Zechariah is an important precursor in the development of apocalyptic.

Zechariah 1–8 has three parts, each of which is introduced by a dating notice (1:1; 1:7; 7:1). The first part, therefore, is 1:1-6. These six verses are a call for repentance based on Yahweh's past dealings with Israel. The second section, the bulk of the book, consists of 1:7–6:15. These chapters report a series of eight visions interspersed with prophetic oracles, which are sometimes incorporated within them. The visions typically follow the pattern: vision, question about the meaning of the vision, and angel's explanation. The eight visions are the following:

1. horses patrolling the earth (1:7-17);
2. four horns representing oppressive powers and four smiths to destroy them (1:18-21);
3. a man with a measuring cord for measuring Jerusalem, which will be resettled by a large population (2:1-5 [Hebrew 2:5-9]);
4. Joshua, the high priest, and his priestly garments, both of which will be consecrated (3:1-10);
5. a lampstand and two olive trees representing Zerubbabel and Joshua (4:1-14);
6. a flying scroll with a curse on thieves and those who swear falsely (5:1-4);
7. a basket with a woman in it representing the removal of Judah's sin (5:5-11);
8. four chariots (6:1-8).

Scholars have noticed correspondences between different pairs of these visions that indicate a pattern in their arrangement. Thus, the first and last visions both involve horses and both deal with Yahweh's universal dominion. The second and seventh both have two parts to their visions; they also both concern Judah. The third and sixth both describe measurements and contain an oracle from God. The third one takes place in Jerusalem, which also seems to be the point of origin of the scroll in the sixth vision. This narrowing of focus indicates that the subject of the central visions, the fourth and fifth, is the primary interest of the author. That subject is the political and religious leadership in Jerusalem and its temple.

The third section of Zechariah 1–8 is the oracles in chapters 7–8. Like the visions, this section has its own organization in four parts, each introduced by the expression "the word of [Yahweh] came" (7:1, 8; 8:1, 18). The first part raises a question from the people of Bethel about fasting (7:3). The next three parts progress from past to future leading up to the answer to the question in 8:19. The overall tone of this section, like all of Zechariah 1–8, is optimistic and upbeat.

Zechariah 9–14 itself consists of two halves, each introduced with the heading, "an oracle" (9:1; 12:1). The overarching theme of the oracles in both halves is "the Day of Yahweh." The oracles in chapters 9–11 describe the coming "Day of Yahweh" as a time when the divine warrior will defeat Judah's enemies. Chapters 12–14 continue the "Day of Yahweh" theme, using that expression and "on that day" a total of seventeen times. Here, however, the focus is less on foreigners and more on Israel as Yahweh's target. Still, the contents of both halves are diverse; there is even an oracle against prophets (13:2-6).

GROWTH

The two parts of Zechariah (chs. 1–8 and 9–14) are different enough that the book is generally regarded by scholars as two distinct literary works. Zechariah 9–14 is more similar in some ways to Malachi than to Zechariah 1–8. Thus, much like Isaiah, Zechariah is considered composite, and Zechariah 9–14 is often referred to, on the model of Isaiah, as "Second" or "Deutero-" Zechariah. The oracles about the "Day of Yahweh" in Second Zechariah were evidently attached to First Zechariah because of the latter's visionary depictions of the future.

The first two chronological notices in First Zechariah refer to the second year of Darius or 520 B.C.E., the same year as Haggai's oracles. The third notice gives a date two years later (518), and the combined book of Haggai plus Zechariah 1–8 must have been put together not too long after that—most likely before the completion of the temple in 516–515, which neither prophet mentions. Then, Second Zechariah was added at some point after 515. The growth of the book of Zechariah, therefore, may be charted in the following four stages:

Stage 1: Haggai's oracles delivered (520 B.C.E.)
Stage 2: Zechariah's oracles delivered (520–518 B.C.E.)
Stage 3: Haggai's and Zechariah's oracles combined (518–515 B.C.E.)
Stage 4: oracles in Zechariah 9–14 added some time after 515

CONTEXT

The difference between the contexts of First and Second Zechariah is a study in contrasts. As we have seen, the setting that produced First Zechariah is clear and can be described fairly precisely. Like Haggai, Zechariah was a prophet who advocated the construction of the temple by the postexilic community. Zechariah apparently followed Haggai's lead. According to the dates of their oracles, both prophets began their careers in 520, but Haggai began prophesying first. Also, Zechariah continued beyond that year to at least 518, the date of the latest oracle in First Zechariah. Since neither Haggai nor First Zechariah mentions the completion of the temple in 515 B.C.E., the two books were probably combined into one before that date.

By way of contrast, the setting of Second Zechariah is very uncertain. There is widespread agreement that it reflects disillusionment and even conflict within the postexilic community. But the exact nature of those conflicts remains a mystery. It may be that the book reveals disappointment with restoration efforts, which had failed to live up to the idealized vision of Second Isaiah and even of Haggai and First Zechariah. Zechariah 11:4-17 and 13:7-9, in particular, attack Judah's leaders ("shepherds") and depict a community in disarray. But the precise issues remain unknown, since the symbols in the book cannot be correlated for certain with any specific event(s) or individual(s).

Even the date of Second Zechariah is debated, with some dating the book to the late fifth century and others placing it a century or more later. There is a reference to Greece (9:13), which has been construed as indicating a date after Alexander the Great's conquest of Palestine in 333 B.C.E. But the reference is too vague to pinpoint any specific date. In fact, it is possible that the oracles in Second Zechariah were produced over different decades by different individuals.

INTERPRETATION

Both First and Second Zechariah reflect familiarity with and thus reuse and reinterpret other prophetic writings. For instance, Zechariah's third vision of a man measuring Jerusalem with a measuring cord (Zech 2:1-5 [Hebrew 2:5-9]) is similar to Amos's vision of a plumb line (Amos 7:7-10) and to Ezekiel's vision of a man measuring the temple (Ezek 40–48). Similarly, Second Zechariah makes use of the "Day of Yahweh" imagery and language from prophets such as Amos, Joel, and Second Isaiah. Second Zechariah has features that resemble Amos in other respects as well. Its oracles against foreign nations focus on cities, as do those in Amos 1–2. Second Zechariah even refuses to identify with other prophets, as does Amos (cf. Zech 13:4-5; Amos 7:14-15).

Despite these similarities to previous prophets, however, there is something different about both First and Second Zechariah. Both works use language and symbols that are apocalyptic-like. The contrast is easily seen in comparing Zechariah 1–8 with Haggai. Although the message of both works is essentially the same, Zechariah makes use of visions and symbols rather than straightforward oracles as in Haggai. The material in Zechariah 1–8 is often referred to as a precursor to apocalyptic or "proto-apocalyptic." The oracles in Zechariah 9–14 are even closer to "full-blown" apocalyptic with their use of cosmic language describing Yahweh as a warrior about to execute judgment on the entire earth. Zechariah 9–14 bears striking similarity to other prophetic passages, especially Isaiah 24–27 and Joel 2:28–3:21. The term "proto-apocalyptic," therefore, is even more appropriate for these texts—including Second Zechariah—than it is for First Zechariah. Each of these two sections of the present book of Zechariah reflects a different stage in the development of apocalyptic thought and literature out of prophecy, though it is important to add that prophecy was not the only source of apocalyptic's development.

MALACHI

Malachi is the final prophetic installment in the Book of the Twelve and the last book in the Old Testament. It is important to note, though, that because of a different arrangement of books, Malachi is not the last book in the Hebrew Bible. That place falls to Chronicles. The difference lends itself to different expectations on the part of Jewish and Christian readers, as will be explored below.

CONTENT

The book of Malachi contains six oracles, each of which has a distinct dialogue built around a set of questions and answers:

1:2-5 reaffirms Yahweh's continuing love and faithfulness to Jacob/Israel in contrast to Esau/Edom.

1:6–2:9 indicts the priests in Jerusalem for their offerings of inferior animals and their failure to instruct the people properly.

2:10-16 condemns the people for unfaithfulness to God and to each other, focusing on divorce.

2:17–3:5 scolds the people for accusing God of injustice and promises a "messenger of the covenant" who will refine and purify the priests so that they can offer proper sacrifices before God approaches for judgment.

3:6-12 calls for repentance for "robbing God" by failing to tithe and promises prosperity if the full tithe is brought in.

3:13–4:3 (Hebrew 3:13-24) again raises the question of God's justice since evildoers prosper, before launching into a description of God's coming judgment on the wicked and vindication of the righteous.

The book begins with a brief heading or preface (1:1) and concludes with two widely recognized appendices, recalling two of Israel's greatest heroes. The first calls upon the audience to remember the law of Moses (4:4); the second promises the coming of Elijah as a herald of the horrific "Day of Yahweh" (4:5-6).

GROWTH

The growth of the book of Malachi is intimately associated with the development of the "Book of the Twelve," the scroll containing the twelve "minor" prophets as a part of the Hebrew canon. Malachi may not have been written as an independent book, and may not have been the name of a prophet. The heading that begins Malachi (1:1) is very similar to the headings of the two principal oracles that comprise Second Zechariah:

Mal 1:1: "An oracle. The word of [Yahweh] to Israel by Malachi "
Zech 9:1: "An oracle. The word of [Yahweh] is against the land of Hadrach"
Zech 12:1: "An oracle. The word of [Yahweh] concerning Israel"

What has become the book of Malachi may have originated as the third anonymous oracular writing appended to Zechariah or to the collection of prophetic writings. "Malachi" means "my messenger" and may have originated as a title rather than a proper name. This could help to explain the complete absence of personal information about Malachi both inside the book and elsewhere in the Bible. The Greek translation of the Old Testament, the Septuagint (LXX), takes it as a title, rendering "his messenger" instead of "my messenger" in Mal 1:1. The name may have been formulated from Mal 3:1: "See, I am sending my messenger to prepare the way before me." The motive for construing it as a proper name and the book as an independent work may have been as simple as the desire to achieve a total of twelve prophets in the scroll in parallel to the twelve tribes of Israel.

On a smaller scale, the three verses that contain the two appendices to Malachi were likely additions to the "Book of the Twelve." They evoke two of the best-known prophets of the Old Testament: Moses, who received the law, which served as the foundation for prophetic calls to obedience, and Elijah, who embodied the spirit and boldness of the ideal prophet.

There is also some indication that the final section of Malachi (3:13–4:3) may be an addition to the previous materials in the book. This final section (especially 3:16–4:3) differs in three striking ways from the preceding sections. First, in contrast to 1:1–3:12, this last section lacks any reference to Jerusalem, Judah, the temple, the priests, or any specific sin. Second, 3:16–4:3 presumes an inner-Israelite dichotomy between the "righteous" and the "wicked" not found in the earlier portions of Malachi where all the people are reproved. Third, 3:16–4:3 offers no opportunity for repentance or hope of salvation for the "wicked" but simply looks forward to the "Day of Yahweh" when he will destroy them. These differences raise the possibility that this final section of Malachi may be a kind of apocalyptic addition to the book along the lines of Second Zechariah. However, this addition is not as widely recognized in Malachi as is Second Zechariah in that book.

CONTEXT

The date and historical circumstances of Malachi are difficult to ascertain with precision. The references to the priests and sacrifices as well as to tithing indicate that the temple has been rebuilt and is functioning, so that the prophecies in Malachi followed those of Haggai and Zechariah and the completion of the temple in 515 B.C.E. The oracle on tithing (3:6-12) connects prosperity with bringing in the full tithe. It suggests that the idealistic visions of Haggai and Zechariah had not been realized and that the people were beginning to question Yahweh's faithfulness to his promises. Malachi responds by explaining that the source of the problem lies not in Yahweh's unfaithfulness but in Judah's robbing of God by failing to tithe properly.

> Bring the full tithe into the storehouse, so that there may be food in my house, and thus put me to the test, says the LORD of hosts; see if I will not open the windows of heaven for you and pour down for you an overflowing blessing. (Mal 3:10)

This oracle in particular might suggest a date not long after Haggai and Zechariah, say around 500 B.C.E.

Other prophecies in Malachi, however, have suggested a later setting to some scholars. The deterioration in worship activities might indicate a further distance from the completion of the temple. Perhaps more compelling is the fact that Malachi shares certain concerns, including proper tithing, with Ezra and Nehemiah, who worked in Jerusalem around the middle of the fifth century. Among these concerns are those of mixed marriage and divorce, which may both be addressed in Mal 2:10-16. Unfortunately, it is not entirely clear what Malachi means with the accusation that the people have profaned Yahweh's sanctuary by marrying the "daughter of a foreign god" (2:11). Is the offense apostasy, that is, worshiping other gods, or mixed marriage, meaning marrying foreign women? If the latter, it is the same problem faced by Ezra and Nehemiah. But even if this is so, Malachi's response to the problem would seem to be very different from theirs. Ezra and Nehemiah demanded that those returnees who had intermarried with the people in the land put away both their wives and children. Malachi, on the other hand, gives the strongest condemnation of divorce in the Old Testament (2:14-16). Malachi's position is the opposite of Ezra's and Nehemiah's and may even be a response to them. If so, Malachi would date from sometime in the second half of the fifth century.

INTERPRETATION

The principal, overarching theme in the book of Malachi is covenant. Three covenants are mentioned specifically: the covenant with Levi (2:8), the covenant with the ancestors (2:10), and the covenant of marriage (2:14). The middle one, the covenant with the ancestors, is ambiguous and may refer to the covenant with the patriarchs (Abraham, Isaac, and Jacob) or the covenant with the Sinai/Horeb generation—or both. The "messenger of the covenant" (3:1) is probably also a reference to the Mosaic covenant on Sinai/Horeb. The "messenger of the covenant" seems to refer to a prophetic figure. His task is to prepare the way for Yahweh's coming in judgment and to refine and purify the Levites (3:1-3).

In addition to these specific references to covenants, there are a number of other allusions to covenants in Malachi. In fact, the idea of Yahweh's covenant relationship with Israel pervades the book, at least in the background of each of its oracles. For instance, the discussion of Yahweh's love for Israel (1:2-5) makes use of ancient treaty/covenant language and imagery in which "love" is to be understood in terms of loyalty and faithfulness, demonstrated by adherence to the terms of the treaty or covenant.

Covenant terminology and ideology saturate the rest of the book as well. "Master" and "servant" and "father" and "son" (1:6) are terms that occur frequently in covenants, as do the words "cursed" and "great king" (1:14). Similarly, the term translated "special possession" in 3:17 is used elsewhere in the Old Testament and ancient Near Eastern literature to refer to the vassal in a treaty relationship (Exod 19:5; Deut 7:6; 14:2; 26:18; Ps 135:4; Qoh 2:8). Perhaps more important than these specific terms are the implications of Yahweh's covenant with Israel that Malachi emphasizes.

Above all, the oracles in Malachi stress the conditionality of the covenant between Yahweh and Israel and the obligations that it imposes upon Israel. Malachi makes the point that Yahweh has kept his side of the bargain while Israel has strayed, and the prophecies call Israel to remember its covenant commitment and be obedient. Only then will the blessings promised in the covenant for loyalty to its terms accrue. It goes without saying that the predominance of covenant ideology in Malachi reflects familiarity with Israel's covenant traditions—the stories about the patriarchs in Genesis as well as the law of Moses and the covenant with the Levites—on the part of its author(s). It is fair to say that, as the final work in the Book of the Twelve, Malachi utters the last word of prophetic interpretation of Israel's earliest traditions, and that word is "covenant."

Malachi also well illustrates a key difference between Judaism and Christianity in the interpretation of the Hebrew scripture and the expectations arising from it. In the Hebrew Bible, Chronicles, not Malachi, is the last book, and Chronicles ends with the edict of Cyrus freeing the Babylonian exiles to return to Jerusalem and rebuild the temple (2 Chr 36:22-23). The expectation of the Hebrew Bible, therefore, lies in the restoration of Israel's religious and political institutions, which Judaism seeks to fulfill in a reinterpreted form (e.g., synagogue for temple and prayer for sacrifice). The Christian Old Testament, on the other hand, ends with Malachi's admonition to recall the Mosaic law (Mal 4:4), to be sure. But this is followed by the promise of the coming of a prophetic figure, "Elijah," who will lead the people to repentance before the "great and terrible day of [Yahweh]." This appendix to Malachi has lent itself well in Christian reinterpretation to the expectation of Jesus, preceded by John the Baptist, whose lifestyle resembled Elijah's and who proclaimed a message of repentance.

PART FOUR

Writings

INTRODUCTION TO THE WRITINGS

The third section of the Hebrew Bible is known as the Writings (Hebrew *ketuvim*), a catchall term that categorizes a set of books sharing very little in common. The wide range of genres and styles of literature found in the Writings is probably the most distinguishing feature of the collection. These works are generally among the latest books of the Hebrew Bible, and so they can provide a valuable window into later stages of the community's development.

The following books comprise the Writings: Psalms, Proverbs, Job, Song of Solomon, Ruth, Lamentations, Qoheleth, Esther, Daniel, Ezra–Nehemiah, and 1–2 Chronicles. Books within this group are sometimes joined to form subgroups that are brought together due to common themes or usage. Forming one such subgroup are the Wisdom books—Proverbs, Job, and Qoheleth. These three works stem from the Israelite wisdom tradition, which attempts to address questions and issues about life arising from common human experience. Proverbs is a collection of aphorisms and maxims that offer insights about how the world works and that give instruction on how to live. Job is a work that explores the problem of innocent suffering and God's role in it. Qoheleth, also known as Ecclesiastes, contains the musings of a man who is resigned to the absurdity and emptiness of life.

Another subgroup is the *megillot,* a Hebrew word meaning "scrolls" that refers to five books that are each read on a particular Jewish feast day. The name derives from the fact that the five books can all easily fit on one scroll. Qoheleth is one of these books. The Song of Solomon is an unusual biblical book—it is erotic literature that addresses issues of human longing and desire. Ruth is a survival story that recounts the experiences of two women who must make their way in a world that tends to marginalize people in their position. As its name suggests, Lamentations gives expression to the intense emotional pain that is part of the grieving process. Esther, the last of the *megillot,* is another short story that tells the tale of a young Jewish woman who rises to a position of power in a foreign land and is thus able to save her people from destruction.

The remaining books of the Writings give further evidence of the diverse nature of this section of the Hebrew Bible. Psalms contains a collection of prayers and hymns that articulate the richness and depth of Israelite spirituality. The book of Daniel is an interesting mix of court tales and visions that center around a legendary figure. It also contains the Hebrew Bible's only example of apocalyptic, a style of writing that tries to respond to the needs and concerns of people who are experiencing oppression and persecution. Both Ezra–Nehemiah and 1–2 Chronicles are examples of historiography. The former describes events surrounding the return from exile, whereas Chronicles presents a theological account of history that is like, yet unlike, that found in the Deuteronomistic History.

A theme that is addressed by a number of these works—Ruth, Esther, Ezra–Nehemiah, Daniel, and some sections of Proverbs in particular—concerns relations with non-Israelites and non-Jews. In the case of Ruth, an openness to foreigners encourages peaceful coexistence, even to the point of welcoming them as full members of the community. But more often than not the Writings warn against the dangers of mixing with those who are different, in some places legislating against certain types of interaction with foreigners. This is probably due to the relatively late date of composition for much of this material, which probably took final shape in the exilic period when issues of identity and assimilation were especially critical.

Despite that push toward exclusivity, there is a multicultural dimension to the Writings, like the rest of the Hebrew Bible, because of its familiarity with—even indebtedness to—the literature found in other parts of the ancient Near East. The various genres and types of writing mentioned above—wisdom, erotica, novella, lament, prayer, apocalyptic, historiography—are all found among the writings of Israel's neighbors, and some of these parallels will be discussed in the pages that follow. They are an important reminder to us that the biblical literature, and Israelite thought more broadly, did not develop in a vacuum, divorced from the larger world around it.

What the Hebrew Bible's final section lacks in coherence is more than made up for by its breadth and depth. The Writings, more than the Torah or the Prophets, allow us to experience the remarkable variety of forms and styles that are part of the biblical tradition. Here we encounter the true artistry of the text and can better appreciate the astonishing creativity of its authors.

CHAPTER 28

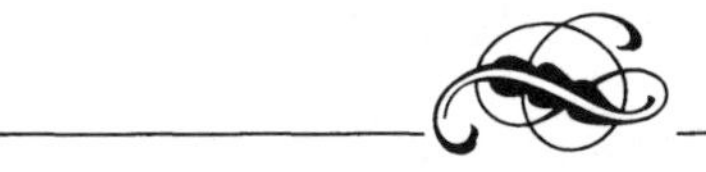

WISDOM LITERATURE: JOB

The character of Job is known in modern parlance for his long-suffering nature and endurance, as when a person is credited with having "the patience of Job." To be sure, faithful endurance through suffering is an important part of the book of Job. But it is a multifaceted book, and Job is a multidimensional character. Part of this character is reflected in Job's very name, which means something like, "Where is the father [i.e., God]?" Job desperately inquires about God's presence and role in his agony.

CONTENT

The book of Job has three distinct parts: a prologue (1:1-13), a series of dialogues (3:1–42:6), and an epilogue (42:7-17). The prologue and epilogue are in prose, while the dialogues are in poetry.

The prologue sets the stage for the story by introducing Job as a "blameless and upright" man. He does not sin himself, and he offers sacrifices on behalf of his children just in case they have sinned. Then, the scene shifts to the divine realm, where the divine beings (lit. "sons of God") in the heavenly court are presenting themselves before Yahweh. Among them is a figure called "the enemy," which is the meaning of the Hebrew word *śatan*. This is not a proper name here, though it is often misleadingly translated as such. Rather, the fact that the word has the definite article indicates that it is a title. It also does not refer to the devil; the concept of such a representative of evil is a later development in Judaism carried over into Christianity. The role of "the enemy" in this story seems to be that of a sort of prosecuting attorney, whose job it is to wander the earth looking for people to accuse of sin before God. Hence, he is sometimes referred to here as "the Accuser" or "the Adversary."

Yahweh challenges the Accuser to consider Job in his blamelessness. The Accuser responds that Job serves God only because God has blessed him. He contends that if God were to take away Job's possessions, Job would curse God. Yahweh grants the Accuser permission to do just this, with the provision that he may not harm Job's person. The story then explains how Job lost all that he had, including his children, on a single day. Yet, this episode concludes with Job accepting his situation and blessing, rather than cursing, Yahweh. He does not sin. God has won the wager.

The second chapter of the book begins with another gathering of the divine beings with the Accuser once more among them. This time, the Accuser alleges that Job serves God because God protects him and that if Job's health were threatened he would curse God. Yahweh again grants the Accuser permission, this time to harm Job's person, though with the provision that he may not kill Job (though Job does not know this!). Job is afflicted with horrible sores, so much so that even his wife encourages him to curse God and end his suffering. But Job refuses and does not "sin with his lips."

At this point, Job's three friends, Eliphaz, Bildad, and Zophar, arrive. They are in shock at his condition and sit speechless with him for seven days. Then, a debate ensues over the question of the reason for Job's suffering. Job begins by cursing the day he was born and wishing he had died at birth because of the terrible suffering he is experiencing (ch. 3). Eliphaz responds (chs. 4–5) by suggesting that Job is blind to his faults. Surely, he argues, Job must have sinned.

> Think now, who that was innocent ever perished?
> Or where were the upright cut off?
> As I have seen, those who plow iniquity
> and sow trouble reap the same. (4:7-8)

Eliphaz says that if he were in Job's shoes, he would repent and rely on God's mercy:

> As for me, I would seek God,
> and to God I would commit my cause. (5:8)

He even says that Job should be happy that God is disciplining him

> How happy is the one whom God reproves;
> therefore do not despise the discipline of the Almighty. (5:17)

Job answers in chapters 6–7, saying that his suffering is greater than his interlocutors appreciate and that they are not true friends to him because they are forsaking him in his time of need—something for which God will judge them.

> Those who withhold kindness from a friend
> forsake the fear of the Almighty.
> My companions are treacherous like a torrent-bed,
> like freshets that pass away. (6:14-15)

He asks why God torments him and why, if he has sinned, God will not just forgive him.

> If I sin, what do I do to you, you watcher of humanity?
> Why have you made me your target?
> Why have I become a burden to you?
> Why do you not pardon my transgression
> and take away my iniquity? (7:20-21)

Bildad speaks next (ch. 8), reaffirming Eliphaz's point. Bildad defends God's justice and says Job needs to repent of his sin. He even says that Job's children got what they deserved because they did wrong.

> Does God pervert justice?
> Or does the Almighty pervert the right?
> If your children sinned against him,
> he delivered them into the power of their transgression.
> If you will seek God
> and make supplication to the Almighty,
> if you are pure and upright,
> surely then he will rouse himself for you
> and restore you to your rightful place. (8:3-6)

Job's answer to Bildad (chs. 9–10) is that a human being cannot be righteous before God. What is more, God is so much more powerful that Job says he cannot answer God or reason with him. Job continues to affirm his innocence, but there is no third party to whom he can appeal for justice. He addresses God, asking why God brought him into the world just to torment and kill him.

Zophar is incensed by Job's remarks and responds with trite aphorisms in chapter 11. He says that if Job will change his attitude, God will make his life "brighter than the noonday" (11:17).

Job (chs. 12–14) says that the platitudes of his "friends" are useless compared to his experience: "Your maxims are proverbs of ashes" (13:12). He accuses them of misrepresenting the truth in order to defend God in 13:7: "Will you speak falsely for God, /and speak deceitfully for him?"

All of this represents one cycle of the dialogues, with each of the friends speaking in turn, followed by a response from Job. There are two more cycles encompassing chapters 15–21 and 22–26, respectively. The third cycle, however, is incomplete; Bildad's speech is brief, and Zophar does not speak a third time. Chapter 27 then begins with the statement that "Job again took up his discourse." Chapter 28 stands out as a hymn to Wisdom and does not appear to be attributed to any speaker. In chapter 29, Job again "took up his discourse." His speech runs through chapter 31, where "the words of Job are ended." At this point, a new character named Elihu is introduced. His speech continues through chapter 37. The rest of the dialogues (38:1–43:6) are God's speeches with brief, contrite replies from Job (40:3-5; 42:1-6).

The book ends in the epilogue with Yahweh telling Eliphaz that he is angry with the three friends because they "have not spoken of me what is right, as my servant Job has done" (42:8). Yahweh tells them to get Job to offer a sacrifice for them to atone for their wrong. Yahweh also restores Job's health and prosperity, giving him twice as much as he had before.

GROWTH

Scholars generally regard the prose sections in the prologue and epilogue as the oldest version of the book. The two parts together (1:1–2:10; 42:10-17) form a complete story that is likely based on an old folktale. The Accuser questions Job's integrity, alleging that he serves God only for the rewards. Job is tested twice and proves his faithfulness; he serves God because it is the right thing to do and not because he is blessed. It is, therefore, entirely appropriate for God to bless him, since the blessing is not the reason for his loyalty.

This folktale was used to provide the setting for a debate over the question of the cause of human suffering. The dialogues were inserted into the story, turning it into a prose framework around the poetic speeches of Job and his friends. The main issue of the book was thereby changed from the question of why a person (here Job) should serve God to why human beings suffer.

Additionally, most scholars believe that the hymn to Wisdom in chapter 28 and the speeches of Elihu were added even later to the book. The hymn to Wisdom interrupts the speeches of Job in chapters 27 and 29 and is at least an interlude. As for Elihu, he is not mentioned elsewhere in the book outside of his speeches, nor does Job or any of the other characters interact with him or respond to him. His speeches vary in style and vocabulary from the rest of the book. In content, his speeches are basically a defense of God. They thus anticipate the speeches of God. To the extent that their attitude toward Job is not that different from that of his friends, Elihu's speeches are repetitive. Finally, Elihu is the only Israelite among the book's human characters. These speeches, therefore, may have been added by a later writer who was not content with the book's ending.

CONTEXT

There are at least three relevant contexts for the book of Job. The first is the context in which the story is set. This is the distant past, perhaps the time in which the patriarchs are envisioned as living. Like them, Job's wealth is measured in terms of livestock. Job is also not Israelite but lives in the land of Uz, which may have been in Edom. This setting in a distant place and time hints at the legendary nature of the story. Job's legendary status is also reflected in references to him, along with Noah and Dan(i)el, as a model of righteousness in the book of Ezekiel (Ezek 14:14, 20).

A second context is that in which the book was written. Job is extremely difficult to date. Most scholars place it in the exile (sixth–fifth centuries B.C.E.). It has been argued that the book was written as a response to the Deuteronomistic History, disputing its claim that the exile was punishment for sin. It is true that Job's message would call into question the equation of suffering with punishment that is typical of the prophets and the Deuteronomistic History. However, there is no clear indication that the book of Job was designed specifically to counter the Deuteronomistic History. The focus of Job is on individual suffering rather than the experience of a nation or community.

Finally, there is the broader, theological context of the book. Suffering, especially at an individual level, was certainly not limited to the exile, and questioning the reason for it is a common human response, which cannot be limited to any particular time or event. Rather than trying to isolate a historical context for Job, we may do better to be content with understanding the book in the social and literary context of Wisdom thought and literature, which seeks to tackle the big questions of life—such as the struggle to comprehend human suffering and its cause(s). Coupled with this question is that of the justice or fairness of God (theodicy). These issues are timeless and simply an integral part of the human experience. Not surprisingly, therefore, ancient works of Wisdom from both Egypt and Mesopotamia bear similarities to the book of Job. The similarities are only general. That is, there is no indication of literary dependence. Still, they show that the gap between certain religious teachings and human experience, reflected in Job, was felt across various cultures and belief systems in the ancient Near East.

INTERPRETATION

The issue of theodicy is one of the most enduring and difficult of problems faced by theologians. The basic question is easy to frame: if God is benevolent (all good) and omnipotent (all powerful), where do suffering and evil come from? If God is benevolent, he would presumably not want to bring harm on people. If God is omnipotent, he could do away with suffering and evil or not allow them to exist in the first place.

The philosophical and theological complexities of this question go far beyond Job, which deals with the question at a very basic level—the case of one man. Job holds fast to his integrity and denies that he has done anything wrong, while his friends claim that he must have sinned or he would not be suffering. Job's friends, therefore, represent the traditional view that the book's author wishes to call into question. To the extent that Job says he has done nothing deserving punishment, he also buys into the traditional view. He speaks, though, from his personal experience and situation. He knows he has not sinned. Therefore, he reasons, God is afflicting him without cause. At points, he goes so far as to express a wish to summon God in order to argue his case before God and to compel God to defend his actions (13:3, 18-23). He also wishes for an impartial mediator who would hear both sides—God's and Job's—and adjudicate (9:33). The fear Job articulates in both of these passages is that God will overpower him and prevent him from fully defending himself or expressing his position.

As is typical of Wisdom literature, the book of Job, as it now stands, is a debate on the question of the cause of suffering. The two positions are represented by Job and his friends. The friends take the view that suffering is the consequence of sin. Job counters, in effect, that this is not always so, since he has not sinned yet is suffering. The fact that the end of the book has God saying that Job has spoken rightly of him but the friends have not suggests that the author of the book sides with Job. That is, the book was evidently written to challenge the traditional or at least common explanation of suffering as the result of sin.

Nevertheless, the ending of the book of Job contains some intriguing features that complicate its message. First of all, God does not really answer Job's questions. That is, God never explains to Job why he suffered or why suffering exists at all and what its potential causes may be. Perhaps that is part of the book's point—that God does not have to explain himself or justify his actions to humans. In a sense this is precisely what Job admits in his speeches—that God can simply overpower him. But God does not address the heart of Job's concerns, his demand to know the cause for his ills.

A second intriguing feature of the ending is the way that it seems to undercut the book's primary contention. As we saw above, Job's restoration fits perfectly as the conclusion to the folktale. Its topic was not suffering or theodicy but human integrity, the idea that one should serve God regardless of reward. With the insertion of the dialogues, however, the ending becomes inappropriate. The point of the dialogues is to dispute the notion that suffering is the result of sin. The flip side of this notion, which the dialogues must also call into question, is that prosperity is the result of righteousness. But Job's restoration seems to support this latter idea and therefore, indirectly, the notion of the correlation between sin and suffering. Still, one need not regard the ending as a blatant contradiction. Rather, one might see it as a way of leaving the debate about the reason for suffering open. As with Job's question of God, the answer is never given. The reason for suffering is never explained, and the debate about it remains open-ended. This kind of open debate is also typical of Wisdom literature.

CHAPTER 29

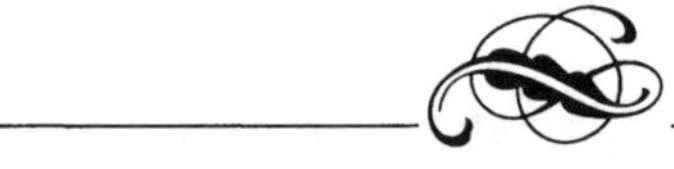

WISDOM LITERATURE: PROVERBS

The title of this book comes from the Hebrew term *māšāl*. Although "proverb" is typically used to translate *māšāl*, it would be a mistake to assume that the two words convey the same meaning. There are proverbs in the book of Proverbs, but it also contains other literary forms like allegories, similes, lists, and pronouncements that make the work more diverse than its English name might suggest. The Hebrew root of the word *māšāl* has to do with likeness and comparison, and this is the best way to understand the aim of the book—it invites its readers to reflect on its contents in order to see similarities and make connections with the everyday world around them.

CONTENT

The book of Proverbs, as one of the Wisdom writings, attempts to explain what common experience can teach us about life and human nature. It contains a collection of sayings and aphorisms that are mostly observations about social relations and how the world works. Although the book tends to avoid legislating behavior or being overtly dogmatic, it consistently reinforces certain ideas and practices in a way that leaves little doubt as to how the reader should order and conduct his or her life.

Traditionally, the book has been associated with King Solomon. A very obvious reason for this is that the first two collections of proverbs it contains are attributed to him (1:1; 10:1). Similarly, a later collection is identified as originating with Solomon but copied down by officials of King Hezekiah (25:1). The description of Solomon's reign elsewhere in the Bible also helps to account for the link between him and the book of Proverbs. In 1 Kings 3 he requests of God that he be given a discerning mind, and his wish is granted. Later in the same chapter the legendary wisdom of Solomon is displayed in the famous story of the two women who each claim to be the mother of the same child. The dispute is resolved only when the king proposes to have the baby cut in half, thereby revealing the identity of the true mother. The clearest connection between Solomon and

Proverbs is found in 1 Kgs 4:32, which claims he authored many of them. "He composed three thousand proverbs, and his songs numbered a thousand and five."

However, scholars generally agree that there is no real support for the claims of Solomonic authorship for Proverbs. It has already been noted that the book contains a number of collections that are clearly marked by titles or superscriptions. Even though some of the headings are associated with Solomon, these attributions are from a later period and should not be dated to his reign. These collections were compiled at various times and joined together during a complex process of growth and editorial work. There are at least seven sections to the book of Proverbs, each with its own distinct history and features.

The first collection (1:1–9:18) bears the title "the proverbs of Solomon son of David, king of Israel." The opening section of this part might be the introduction to the entire book because it appears to describe the purpose of the work and the effects it can have on its reader. These opening verses contain many terms and ideas that are basic to the biblical wisdom tradition.

> For learning about wisdom and instruction,
> for understanding words of insight,
> for gaining instruction in wise dealing,
> righteousness, justice, and equity;
> to teach shrewdness to the simple,
> knowledge and prudence to the young—
> let the wise also hear and gain in learning,
> and the discerning acquire skill,
> to understand a proverb and a figure,
> the words of the wise and their riddles.
> The fear of the LORD is the beginning of knowledge;
> fools despise wisdom and instruction. (1:2-7)

The last sentence of the passage is interesting for a couple of reasons. It is the first reference in Proverbs to "the fear of the LORD," a theme that appears a number of times throughout the book (9:10; 15:33; 31:30) and expresses the proper attitude of a wise person. Its second occurrence in 9:10 is found at the end of this first section, forming an inclusio that helps to establish a central message of the book. The last line also highlights the choice that is implicitly present throughout much of the book of Proverbs. Each person must make a conscious decision to follow wisdom or run the risk of being a fool who is doomed to destruction.

Much of the rest of the first part is presented as a set of instructions from a parent to a child, with the address "my child/children" recurring throughout the section and uniting it (1:8, 10, 15; 2:1; 3:1, 11, 21; 4:1, 10, 20;

5:1, 7; 6:1, 3, 20; 7:1, 24; 8:32). The older, parental side functions as an authority figure who tries to encourage the younger addressee to live properly by engaging in certain activities and avoiding others. Interestingly, the child never responds to the message of the parent. An aspect of this section that will be discussed below is the personification of wisdom as a female figure.

The second section (10:1–22:16) is titled "the proverbs of Solomon" and differs in style and content from the first. It contains brief comments on life that are usually presented in bicola form, that is, two lines to each verse. Unlike the first part, hardly any family language is found here, and it is comprised of observations on experience rather than imperatives to act or not act in a certain way. For the most part, this section does not speak of the evils or dangers present in life, and it possesses a more upbeat quality. This part of the book contains many examples of what a modern reader would identify as parables.

The third section of the book (22:17–24:34), titled simply "the words of the wise," has generated much discussion among scholars because of its striking similarity to the Instruction of Amenemope, an Egyptian wisdom text of the eleventh century B.C.E. The two texts follow the same general outline and often closely parallel each other in specific content. Each calls attention to the fact that it is divided into thirty sections, and each identifies a purpose that they both share. The final chapter of the Egyptian work begins,

> See thou these thirty chapters:
> They entertain; they instruct;
> They are the foremost of all books;
> They make the ignorant to know. (ANET)

This is quite similar to what the biblical author says in 22:20-21.

> Have I not written for you thirty sayings
>   of admonition and knowledge,
> to show you what is right and true,
>   so that you may give a true answer to those who sent you?

It is generally held that the Instruction of Amenemope served as a source or model for this part of Proverbs.

The fourth section of Proverbs (25:1–29:27) carries the superscription "these are other proverbs of Solomon that the officials of King Hezekiah of Judah copied." Like other parts of the book, it contains words of advice and observations on life. "Whoever gives to the poor will lack nothing, / but one who turns a blind eye will get many a curse" (28:27). "A fool gives full vent to anger, / but the wise quietly holds it back" (29:11). It is also distinguished by a great many similes and comparisons, some of which are quite graphic and memorable. "Like a dog that returns to its vomit / is a fool who reverts to his folly" (26:11). "As a door turns on its hinges, / so does a lazy person in bed" (26:14). "Like a bird that strays from its nest is / one who strays from home" (27:8). The teaching function of these proverbs and the points they attempt to convey are readily apparent in such images. The fourth part of the book also contains a number of references to the king and the royal court, a context that is not frequently mentioned elsewhere in the book (25:1-7; 28:2-3, 15-16; 29:4, 12, 14, 26).

The final three sections of the book are briefer than the first four. The "words of Agur son of Jakeh" (30:1-33) begin on a somewhat skeptical note as the author wonders if it is possible to attain true wisdom. The section concludes with a series of numerical sayings, which are riddle-like statements meant to list examples of particular qualities.

> Three things are stately in their stride;
> four are stately in their gait:
> the lion, which is mightiest among wild animals
> and does not turn back before any;
> the strutting rooster, the he-goat,
> and a king striding before his people. (30:29-31)

"The words of King Lemuel," an unknown figure, are found in 31:1-9 in the form of a series of admonitions from the king's mother urging him to avoid wine and women because they will distract him from the duties of his office. The final section (31:10-31) is a poem that describes the qualities of the perfect woman. It is written as an acrostic, with the first word of each line beginning with the next letter in the Hebrew alphabet.

GROWTH

The discussion of the content of Proverbs has identified a number of ways in which it is possible to discern in general terms the growth and development of the book. The easily identifiable collections that are marked off by their superscriptions underscore the composite nature of the work. Each of these sections has its own distinct history of formation and transmission, which is now impossible to trace with any confidence. The similarity between 22:17–24:34 and the Egyptian Instruction of Amenemope is also a clear indication that the book has evolved over time. The author(s) of Proverbs almost certainly drew on wisdom literature from Egypt, and perhaps elsewhere in the ancient Near East, in the process of compiling the work. Similarly, the version of the book that is preserved in the Septuagint is different from the Hebrew one in some significant ways. The Greek text presents the material in a different order and contains over one hundred proverbs that are not in the Hebrew, and these differences attest to the complex development of the book.

There is not a great deal of theological language in the book of Proverbs. For example, the covenant is not mentioned at all and there are very few references to the cult or the details of worship. The first section (chs. 1–9) occasionally asserts that there is a connection between wisdom and faith in God (1:7; 2:1-11; 3:5-7; 8:12-31, 35-36), but the theological language in latter chapters is less frequent and more general (16:9; 19:21; 21:30-31). This has led some scholars in the past to suggest that the material in the book was originally secular in nature and over time a theological veneer was added to it in places. This view is no longer popular, and it is now assumed that the relatively rare religious elements in the text are original to it. In other words, more scholars have become convinced that the wisdom tradition in Israel did not begin as a totally secular movement but rather are inclined to think that there was a theological component in some streams of it from the beginning.

The presence of different collections in the book indicates that Proverbs took shape over an extended period of time, but the details of that process are impossible to reconstruct. It is quite likely that it reached its final form sometime in the early postexilic period (the first half of the sixth century B.C.E.), but the various sections that compose it are probably much older than that.

CONTEXT

As just noted, it is extremely difficult to date Proverbs with any precision. This is partly due to the nature of the material it contains. Most of the aphorisms and maxims in the book reflect common human experience in all times and places and therefore cannot be easily associated with a particular period or location. This being the case, is it possible to at least identify the social context out of which such a work might have emerged and responded to? This is an issue that has occupied the attention of many scholars, but the results are far from conclusive. In all likelihood, the various collections that comprise Proverbs arose out of a number of different contexts.

The high concentration of terms like "father," "mother," and "child/children" in the first section and elsewhere in the book suggests that the family was the origin of some of the material in Proverbs. Israelite parents educated their children on proper living and behavior by instructing them through proverbs and similar sayings, not unlike what continues to happen into the present day. Some sections of Proverbs probably trace their roots back to this age-old way of communicating advice from one generation to the next. They may have circulated orally for some time before they were written down and eventually became a part of the book as we now have it.

Another context that gave rise to some of this material was the royal court. The book's explicit link to Solomon shows that biblical Israel followed other ancient Near Eastern cultures in associating kings with wisdom. Some scholars have suggested that this might have been done in order to legitimate Solomon's harsh style of rule. In this view, God's granting wisdom to Solomon in 1 Kings 3 gives him divine approval and serves as an apology or defense for his later actions in a way similar to how the Deuteronomistic History functions for King David.

The superscriptions referring to the "proverbs of Solomon" (1:1; 10:1; 25:1) do not necessarily imply that we are to think he wrote them all. More likely, it is a way of claiming that the proverbs were collected during Solomon's reign and approved by him. The actual tasks of composing and writing the proverbs would have fallen to professional scribes and other members of the royal court charged with handling the demands of an expanding society. We see a reference to this group in 25:1, which speaks of the officials of King Hezekiah of Judah who copied down the proverbs of Solomon. These individuals were well-educated, literate members of society who were familiar with other cultures of the ancient Near East and proficient in the languages spoken throughout the area. They were probably also involved in the education of princes and other members of nobility. Most likely some portions of the book were first written down by these court officials, who were preserving these traditions for the king or using them for instructional purposes.

An argument against a royal context for Proverbs is that there are not many references to the king and the court in the book. The bulk of the work is dominated by themes that center on personal morality and interpersonal relations, while only a small percentage of it addresses issues related to kingship. This has caused some scholars to argue that the connection to Solomon and the court is a late addition to the book that might date from the exilic period. As noted earlier, assigning dates to Proverbs is a highly speculative undertaking, but it is not unreasonable to suggest that some portions of the work have their origin in the royal court.

The fact that neighboring cultures associated wisdom with kingship suggests that the same thing was probably true for ancient Israel. It has already been noted that a section of the book of Proverbs (22:17–24:34) is dependent upon the Egyptian Instruction of Amenemope. Another wisdom text, "The Book of Ahiqar," attests more directly to the connection between wisdom and the court. This work was written in Aramaic in the fifth century B.C.E. and was discovered in the ruins of the Jewish exilic settlement of Elephantine in southern Egypt. It describes the adventures of Ahiqar, a wise scribe who worked in the court of the Assyrian ruler Esarhaddon (680–669 B.C.E.). Part of the book contains a collection of proverbs and other wisdom-like material not unlike what is found in the Bible.

It seems, then, that the two social contexts most clearly associated with the book of Proverbs are the family and the royal court. Basing their arguments on evidence from other ancient Near Eastern societies, some scholars have proposed that another likely setting would have been the school. Theoretically, this makes perfect sense because there is a clear pedagogic quality and purpose to Proverbs. But the problem with this theory is the lack of any evidence supporting the existence of schools in the preexilic period. Until it can be conclusively demonstrated that there were schools in Israel, it is better not to speculate on their possible connection to the book of Proverbs.

INTERPRETATION

Several times in the first section of the book, wisdom is personified as a female figure who interacts with people. The first of these is in Prov 1:20-33, most of which is a warning to those who have rejected Wisdom's call to follow her ways.

> Because I have called and you refused,
> have stretched out my hand and no one heeded,
> and because you have ignored all my counsel
> and would have none of my reproof,
> I also will laugh at your calamity;
> I will mock when panic strikes you. (1:24-26)

Only those who listen to Wisdom and take her advice will enjoy a secure and happy life that is free of trouble.

The passage opens with a description of where Wisdom makes her plea.

> Wisdom cries out in the street;
> in the squares she raises her voice.
> At the busiest corner she cries out;
> at the entrance of the city gates she speaks. (1:20-21)

The street, square, and city gate are the most public spaces in a society. In ancient Israel these locations were where people met, business was transacted, and court cases were decided. Wisdom is present and available in all these places; people only need to listen for her and conduct their lives according to her message.

Wisdom's authority is underscored by the similarities between her words and what the prophets say elsewhere in the Bible. Her cry "How long?" (v. 22) is echoed in Jeremiah (4:14, 21). The complaint that her call has been ignored is similar to the one voiced by the prophets (Isa 65:12; 66:4; Jer 7:13). The Hebrew word translated "give heed" at the beginning of verse 23 might better be rendered as "turn" or "return," an important concept in the prophetic writings that urges people to reorient their lives. These and other connections with the prophets contribute to the overall image of Wisdom as an authoritative spokeswoman for God.

Wisdom also speaks in 8:1-36, a passage that is less closely affiliated with the prophetic tradition and lacks the somewhat threatening tone of her first speech. Here, too, she cries out in the main thoroughfares and at the entrances to the city (8:1-3). She begins by singing her own praises and listing the many outstanding qualities she possesses, including prudence, intelligence, truth, righteousness, and discretion. She boasts that wisdom is better than gold or jewels and that it is only through her that kings are able to rule properly (8:4-21).

She then goes on to explain her role in creation (8:22-31). Wisdom was with God from the beginning of time, before anything else had been formed, and was present when God created the heavens, the waters, and the earth. She enjoys a unique intimacy with God, who experiences great pleasure from her presence.

> Then I was beside him, like a master worker;
> and I was daily his delight,
> rejoicing before him always,
> rejoicing in his inhabited world
> and delighting in the human race. (8:30-31)

The precise nature of the relationship between Wisdom and God in this text is difficult to determine because the description of how it began in 8:22 is ambiguous. "The LORD created me at the beginning of his work, /the first of his acts of long ago." The Hebrew word translated here as "created" can also mean "begot," "brought forth," or even "acquired." Commentators have usually been careful to avoid giving the impression that Wisdom is a preexistent being or a child conceived by God, but in fact the exact meaning of the verb is a point of debate.

Wisdom is also personified in 9:1-6, where she builds a house, prepares a meal, and invites people to partake.

Come, eat of my bread
   and drink of the wine I have mixed.
Lay aside immaturity, and live
   and walk in the way of insight. (9:5-6)

Here she is contrasted with the foolish woman, who attempts to seduce people into abandoning the proper path and embracing a life of folly (9:13-18). This juxtaposition captures well the theme of choice that is at the heart of these depictions of Lady Wisdom and the book of Proverbs as a whole. Every person is continually confronted with a choice—he or she must make the decision to either follow wisdom or reject it. At the end of her second speech, Wisdom reminds us that the stakes are high and it is ultimately a matter of life or death.

For whoever finds me finds life
   and obtains favor from the LORD;
but those who miss me injure themselves;
   all who hate me love death. (8:35-36)

Underlying these texts is an unshakable confidence in the reliability of the law of cause and effect. They reflect a certainty that if someone chooses a particular path it will lead to only one destination. In other words, according to this worldview the person who opts for wisdom can be assured of success and a happy life. This understanding of acts and consequences is characteristic of the book of Proverbs, but it does not typify the biblical wisdom tradition as a whole. The other two wisdom books, Job and Qoheleth, recognize that this isn't the way things work because good people are not always rewarded and evil people often flourish. The authors of Proverbs were undoubtedly well aware of this fact, but for their own reasons or those of their audiences they chose to express a belief in a more predictable world.

CHAPTER 30

WISDOM LITERATURE: QOHELETH

Qoheleth is one of the five *megillot* ("scrolls") that make up a section of the Writings in modern editions of the Hebrew Bible. The other books that comprise the *megillot* are Song of Solomon, Ruth, Lamentations, and Esther. Each of the members of that group is read in conjunction with a particular Jewish feast, and Qoheleth is associated with the Feast of Booths, or *Sukkoth,* celebrated in the fall as a commemoration of the Israelites' journey from Egypt to the promised land.

CONTENT

In the view of most scholars the language and vocabulary of Qoheleth suggest that it was composed at a relatively late date. Many of the ideas and thoughts expressed in the book reflect a postexilic context in which the beliefs and attitudes of earlier times are being questioned. In addition, some of the words in the book are Aramaisms, which means that they show influence from Aramaic on the Hebrew forms. Aramaisms are characteristic of later compositions. The same can be said about the Persian words that are occasionally found in the text. An example of this is the term *pardes,* a Persian word found in 2:5 meaning "park" that is etymologically related to the English word "paradise."

The superscription that opens the book identifies the author as the "son of David," a designation that has led to the idea that Solomon wrote the work. But Solomon is never mentioned by name anywhere in the book, so the opening verse is best understood as an attempt to associate the work with a venerable figure of the past. The superscription also refers to the author as *qoheleth,* a word found nowhere else in the Hebrew Bible. It is variously translated as "teacher" and "preacher," but it is perhaps best rendered as "gatherer," which could possibly be an allusion to the wisdom and personal wealth the author has accumulated. The Greek translation of *qoheleth* is *ekklesiastes,* which is the basis for the other title by which the book is commonly known—Ecclesiastes.

Sometimes referred to as the most pessimistic book in the Hebrew

Bible, Qoheleth contains a variety of different literary genres and styles of writing, including autobiography, story, parable, and proverb. There is some debate regarding how best to divide up the central part of the book that makes up its main body, but there is a general consensus regarding the arrangement of the material at the two ends of the work. The superscription (1:1) precedes an opening statement (1:2) that is presented as an instruction from the author expressing one of the central themes of the book: "Vanity of vanities, says the Teacher, vanity of vanities! All is vanity!" This is followed by a poem in 1:3-11 that discusses the circularity and predictability of nature that is neatly summed up in verse 9:

> What has been is what will be,
> and what has been done is what will be done;
> there is nothing new under the sun.

The end of the book begins with a section that urges the reader to make the most of life before it is too late (11:7–12:7). "Remember your creator in the days of your youth, before the days of trouble come, and the years draw near when you will say, 'I have no pleasure in them'" (12:1). There then follows a statement that is virtually identical to the one found in 1:2. "Vanity of vanities, says the Teacher; all is vanity" (12:8). These two verses function as an inclusio that frames the entire book and reinforces the idea that this is a central message of the work. Qoheleth concludes with an epilogue that some scholars divide into two (12:9-11, 12-14).

The main body of the book opens with a section (1:12–2:26) in which the author speaks in the first person as a king of Israel that has been compared with royal annals and inscriptions found in other parts of the ancient Near East. He describes his personal quest for wisdom and riches that left him feeling hollow and unsatisfied, causing him to conclude that life is ultimately meaningless. "So I hated life, because what is done under the sun was grievous to me; for all is vanity and a chasing after wind" (2:17). After this point the author never again speaks of himself as a king or uses language associated with royalty to describe himself.

Various theories have been put forward regarding how the rest of the central part of the book (3:1–12:7) is organized and should be divided. A few sections are fairly well-defined, like the poem in 3:1-8 whose opening words are "For everything there is a season, and a time for every matter under heaven." This brief composition provided the lyrics for a popular song written by folksinger Pete Seeger and recorded by the band The Byrds in the 1960s. But most of the units, if they exist at all, are very hard to identify. Some scholars have argued that the work is organized around a series of seven refrains that urge readers to eat, drink, and enjoy themselves (2:24-26; 3:12-13; 3:22; 5:18-19; 8:15; 9:7-10; 11:7-10). Another has claimed that there are a number of refrains that are found in different parts of the book that reveal an elaborate system of numerical patterns. Others have seen a structure that is thematic in nature, or an organization that is based on Greek styles of argument.

Despite the lack of agreement on the precise structure of the middle section of Qoheleth, certain themes and ideas reappear with frequency, giving the work a semblance of organization and cohesiveness. The author believes that the conventional wisdom and pat answers that characterized the past no longer apply because the world lacks moral order since human experience is dominated by chance and randomness. "Again I saw that under the sun the race is not to the swift, nor the battle to the strong, nor bread to the wise, nor riches to the intelligent, nor favor to the skillful; but time and chance happen to them all" (9:11). Futility and emptiness result from the constant search for the meaning of life. In particular, the attempt to understand God's purpose in the world is pointless. God is referred to throughout the course of the work (1:13; 2:24-26; 3:10-19; 5:1-7, 18-20; 7:13-14, 29; 8:12-13; 9:7; 11:5; 12:13-14), but the author ultimately finds the deity incomprehensible and does not believe human beings have a special relationship with God. "He has made everything suitable for its time; moreover he has put a sense of past and future into their minds, yet they cannot find out what God has done from the beginning to the end" (3:11). Death awaits us all, and once we are gone we are soon forgotten.

The word Qoheleth uses to describe this absurd and tragic condition that all humans share is *hebel*. It is a term, found thirty times in the book, that can describe a breath or vapor, and also carries the connotation of something fleeting that lacks permanence. As in the texts cited above, it is often translated as "vanity," which conveys the sense of futility that is at the heart of the Hebrew word. Reflecting upon his experiences and hollow accomplishments causes Qoheleth to conclude that all of life is vanity and as fleeting as a breath.

GROWTH

As already stated, there is a general scholarly consensus that the text of Qoheleth as we have it is a relatively late document. This conclusion has been reached largely on the basis of the language and vocabulary of the book. The Aramaisms and Persian words it contains point in this direction, as do the linguistic features it shares with later forms of the Hebrew language. Some scholars have suggested that the Hebrew of Qoheleth has certain affinities with the Mishnaic Hebrew that developed after the return from exile and took definitive shape during the rabbinic period. Based on this linguistic evidence and other factors, most date Qoheleth to the third century B.C.E.

It is likely that the book in its present form does not come from its original author but is the result of editorial and redactional activity. It is even possible that more than one editor contributed to the work. The superscription in 1:1 that attributes the book to the "son of David" is most likely a later addition like the superscriptions found on many of the psalms. The epilogue that closes the work is also probably not original to the book. As noted above, some have claimed that there are actually two epilogues. The first, in 12:9-11, repeats the title *qoheleth* that first appears in the book's opening verse and explains how the author is a typical wise man who instructs his audience to take his message to heart.

The proposed second epilogue (12:12-14) adopts a very different tone. "Of anything beyond these, my child, beware. Of making many books there is no end, and much study is a weariness of the flesh. The end of the matter; all has been heard. Fear God, and keep his commandments; for that is the whole duty of everyone. For God will bring every deed into judgment, including every secret thing, whether good or evil." The last two sentences, which both mention God, do not fit very well with the rest of the book, and are seen by many scholars to be a later addition that does not come from the hand of the original author. The call to fear God is something found in other parts of the book (3:14; 5:7; 8:12-13), but nowhere else is the reader told to follow God's commandments. Similarly, the confident note on which the book closes, that God will judge every act, runs counter to Qoheleth's repeated complaint that God is inscrutable and human existence is pointless.

These final sentences put the book more in line with the theology and perspective of most of the rest of the Hebrew Bible, and they were likely influential in the decision to accept Qoheleth into the canon of received writings. It has sometimes been claimed that its association with Solomon played a more significant role in the book's acceptance, but this is probably not correct. As already pointed out, Solomon's name never appears anywhere in the text. In addition, a number of other works, like the Wisdom of Solomon and the Odes of Solomon, are clearly attributed to him but are not part of the canon. More likely, Qoheleth's status as a canonical book is due to its final lines that stress the importance of being faithful to the law and commands of God.

This is related to a larger issue that will be treated in more detail in the section below on interpretation. In a number of places statements are made that seem to go against the dominant view that Qoheleth advocates throughout most of the book. This has sometimes been explained by positing a later editor who added material in an effort to have the book better reflect traditional Israelite beliefs and attitudes. Some scholars have suggested that this might be the same editor who was responsible for the epilogue in 12:12-14. An example of this can be seen in 3:17, which differs from most of the book in that it describes God as intimately involved in human existence. "I said in my heart, God will judge the righteous and the wicked, for he has appointed a time for every matter, and for every work." An even clearer instance of this is in 11:9, where the carpe diem attitude that characterizes much of the book is found in the first half of the verse, only to be followed by a caution that God is keeping score and there will be an ultimate price to pay. "Rejoice, young man, while you are young, and let your heart cheer you in the days of your youth. Follow the inclination of your heart and the desire of your eyes, but know that for all these things God will bring you into judgment."

The presence of these multiple voices and perspectives might be evidence of the growth and evolution of the book as it was reworked by editors who attempted to respond to the needs of changing times and circumstances. Another clue pointing to the text's development could be the different ways the author is referred to in the book. Most of the time, he speaks in the first person as he instructs the reader on wisdom or relates his own experiences. "In my vain life I have seen everything; there are righteous people who perish in their righteousness, and there are wicked people who prolong their life in their evildoing" (7:15). But in some places—particularly in the opening and closing verses of the book—he is spoken of in the third person, and this might be evidence of editorial hands at work.

CONTEXT

It is hard to pinpoint with any precision the exact time and location in which the book of Qoheleth was written. A few passages are quasi-narratives and could possibly be based on actual events, but they are too vague and lacking in detail to be of any help in dating them. Interestingly, they all make reference to a king but do not identify him with the author. "There was a little city with few people in it. A great king came against it and besieged it, building great siegeworks against it. Now there was found in it a poor wise man, and he by his wisdom delivered the city. Yet no one remembered that poor man" (9:14-15; see also 4:13-16; 8:2-4; 10:16-17). It is possible, perhaps likely, that such texts are simply parables that are meant to make a point and have no basis in history. Much more useful is the linguistic and vocabulary evidence mentioned earlier that at least allows us to date the text within a given range. Egypt and Phoenicia have been proposed as possible settings in which Qoheleth was written, but nothing in the text rules out a provenance in Palestine.

Some scholars have argued that Qoheleth must have belonged to the upper class. According to the text, he was a man of means who had accumulated more wealth than anyone in Jerusalem (2:4-9). He may have been speaking from personal experience with his repeated reminders that money and possessions do not prevent one from experiencing the same fate of death and anonymity that awaits every person. "The lover of money will not be satisfied with money; nor the lover of wealth, with gain. This also is vanity" (5:10). It is likely that Qoheleth's pupils came from wealthy backgrounds and he was trying to warn them against becoming complacent in their prosperity and good fortune. The Zenon Archive, a collection of documents that offer valuable insights into daily life and society in mid-third century B.C.E. Palestine and the rest of the Greek world, supports this idea. According to some of these writings, privileged Jews around 250 B.C.E. enjoyed a tremendous amount of economic prosperity, and it is possible that this is the very audience to whom Qoheleth directed his message.

The author was likely influenced by certain ideas and ways of thinking that were popular within the Greek culture of his time. Concepts like absurdity and randomness certainly had their counterparts in the Greek world. Given the date of the book's composition, it is not inconceivable that Qoheleth had been exposed to them.

A number of literary works from the ancient Near East address issues similar to those found in Qoheleth. From Egypt there is a composition titled "A Dialogue between a Man and His Soul," which comes from the Middle Kingdom period (ca. 2000 B.C.E.) and describes a conversation between a man and his soul. The man is despondent over his lack of good fortune despite the fact that he has behaved in an upright and moral fashion. He raises the possibility of suicide, and his soul responds by telling him that one who commits suicide does not enjoy the benefits of the afterlife. The soul recommends instead that the man stop trying to measure up to the rules set by society and simply live in a way that will allow him to enjoy life. The book of Qoheleth never puts forth suicide as a solution to the meaninglessness of human existence, but the connections between it and this Egyptian text are apparent.

Another parallel is seen in a section of the Gilgamesh story, an epic that purports to describe the life and adventures of Gilgamesh, a legendary king of Uruk in Mesopotamia around the year 2600 B.C.E. It has survived in a number of different versions and was originally written in Akkadian. The text is well known to Bible scholars because it makes reference to a figure named Utnapishtim, who survived a devastating flood in a large boat just as Noah does in Genesis. But another part of the story shares a thematic connection with Qoheleth. At one point Gilgamesh, mourning the death of his close friend Enkidu, comes upon a woman who asks him why he is so forlorn. He tells her the reason he is troubled and acknowledges his fear of death. She responds by asking him how he possibly expects to escape death, which is the fate of every mortal. She advises him to be happy with his lot in life, dance, play, and enjoy his children and wife. The call to enjoy life and not worry about what one is unable to control is voiced repeatedly in Qoheleth.

The similarities between these ancient Near Eastern texts—and others like them—and Qoheleth are striking, but they should not cause us to jump to the conclusion that the author of the biblical book was borrowing from the earlier works. Throughout history human beings have sought to understand the purpose of life and have struggled with the painful fact of mortality. Many have attempted to articulate their fears and views by composing speculative texts that have wrestled with these issues. Qoheleth is just one example of many such efforts that extend throughout the ancient Near East and beyond.

INTERPRETATION

The overall message of Qoheleth is fairly consistent, but it contains passages that contradict what is said elsewhere. This phenomenon was noted above in relation to 3:17 and 11:9. Another example can be seen by comparing 7:2 with 9:7. The first text rejects celebration in favor of grief and sorrow.

> It is better to go to the house of mourning
>   than to go to the house of feasting;
> for this is the end of everyone,
>   and the living will lay it to heart.

This is the opposite advice offered in 9:7 and several other passages that call for celebration and taking pleasure in the moment. "Go, eat your bread with enjoyment, and drink your wine with a merry heart; for God has long ago approved what you do."

These inconsistencies can be understood in several different ways. It might be that Qoheleth cites traditional wisdom only to criticize and reject it. He presents the popular, dominant teachings, and then proposes alternatives that challenge them. In 8:17 he disapproves of those who think they have all the answers to life's mysteries, and his work may be an attempt to refute their claims to certainty. Note the not-so-subtle slap at the wise contained in the passage. "Then I saw all the work of God, that no one can find out what is happening under the sun. However much they may toil in seeking, they will not find it out; even though those who are wise claim to know, they cannot find it out." As appealing as this explanation might be, the author does not explicitly state that he is critiquing received wisdom. He never says, "You've been taught this, but here's what I teach," so we are forced to read between the lines to adopt this interpretation.

Some scholars have argued that Qoheleth is engaging in debate with an adversary throughout the book. In their view the conflicting viewpoints reflect the different perspectives of the author and his opponent, whether real or imaginary. This is an attractive explanation because many writings from the ancient world adopt such a dialogue format to treat complex, difficult-to-solve issues like those addressed in Qoheleth. But the problem here is similar to the one encountered above. Nowhere does the author suggest that such a debate is taking place, so the reader must infer it from the text. In addition, the contradicting passages are relatively few, so the debate, if it exists, is not sustained throughout the entirety of the book.

It is possible that the entire book comes from the author, and the different outlooks are due to his shifting views over an extended period of time. Here, too, he never tells us this is the case, but the autobiographical material suggests that the book's content took shape over many years. The section in which the author speaks of himself as king (1:12–2:27) is probably not meant to be taken literally, but if it has any basis in historical events it tells us that Qoheleth experienced many years of success and prosperity that left him feeling empty and unfulfilled. Perhaps the book records his conflicting feelings as he made the long journey through his many accomplishments to ultimate disillusionment.

Equally plausible is the possibility that has already been mentioned several times—the different perspectives reflect editorial activity after the time of the original author. A later redactor could have added material in an effort to put the work more in line with mainstream Israelite theology and beliefs. This is likely the case with the last two verses of the book (12:13b-14) that exhort the reader to keep God's commandments, a notion not found elsewhere in the book, and it could apply to other sections that introduce opposing viewpoints.

The contradictions in the text might be Qoheleth's way of underscoring his point that truth is elusive and the quest for meaning and understanding will never succeed. Is he quoting accepted wisdom in order to critique it? Is he engaging in a debate with an interlocutor? Did his views shift over time? Or did a later editor rework portions of the text? We will never know for certain which, if any, of these explanations is correct. But the uncertainty and ambiguity such questions create suit the purposes of the book perfectly by making an ironic comment on the limitations of human reason.

CHAPTER 31

ADDITIONAL WRITINGS: PSALMS

The book of Psalms has played an important role in Judaism and Christianity throughout history because it is a collection of prayers, hymns, and other works that are commonly used for worship in both faiths. The oldest Hebrew manuscripts do not have a title for the collection, but later ones identify it as *tehillim* ("praises"), a word used to describe some of the pieces that comprise the book. The Hebrew root *hll* from which this word derives is the etymological basis for the word hallelujah, literally "Praise Yahweh!" The word "psalm" comes from the Greek *psalmos*, which is how the Greek translation, or Septuagint (LXX), translates the Hebrew term *mizmor* ("song") that is the title of fifty-seven compositions in the book.

CONTENT

In the Masoretic Text (MT) upon which most English translations are based, the book contains 150 compositions, each comprising a separate section or chapter. The LXX, has an additional psalm at the end of the collection that is not found in the MT. The Septuagint also divides the psalms differently in places, with the result that the numbers assigned to them vary slightly depending on what type of Bible one is using. The LXX combines Psalms 9 and 10 into one, joins Psalms 115 and 114 as Psalm 113, divides Psalm 116 into Psalms 114 and 115, and divides Psalm 147 into Psalms 146 and 147. The Roman Catholic and the Orthodox churches tend to follow the Greek numeration, so in most of the Psalter the psalm numbers in their Bibles do not match perfectly with what is found in the Protestant and Jewish traditions.

It is impossible to neatly categorize the content of a work that is as varied as the book of Psalms. Prayer, praise, request, complaint, thanksgiving, and remembrance are some of the most frequent modes and forms present throughout the collection. Because these different types of writing are usually easily identifiable, the common tendency among scholars has been to classify the psalms by genre and to study them as members of groups that share particular characteristics and traits. Despite their differences, however, certain themes and features are found in many psalms of various types and genres.

The most important thing all the psalms have in common is that they are works of poetry, a fact that is immediately apparent in most English translations because the material is arranged in verse form. Biblical Hebrew poetry exhibits some qualities that are found in poetry from other places and times. Elements like meter and rhythm, and literary devices such as metaphor and rich imagery, are present in Hebrew poetry just as they are found in poetry throughout much of the world. But the characteristic that is the defining feature of biblical Hebrew poetry is something scholars refer to as parallelism.

The standard unit of poetry in the Hebrew Bible is the line, which is typically divided into two cola (singular "colon") although it is not uncommon to find a line with three or more cola. This structure can be seen in Ps 51:2, where the first colon reads "Wash me thoroughly from my iniquity," and the second follows, "and cleanse me from my sin." There is an obvious semantic connection between these two statements, but they are not saying exactly the same thing. Sometimes, as in 51:5, the second colon highlights a particular aspect of the first colon or advances its meaning in some way. "Indeed, I was born guilty, /a sinner when my mother conceived me." Here, the psalmist takes the idea in the first colon further by pushing it back nine months earlier to the moment of his conception. In these two examples the two cola have a similar meaning, but this is not always the case. Elsewhere, the parallelism can be antithetical as the second colon reverses or negates what was said in the first one. The final verse of the first psalm (1:6) provides an instance of this. "For the LORD watches over the way of the righteous, / but the way of the wicked will perish." Scholars debate the various forms and functions of parallelism found in the poetry of the Hebrew Bible, but there is no denying that parallelism is its dominant trait and that it has a profound impact on the reader's experience of a work like the book of Psalms.

There are five parts to the book: Psalms 1–41, 42–72, 73–89, 90–106, and 107–150. These sections are clearly delineated by the presence of a doxology at the end of the first four. The first (41:13) and the third (89:52) are the briefest, and they share a common structure—"Blessed be the LORD, the God of Israel, /from everlasting to everlasting. Amen and Amen." "Blessed be the LORD forever. Amen and Amen." The other two (72:18-20; 106:48) also contain a command to bless God and conclude with "Amen." These passages are obviously meant to be dividers because they do not bear any connection to the content of the psalms they conclude and they are the only places where the word "Amen" is found in the entire book.

Superscriptions, or headings, are found at the beginning of 116 psalms. These titles vary in length from a single Hebrew word that connects the composition with a particular individual ("Of Solomon" in Psalm 72) to lengthier statements that offer instructions and attempt to contextualize the psalm at a certain moment in time. The heading of Psalm 60 reads, "To the leader: according to the Lily of the Covenant. A Miktam of David; for instruction; when he struggled with Aram-naharaim and with Aram-zobah, and when Joab on his return killed twelve thousand Edomites in the Valley of Salt." As this example illustrates, the superscriptions sometimes contain notations to the song leader, or choirmaster (who is mentioned in more than one-third of the psalms), indicating what instruments to use or, as in this case, what kind of composition it is (a miktam) and what tune it should be set to ("according to the Lily of the Covenant"). King David is mentioned in the superscriptions of 73 psalms and 14 of them, like Psalm 60, mention particular events in his life.

The majority of the untitled psalms are found in the latter part of the book, but Psalm 10 is an interesting exception that deserves some comment. It has already been noted that the Septuagint combines Psalms 9 and 10, and their common format supports this arrangement. They form an acrostic poem, a form sometimes found in the Hebrew Bible in which the Hebrew alphabet is spelled out in order by the first letter of each stanza or line. In this case not all the letters are present, but there is no doubt that here, as in Psalms 25, 34, 37, 111, 112, 119, and 145, an acrostic pattern is present. The lack of a heading for Psalm 10 is most likely due to the fact that it continues the acrostic begun in Psalm 9 and therefore constitutes its second part.

GROWTH

Editorial activity is evident in the division of the book into five sections and the similar doxologies that conclude the first four of those sections. Some scholars have proposed that this structure may be modeled on the five books of the Torah. If so, then perhaps one function of the collection is to celebrate and reflect upon the relationship between God and humanity that is first established in the Torah. The first two psalms, which both lack superscriptions, are commonly understood to serve as an introduction to the entire collection, and the references to the law and the benefits of observing it in the first psalm help to strengthen the proposed connection to the Torah (1:2, 3, 6).

Some of the material may have originally circulated as separate collections before becoming part of the book. An example of this are the psalms of the "sons of Korah," a group of eleven compositions that are so identified in their superscriptions (42, 44–49, 84–85, 87–88). The reason they were broken up and are now found in different parts of the book is unknown.

Psalms 42–83 are often referred to as the Elohistic psalms because throughout this section God is referred to as Elohim much more frequently than elsewhere in the book. In these forty-two psalms God is called Elohim approximately 240 times and is called Yahweh 43 times. This is more or less the opposite of the ratio of the use of the two names that is found in the first section of the book (Pss 1–41), where the title Yahweh dominates. If the Elohistic psalms were originally an independent collection, the five-part structure imposed by the editors has disrupted its unity somewhat because they make up the entirety of the second section (Pss 42–72) but conclude partway through the third section (73–89).

Another easily identified group of psalms are the "Songs of Ascent" (120–134), which all share that title and, when taken as a whole, describe the various stages of a journey to Jerusalem. The section ends with the lament of an Israelite who has been forced to live far from the land and concludes at the temple with a doxology.

> Come, bless the LORD, all you servants of the LORD,
> who stand by night in the house of the LORD!
> Lift up your hands to the holy place,
> and bless the LORD.
> May the LORD, maker of heaven and earth,
> bless you from Zion.

The collection may have functioned as a spiritual guide or prayer book for those making the pilgrimage to Jerusalem.

Psalm 119, which is found just before the Songs of Ascent, is an interesting and important composition for a number of reasons. It is a complex acrostic divided into twenty-two stanzas of eight lines each. Each of the eight lines in every stanza begins with the same Hebrew letter, and the twenty-two stanzas are arranged in alphabetic order. It is also the longest psalm in the entire book, and its emphasis on observing the law establishes a link between it and the first psalm. This is clearly seen when we compare the first two verses of the two psalms.

> Happy are those
> who do not follow the advice of the wicked,
> or take the path that sinners tread,
> or sit in the seat of scoffers;
> but their delight is in the law of the LORD,
> and on his law they meditate day and night.
> (1:1-2)

> Happy are those whose way
> is blameless,
> who walk in the law
> of the LORD.
> Happy are those who keep
> his decrees,
> who seek him with
> their whole heart. (119:1-2)

The law is not a very common theme in the book, and its presence in both these psalms has led some scholars to suggest that the collection might have originally concluded with Psalm 119, thereby creating an inclusio, or bookend effect, with the opening. In this scenario, the Songs of Ascent were added at a later point followed by the subsequent material that concludes the book as we presently have it.

The superscriptions are not original to the psalms, but their precise origin is unknown. The many references to David in them, particularly the fourteen historical headings that link a psalm with a particular moment in his life (Pss 3, 7, 18, 30, 34, 51, 52, 54, 56, 57, 59, 60, 63, 142), have contributed to the notion that David was the author of the psalms. But no internal evidence supports this view, and scholars reject the theory of Davidic authorship. The Greek (Septuagint) and Syriac translations have more headings than are found in the MT and most of them are related to David, which suggests that as time went on there was a tendency to associate more and more of the psalms with him.

In 2 Samuel 22 David's rescue from his enemies causes him to break into song and recite Psalm 18, an action that could be interpreted as support for the idea that he composed the psalms. In fact, Psalm 18 was written long after David's time but the editor of the Deuteronomistic History introduced it in 2 Samuel 22 because its content speaks to the circumstances of David's situation at this point in the narrative. It should be noted that the DH does not refer to the composition as a psalm. A related phenomenon is the occasional presence of part of a psalm in another psalm. For example, Ps 40:14-18 and Ps 70:2-5 mirror each other so closely that they are virtually identical. Examples such as these suggest that entire psalms or parts of psalms might have circulated independently or were available as source material for those composing other writings that became part of the Hebrew Bible.

A final example of the fluidity and evolving nature of the Psalter can be seen in the Dead Sea Scrolls found at Qumran. Approximately thirty different Psalms manuscripts were discovered there, and they do not differ markedly from the MT in terms of the textual content, but there are some variations in the order of the psalms. In addition, a manuscript containing Psalm 151 was also found at Qumran, which is important evidence from the Hebrew-writing community from the beginning of the Common Era in support of the Septuagint, which also concludes with Psalm 151.

Editorial hands are noticeably present in the book of Psalms. The overall structure of the work, the various parts that comprise it, and the evidence from the translations and versions all testify to its complex history of transmission. Scholars debate the issue of when the book reached its final form, but some point to the reference to Babylon in 137:1 as an important clue. The verse clearly presumes an exilic context and therefore the book of Psalms must have reached its present shape sometime after 586 B.C.E.

CONTEXT

It has already been noted that one of the most common ways scholars have studied the book of Psalms is through categorizing the material by genres and then studying individual psalms or groups of psalms as representatives of a particular type. With this approach it is important to try to determine the *Sitz im Leben* (situation in life), or context of a given composition. In what kind of setting or environment might such a psalm have been used? What is the likely mind-set or circumstances of someone who would recite a psalm like this? What does the content of the psalm tell us about how it might have functioned for the individual or community? These and similar questions are the ones posed when one engages in a method of biblical study referred to as form criticism, which seeks to understand a given passage in light of the role it played for the people and institutions of the biblical world.

The development of form criticism has been strongly influenced by scholarly work on the book of Psalms. The details of that contribution will be outlined in the next section on interpretation. At this point our main interest is in illustrating how and why questions about context naturally arise from a careful reading of the Psalter. In many cases the text of a given psalm provides clues and information as to its possible use and function.

Some psalms appear to be related to worship services and the cultic life of ancient Israel. They typically call the people to praise God by listing the actions or qualities of God that merit that praise. The beginning of Psalm 33 offers a good example of this, complete with a reference to the musical instruments that might have been used during worship.

> Rejoice in the LORD, O you righteous.
> Praise befits the upright.
> Praise the LORD with the lyre;
> make melody to him with the harp of ten strings.
> Sing to him a new song;
> play skillfully on the strings, with loud shouts.
> For the word of the LORD is upright,
> and all his work is done in faithfulness.
> He loves righteousness and justice;
> the earth is full of the steadfast love of the LORD. (33:1-5)

Psalm 136 also probably functioned in this way. Each of its twenty-six verses is comprised of two lines, the first of which identifies some reason God should be thanked, while the second is identical throughout the psalm: "for his steadfast love endures forever." This repeated antiphon was probably recited over and over again by the congregation or a portion of them. Other psalms that might have been part of the temple ritual include 19, 65, 76, 87, 98, 103, 114, 135, and 150.

Certain psalms offer thanks to God, and the references to sacrifices and vows in them suggest they may have originated in rituals of thanksgiving. "I will come into your house with burnt offerings; I will pay you my vows, those that my lips uttered and my mouth promised when I was in trouble. I will offer to you burnt offerings of fatlings, with the smoke of the sacrifice of rams; I will make an offering of bulls and goats" (66:13-15; see also 18, 34, 92, 116, 138).

Other psalms seem to be responses to crises either within the community or on the individual level. In the former case, the psalm begins with a complaint followed by a prayer to God to remove the difficulty. It usually ends on a note of confidence that God will hear the community's petition. Psalm 74 is an example of this type of composition, and its opening verses indicate it is responding to the devastating effects of the destruction of the temple and the exile.

> O God, why do you cast us off forever?
>   Why does your anger smoke against the sheep of your pasture?
> Remember your congregation, which you acquired long ago,
>   which you redeemed to be the tribe of your heritage.
>   Remember Mount Zion, where you came to dwell.
> Direct your steps to the perpetual ruins;
>   the enemy has destroyed everything in the sanctuary. (Ps 74:1-3)

Psalms of this sort also attempt to respond to communal loss as a result of famine, pestilence, attack, or drought (see Pss 44, 79, 80, and 83).

Elsewhere the troubles are of a more personal nature as the psalmist tries to persuade God to come to his aid in the midst of his affliction. More psalms fit into this category than any other, and Ps 140:1-4 gives a good sense of the tone they usually adopt.

> Deliver me, O LORD, from evildoers;
>   protect me from those who are violent,
> who plan evil things in their minds
>   and stir up wars continually. They make their tongue sharp as a snake's,
>   and under their lips is the venom of vipers.
> Guard me, O LORD, from the hands of the wicked;
>   protect me from the violent
> who have planned my downfall.

Among the many other examples of this type psalm are 5, 7, 22, 26, 31, 51, 57, 63, 70, 88, 109, and 143.

The "royal psalms" comprise another group that is easily identifiable because they mention the king and are best understood within the context of the royal court. These can be in the form of a thanksgiving hymn by the king upon return from battle (18) or a recollection of the promise God made to David to be with him and his descendants forever (132). Others sound like they might be appropriate for an occasion like a coronation or enthronement celebration.

In your strength the king rejoices, O LORD,
  and in your help how greatly he exults!
You have given him his heart's desire,
  and have not withheld the request of his lips.
For you meet him with rich blessings;
  you set a crown of fine gold on his head. (21:1-3; see also Pss 2, 72, 110)

INTERPRETATION

These are some of the major groups that have been identified to show that the psalms can be categorized based on their form and likely function. The scholar who engaged in the first detailed, systematic study of the book along these lines was Hermann Gunkel (1862–1932), who determined that there were five main categories of psalms: (1) hymn, (2) community lament, (3) royal, (4) individual lament, and (5) personal thanksgiving. In addition to these groupings, Gunkel identified a number of minor genres like wisdom psalms, liturgies, and communal thanksgiving.

Although Gunkel focused his attention on the content and tone of individual psalms, he did not have much to say about their likely context or how they might have functioned for the ancient Israelites. This was the major contribution of Sigmund Mowinckel (1884–1965), who pursued questions regarding the *Sitz im Leben* of the psalms that his predecessor had not asked. Mowinckel stressed the importance of understanding how the Israelite cultic system functioned, and he was able to draw upon advancements in the study of Babylon and other neighboring cultures that were unavailable during Gunkel's time.

Taking the Babylonian system as a model, Mowinckel believed that there was an annual enthronement of Yahweh in Israel during the fall festival of the new year, and he thought many of the psalms could be connected to that celebration. Each year the Israelites would symbolically reenact Yahweh's defeat of their enemies and would enthrone Yahweh as king after a ritual procession. Mowinckel maintained that the book of Psalms is best understood as a collection of compositions that centered on the ritual activities associated with this annual event.

His ideas have been very influential, but many scholars have found problems with Mowinckel's reconstruction and theory. Whereas certain psalms easily fit a cultic context and could plausibly be related to an enthronement ceremony, others seem out of place in such a setting. Many psalms do not mention the cult at all, and it appears that their primary purpose is to give voice to a person's needs and concerns. The individual laments, which constitute the largest group of psalms, are an example of this. How might they have functioned in Mowinckel's envisioned enthronement ceremony? Many scholars think it unlikely that compositions like these would have served any purpose in the new year celebration.

The way the material in the book is organized is important in this regard as well. As noted earlier, some scholars have argued that the book originally ended with Psalm 119, which shares the theme of the law with Psalm 1, thereby giving a thematic focus to the whole work. This downplays the connection with the cult and raises questions about Mowinckel's ideas. Others have claimed that there is a gradual shift in tone throughout the course of the book as the laments that dominate the first half give way to more praises in the second half, leading the reader from one mode to another. If this is the case, it too de-emphasizes the cult and highlights more the role and experience of the individual reader.

The work of Gunkel and Mowinckel continues to be influential and debated by scholars, but there is no evidence for exactly how the psalms were used or read by ancient people. Ultimately, any attempt to reconstruct the cult or another element of Israelite society and propose a connection between it and the book of Psalms must remain speculative.

CHAPTER 32

ADDITIONAL WRITINGS: THE SONG OF SOLOMON AND LAMENTATIONS

THE SONG OF SOLOMON

The Song of Solomon is also known as Song of Songs and Canticles. All three names come from the first line of the book (v. 1): "The Song of Songs, which is to/for/by Solomon." The expression "song of songs" is a superlative in Hebrew and means the greatest or best song. "Canticles" comes from the Latin word for songs and originates with the Vulgate, or Latin translation of the Bible.

Song of Solomon is one of the *megillot*, or five *scrolls* (the others are Ruth, Esther, Qoheleth [or Ecclesiastes], and Lamentations), in the Bible that came to be associated with Jewish holidays. Song of Solomon is read at Passover.

CONTENT

Simply put, Song of Solomon is erotic poetry. It is not pornographic; the act of sexual intercourse is never explicitly described. The poetry, rather, expresses desire and longing, admiration and physical attraction. It is also not exploitative but mutual and egalitarian between woman and man.

There is no clear structure or organization to Song of Solomon, at least none upon which scholars have agreed. Some believe it to be a single poem by a single author, while others see it as a collection or anthology of different poems. Some have argued for a tightly organized structure—though it must be said, without convincing the majority of scholars. It is probably fair to say that most scholars today view the book as a collection of love poems without any clear, discernible organization. There is no agreement even on the number of poetic units contained in the book, making it impossible to outline. However, it is possible to distinguish between speakers or voices based on content and masculine and feminine forms in Hebrew.

1:1 – Heading
1:2-8 – Female

1:9-11 – Male
1:12-14 – Female
1:15-16a – Male
1:16b–2:1 – Female
2:2 – Male
2:3–3:5 – Female
3:6-11 – Unclear
4:1-15 – Male
4:16 – Female
5:1a – Male
5:1b – Plural
5:2-8 – Female
5:9 – Plural
5:10-16 – Female
6:1– Plural
6:2-3 – Female
6:4-10 – Male
6:11-12 – Female
6:13 (Hebrew 7:1) – Plural
7:1-9 (Hebrew 7:2-10) – Male
7:10 (Hebrew 7:11)–8:7 – Female
8:8-9 – Plural
8:10-12 – Female
8:13 – Male
8:14 – Female

Sometimes, the speakers are in dialogue. For instance, 5:10-16 answers questions in 5:9 about the appearance of the beloved, and 6:2-3 answers questions in 6:1 about where he has gone. There are also repeated verses or "refrains," most notably:

> I adjure you, O daughters of Jerusalem,
>   by the gazelles or the wild does,
> do not stir up or awaken love
>   until it is ready. (2:7; cf. 3:5; 8:4)

The "daughters of Jerusalem" may be the chorus of plural voices that speaks from time to time, although in some cases the plural speakers might just as easily be males, friends of the male beloved. It is possible that the male and female speakers are the same throughout—that is, that the book envisions two principal characters, an individual female lover and an individual male lover. But it is just as possible that it is a collection of separate poems from different males and females. In either case, the female voice clearly dominates.

GROWTH

Because the number of poems and their organization are so uncertain, it is also unknown how the book came into existence. The connection of the book with Solomon is probably based on the reference to Solomon as the author of 1005 songs (1 Kgs 4:32 [Hebrew 5:12]) and the tendency to tie anonymous writings with known biblical figures. The reference to Solomon in the heading is ambiguous. Like the headings of the psalms that mention David, it might imply a dedication or the like and is not necessarily a claim of authorship. Solomon is mentioned by name six additional times in the book (1:5; 3:7, 9, 11; 8:11, 12). These play upon the tradition of Solomon as the wealthiest, most luxuriant king of Israel and do not necessitate any affinity with the historical figure.

The book has also been assigned to a whole range of dates from the tenth to the second century B.C.E. Most scholars today favor a date toward the end of this spectrum, in the fourth or third century B.C.E. This relatively late date is suggested by the presence of Song of Solomon in the Writings, which generally contains the latest materials in the Hebrew Bible. It is also indicated by linguistic considerations, specifically the influence of Aramaic in the book and the presence of what appear to be loan words from Persian and perhaps even Greek. Despite the probable lateness of the actual writing of the book, its poetry incorporates themes, ideas, and even language attested in much earlier times.

CONTEXT

Whenever Song of Solomon was written, it emerged from a rich background of love poetry in the ancient Near Eastern world, especially from Mesopotamia and Egypt. The former has yielded texts from as early as the third millennium that deal with "sacred marriage" between two gods, represented in cultic ceremonies by the king and a priestess. The similarities that these texts bear to Song of Solomon tend to be broad and general and stem from common subject matter. The Egyptian texts, primarily from the fourteenth to the twelfth centuries, are more instructive.

The Egyptian poems were often written to be sung at banquets and hence raise the possibility that the Song of Solomon was composed for a similar setting. Like the Song of Solomon, these poems make use of sensuous imagery describing all five senses. They are comparable in terms of genre, expressing admiration, yearning, physical attraction, and even boasting. They also portray the lovers using the same terms of endearment for one another ("brother" and "sister"). Above all, these texts have helped to identify the nature of the poetry in the context of Song of Solomon simply as erotic poetry voicing love and desire between young, unmarried, heterosexual lovers. The possibility of additional settings and meanings to the book has given rise to a colorful history of interpretation.

INTERPRETATION

The recognition of Song of Solomon as erotic literature naturally provokes the question, "What is it doing in the Bible?" The question is sharpened all the more by the fact that the book never refers to God. Discussions about it among early rabbinic sources hint that its acceptance as canon was contested. There are three likely reasons for its ultimate canonization. Two of these are the traditional connection with Solomon and the high praise it received from certain interpreters. Rabbi Aqiba (ca. 135 C.E.), for instance, is famously quoted as saying, "The whole world is not worth the day on which the Song of Songs was given to Israel, for all the Scriptures are holy, but the Song of Songs is the Holy of Holies."

The third reason for the Song's acceptance had to do with the symbolic interpretation it received. Until the modern era, both Jewish and Christian interpreters have read the book allegorically. For Jews, the male and female characters represent God and Israel, respectively. For Christians, they stand for Christ and the church. Christian mystics have found the book to express the soul's longing for union with God.

Modern scholars generally agree that Song of Solomon is fundamentally erotic poetry about young people in love. But there are a number of proposals for narrowing down the setting in which the poems in the book were originally formulated or used. Some have hypothesized that the poems grew out of a liturgical, sacred marriage ritual much like those celebrated between Mesopotamian gods. In addition to being highly theoretical, though, this idea would apply only to the "prehistory" of the poetry in Song of Solomon before it was adopted by worshipers of Yahweh. Some interpreters have tried to read the Song as a drama. As we have seen, however, there is no agreement on the identity of the characters or their speeches. There is also no obvious plot. Yet other proposals include a wedding or funeral setting. In support of the former, modern Arab weddings still make use of poems (called *wasfs*) in which the couple describes each other's body in highly metaphorical language, akin to certain passages in Song of Solomon. The latter envisions a funerary orgy celebrating life over death.

Literary theory has recognized that a reader brings meaning to a text as well as drawing from it. It may be legitimate, therefore, to acknowledge at least the possibility of various levels of meaning in the Song. Perhaps even more appropriate would be the appreciation of the book on the aesthetic level. In the end, perhaps the Song of Solomon is more to be enjoyed than to be dissected. After all, readers unfamiliar with all of the names of places, plants, and animals in the book can still understand and appreciate it as the beautiful expression of the experience of human love with all of the joys and pains that accompany it.

LAMENTATIONS

Like Song of Solomon, as well as Ruth, Esther, and Qoheleth (Ecclesiastes), the book of Lamentations is one of the *megillot*, or scrolls, read in connection with Jewish holidays. Lamentations is read during *Tisha B'av* ("the ninth of Av"), which takes place in the summer, usually in

August, and commemorates tragedies in Jewish history, particularly the destructions of Jerusalem and the temple. Following in the same vein, Christians sometimes read Lamentations on Good Friday.

As one of the *megillot,* Lamentations is in the Writings section of the Hebrew Bible rather than the Prophets. Its placement following Jeremiah in English Bibles follows the Septuagint, or Greek translation of the Hebrew Bible, and is based on the tradition that Jeremiah wrote it. The English title "Lamentations" is also a translation of the Greek name for the book (*Threnoi*). In Hebrew, the book is known simply by its first word, *'ekah,* "Hoẉ."

CONTENT

Lamentations consists of five poems occupying a chapter apiece in English translations. Each poem deals in some way with the destruction of Jerusalem by the Babylonians in 586 B.C.E. The poems do not describe the events surrounding the fall of the city in chronological order but give glimpses of and reactions to those horrific events and their consequences. The first poem describes the city's destruction from both the perspective of the poet as observer and of Jerusalem itself, envisioned as a woman. The second focuses on the destruction as the direct attack of Yahweh. Poem three is primarily an individual lament with fewer allusions to Jerusalem's fate. The fourth poem returns to a description of Jerusalem and the suffering of its residents during its siege and after its fall. The final poem is a communal lament that calls upon Yahweh to remember what has befallen Jerusalem and to restore it.

The organizational principle of the five poems is alphabetic. The first, second, and fourth poems are acrostics, each verse beginning with a successive letter of the alphabet. Note that these chapters all have twenty-two verses, the number of letters in the Hebrew alphabet. In the third poem, every three verses begin with the same letter, so chapter three has sixty-six verses. The fifth poem, though not an acrostic, also has twenty-two verses. The third poem offers some muted hope for rescue. All of the poems make frequent use of a distinctive meter, dubbed *qinah* ("lament") meter, in which a shorter line, consisting of two metrical beats, follows one or more lines of three beats. This uneven meter can sometimes be perceived in English translation:

> Our heritage has passed to aliens,
> Our homes to strangers. (5:2, *TANAKH*)

GROWTH

There is no clear indication within the poems as to the order in which they were written or the process by which they came to comprise the present book. There is some analogy to Lamentations in a series of works in Sumerian that are also poetic laments over the ruin of cities and temples by foreign enemies. These works date from ca. 2000–1700 B.C.E., so that they are much older than the Bible's Lamentations, though they were likely recopied over the centuries in the Babylonian scribal school curriculum.

As with the biblical book, these Sumerian works articulate the physical, social, and spiritual trauma caused by the destruction of city and temple, which they understand as a crisis brought or allowed by the native god. The works also share many similarities in expression and imagery with Lamentations. Unlike the major Sumerian texts, however, Lamentations does not describe a "happy ending" in which God restores favor and the city again flourishes. In fact, the Sumerian laments are apparently intended to curry the favor of the deity to allow the temple to be razed and then rebuilt and never again destroyed. Lamentations betrays no such intent. Scholars, therefore, debate the question of whether the similarities between Lamentations and the Sumerian laments are the result of actual literary dependence and participation in the same genre or are simply due to their setting and origin in the comparable situation of coping with the devastation of a ruined city.

CONTEXT

Tradition ascribes the book of Lamentations to the prophet Jeremiah. The tradition goes back at least to the Septuagint (ca. 250 B.C.E.), which places the two books together and begins Lamentations with the following superscription: "After Israel was captured and Jerusalem was laid desolate, Jeremiah sat weeping and composed this lament over Jerusalem" (AT).

The link with Jeremiah is probably based on the depiction of the prophet mourning over Jerusalem within the book that bears his name (Jer 7:29; 8:18-9:1; 9:17-22) and on the note in Chronicles that he lamented or composed a lament over the death of King Josiah (2 Chr 35:25). The tradition of Jeremiah as the "weeping prophet" continued in Judaism and Christianity and is well represented in Rembrandt's famous painting of him.

Despite the tradition, biblical scholars are almost unanimous in considering the book of Lamentations as anonymous. There are several good reasons for this. First, in the Hebrew Bible, Lamentations is found among the Writings, as we have seen, and not after Jeremiah. In addition, the Hebrew text of Lamentations makes no reference to Jeremiah. Hence, the earliest tradition draws no connection between the two.

Furthermore, contrasts between Lamentations and Jeremiah militate against their common authorship. For one thing, the focus in Lamentations is more on the community than on any individual. More important are the contrasts in language and especially ideas and perspectives between the two books. For example, Lamentations reflects a positive view of the religious and political leadership in Jerusalem, even calling the last king of Judah, Zedekiah, "[Yahweh's] anointed, the breath of our life" (Lam 4:20). Jeremiah takes a much dimmer view of Zedekiah and the rest of Jerusalem's elite (Jer 37:17-21). Jeremiah (7:14) prophesied the destruction of the temple by foreigners, while Lamentations (1:10) says that God had forbidden their entry into the sanctuary. Jeremiah (2:18) denounced efforts to seek help from other nations, but Lamentations (4:17) would welcome such help. It also seems unlikely that Jeremiah would have admitted that Jerusalem's prophets received no vision from Yahweh (Lam 2:9).

Although the tradition that Lamentations was written by Jeremiah is probably a result of the tendency, also at work in Song of Solomon (as well as Psalms [David] and Proverbs [Solomon]), to ascribe anonymous books to well-known Bible heroes, it reflects the most likely date for the book. The content of Lamentations indicates that it was written shortly after the destruction of Jerusalem in 586 B.C.E., probably by someone in Palestine who witnessed the catastrophe. There is no good evidence to confirm this date or to pinpoint it more precisely, but there is also no good reason to doubt it. The book would have been written considerably before the end of the exile (ca. 538 B.C.E.), especially since it betrays no real optimism about Jerusalem's future restoration.

INTERPRETATION

There is no consistent, overall message to be found in Lamentations—no lesson of hope or reassurance. There is no word from God, who is absent throughout. All expression in the book comes from the human side. The author makes use of laments, both individual and communal, and dirges to express sorrow and pain, and finally to appeal to God for restoration. What hope the book implies is subdued and ambiguous and found in the experience of God's mercy and previous rescue in chapter three.

The literary structure of Lamentations embodies and illustrates its valuable role as human expression. The book is a catharsis—an expression of grief. But the acrostic form of its content serves to limit the sorrow that it expresses and to channel its emotion into creativity. The creative form also serves the function of bringing order out of the chaos of destruction. With catharsis and order, the process of healing for the ruined Jerusalem community and the individual author might begin, even in the absence or delay of a divine response.

CHAPTER 33

ADDITIONAL WRITINGS: RUTH AND ESTHER

The books of Ruth and Esther are both part of the *megillot*, the five scrolls traditionally read one each in conjunction with the five Jewish festivals. Ruth is read at the harvest Festival of Weeks, or *Shevu'ot* (Pentecost), and Esther at Purim. Both are short stories whose hero or main character is a woman. Both also deal with the relationship between Israelites or Jews and foreigners.

RUTH

The book of Ruth is set during the period of the judges, but its story in many ways is timeless. A tale about love and loyalty, it is remarkable for the simple fact that there is no villain in the book. Nor are the characters people of power or fame. On one level, it is a simple story about common people facing the everyday problem of survival. On other levels, it is fascinating for the glimpses it affords at daily life in ancient Israel, and its message is profound.

CONTENT

The folktale in the book of Ruth begins with a famine in Israel that forces a family from Bethlehem to move to Moab, on the other side of the Dead Sea. Over a space of ten years, the husband, Elimelech, dies, followed by his sons, whose fate is heralded by their names, Mahlon ("sickly") and Chilion ("weak"). This series of disasters leaves Naomi, the wife and mother, whose name means "pleasant," in a most unpleasant situation. Hearing that the famine in Israel has abated, she decides to return home. She urges her two daughters-in-law, both Moabites, to remain in their native land. One of them, Orpah, eventually heeds her mother-in-law and returns home, but the other one, Ruth, expressing undying loyalty, stays with Naomi. Their arrival in Bethlehem causes a stir among the women of the town, whom Naomi tells to call her Mara ("bitter") because of the way God has dealt with her.

Since they have returned at the time of the barley harvest, Ruth volunteers to glean—that is, pick up stalks of grain missed by the reapers—and Naomi recommends the field of a kinsman named Boaz. Impressed by

Ruth's industry and loyalty to her mother-in-law, Boaz treats Ruth with special favor, allowing her to eat and drink from the provisions for his workers and ordering them not to bother her and even to leave some of what they have picked for her.

At the end of the harvest, Naomi tells Ruth to dress up at night and go to the threshing floor, typically a flat, open, elevated place where grain was winnowed, that is, the kernels separated from their hulls. Boaz and his workers would be celebrating the harvest. Ruth is to go to Boaz when he lies down, "uncover his feet," and wait for instructions. When Boaz is startled awake in the middle of the night and finds Ruth lying at his feet, she asks him to "spread his cloak" over her because he is the next of kin. He praises her for her loyalty and then informs her that there is a nearer kinsman than he who may choose to act as redeemer. He assures her that he will redeem if the nearer kinsman does not. She stays the night, and in the morning he sends her back to Naomi with a gift of grain.

Boaz goes to the city gate and finds the other kinsman. In front of the city elders, he invites the man to redeem a plot of land belonging to Naomi. The other kinsman is interested until he learns that Ruth comes with the land. Boaz then assumes the place of redeemer. He marries Ruth and fathers a son, Obed, David's grandfather. The book closes with a genealogy tracing David's genealogy from Perez, son of Judah.

GROWTH

The story is set during the time of the judges but obviously arose later. The genealogy of David at the end of the book (4:18-22) is generally considered a later addition, but David is still mentioned at the end (4:17). The book has been assigned widely divergent dates, ranging from the time of David or Solomon (tenth century B.C.E.) to the Hellenistic period (third–second century B.C.E.). Its language seems to support a date in the fifth or fourth century, though this has been disputed. Those who favor a date in the postexilic period (fifth century on) point to the theme of universalism, God's concern for all people, in the book. Others emphasize the story's connection with David and its references to Israelite custom, both of which they say indicate a compositional setting during or before the exile of 586 B.C.E., when the monarchy was still in existence. Both positions may have some validity. The basic folktale could have arisen and circulated orally during the time of the monarchy but the story only have been written down at a relatively late date, after the end of the monarchy and the start of the exile.

CONTEXT

More intriguing than the question of historical setting is the social context of the story, especially as it relates to Israelite customs and law. There are references throughout the story to a number of social practices and customs, especially associated with an agricultural setting, for which there are sometimes prescriptions in biblical law. However, the practices in Ruth do not always match the legal prescriptions.

Gleaning

Gleaning represented a kind of ancient charity, designed to provide food for the poor, especially in three classes: widows, orphans, and aliens. These were people who did not have access to the usual sources of work and income. Widows and orphans lacked providers in the patriarchal culture. Aliens were foreigners who had taken up residence in Israel but were disadvantaged because they were unfamiliar with its laws and customs. Biblical law commanded leaving the edges and corners of fields unharvested as well as leaving some cut stalks in the field for the poor to gather (Deut 24:19; Lev 19:9; 23:22). Although the story of Ruth does not specifically mention the corners and edges of the field, her gleaning seems to fit with the law. Ruth is both a widow and an alien. Boaz's order to let her glean among the sheaves (standing bundles), where grain would have fallen, and even to pull some out for her (Ruth 2:15-16) exhibits his generosity.

Levirate Marriage and the Redeemer

Levirate marriage was a custom practiced among ancient Israelites and other peoples. The rules for it are spelled out in Deut 25:5-10 and illustrated in a story in Gen 38:1-10. Basically, if a man died childless it became his brother's (the levir) responsibility to marry the widow and father children who would receive the property and carry on the name (lineage) of the dead man. It is unclear whether this practice lies behind the story in Ruth. On the one hand, Naomi's rhetorical questions to Orpah and Ruth about waiting until other sons grew up (Ruth 1:12-13) seems to assume levirate practice. So does Boaz's statement to the elders about maintaining the dead man's name and inheritance (4:10). Then, Ruth's petition to Boaz to "spread his cloak" over her because he is the next-of-kin seems to be a marriage proposal (Ezek 16:8). Also, when Obed, the son of Ruth and Boaz, is born, he is referred to as Naomi's son, and she seems to adopt him as her son or grandson (4:16-17). But there are significant differences: Any further children Naomi might have would not be Elimelech's. Boaz is not the brother of Mahlon and Chilion but simply a close relative—and not even the closest—of Elimelech. Most of all, at the end of the book, the lineage of Obed is traced through Boaz rather than through Ruth's dead husband. Obed is not Naomi's blood relative at all.

A more fitting legal or cultural context to the story may be the process of redemption of land (Lev 25:25-27), since Boaz is *go'el* ("redeemer" or "next-of-kin"), and he claims the right to buy back Naomi's plot of land. But this leaves Boaz's marriage to Ruth unexplained. It is not clear why marriage to Ruth should go together with redemption of the land. Perhaps it is Boaz's ploy to ensure that Ruth and Naomi are cared for. But it is also surprising that Naomi owns land at this point in the story, since it has not been mentioned before, and she is destitute.

Justice in the Gate

Boaz goes to the city gate to make legal arrangements for his redemption of Naomi's field and of Ruth (Ruth 4:1) because the chambered gateways of walled cities were the places where business and legal transactions occurred (Amos 5:15). The transaction is confirmed by the closer next-of-kin removing his sandal and handing it to Boaz, as explained in Ruth 4:6. This may be another divergence with the levirate marriage law, where the widow is to remove the sandal of the brother who refuses to act as redeemer and spit in his face (Deut 25:9). Alternatively, it may have been a practice for completing any transaction.

These divergences between the descriptions in Ruth and the prescriptions in the law may reflect variations in certain customs as practiced in different contexts, that is, different times or places in Israel. In addition to them, the context of the scene at the threshing floor deserves special mention. The term "feet" is often used in the Hebrew Bible as a euphemism for the genitals, and it is usually so understood here. That is, Ruth exposes Boaz's genitals, or even, if the expression has the same sense as the idiom "uncover the nakedness of" (Lev 18), has sexual relations with him. The reason for this sexually oriented act (if this is the correct interpretation) is not entirely certain. Perhaps it is to make clear that Ruth's request that Boaz "spread his cloak" over her is a proposal of marriage.

INTERPRETATION

Aside from the interpretive issues discussed above, the main question of the book of Ruth is its purpose. Scholars have proposed three answers to this question: (1) Ruth is a pleasant folktale written purely for entertainment; (2) the book was written to legitimate David's kingship; (3) it was written to advocate universalism, God's concern for all people. The third of these seems most likely. The story clearly extols the virtue of loyalty. Naomi, Ruth, and Boaz all exhibit it—Naomi by looking out for Ruth's welfare, first by suggesting that she stay in Moab and then by instructing Ruth to seek marriage with Boaz; Ruth by sticking with her mother-in-law and then marrying Boaz because he was Naomi's relative, thereby ensuring that Naomi would be cared for; and Boaz because he rewards Ruth's loyalty and then is himself dependable when it comes to making the arrangements for Naomi and Ruth.

The likeability of the main characters is one of the reasons for the story's popularity. But the book was written for more than its entertainment value. This is indicated by the subtle theology of the book. Ruth just "happens" to go to the field of Boaz, Naomi's kinsman, to glean (2:3), and the closer kinsman comes to the city gate when Boaz is there (4:1). These "coincidences" hint at Yahweh's working "behind the scenes" and again indicate that the story, though it may have arisen as a folktale, was written for more than entertainment.

The hints of the divine in this story might indicate God's guidance and favor toward David's ancestors leading to his birth. In the same vein, the loyalty displayed by them might illustrate the worth of the stock that produced the great king. But Ruth's Moabite heritage cannot be ignored, and this fact is decisive for the story's interpretation. The Moabites were often enemies of Israel. David, in fact, is credited with conquering them (2 Sam 8:2). If David had a Moabite heritage it seems doubtful that an Israelite writer would want to highlight it. The book of Ruth does more than simply admit the brute fact of David's ancestry; it holds Ruth up as the epitome of loyalty. Ruth also adopts Yahweh as her God and thus becomes a faithful adherent of Israelite religion. These elements of the story demonstrate the potential value and virtue of non-Israelites as well as Yahweh's interest in them. The successful union of Boaz and Ruth is also a strong argument in favor of Israelites interacting with other peoples, a practice strongly opposed by Ezra and Nehemiah, whose views the book of Ruth may have been written to counter.

ESTHER

The book of Esther is like Ruth in telling a story with a limited cast of characters in which the hero is a woman and God is not explicitly mentioned. Unlike Ruth, however, Esther is set among the highest echelons of power, and there is a definite villain. Thus, there is an "edginess" to the story of Esther that is quite foreign to Ruth.

CONTENT

The story of Esther revolves around four central characters: Esther; her cousin Mordecai, who raised her; the Persian king Ahasuerus; and his ambitious advisor, Haman. The story begins with an extravagant banquet—really a drinking bout—given by Ahasuerus. On the seventh day, the king summons his queen, Vashti, to appear before him and his guests wearing her crown—and perhaps nothing else—so that he can show off her beauty. She refuses, to the great consternation of the king and his officials, and the decision is taken to replace her. The king decrees that all the beautiful young virgins in the empire should be gathered to the harem to undergo beauty treatments and that the woman who most pleases the king will become the new queen. Esther is chosen, but she does not reveal her Jewish identity.

Afterwards, Haman launches a plot to destroy all the Jews because he hates Mordecai, who refuses to bow down to him. Haman convinces the king to allow him to issue a decree mandating the destruction of the Jews throughout the kingdom on a day chosen by casting the lot (*pur*). Persuaded by Mordecai to intercede on behalf of her people, Esther risks her life by appearing uninvited before the king on his throne. Ahasuerus holds out his scepter to Esther, saving her life, and she requests that he and Haman join her for a banquet that she has prepared for them. When they come, she invites them again for the next day and promises to make her real request then.

Haman is pleased about the banquet and the invitation until he sees Mordecai. Then he becomes angry and depressed. At his wife's suggestion he has an enormous gallows built upon which to hang Mordecai. Meanwhile, when Ahasuerus cannot sleep that night, he has the annals read to him and discovers that Mordecai was never rewarded for thwarting an assassination plot against the king. Ahasuerus asks Haman what should be done for someone the king wishes to honor. Thinking that he is the honoree, Haman suggests parading the man through the city in royal robes and on a royal horse. The king then orders Haman to do this to Mordecai. Haman is, therefore, extremely frustrated when he goes to Esther's second banquet. She accuses Haman before the king of plotting to destroy her and her people. Angry, the king steps out. Haman falls on Esther's couch pleading for his life. Ahasuerus returns and thinking that Haman is assaulting the queen orders his immediate execution upon the gallows he had built for Mordecai.

The king permits Esther and Mordecai to issue a decree and letters in his name reversing his earlier decree. On the very day meant for their destruction, the Jews are allowed to defend themselves and even to destroy their enemies. The book ends by explaining how the Jewish holiday of Purim is a memorial and celebration of this occasion when the day chosen by lot (*pur*) for the Jews' destruction was reversed and became a day of triumph over their enemies.

GROWTH

There is good evidence that the book of Esther as we now have it developed in two stages. One of the Greek translations of the book of Esther lacks the material in chapter 9, indicating that the story originally ended without the reference to the holiday of Purim (the reference to the lot, *pur*, in 3:7 is usually regarded as a later addition).

There have also been attempts to trace the origin of the story in chapters 1–8. One prominent view is that this story represents a combination of three originally distinct stories—one about Mordecai and his conflicts and triumphs over enemies in a series of court intrigues, a second about Esther's salvation of the Jewish people from planned annihilation, and a third about Queen Vashti.

In addition to the current story, there are, as in the case of Daniel, a series of additions to the story of Esther found in the Greek translations of the book. There are six of these additions totaling 107 verses. They are included in the Apocrypha, or Deuterocanonical works. They include such things as prayers, dreams, and edicts referred to and associated with the main characters in Esther.

In sum, then, the growth of the book of Esther can be described in four stages: (1) sources—the independent stories of Mordecai, Esther, and Vashti; (2) the "original" version of Esther behind chapters 1–8; (3) the second edition represented by the version found in the Hebrew Bible; and (4) the "supplemented" version of the story with the additions in the Greek translations of the book.

CONTEXT

As with the book of Daniel, there are two main levels to the historical context of Esther—the late Persian or early Hellenistic period (late fourth century B.C.E.) for the "original" edition of the book (chs. 1–8) and later in the Hellenistic period (third or perhaps second century) for the version in the Hebrew Bible. These dates are indicated by the vocabulary of the book and by the different attitudes toward foreigners reflected in it. Specifically, there are numerous Persian words in the book but a complete absence of Greek words. In regard to the attitude toward foreigners, chapters 1–8 depict Ahasuerus as foolish and easily manipulated, a lush but not really evil. Haman alone is wicked, and he is something of a stereotypical villain. Chapters 9–10, on the other hand, display and indeed celebrate a bloodthirsty vengefulness toward all "enemies of the Jews." The latter attitude seems well suited to the oppression under Hellenistic rulers, while the former fits better with the more tolerant Persians.

In terms of its literary context, the book of Esther is a novella, that is, a short story in which a series of episodes involving the same set of characters leads to a conclusion or resolution of a problem that has arisen. It is similar to other novellas in the Bible, especially the book of Ruth and the Joseph story in Genesis. In fact, scholars have observed numerous instances in which the wording and themes of Esther are dependent on the Joseph story. For instance, Ahasuerus's passing of authority through his signet ring (Esth 3:10; 8:2) is similar to Pharaoh's gift to Joseph (Gen 41:42).

INTERPRETATION

Esther has a very controversial history of interpretation. Leading Jewish and Christian interpreters, among them Martin Luther, have expressed strong dislike for the book and doubt about its worth as scripture. The canonicity of the book was contested from the beginning, as suggested by the absence of any fragment of it among the Dead Sea Scrolls. There are several reasons for this disdain, including the complete lack of any reference to God in the book. There may be hints of "providence" at work, as when Mordecai suggests to Esther that she may have been chosen queen in order to save her people (4:14) and when Haman's wife tells him that he will fail due to Mordecai's Jewish heritage (6:13). But even these allusions to the divine seem further removed from Esther than similar references from Ruth do.

As it now stands, with the inclusion of chapters 9–10, the book of Esther is clearly an etiology for the Jewish holiday of Purim. This is another reason for criticism of the book on the part of interpreters. It is not so much that Purim was and is a celebration of overindulgence and intoxication or even that it was probably a "pagan" holiday in Babylonia or Persia that was adopted by Jews, though these features have been found objectionable. But the main issue that interpreters have with the book concerns the bloodshed that it advocates in its final two chapters. Even though scholars are virtually unanimous in doubting the historicity of these events, the legitimation and celebration of such violence is still disturbing.

The original edition of Esther, that is, without the final two chapters, was written for a purpose unrelated to Purim—perhaps to show that it was possible for Jews to assimilate to an extent to life in a foreign country while still maintaining their identity and traditions. The story contains a number of unrealistic features that at once indicate its historical improbability and also illustrate its literary artistry. One of the story's most intriguing features noted by modern scholars is its humorous elements that are the result of its characterizations and exaggerations. There is an enormous amount of drinking in the book. The opening scene has King Ahasuerus throw an extravagant banquet—really a drinking party—lasting 180 days! The beauty treatment given to all the young virgins, from whom the king has his pick, lasts an entire year. Then there is the ludicrousness of the imperial disaster and the solution to it that arises from Queen Vashti's refusal to appear when summoned. The king's advisors are terrified that this will lead all of the women in the kingdom to despise their husbands. Their proposal, which pleases the king, is the issuance of an edict commanding all women to honor their husbands. There are also ironies, such as Haman choosing Mordecai's reward because he thinks it is for him and Haman being hung on the gallows that he had built for Mordecai. The humor of the book and its optimism about the ultimate triumph of goodness are two of the reasons for its continued appeal despite its unhistorical nature and its present, unsavory conclusion.

CHAPTER 34

ADDITIONAL WRITINGS: DANIEL

The book of Daniel is unique in the Hebrew Bible. In the Christian Old Testament, it is placed among the Prophets. But the character of Daniel is not really a prophet, and in the Hebrew Bible Daniel is among the Writings. The book contains a combination of folktales and apocalyptic writings. It is the only example of apocalyptic literature in the Hebrew Bible.

CONTENT

The first six chapters of Daniel consist of stories about the young man Daniel and his friends. The stories are set in the sixth century—actually beginning in 606 B.C.E.—when the young men, who were the "cream of the crop" in Jerusalem, were taken into exile to serve the Babylonian king (Dan 1:1-7). The stories tell how Daniel and his friends maintain their faith and prosper in the courts of foreign rulers. Among them are some of the most popular tales in the Bible, including those of the "fiery furnace," the "handwriting on the wall," and "Daniel in the lion's den." Following is a brief recap of these stories by chapter.

Daniel 1:

Daniel and his friends prove that their diet of vegetables is superior to the king's delicacies. They also show themselves to have greater wisdom than the king's other advisors.

Daniel 2:

King Nebuchadnezzar has a troubling dream, and he demands that his advisors tell him both the dream and its interpretation. Only Daniel is able to do so. The dream was a vision of a large statue with different parts, consisting of different metals, that is pulverized by a large boulder, which then grows into a mountain. Daniel explains that the parts represent successive kingdoms that will arise until God sets up a kingdom that will never be destroyed.

Daniel 3:

Daniel's friends are thrown into a blazing furnace for refusing to bow to a giant statue erected by King Nebuchadnezzar or to worship his gods, but they are protected by God and emerge unharmed.

Daniel 4:

A letter from Nebuchadnezzar recounts another dream interpreted by Daniel, which was fulfilled in Nebuchadnezzar's temporary humiliation by God so that he lived as an animal.

Daniel 5:

In the midst of a drinking festival, King Belshazzar has the sacred vessels taken from the temple in Jerusalem brought out for use by his guests, who are also praising the Babylonian idols. A hand immediately appears and writes mysterious words on the wall. Daniel interprets the words as a prediction that Belshazzar's kingdom will be taken from him and divided between the Medes and Persians. Babylon falls that night to Darius the Mede.

Daniel 6:

Urged by advisors who are jealous of Daniel, King Darius issues an edict prescribing death for anyone who prays to any god or human other than him. Daniel continues to pray to God and is thrown into a den of lions. But God closes the lions' mouths so that Daniel is not harmed.

The apocalyptic visions in the second half of the book are similar to the dream in Daniel 2 in that they relate mostly to international events. However, Daniel is the one who sees the dreams and visions in the book's second half, and he is not able to interpret them himself but requires a heavenly interpreter. There are basically three visions, one each in chapters 7 and 8 and then a single vision in chapters 10–12. The bulk of chapter 9 is a prayer of confession for the sins of Israel, which led to destruction and exile.

The visions all have a similar content in that they use symbols to depict historical events leading to the rise of an oppressive ruler who will in turn be overthrown by God. Thus, in chapter 7, Daniel sees a dream of four beasts, the last of which has ten horns. An eleventh horn arises, speaking arrogantly and warring against the holy ones until the Ancient of Days destroys it and turns the kingdom over to "one like a human being" (7:13). The interpretation reveals the four beasts to represent kingdoms and the horns kings, such that God (the Ancient of Days) will give dominion to the holy ones in the days of the fourth kingdom after a particularly arrogant ruler.

In Daniel 8, the vision is of a ram with two horns that is struck by a male goat with a single horn so that the ram's two horns are broken. The goat's horn is then replaced by four horns, and one of them produces a small horn that grows toward heaven and acts arrogantly. The interpretation identifies the two-horned ram as the kings of Media and Persia and the goat as Greece.

In chapter 9, following Daniel's prayer, the angel Gabriel appears to him announcing that it will take "seventy weeks" (v. 24) to "finish the transgression" (v. 25) of Jerusalem and that after sixty-two weeks there will arise a "prince" (v. 27) who will replace the city's offerings with "an abomination that desolates."

In the last three chapters, Daniel sees a vision of a "man," likely the angel Gabriel, who tells him about international events that are about to take place. The focus of his message is on relations between the "king of the north" and the "king of the south" leading to the rise of a "contemptible person" (11:21) who will profane the temple and set up the "abomination that makes desolate" (11:31) in it until the angel Michael arises as Israel's protector at the "time of the end" (11:35).

GROWTH

The book of Daniel had a complex development, beginning with the figure of Daniel, who was already legendary in Canaanite (Ugaritic) literature. Hence, he is mentioned in Ezekiel (14:14; 28:3) as a hero of the distant past, along with Noah and Job, known for his righteousness and wisdom. In the book of Daniel, "Daniel" is a pseudonym. That is, authors of apocalyptic works typically did not use their real names but chose instead to record their visions as received by well-known characters from the distant past, usually a highly regarded figure from the Bible. This bolstered the author's credibility and added a sense of certainty to the visions in that the events they foresaw were determined from ages long past. Thus, there are apocalypses ascribed to Adam, Seth, Enoch, Moses, Abraham, and others. Daniel's name may have been used first for the recipient of the visions and then secondarily applied to the hero of the stories. Alternatively, both the stories and the visions may have been associated with Daniel from the start, and this association would have been an important factor leading to their combination in the present book.

The two halves of the book, the stories and the apocalyptic visions, had independent origins. This is indicated by the different attitudes they reflect toward foreign rulers. The kings in the stories are basically favorably disposed toward Daniel and his friends. Though often pompous and foolish, they are not thoroughly evil or oppressive. The heroes—Daniel and his friends—are part of the royal administration as advisors to the kings. On the other hand, the terms "evil" and "oppressive" describe precisely the rulers in the visions, especially the last one who is the focus of the visions—the eleventh or small horn, the "prince" and "contemptible person" who profanes Jerusalem with an "abomination." This figure is a direct opponent of God and a persecutor of God's people.

The court stories in the first half of the book probably arose earlier and independently from one another. Fragments of a document called the *Prayer of Nabonidus* discovered among the Dead Sea Scrolls may represent an earlier version of the story behind Daniel 4. The stories in chapters 3–6 may have been the first to be gathered, since the Greek version of these chapters diverges from its predecessor more extensively than the other chapters in Daniel. The stories in chapters 1–6 as a whole were adopted by the author of the apocalyptic part of Daniel.

But there are yet further complications. Daniel is actually written in different languages—1:1–2:4a and chapters 8–12 are in Hebrew, whereas the middle of the book, essentially chapters 2–7, is in Aramaic—and the different languages probably result from stages of development. Scholars generally think that chapters 8–12 were the last section of the book to be written (in Hebrew) and that chapter 1 (plus 2:1-4a) was written or translated into Hebrew to provide a frame for the Aramaic section.

Finally, the Greek translation of Daniel contains four passages not found in the received text of the Hebrew Bible but included in the Apocrypha, or Deuterocanon: the Prayers of Azariah, the Song of the Three Young Men, Susanna, and Bel and the Dragon. The exact origin of these works is uncertain, but they indicate continued development surrounding the book of Daniel.

CONTEXT

Two contexts are crucial for understanding the book of Daniel: its literary context as apocalyptic literature and the historical context in which it was written. The two are related, since discernment of the historical context of an apocalyptic work can only be done through comprehending how the genre of apocalyptic functions. Apocalyptic (from a Greek word meaning "revelation") flourished as a genre between ca. 200 B.C.E. and 200 C.E. Daniel is one of the earliest examples of the genre. Its revelation comes in the form of a report of a vision or journey to heaven by the human author. What the author sees is typically interpreted by a supernatural guide as relating to earthly realities, specifically, the events leading up to a crisis, which God will resolve by intervening and bringing a close to the age and destruction of the evil forces that afflict the righteous.

The visions of the future in apocalyptic are mostly *ex eventu,* meaning "after the fact." That is, they are events that have already taken place by the author's time and indeed lead up to that time. This is because the real purpose of apocalyptic is not to foretell the future or the end of the world but to encourage and console people in crisis. Authors of apocalyptic seek to address their contemporaries by imparting to them the special "revelation" that the trials they are currently experiencing will soon end and that God will justify and exalt the righteous who remain loyal to him.

Historically, there are two contexts for Daniel—one for the stories and another for the visions. The stories are set in the Babylonian and Persian periods, essentially the sixth century B.C.E. However, the stories present several serious historical problems: (1) Dan 1:1 states that Nebuchadnezzar invaded Jerusalem in the third year of Jehoiakim = 606 B.C.E., when it is known from other sources, such as the Babylonian Chronicles, that Nebuchadnezzar did not come to power until 605 (cf. Jer 25:1) and did not invade Jerusalem until 598–597. (2) Contrary to Daniel 5, Belshazzar was not the son of Nebuchadnezzar or even his descendant, but the son of another Babylonian king, Nabonidus. Furthermore, though he was an important prince, Belshazzar was never actually king of Babylon. (3) There was no Darius the Mede who conquered Babylon (Dan 5:31; 9:1; 11:1). It was the Persian king Cyrus who defeated Babylon. One of his successors, Darius I, did organize the kingdom into 120 satrapies (Dan 6:1), but he was also a Persian. In fact, there was no independent empire of the Medes. These inaccuracies indicate that the stories in Daniel 1–6 did not originate close to the events that they portray but were significantly removed from the sixth century. Many scholars date them to the late Persian or early Hellenistic period, in the second half of the fourth century B.C.E.

The second historical context of Daniel is that of the visions in chapters 7–12 and the period when the book reached its final form. This context was the persecution of the Jews by the Seleucid ruler, Alexander IV "Epiphanes" in ca. 167–164 B.C.E. Antiochus invaded Jerusalem in 169, robbing the temple, and again in 167, massacring its inhabitants and desecrating the temple by erecting an altar to Zeus and purportedly sacrificing a pig upon it. The visions in Daniel 8–12 allude to these events, especially by their references to the profaning of the temple and the desolating abomination. The accuracy with which these chapters, especially Daniel 11, portray these events is a good indication that they were written in close proximity and in response to the events. The fact that the book envisions Antiochus's death occurring in Israel (11:45) when he actually died in Persia contrasts with the previous accuracy of the chapter and indicates that the book was completed before his death in 164.

INTERPRETATION

To illustrate interpretation in Daniel, we have chosen sample texts from each half—the story of Nebuchadnezzar's dream in chapter 2 and the visions in chapters 7–8.

Daniel 2

The statue in Nebuchadnezzar's dream combines two motifs that were common in ancient literature. One of these, best known from the Greek historian Hesiod, is the notion of ages of history represented by a series of metals declining in value. The other, also attested in Roman as well as Greek literature, is the idea that the Near East was ruled by a sequence of four kingdoms or empires, typically: Assyria, the Medes, the Persians, and the Macedonians. In Daniel, the scheme begins with the Babylonians in order to adapt it to the setting of the figure of Daniel in the court of Nebuchadnezzar. The empire of the Medes was a traditional motif rather than historical fact. Macedonia was the home of Alexander the Great and so is equivalent to Greece in Daniel. The feet of the statue—partly of iron, partly of clay—represent the Greek empire after Alexander's death, which was divided among four of his generals, who each established a dynasty in different places.

The dream presupposes the division of Alexander's empire in 323 B.C.E. but does not go into much historical detail beyond that. Although Daniel tells Nebuchadnezzar that the dream reveals "what will happen at the end of days" (2:28), that is not the real focus of the story. In this respect, the story in chapter 2 differs significantly from the visions in the book's latter half. The real point of the story is theological and literary—to glorify God by showing his control over world empires and to explain how Daniel and his friends came to positions of prominence in Babylonian and Persian courts. The entire story is very similar to and likely dependent on the story of Joseph in Genesis. Both are captives in a foreign land, and both interpret the king's dream, thereby gaining his trust and being promoted to a place of authority.

Daniel 7

The vision of the four beasts draws extensively from Canaanite mythology. Like the sea god, Yamm, the beasts embody the evil force of primordial chaos. There is no other reason for them to be coming out of the sea. The title "Ancient of Days" is similar to that of the chief Canaanite god El, "Father of Years." The "one like a human being" in 7:13 is comparable to the god Baal. He comes with the clouds, as Baal is called the "rider on the clouds" in the Ugaritic texts. He approaches the "Ancient of Days" as Baal approaches El. Most important, he triumphs over the sea monster as Baal defeats Yamm.

The four kingdoms represented by the four beasts are Babylon, Media, Persia, and Greece. The ten horns on the fourth beast represent the rulers of the Seleucid dynasty, and the troublesome eleventh horn is Antiochus IV. The "Ancient of Days" is God, and the "one like a human" is an angel, probably Michael, who is depicted as Israel's guardian (Dan 10:13, 21). The "holy ones" or "saints" who, along with this figure, receive an eternal kingdom may refer to faithful Jews or to angels, or both. This illustrates the idea behind apocalyptic literature that earthly history is determined by heavenly realities. By exalting himself and desecrating the temple, Antiochus really assaults the angels and oppresses them even as he oppresses faithful Jews.

The point of the vision is to encourage the Jews under oppression by assuring them that their persecution is limited, lasting "a time, two times, and half a time" (7:25)—probably three and one-half years, God is in control, the defeat of their oppressor is imminent, and the forces of good will triumph. When that happens, they will receive and possess an eternal kingdom (7:17-18, 21-22).

Daniel 8

The vision of the ram and the goat is especially important for interpretation because it presupposes the one in chapter 7 (8:1), and it explicitly identifies the countries to which both visions refer (8:20-21). The ram with two horns is Media and Persia, and the goat is Greece. The goat's horn, identified as the first king of Greece, is obviously Alexander the Great. The four kingdoms that subsequently arise from the broken horn of the goat (8:22) are Alexander's successors, the generals who divided up his empire after his death. The small horn that became great and arrogant is Antiochus IV. The reference to him halting the regular sacrifice in the temple and setting up the "transgression that makes desolate" (8:13) is an allusion to his installation of an altar and idol to Zeus in 167 B.C.E. The Hebrew word "desolation" or "desolating" (*shōmēm*) is a play on *ba'al shāmayim*, "lord of heaven," one of the titles used for Zeus.

As is typical of apocalyptic literature, the reference to Antiochus's desecration of the temple is *ex eventu*. That is, the vision describes events that have already taken place. This means that the vision was composed sometime after Antiochus's desecration of the temple in 167 B.C.E. Although the vision itself does not describe Antiochus's downfall in detail, it does indicate the temporary nature of his desecration—2300 mornings and evenings or 1150 days (8:14). Also, Daniel is told that the horn will be broken "not by human hands" (8:25). Thus, the message of the vision is that the oppression currently being suffered at the hands of Antiochus will not last long because God is going to intervene to halt it. As with chapter 7, the intent of this vision and indeed of the book of Daniel as a whole is to comfort, encourage, and console the faithful Jews who are suffering under Antiochus's persecution.

A further dimension of that hope and consolation that is of special interest to modern readers is Dan 12:2: "Many of those who sleep in the dust of the earth shall awake, some to everlasting life, and some to shame and everlasting contempt." This is the first (and maybe the only) reference in the Old Testament to the idea of resurrection of the dead. It is a further demonstration of the point that for the author and original audience of Daniel, the only hope was in God and not in the course of history. Even for those who had died, there was hope of ultimate vindication. The notion of resurrection and an afterlife was a very late development in the Old Testament, as indicated by the late date of Daniel, but one that was ripe for further development in the New Testament and Christianity.

CHAPTER 35

ADDITIONAL WRITINGS: EZRA–NEHEMIAH

The books of Ezra and Nehemiah are a single book in the Hebrew Bible. This book recounts the return of Jews from Babylon under Persian authority to their homeland and the rebuilding of the temple. More important in the long run than the temple rebuilding is the reconstitution of Israel as a religious community under the law promulgated by Ezra.

CONTENT

Ezra–Nehemiah begins with the decree of Cyrus, the first king of the Persian Empire, allowing the exiles from Judah and Jerusalem to return home (Ezra 1:1-4). The edict is essentially the same as the last two verses of 2 Chronicles. It is followed by an inventory of the temple treasures brought back by the returnees (1:5-11) and a list of the returnees themselves (Ezra 2).

After these preliminaries, the restoration takes place in three stages. The first is the rebuilding of the temple, narrated in Ezra 3–6. The altar is reconstructed and the temple foundation laid under Jeshua, who is a priest, and Zerubbabel, who is in the royal line of David (Ezra 3). Scheming from local opponents leads to a decree by the Persian king Ahasuerus halting the work (Ezra 4). It is resumed and completed under his successor, Darius, at the urging of the prophets Haggai and Zechariah (Ezra 5–6).

The second stage is the restoration of the community under Ezra's leadership (Ezra 7–10). Ezra the scribe is sent by King Artaxerxes on a mission of religious instruction to the residents of Judah and Jerusalem (7:1-26). Beginning in 7:27, Ezra then reports on his mission in the first person. He tells about his journey and the appointments and preparations that he and his entourage made for their arrival in Jerusalem (7:27–8:36). The rest of Ezra deals with the crisis of intermarriage between Jews and non-Jews that Ezra discovered. He relates the fasting and prayer that he undertook upon hearing about the problem (ch. 9). Returning to the third person, the narrative then lists the men who had married non-Jewish women and who purged their community by sending their foreign wives and children away (Ezra 10).

The third and final stage of restoration is the rebuilding of the rest of the city of Jerusalem under Nehemiah (Neh 1:1–7:5). This section is narrated in the first person and for that reason is often referred to, along with the first-person material in chapters 12–13, as the "Nehemiah memoir." In the first two chapters, Nehemiah reports his status in the court of Artaxerxes, his commission to rebuild Jerusalem's walls, and his journey to and inspection of the city. The next four chapters report the progress made on various sections of the wall and its eventual completion despite economic hardships and opposition from neighboring rulers. With the appointment of guards on the wall (7:1-4), the list of returnees from Ezra 2 is repeated in Nehemiah 7, thus framing the intervening materials and indicating the unity of Ezra–Nehemiah.

Following the long account of restoration, Nehemiah 8–9 report Ezra's reading of the law and instruction based on a recitation of Israel's history. This is followed by a list of signatories to a community pledge to live according to the law (Neh 10). Chapters 11–12 contain lists of names, especially of priests and Levites, representing the repopulation of Jerusalem at the celebration dedicating the city wall. The book ends in chapter 13 with another section of memoirs in which Nehemiah relates a second visit to Jerusalem following his return to Persia. Appalled at several violations of the law and community pledge, including intermarriage, Nehemiah takes corrective steps.

GROWTH

To a large extent, Ezra–Nehemiah is a compilation of sources. The Cyrus edict (Ezra 1:2-4) and the memoirs, that is, first-person accounts, of Ezra and Nehemiah have already been mentioned.

There are also several examples of purported official correspondence with the Persian court: Ezra 4:11-16; 4:17-22; 5:7-17; 6:6-12; 7:12-26. Indeed, Ezra 4:7–6:18 is in Aramaic rather than Hebrew, a fact that may be due to the preponderance of correspondence in it, since Aramaic was the diplomatic language of the day. These letters generally accord with the bureaucratic conventions of the time, suggesting that they are genuine, though they have almost certainly been edited in conformance to Jewish theology.

A third kind of source that is common in the book is lists of names. In addition to the two effectively identical lists of returnees in Ezra 2 and Nehemiah 7 that frame the account of restoration, there are lists of men married to foreign women (Ezra 10:18-44), of builders (Neh 3), of signatories to the pledge (Neh 10:1-27), and of priests, Levites, and leaders (Neh 11:3–12:26), to name the most prominent.

These sources give insight into the nature of Ezra–Nehemiah. The letters indicate that the compilation in Ezra–Nehemiah is thematic rather than chronological. The letters mentioned in Ezra 4:6 and 4:7-16 are dated to the reigns of Ahasuerus (ca. 486–465 B.C.E.) and Artaxerxes (ca. 465–424 B.C.E.). They have nothing to do with opposition to the building of the temple, which was completed in 515 B.C.E. This means that the resumption and completion of the temple rebuilding under Darius (522–486 B.C.E.), which is recounted in Ezra 5–6, actually took place long *before* the letters from Ahasuerus and Artaxerxes that appear to be the cause for stopping the work in Ezra 4. Apparently, the book's compiler is trying to illustrate the methods employed by the opponents of the Jews rather than to narrate history in chronological order. The anachronism may also indicate that the book's author/compiler wrote at a time substantially later than the events it recounts—probably in the middle of the fourth century B.C.E.

In addition to its sources, two other matters are important for understanding the growth of the present book of Ezra–Nehemiah. The first of these is its relationship to 1–2 Chronicles. The two works are obviously related in some way, since Chronicles ends where Ezra–Nehemiah begins, with the edict of Cyrus. For a long time, scholars assumed that both books had been written by the same author and were, in fact, a single work. Hence, Chronicles–Ezra–Nehemiah were grouped together as the "Chronicler's History." Since about 1970, however, this assumption has been increasingly called into question, and scholarly opinion has shifted. It is now generally assumed that Chronicles and Ezra–Nehemiah were by different authors. The main reason for this shift has been the perception of different—often opposite—interests and theological perspectives in the two books. For instance, Ezra–Nehemiah treats the remnant of the northern tribes as foreigners with whom the people of Judah and Jerusalem are not to intermarry. In Chronicles, by contrast, the northerners are viewed as apostates but still a part of God's chosen people, Israel; they only need to renew their allegiance to the Davidic monarchy and the temple in Jerusalem. Despite these differences, though, the link between Chronicles and Ezra–Nehemiah through the Cyrus edict suggests that there may have been an attempt at some point to tie the two works together.

The other issue related to the growth of Ezra–Nehemiah is its relationship to the Apocryphal or Deuterocanonical book of 1 Esdras. First Esdras basically duplicates, with minor variations, material in Chronicles and Ezra–Nehemiah. Specifically, it begins with Josiah's Passover celebration and then recounts the end of Judah (1 Esd 1), parallel to the end of 2 Chronicles (2 Chr 35–36). Then, it relates the account of return and restoration parallel to all of Ezra (1–10) and Nehemiah 8. The only substantial addition is a story about a contest between three bodyguards of King Darius over the question of what the strongest thing is (1 Esd 3:1–5:6). The point of the story is to explain how the winner, Zerubbabel, came to be granted permission to lead the returnees back to Jerusalem.

First Esdras is known only in Greek. But scholars debate whether it is based on a fragment of an earlier, Hebrew edition of Chronicles–Ezra–Nehemiah that treated them as a single work or is a late Greek compilation of portions from the separate books of Chronicles and Ezra–Nehemiah.

CONTEXT

The historical context of Ezra–Nehemiah is the late sixth and fifth centuries when what had been the kingdom of Judah was the province of Yehud in the Persian Empire. The rebuilding of Jerusalem probably took place in four stages. The first wave of returnees came in 538 B.C.E., shortly after the Persians conquered Babylonia in 539 and Cyrus issued the edict permitting the return. This group was led by a man named Sheshbazzar. Little is known of their restoration efforts or what became of them, but they were apparently forced to give up the project after laying the temple's foundation (Ezra 5:16). A second group of returnees under Zerubbabel and Jeshua succeeded in rebuilding the temple in the years 520–515 B.C.E. Again, however, it is unknown what happened to them and their aspirations for the future.

The third wave was led by Ezra, evidently in 458 B.C.E., and the fourth by Nehemiah in 444. Ezra established the moral authority for the restoration through his inculcation of the law. Nehemiah rebuilt the city wall of Jerusalem. The chronological disorder within Ezra–Nehemiah makes this fourfold scheme somewhat uncertain. Some scholars place the return of Ezra after that of Nehemiah, arguing that the Artaxerxes who commissioned Ezra (Ezra 7:1) was Artaxerxes II (404–358 B.C.E.) rather than Artaxerxes I (465–424 B.C.E.). Ezra's mission is dated to the seventh year of this king (Ezra 7:7), making it either 458 or 398 B.C.E.

The Cyrus edict accords with what is known of Persian imperial policy, which entailed tolerance and support for the religions of conquered peoples. Thus, the setting in Judah under Persian rule was one that, contrary to Babylonian policy, fostered restoration of the temple and its institutions in Jerusalem.

The broader cultural context reflected in Ezra–Nehemiah involves the matter of self-identity. Ezra and Nehemiah both confronted opposition to their enterprise from the local inhabitants, the "people of the land," whose assistance in building the temple they refused and who, therefore, opposed the project (cf. Ezra 4:1-5). These were the heirs of those whom the Assyrians had settled in territories of the northern tribes after 721 B.C.E. They probably considered themselves worshipers of Yahweh just like the returnees, but Zerubbabel, followed by Ezra and Nehemiah, had a different viewpoint. They saw the "people of the land" ethnically as foreigners or mongrels, mixed with those imported by the Assyrians, and religiously as apostates who had abandoned or perverted the worship of Yahweh. This was the beginning of the Jewish-Samaritan conflict that lies in the background of the New Testament.

The stories in Ezra–Nehemiah, then, reflect conflict over the question of the identity of the true heirs of Israel, its land, tradition, culture, and promises. Ezra–Nehemiah answers this question by defining the community in exclusivist ethnic and religious terms. In this respect, the book contrasts with other biblical works such as Ruth, Jonah, and Chronicles. All of these books reflect the literary and cultural environment that produced Ezra–Nehemiah. That environment was a community in which there were debates about how it should define itself. Was a true Israelite or Jew narrowly defined, as Ezra–Nehemiah claims, or were those of the northern tribes to be included (Chronicles)? And what about a person like Ruth who perfectly exemplified the "Israelite" virtue of loyalty? Did God really care about non-Israelites, as Ruth and Jonah seem to indicate? Ezra–Nehemiah obviously advances the most conservative perspective in this debate.

INTERPRETATION

The rejection of the "people of the land" in Ezra–Nehemiah is influenced by and based on interpretation of Deuteronomy and the Deuteronomistic History. Ezra–Nehemiah's view of the northern tribes is adopted from the description in 2 Kings 17. In their opposition to foreign marriages both Ezra and Nehemiah quote from Deuteronomy 7 (Ezra 9:11-12; Neh 13:25). But whereas Deuteronomy forbade marriage to indigenous Canaanites, Ezra–Nehemiah applies the prohibition to all non-Israelites. According to this interpretation, Boaz's marriage to Ruth would have been forbidden! Moreover, Ezra 10:2 refers to "foreign women from the peoples of the land" whom the Jewish leaders have married, thereby breaking faith with God. Again, these "people of the land" are evidently the Samaritans, the remnant of the northern tribes. Hence, Ezra–Nehemiah actually applies the law in Deuteronomy to marriage with people of mixed Jewish lineage.

The imposition of a prohibition of "foreign" marriage may seem quite cruel on the surface. The consequences of women and children being "put away" could have been dire. The women would have had little means of sustenance or support beyond begging or prostitution. The children would quite possibly have become suddenly fatherless and homeless with no hope of inheritance. At the same time, such a measure may have been socially or psychologically necessary for the self-preservation of the newly formed community.

In Jewish tradition, Ezra is regarded as the individual who compiled and collated the law. His implementation of the law within the community in a real sense marked the beginnings of Judaism. Although the attempt to regulate daily life and activities according to the law did not succeed for long, the definition of the community of God's people by religious and ethnic criteria has endured. The nation and people of Israel died with the respective exiles of the separate kingdoms of Israel and Judah to Assyria and Babylonia. With Ezra, Israel was reborn as a faith community—Judaism—that defined itself according to adherence to the scripture that Ezra promulgated.

CHAPTER 36

ADDITIONAL WRITINGS: 1–2 CHRONICLES

The book of Chronicles (1–2 Chronicles are two volumes of the same work) has often been ignored by biblical scholars or dismissed as a late work of pious fiction. Starting in the 1960s and 70s, however, the academic study of Chronicles has come into its own as scholars have begun to explore its literary and theological sophistication in depth and to appreciate it more fully.

CONTENT

The book of Chronicles falls into three main sections: 1 Chronicles 1–9, 1 Chronicles 10–2 Chronicles 9, and 2 Chronicles 10–36.

1 Chronicles 1–9

The first nine chapters of Chronicles are a collection of genealogies—the most extensive set of genealogies in the Bible. They serve as an introduction to the author's work, highlighting the identity and unity of the tribes of Israel and providing a synopsis of its history up to David, where the narrative account begins.

1 Chronicles 10–2 Chronicles 9

The second section recounts the reigns of David and Solomon as a single period. This is the "Golden Age" of Israel's united monarchy in Chronicles' presentation. This section can be further divided into three parts: the reign of David (1 Chr 10–21); the transition from David to Solomon, in which David commissions Solomon to build the temple and supplies the materials and personnel for the project (1 Chr 22–29); and the reign of Solomon (2 Chr 1–9). David and Solomon are presented in Chronicles as mirror images of each other. David becomes king (1 Chr 10–12), establishes the worship of Yahweh in Jerusalem (1 Chr 13–17), and gains the military supremacy that ensures the peace needed to build the temple (1 Chr 18–21). Similarly, Solomon is confirmed as king (2 Chr 1), builds the temple (2 Chr 2–7), and enjoys the benefits of his loyalty to Yahweh (2 Chr 8–9).

2 Chronicles 10–36

The remaining section covers the history of Judah from the division of the kingdom following Solomon (ca. 925 B.C.E.) to the edict of Cyrus permitting the people of Judah to return home and rebuild the temple (ca. 538 B.C.E.). In contrast to 1–2 Kings, which recounts the history of both kingdoms, Israel and Judah, Chronicles treats only the history of Judah. This is because Israel is considered an illegitimate kingdom in Chronicles—the result of human rebellion against God's chosen Davidic dynasty and against the chosen city of Jerusalem with its temple.

GROWTH

Although portions of Chronicles, especially in 1 Chronicles 1–9 and 22–29, may reflect later editing, scholars are generally agreed that the book as a whole is the work of a single writer, typically referred to as the "Chronicler." The issue of growth in the book, therefore, has less to do with its authorship than with the materials that the Chronicler drew on as sources.

The Chronicler's main source was the Deuteronomistic History, especially the account of the monarchy in the books of Samuel and Kings. The Chronicler basically made four kinds of revisions in his Samuel-Kings source: omissions, rearrangements, additions, and changes.

Omissions

The Chronicler's use of Samuel and Kings was selective. He omitted material that did not fit his theological agenda. Thus, he began his narrative in 1 Chronicles 10 with the story of the death of Saul simply to show how Yahweh turned the kingdom over to David. In his account of David's reign, he omitted the stories of David's affair with Bathsheba (2 Sam 11–12) and the revolt of David's son Absalom (2 Sam 13–20) because these did not fit with his idealized portrait of David. He also left out the negative material about Solomon (1 Kgs 11) for the same reason. Finally, as noted, he omitted the history of the northern kingdom of Israel, except where it overlapped with Judah, because the latter, which housed the temple and the Davidic dynasty, was his main concern and because he viewed Israel as illegitimate for theological reasons.

Rearrangements

The best example of the Chronicler's rearrangement of his source materials is in 1 Chronicles 11 where the lists and stories about the military heroes in David's army are transferred from the end of Samuel to the episode of David's coronation. The Chronicler made this change in order to stress all Israel's support behind David as king in his conquest of

Jerusalem and his transfer of the ark of the covenant there as a prelude to building the temple.

Additions

All of 1 Chronicles 1–9 and 22–29 represent the Chronicler's additions to the story of David found in 1–2 Samuel. As noted, the genealogies in chapters 1–9 portray Israel as united and serve as a prologue to the focus on the golden age of David and Solomon. David's preparation for the temple and commissioning of Solomon in chapters 22–29 emphasize the centrality of the temple for the Chronicler's version of history. There are other additions in 2 Chronicles, principally in the form of speeches by major characters that express the Chronicler's own theological outlook.

Changes

The Chronicler's evaluation of individual kings in 2 Chronicles is sometimes exactly the opposite of that found in Kings. The best example may be King Manasseh, who is incorrigibly wicked in Kings and seen as the reason for the Babylonian exile (2 Kgs 21), but is repentant in Chronicles and even carries out religious reforms in the second half of his reign (2 Chr 33). One of the reasons for these kinds of changes is the Chronicler's penchant for "periodizing" the reigns of kings by describing the first part of their reigns as righteous and the second part as wicked, or, as in the case of Manasseh, the other way around.

The Chronicler also made use of other canonical works in addition to Samuel and Kings. Thus, he borrowed from Genesis, Exodus, Numbers, Joshua, and perhaps other books for his genealogies. He shows familiarity with the laws in Exodus, Leviticus, Numbers, and Deuteronomy. He borrows from Psalms (see 1 Chr 16, which incorporates parts of Pss 96, 105, and 106), and he alludes to prophetic texts from Isaiah, Jeremiah, Zechariah, and Malachi, among others. Even the Cyrus edict at the end of 2 Chronicles may be taken from the beginning of Ezra.

The composition of Chronicles, then, is a benchmark in the growth of the Hebrew canon. It offers a unique opportunity within the Hebrew Bible to see how one writer made use of and interpreted earlier parts of the Bible. Chronicles, therefore, is important for understanding the growth of the entire canon of the Bible—its diversity as well as its reuse and reinterpretation for later settings.

CONTEXT

Literary

The literary context of Chronicles is the nearly complete Hebrew Bible. The Chronicler's extensive use of canonical sources also relates to the determination of the genre and nature of his work. Is Chronicles an alternative or second version of the history of Israel found in Pentateuch and Deuteronomistic History? Or is it an example of a "rewritten Bible," a retelling of the biblical story, sometimes with paraphrase, sometimes with elaboration? Or is it some other type of literature? This question has not yet been answered definitively, but it is perhaps more a question of terminology than of actual identity. What is important is the recognition of Chronicles' literary uniqueness in the Bible.

In addition to the Chronicler's use of biblical sources, the question of his use of nonbiblical sources is another element of the identification of Chronicles' literary context. Here there is an irony. On the one hand, the Chronicler frequently refers to "official" sources, such as the "book of the kings of Israel" (cf. 1 Chr 9:1; 2 Chr 20:34), and to prophetic sources such as the "history of the prophet Nathan" (2 Chr 9:29), which have proven upon scholarly analysis most likely to be different, creative ways of referring to Samuel and Kings. On the other hand, it seems clear from the content of Chronicles that the Chronicler also used sources of information outside of the Bible that he did not cite by name. The latter sources were sometimes removed from their original settings and placed in entirely different contexts. For example, lists of Levites from the Chronicler's own time are placed in the time of David.

Historical

The literary context of Chronicles is also helpful for determining its historical and social location. The earliest possible date for the book's composition is 539 B.C.E., as set by the reference to the Persian kingdom near its end (2 Chr 36:20). Allusions to or citations from Chronicles in several second-century works indicate that it had to have been written before 200 B.C.E. Within this time frame, there are indications that further narrow the range to 400–250, with a date between 350–300 being the most likely. Such indications include the extent of some of the genealogies in the beginning nine chapters and the dates of biblical materials cited or alluded to in Chronicles. The historical setting of Chronicles, in short, was the period following the Babylonian exile. Under their new Persian overlords, the people of the one-time kingdom of Judah were allowed to return home to rebuild their religious and social institutions in what was now the Persian province of Yehud.

The social makeup of this community has been sketched by some scholars. It may be that its focus was the temple, which had been rebuilt in the years 520–515 B.C.E. At least, in the Chronicler's portrait of the ideal Israelite state, the temple is at the center. The Chronicler may also have hoped for the restoration of the Davidic monarchy over all the tribes of

Israel. Perhaps he believed or hoped that restoration would result from faithful adherence to the law of Moses and the precepts for worship established by David.

The Chronicler himself was probably a member of the elite upper class in Jerusalem. He was obviously well educated and familiar with the religious and literary traditions of his predecessors in Jerusalem. He was, therefore, likely a Levite and a scribe. Likewise, his audience was probably not the general public, most of whom possessed little more than a rudimentary reading knowledge at most. Rather, he wrote for his peers, the political and religious leadership of Jerusalem.

INTERPRETATION

Whatever the genre of Chronicles, it is, above all, a sophisticated work of theology. There are four widely recognized major theological tenets in the work: the temple, the kingship of David and Solomon, all Israel, and divine retribution or reward.

Temple

The temple, its personnel, and the worship activities that occur there comprise the Chronicler's main concern. The genealogy of the Levites who serve in the temple is one of the longest and stands in the center of the genealogies in 1 Chronicles 1–9. The account of the reigns of David and Solomon is focused on their activities in behalf of the temple. David transfers the ark to Jerusalem in 1 Chronicles 13–16. He is prohibited from building the temple because he has shed so much blood in war (1 Chr 17). His successes in war (1 Chr 18–20) bring the tranquility needed to build the temple. The Chronicler even recounts a story about David's sin in taking a census (1 Chr 21) in order to explain the choice of location of the altar. He then stockpiles provisions and makes plans for the temple construction and its ongoing activities at the same time as commissioning Solomon as his successor in order to build the temple (1 Chr 22–29). After Solomon, the kings of Judah are evaluated on religious grounds—whether they maintain proper worship of Yahweh. Hezekiah, for example, is portrayed in Chronicles as a model along with David and Solomon because of his restoration of temple worship.

David and Solomon

The reigns of David and Solomon are presented together in Chronicles as Israel's golden age. The Chronicler idealizes both of them by omitting all of the negative material about Solomon and most of it about David. Through this portrait of their reign he expresses the hope—and perhaps the model—for the restoration of the Davidic kingdom over a united Israel in the postexilic period.

David and Solomon are equals, though each has a different role. David establishes the dynasty and brings about the peace necessary for building the temple. Solomon builds the temple and enhances Israel's international prestige and prosperity. David's role as a founder of Israel's faith in Chronicles is especially remarkable. He supplies not only the provisions and personnel for building the temple, but its very blueprint as well. He also designates the orders of the priests, Levites, musicians, and gatekeepers who carry on the daily rituals at the temple. In the Chronicler's theological outlook, all of these accomplishments by both David and Solomon are attributable not only to their initiative and dedication; they are also gifts from God in reward for their faithfulness.

In addition to their respective roles in establishing Israel's worship, David and Solomon are the founders of Israel's divinely chosen, ruling dynasty. Chronicles is quite clear in expressing the view that kingship belongs to God, and God chose David and his line to rule. God took the kingdom from Saul and turned it over to David (1 Chr 10:14). The covenant with David is a unilateral promise (1 Chr 17). Then, in contrast to 1 Kings 1–2, where it is uncertain who David's successor will be, Solomon is designated and placed on the throne by David himself before his death without even the mention of another candidate. Thus, the revolt of Jeroboam and the northern tribes against the Davidic dynasty is rebellion against God, and the northern kingdom of Israel is illegitimate (see 2 Chr 13:5-7).

All Israel

Even though the northern kingdom is religiously and politically illegitimate in the Chronicler's view and therefore does not merit a distinct record, its citizens still have a heritage in the ideal kingdom of Israel. Hence, the Chronicler's vision for restoration is the reuniting of "all Israel" (13:4) under its Davidic king. Thus, the genealogy that opens the book of Chronicles includes the northern tribes and characterizes the ideal extent of Israel. The enthronements of David and Solomon are celebrated by all Israel. The entire nation is also involved in the conquest of Jerusalem, the transfer of the ark, and the construction and dedication of the temple.

The clearest expression of the Chronicler's view of the "all Israel" ideal in light of the divided kingdom is found in the address of King Abijah of Judah to the Israelite army in 2 Chronicles 13. Through Abijah the Chronicler explains that the division of the kingdom was an act of rebellion against Yahweh, but it was perpetrated by Jeroboam and "certain worthless scoundrels" (13:7) who followed him, not by all the northerners. True Israel is preserved in the people of Judah who remain faithful to

God and to the institutions that God established in Jerusalem. Even though the northern kingdom of Israel is apostate, the people of the north are still part of Israel, part of the people of Yahweh, the brothers and sisters of Judah. They can still repent and return to God; indeed, Abijah invites them to do so. The Chronicler later holds up the model of King Hezekiah, who restores worship on the part of united Israel in Jerusalem.

Retribution/Reward

This basic principle of the Chronicler is articulated in David's commission to Solomon (1 Chr 28:9): "If you seek him, he will be found by you; but if you forsake him, he will abandon you forever." The principle is first illustrated with Saul, who was put to death by Yahweh for his unfaithfulness and his kingdom handed over to David (1 Chr 10:13-14). It is most apparent, though, in the Chronicler's treatments of kings of Judah in 2 Chronicles. It is usually "immediate" retribution or reward because it takes place in the king's lifetime. In fact, as already noted, the Chronicler typically "periodizes" the reigns of kings by dividing them into a time of faithfulness followed by reward and a subsequent time of unfaithfulness followed by punishment. Rewards come in the form of "rest" and "quiet" from warfare, military strength, building activity, a large family, wealth, international reputation, and respect from subjects. Disasters that befell certain kings are interpreted as retribution for sin.

Other Themes

These four major interests of the Chronicler are supported by additional themes. For instance, prophets play an important role in Chronicles, reflected in the dual admonition to believe in Yahweh and to believe the prophets (2 Chr 20:20). Prophets pronounce judgment for sin and warn of impending punishment. Thus, although retribution is immediate, there is always the chance to avoid it by repenting.

Particularly noteworthy is the Chronicler's emphasis on personal attitudes and piety. Despite his emphasis on proper ritual obedience, the Chronicler is not a rigid legalist. Thus, God makes special allowance at Hezekiah's Passover celebration for people whose heart is in the right place even though they are ceremonially unclean (2 Chr 30:18-20). Along these lines, joy is a regular element of cultic celebrations in Chronicles. Such occasions also showcase the generosity and volunteerism of the people. Humility is an especially important virtue for the Chronicler. The penitent "seek" God, which is the Chronicler's term for personal devotion and is also a key to avoiding divine wrath when one has sinned, since Yahweh will never remove his "steadfast love" or loyalty for his people.

Bibliography

TORAH

The Beginning (Genesis 1:1–2:3)

Anderson, Bernhard W. "Creation," *Interpreter's Dictionary of the Bible.* Nashville/New York: Abingdon Press, 1962.

Clifford, Richard J. *Creation Accounts in the Ancient Near East and in the Bible.* Catholic Biblical Quarterly Monograph Series 26. Washington, D.C.: Catholic Biblical Association, 1994.

Garr, Randall W. *In His Own Image and Likeness: Humanity, Divinity, and Monotheism.* Leiden, Netherlands: Brill Academic Publishers, 2003.

Heidel, Alexander. *The Babylonian Genesis: The Story of Creation.* Second ed. Chicago: University of Chicago Press, 1951.

Löning, Karl, and Erich Zenger. *To Begin With, God Created . . . : Biblical Theologies of Creation.* Collegeville, Minn.: Liturgical Press, 1989.

Pritchard, James B., ed. *Ancient Near Eastern Texts Relating to the Old Testament.* Third ed. Princeton, N.J.: Princeton University Press, 1969.

Adam and Eve (Genesis 2:4b–3:24)

Anderson, Gary A. *The Genesis of Perfection: Adam and Eve in Jewish and Christian Imagination.* Louisville: Westminster John Knox Press, 2001.

Barr, James. *The Garden of Eden and the Hope of Immortality.* Minneapolis: Fortress Press, 1993.

Kvam, Kristen E., Linda S. Schearing, and Valarie H. Ziegler. *Eve & Adam: Jewish, Christian, and Muslim Readings on Genesis and Gender.* Bloomington/Indianapolis: Indiana University Press, 1999.

Meyers, Carol L. *Discovering Eve: Ancient Israelite Women in Context.* New York: Oxford University Press, 1988.

Trible, Phyllis. *God and the Rhetoric of Sexuality.* Philadelphia: Fortress Press, 1978.

After the Garden (Genesis 4–11)

Bailey, Lloyd R. *Noah: The Person and the Story in History and Tradition. Studies on Personalities of the Old Testament.* Columbia: University of South Carolina Press, 1989.

———. *Where Is Noah's Ark? Mystery on Mount Ararat.* Nashville: Abingdon Press, 1978.

Lambert, W. G., and A. R. Millard. *Atrahasis: The Babylonian Story of the Flood.* Winona Lake, Ind.: Eisenbrauns, 1999.

L'Heureux, Conrad E. *In and Out of Paradise: The Book of Genesis from Adam and Eve to the Tower of Babel.* New York: Paulist Press, 1983.

Abraham

McCarter, P. Kyle. "The Patriarchal Age." Pages 1-29 in H. Shanks, *Ancient Israel: A Short History from Abraham to the Roman Destruction of the Temple.* Washington, D.C.: Biblical Archaeological Society, 1988.

Thompson, Thomas L. *The Historicity of the Patriarchal Narratives.* Beihefte zur Zeitschrift für die alttestamentliche Wissenschaft 133. Berlin: Walter de Gruyter, 1974.

Van Seters, John. *Abraham in History and Tradition.* New Haven, Conn./London: Yale University Press, 1975.

Jacob

Hendel, Ronald S. *The Epic of the Patriarch: The Jacob Cycle and the Narrative Traditions of Canaan and Israel.* Harvard Semitic Monographs 42. Atlanta: Scholars Press, 1988.

McKenzie, Steven L. "The Jacob Tradition in Hosea 12:4-5." *Vetus Testamentum 36* (1986): 311-22.

Walters, Stanley D. "Jacob Narrative." Pages 599-608 in vol. 3 of *The Anchor Bible Dictionary.* Edited by David N. Freedman. 6 vols. New York: Doubleday, 1992.

Walton, Kevin. *Thou Traveller Unknown: The Presence and Absence of God in the Jacob Narrative.* Waynesboro, Ga.: Paternoster, 2003.

Joseph

Coats, George W. *From Canaan to Egypt: Structural and Theological Context for the Joseph Story.* Catholic Biblical Quarterly Monograph Series 4. Washington, D.C.: Catholic Biblical Association, 1975.

Humphreys, W. Lee. *Joseph and His Family: A Literary Study. Studies on Personalities of the Old Testament.* Columbia: University of South Carolina Press, 1989.

Kaltner, John. *Inquiring of Joseph: Getting to Know a Biblical Character through the Qur'an.* Interfaces. Collegeville, Minn.: Liturgical Press, 2003.

Redford, Donald B. *A Study of the Biblical Story of Joseph (Genesis 37-50).* Supplements to Vetus Testamentum 20. Leiden, Netherlands: Brill Academic Publishers, 1970.

Exodus

Assmann, Jan. *Moses the Egyptian.* Cambridge, Mass.: Harvard University Press, 1997.

Childs, Brevard S. *The Book of Exodus.* Old Testament Library. Philadelphia: Westminster Press, 1974.

Dozeman, Thomas B. *God at War: A Study of Power in the Exodus Tradition.* New York: Oxford University Press, 1996.

Propp, William H. C. *Exodus 1-18.* Anchor Bible. New York: Doubleday, 1998.

Van Seters, John. *The Life of Moses: The Yahwist as Historian in Exodus–Numbers.* Louisville: Westminster John Knox Press, 1994.

The Law

Alt, Albrecht. "The Origins of Israelite Law." Pages 101-71 in *Essays on Old Testament History and Religion.* Garden City, N.Y.: Doubleday, 1968.

Greengus, Samuel. "Law." Pages 242-52 in vol. 4 of *The Anchor Bible Dictionary.* Edited by David N. Freedman. 6 vols. New York: Doubleday, 1992.

Harrelson, Walter. *The Ten Commandments and Human Rights.* Philadelphia: Fortress Press, 1980.

Levenson, Jon D. *Sinai & Zion: An Entry into the Jewish Bible.* San Francisco: Harper & Row, 1985.

Patrick, Dale. *Old Testament Law.* Atlanta: John Knox Press, 1985.

Roth, Martha T. *Law Collections from Mesopotamia and Asia Minor.* Society of Biblical Literature Writings from the Ancient World 6. Atlanta: SBL, 1997.

Wilderness Traditions

Coats, George W. *Rebellion in the Wilderness: The Murmuring Motif in the Wilderness Traditions of the Old Testament.* Nashville: Abingdon Press, 1968.

Davies, Graham I. *The Way of the Wilderness: A Geographical Study of the Wilderness Itineraries in the Old Testament.* Society for Old Testament Study Monograph Series 5. Cambridge: Cambridge University Press, 1979.

———. "Wilderness Wanderings." Pages 912-14 in vol. 6 of *The Anchor Bible Dictionary.* Edited by David N. Freedman. 6 vols. New York: Doubleday, 1992.

Levine, Baruch A. *Numbers 1-20.* Anchor Bible 4A. New York: Doubleday, 1993.

———. *Numbers 21-36.* Anchor Bible 4B. New York: Doubleday, 2000.

Wenham, Gordon J. *Numbers.* Old Testament Guides. Sheffield, England: Sheffield Academic Press, 1997.

FORMER PROPHETS

Deuteronomy

Levinson, Bernard M. *Deuteronomy and the Hermeneutics of Legal Innovation.* New York: Oxford University Press, 1997.

Mayes, A. D. H. *Deuteronomy.* New Century Bible. Grand Rapids, Mich.: Wm. B. Eerdmans Publishing Company, 1981.

McCarthy, Dennis J. *Treaty and Covenant: A Study in Form in the Ancient Oriental Documents and in the Old Testament.* 2d ed. Analecta Biblica 21A. Rome: Pontifical Biblical Institute, 1978.

Nelson, Richard D. *Deuteronomy.* Old Testament Library. Louisville: Westminster John Knox Press, 2002.

Tigay, Jeffrey. *Deuteronomy.* JPS Torah Commentary. Jerusalem: Jewish Publication Society, 1996.

Weinfeld, Moshe. *Deuteronomy and the Deuteronomic School.* Oxford: Clarendon Press, 1972.

———. *Deuteronomy 1-11.* Anchor Bible 5. New York: Doubleday, 1991.

Joshua

Campbell, Antony F., and Mark A. O'Brien. *Unfolding the Deuteronomistic History: Origins, Upgrades, Present Text.* Minneapolis: Augsburg Fortress Publishers, 2000.

Dever, William G. *Who Were the Early Israelites and Where Did They Come From?* Grand Rapids, Mich.: Wm. B. Eerdmans Publishing Company, 2003.

McKenzie, Steven L. "Deuteronomistic History." Pages 160-68 in vol. 2 of *The Anchor Bible Dictionary.* Edited by David N. Freedman. 6 vols. New York: Doubleday, 1992.

Nelson, Richard D. *Joshua.* Old Testament Library. Louisville: Westminster John Knox Press, 1997.

Noth, Martin. *The Deuteronomistic History.* Journal for the Study of the Old Testament Supplement Series 15. Sheffield, England: JSOT Press, 1981.

Pury, Albert de, Thomas Römer, and Jean-Daniel Macchi. *Israel Constructs Its History: Deuteronomistic Historiography in Recent Research.* Journal for the Study of the Old Testament Supplement Series 306. Sheffield, England: Sheffield Academic Press, 2000.

Judges

Ackerman, Susan. *Warrior, Dancer, Seductress, Queen.* Anchor Bible Reference Library. New York: Doubleday, 1998.

Bal, Mieke. *Death and Dissymmetry: The Politics of Coherence in the Book of Judges.* Chicago: University of Chicago Press, 1988.

Boling, Robert G. *Judges.* Anchor Bible 6A. New York: Doubleday, 1975.

Halpern, Baruch. *The First Historians: The Hebrew Bible and History.* San Francisco: Harper & Row, 1988.

Van Seters, John. *In Search of History: Historiography in the Ancient World and the Origins of Biblical History.* New Haven, Conn.: Yale University Press, 1983.

Yee, Gale A., ed. *Judges and Method: New Approaches in Biblical Studies.* Minneapolis: Fortress Press, 1995.

The Beginning of Monarchy in Israel (1 Samuel 1–15)

Ehrlich, Carl S., and Marsha C. White, eds. *Saul in Story and Tradition.* Forschungen Zum Alten Testament 47. Tübingen, Germany: Mohr Siebeck, 2006.

Gunn, David M. *The Fate of King Saul: An Interpretation of a Biblical Story.* Journal for the Study of the Old Testament Supplement Series 14. Sheffield, England: JSOT Press, 1980.

Klein, Ralph W. *1 Samuel.* Word Biblical Commentary 10. Dallas: Word Books, 1983.

McCarter, P. Kyle. *1 Samuel.* Anchor Bible 8. New York: Doubleday, 1980.

The Rise of David (1 Samuel 16–2 Samuel 5)

Alter, Robert. *The David Story: A Translation with Commentary of 1 and 2 Samuel.* New York: W. W. Norton & Company, 1999.

Gunn, David M. *The Story of King David: Genre and Interpretation.* Journal for the Study of the Old Testament Supplement Series 6. Sheffield, England: JSOT Press, 1978.

Halpern, Baruch. *David's Secret Demons: Messiah, Murderer, Traitor, King.* Grand Rapids, Mich.: Wm. B. Eerdmans Publishing Company, 2001.

Isser, Stanley. *The Sword of Goliath: David in Heroic Literature.* Atlanta: Society of Biblical Literature, 2003.

McKenzie, Steven L. *King David: A Biography.* New York: Oxford University Press, 2000.

Steussy, Marti J. *David: Biblical Portraits of Power. Studies on Personalities of the Old Testament.* Columbia: University of South Carolina Press, 1999.

The Reigns of David and Solomon (2 Samuel 5–1 Kings 11)

Finkelstein, Israel, and Neil Asher Silberman. *David and Solomon: In Search of the Bible's Sacred Kings and the Roots of the Western Tradition.* New York: Free Press, 2006.

Handy, Lowell K., ed. *The Age of Solomon: Scholarship at the Turn of the Millennium.* Leiden, Netherlands: Brill Academic Publishers, 1997.

Knoppers, Gary N. *Two Nations Under God: The Deuteronomistic History of Solomon and the Dual Monarchies.* Vol. 1. *The Reign of Solomon and the Rise of Jeroboam.* Harvard Semitic Monographs 52. Atlanta: Scholars Press, 1993.

McCarter, P. Kyle. *II Samuel.* Anchor Bible 9B. New York: Doubleday, 1984.
Rost, Leonhard. *The Succession to the Throne of David.* Sheffield, England: Almond Press, 1982.

The Division and Its Consequences (1 Kings 12–22)
Cogan, Mordechai. *I Kings.* Anchor Bible 10. New York: Doubleday, 2000.
Knoppers, Gary N. *Two Nations Under God: The Deuteronomistic History of Solomon and the Dual Monarchies.* Vol. 2. *The Reign of Jeroboam, the Fall of Israel, and the Reign of Josiah.* Harvard Semitic Monographs 52. Atlanta: Scholars Press, 1994.
Long, Burke O. *1 Kings, with an Introduction to Historical Literature.* Forms of the Old Testament Literature 9. Grand Rapids, Mich.: Wm. B. Eerdmans Publishing Company, 1984.
McKenzie, Steven L. *The Trouble With Kings: The Composition of the Book of Kings in the Deuteronomistic History.* Supplements to Vetus Testamentum 42. Leiden, Netherlands: Brill Academic Publishers, 1991.
Walsh, Jerome T. *1 Kings.* Berit Olam. Collegeville, Minn.: Liturgical Press, 1996.

From Ahab to the Fall of Israel (2 Kings 1–17)
Brueggemann, Walter. *1 & 2 Kings.* Smyth & Helwys Bible Commentary. Macon, Ga.: Smyth & Helwys, 2000.
Dietrich, Walter. "1 and 2 Kings." Pages 232-66 in *The Oxford Bible Commentary.* Edited by J. Barton and J. Muddiman. Oxford: Oxford University Press, 2000.
Fritz, Volkmar. *1 and 2 Kings.* Minneapolis: Augsburg Fortress Publishers, 2003.
Rofé, Alexander. *The Prophetical Stories.* Jerusalem: Magnes Press, 1988.

The End of Judah (2 Kings 18–25)
Cogan, Mordechai, and Hayim Tadmor. *II Kings.* Anchor Bible 11. New York: Doubleday, 1988.
Hobbs, T. R. *2 Kings.* Word Biblical Commentary 12. Dallas: Word Books, 1985.
Provan, Iain W. *Hezekiah and the Books of Kings: A Contribution to the Debate about the Composition of the Deuteronomistic History.* Beihefte zur Zeitschrift für die alttestamentliche Wissenschaft 172. Berlin: Walter de Gruyter, 1988.
Sweeney, Marvin A. *King Josiah of Judah: The Lost Messiah of Israel.* New York: Oxford University Press, 2001.

LATTER PROPHETS

First Isaiah and Micah
Isaiah
Barton, John. *Isaiah 1-39.* Old Testament Guides. Sheffield, England: Sheffield Academic Press, 1995.
Blenkinsopp, Joseph. *Isaiah 1-39.* Anchor Bible 19. New York: Doubleday, 2000.
Childs, Brevard. *Isaiah.* Old Testament Library. Louisville: Westminster John Knox Press, 2001.
Clements, R. E. *Isaiah 1-39.* New Century Bible. Grand Rapids, Mich.: Wm. B. Eerdmans Publishing Company, 1980.
Seitz, Christopher R. "Isaiah, Book of (First Isaiah)." Pages 472-88 in vol. 3 of *The Anchor Bible Dictionary.* Edited by David N. Freedman. 6 vols. New York: Doubleday, 1992.

Micah

Anderson, Francis I., and David Noel Freedman. *Micah.* Anchor Bible 24E. New York: Doubleday, 2000.

Ben Zvi, Ehud. *Micah.* Forms of the Old Testament Literature 21B. Grand Rapids, Mich.: Wm. B. Eerdmans Publishing Company, 2000.

Hillers, Delbert R. *Micah.* Hermeneia. Philadelphia: Fortress Press, 1984.

Wolff, Hans Walter. *Micah the Prophet.* Translated by R. D. Gehrke. Philadelphia: Fortress Press, 1981.

Hosea and Amos

Hosea

Davies, Graham I. *Hosea.* Grand Rapids, Mich.: Wm. B. Eerdmans Publishing Company, 1992.

Seow, Choon-Leon. "Hosea." Pages 291-99 in vol. 3 of *The Anchor Bible Dictionary.* Edited by David N. Freedman. 6 vols. New York: Doubleday, 1992.

Sherwood, Yvonne M. *The Prostitute and the Prophet: Hosea's Marriage in Literary-Theoretical Perspective.* Journal for the Study of the Old Testament Supplement Series 212. Sheffield, England: Sheffield Academic Press, 1996.

Wolff, Hans Walter. *Hosea.* Translated by G. Stansell. Hermeneia. Philadelphia: Fortress Press, 1974.

Amos

Carroll, M. Daniel R. *Amos the Prophet and His Oracles: Research on the Book of Amos.* Louisville: Westminster John Knox Press, 2002.

King, Philip J. *Amos, Hosea, Micah: An Archaeological Commentary.* Philadelphia: Westminster Press, 1988.

Paul, Shalom M. *Amos.* Hermeneia. Minneapolis: Augsburg Fortress Publishers, 1991.

Wolff, Hans Walter. *Amos the Prophet.* Translated by Fr. R. McCurley. Philadelphia: Fortress Press, 1973.

Nahum, Habakkuk, Zephaniah

Anderson, Francis I. *Habakkuk: A New Translation with Introduction and Commentary.* Anchor Bible. New York: Doubleday, 2000.

Baker, David W. *Nahum, Habakkuk, Zephaniah.* Tyndale Old Testament Commentaries. Downers Grove, Ill.: InterVarsity Press, 1988.

Berlin, Adele. *Zephaniah.* Anchor Bible 25A. New York: Doubleday, 1994.

Roberts, J. J. M. *Nahum, Habakkuk, and Zephaniah.* Old Testament Library. Louisville: Westminster John Knox Press, 1991.

Sweeney, Marvin A. *The Twelve Prophets.* Berit Olam. Collegeville, Minn.: Liturgical Press, 2000.

Jeremiah

Carroll, Robert P. *Jeremiah.* Old Testament Library. Philadelphia: Westminster Press, 1986.

Holladay, William L. *Jeremiah.* 2 volumes. Hermeneia. Philadelphia: Fortress Press, 1986-89.

Miller, Patrick D. "The Book of Jeremiah." Pages 555-1072 in vol. 7 of *The New Interpreter's Bible.* Edited by Leander Keck. 12 vols. Nashville: Abingdon Press, 1996.

O'Connor, Kathleen M. *The Confessions of Jeremiah: Their Interpretation and Role in Chapters 1-25.* Society of Biblical Literature Dissertation Series 94. Atlanta: Scholars Press, 1988.

Stulman, Louis. *Order amid Chaos: Jeremiah as Symbolic Tapestry.* Sheffield, England: Sheffield Academic Press, 1998.

Ezekiel

Block, Daniel I. *The Book of Ezekiel.* 2 volumes. New International Commentary on the Old Testament. Grand Rapids, Mich.: Wm. B. Eerdmans Publishing Company, 1997-98.

Boadt, Lawrence. "Ezekiel, Book of." Pages 711-22 in vol. 2 of *The Anchor Bible Dictionary.* Edited by David N. Freedman. 6 vols. New York: Doubleday, 1992.

Greenberg, Moshe. *Ezekiel 1-20.* Anchor Bible 22. New York: Doubleday, 1983.

———. *Ezekiel 21-37.* Anchor Bible 22A. New York: Doubleday, 1997.

Klein, Ralph W. *Ezekiel: The Prophet and His Message.* Columbia: University of South Carolina Press, 1988.

Zimmerli, Walther. *Ezekiel.* Translated by R. E. Clements. 2 vols. Hermeneia. Philadelphia: Fortress Press, 1979-83.

Second Isaiah

Blenkinsopp, Joseph. *Isaiah 40-55.* Anchor Bible 19A. New York: Doubleday, 2002.

Childs, Brevard S. *Isaiah.* Old Testament Library. Louisville: Westminster John Knox Press, 2001.

Hanson, Paul D. *Isaiah 40-66.* Louisville: Westminster John Knox Press, 1995.

Sommer, Benjamin D. *A Prophet Reads Scripture: Allusion in Isaiah 40-66.* Stanford, Calif.: Stanford University Press, 1988.

Joel and Obadiah

Joel

Coggins, Richard. *Joel and Amos.* The New Century Bible Commentary. Sheffield, England: Sheffield Academic Press, 2000.

Crenshaw, James L. *Joel: A New Translation with Notes.* Anchor Bible 24C. New York: Doubleday, 1995.

Hiebert, Theodore. "Joel, Book of." Pages 873-80 in vol. 3 of *The Anchor Bible Dictionary.* Edited by David N. Freedman. 6 vols. New York: Doubleday, 1992.

Wolff, Hans Walter. *Joel and Amos.* Translated by W. Janzen, S. D. McBride, and C. A. Muenchow. Hermeneia. Philadelphia: Fortress Press, 1977.

Obadiah

Barton, John. *Joel and Obadiah.* Old Testament Library. Louisville: Westminster John Knox Press, 2001.

Ben Zvi, Ehud. *A Historical-Critical Study of the Book of Obadiah.* Beihefte zur Zeitschrift für die alttestamentliche Wissenschaft 242. Berlin: Walter de Gruyter, 1996.

Raabe, Paul R. *Obadiah.* Anchor Bible 24D. New York: Doubleday, 1996.

Simundson, Daniel J. *Hosea, Joel, Amos, Obadiah, Jonah, Micah.* Nashville: Abingdon Press, 2005.

Jonah

Green, Barbara. *Jonah's Journeys.* Interfaces. Collegeville, Minn.: Liturgical Press, 2005.

Limburg, James. *Jonah*. Old Testament Library. Louisville: Westminster John Knox Press, 1993.
Sasson, Jack M. *Jonah*. Anchor Bible 24A. New York: Doubleday, 1990.
Simon, Uriel. *Jonah*. The JPS Bible Commentary. Jerusalem: Jewish Publication Society, 1999.
Trible, Phyllis. "Jonah." Pages 463-529 in vol. 7 of *The New Interpreter's Bible*. Edited by Leander Keck. 12 vols. Nashville: Abingdon Press, 1996.

Haggai, Zechariah, Malachi

Hill, Andrew E. *Malachi*. Anchor Bible 25D. New York: Doubleday, 1998.
Meyers, Carol L., and Eric M. Meyers. *Haggai, Zechariah 1-8*. Anchor Bible 25B. New York: Doubleday, 1987.
———. *Zechariah 9-14*. Anchor Bible 25C. New York: Doubleday, 1993.
Petersen, David L. *Haggai and Zechariah 1-8*. Old Testament Library. Philadelphia: Westminster Press, 1985.
———. *Zechariah 9-14 and Malachi*. Old Testament Library. Louisville: Westminster John Knox Press, 1995.
Redditt, Paul L. *Haggai, Zechariah, Malachi*. New Century Bible. Grand Rapids, Mich.: Wm. B. Eerdmans Publishing Company, 1995.

WRITINGS

Job

Gutiérrez, Gustavo. *On Job: God-Talk and the Suffering of the Innocent*. Maryknoll, N.Y.: Orbis Books, 1987.
Habel, Norman C. *The Book of Job*. Old Testament Library. Philadelphia: Westminster Press, 1985.
Newsom, Carol A. "The Book of Job." Pages 319-637 in vol. 4 of *The New Interpreter's Bible*. Edited by Leander Keck. 12 vols. Nashville: Abingdon Press, 1996.
Pope, Marvin H. *Job*. Anchor Bible 15. Garden City, N.Y.: Doubleday, 1973.
Wharton, James A. *Job*. Westminster Bible Companion. Louisville: Westminster John Knox Press, 1999.

Proverbs

Camp, Claudia V. *Wisdom and the Feminine in the Book of Proverbs*. Sheffield, England: Almond Press, 1985.
Clifford, Richard J. *Proverbs*. Old Testament Library. Louisville: Westminster John Knox Press, 1999.
Crenshaw, James L. "Proverbs, Book of." Pages 513-30 in vol. 5 of *The Anchor Bible Dictionary*. Edited by David N. Freedman. 6 vols. New York: Doubleday, 1992.
Fox, Michael V. *Proverbs 1-9*. Anchor Bible 18A. New York: Doubleday, 2000.
Murphy, Roland E. *Proverbs*. Word Biblical Commentary. Dallas: Word Books, 1998.
Pritchard, James B., ed. *Ancient Near Eastern Texts Relating to the Old Testament*. Third ed. Princeton, N.J.: Princeton University Press, 1969.

Qoheleth

Crenshaw, James L. *Ecclesiastes*. Old Testament Library. Philadelphia: Westminster Press, 1987.

Fox, Michael V. *A Time to Tear Down and a Time to Build Up: A Rereading of Ecclesiastes*. Grand Rapids, Mich.: Wm. B. Eerdmans Publishing Company, 1999.

Garfunkel, Stephen. *Qoheleth*. Berit Olam. Collegeville, Minn.: Liturgical Press, 2000.

Limburg, James. *Encountering Ecclesiastes: A Book for Our Time*. Grand Rapids, Mich.: Wm. B. Eerdmans Publishing Company, 2006.

Seow, Choon-Leon. *Ecclesiastes*. Anchor Bible 18C. New York: Doubleday, 1997.

Psalms

Clifford, Richard J. *Psalms 1-72*. Abingdon Old Testament Commentaries. Nashville: Abingdon Press, 2002.

———. *Psalms 73-150*. Abingdon Old Testament Commentaries. Nashville: Abingdon Press, 2003.

Gunkel, Hermann. *An Introduction to the Psalms: The Genres of the Religious Lyric of Israel*. Translated by J. D. Nogalski. Macon, Ga.: Mercer University Press, 1998.

Kraus, Hans-Joachim. *Psalms*. Translated by H. C. Oswald. 2 volumes. Minneapolis: Augsburg Fortress Publishers, 1988-89.

Miller, Patrick D. *They Cried to the Lord: The Form and Theology of Israelite Prayer*. Minneapolis: Augsburg Fortress Publishers, 1994.

Mowinckel, Sigmund. *The Psalms in Israel's Worship*. Translated by D. R. Ap-Thomas. 2 volumes. Nashville: Abingdon Press, 1962.

The Song of Solomon and Lamentations

The Song of Solomon

Carr, David M. *The Erotic Word: Sexuality, Spirituality, and the Bible*. New York: Oxford University Press, 2002.

Murphy, Roland E. *The Song of Songs*. Hermeneia. Minneapolis: Fortress Press, 1990.

Pope, Marvin H. *Song of Songs*. Anchor Bible 7C. New York: Doubleday, 1977.

Walsh, Carey Ellen. *Exquisite Desire: Religion, the Erotic, and the Song of Songs*. Minneapolis: Augsburg Fortress Publishers, 2000.

Lamentations

Berlin, Adele. *Lamentations*. Old Testament Library. Louisville: Westminster John Knox Press, 2002.

Linafelt, Tod. *Surviving Lamentations: Catastrophe, Lament and Protest in the Afterlife of a Biblical Book*. Chicago: University of Chicago Press, 2000.

O'Connor, Kathleen M. *Lamentations and the Tears of the World*. Maryknoll, N.Y.: Orbis Books, 2002.

Ruth and Esther

Ruth

Campbell, Edward F. *Ruth*. Anchor Bible 7. Garden City, N.Y.: Doubleday, 1975.

LaCocque, André. *Ruth*. Translated by K. C. Hanson. Continental Commentaries. Minneapolis: Augsburg Fortress Publishers, 2004.

Linafelt, Tod, and Timothy K. Beal. *Ruth and Esther*. Berit Olam. Collegeville, Minn.: Liturgical Press, 1999.

Trible, Phyllis. "Ruth, Book of." Pages 842-47 in vol. 5 of *The Anchor Bible Dictionary*. Edited by David N. Freedman. 6 vols. New York: Doubleday, 1992.

Esther

Fox, Michael V. *Character and Ideology in the Book of Esther.* Columbia: University of South Carolina Press, 1991.

Levenson, Jon D. *Esther*. Old Testament Library. Louisville: Westminster John Knox Press, 1997.

Moore, Carey. "Esther, Book of." Pages 633-43 in vol. 2 of *The Anchor Bible Dictionary*. Edited by David N. Freedman. 6 vols. New York: Doubleday, 1992.

Tull, Patricia K. *Esther and Ruth.* Interpretation Bible Studies. Louisville: Westminster John Knox Press, 2003.

Daniel

Collins, John J. *The Apocalyptic Imagination.* 2d ed. Grand Rapids, Mich.: Wm. B. Eerdmans Publishing Company, 1998.

———. *Daniel*. Hermeneia. Minneapolis: Fortress Press, 1993.

Gowan, Donald E. *Daniel*. Abingdon Old Testament Commentaries. Nashville: Abingdon Press, 2001.

Seow, Choon-Leon. *Daniel*. Westminster Bible Companion. Louisville: Westminster John Knox Press, 2003.

Smith-Christopher, Daniel L. "Daniel." Pages 17-194 in vol. 7 of *The New Interpreter's Bible.* Edited by Leander Keck. 12 vols. Nashville: Abingdon Press, 1996.

Ezra-Nehemiah

Blenkinsopp, Joseph. *Ezra–Nehemiah*. Old Testament Library. Philadelphia: Westminster Press, 1988.

Clines, David J. A. *Ezra, Nehemiah.* New Century Bible. Grand Rapids, Mich.: Wm. B. Eerdmans Publishing Company, 1984.

Davies, Gordon F. *Ezra and Nehemiah*. Berit Olam. Collegeville, Minn.: Liturgical Press, 1999.

Klein, Ralph W. "The Books of Ezra and Nehemiah." Pages 663-851 in vol. 3 of *The New Interpreter's Bible*. Edited by Leander Keck. 12 vols. Nashville: Abingdon Press, 1999.

Van Wijk-Bos, Johanna W. H. *Ezra, Nehemiah and Esther.* Westminster Bible Companion. Louisville: Westminster John Knox Press, 1998.

1–2 Chronicles

Japhet, Sara. *I and II Chronicles.* Old Testament Library. Louisville: Westminster John Knox Press, 1993.

Klein, Ralph W. *1 Chronicles.* Hermeneia. Minneapolis: Fortress Press, 2006.

Knoppers, Gary. *I Chronicles 1-9.* Anchor Bible 12. New York: Doubleday, 2004.

———. *1 Chronicles 10-29*. Anchor Bible 12A. New York: Doubleday, 2004.

McKenzie, Steven L. *1-2 Chronicles.* Abingdon Old Testament Commentaries. Nashville: Abingdon Press, 2004.

Wright, John W. *1 and 2 Chronicles.* Berit Olam. Collegeville, Minn.: Liturgical Press, 2000.